CONDUCTING
Business Ethically
A PHILOSOPHICAL APPROACH

SECOND EDITION

Martin J. Lecker, Ed.D.

Kendall Hunt
publishing company

Cover image © Shutterstock, Inc.

Kendall Hunt
publishing company

www.kendallhunt.com
Send all inquiries to:
4050 Westmark Drive
Dubuque, IA 52004-1840

Copyright © 2010, 2015 by Martin J. Lecker

ISBN 978-1-4652-7326-0

Printed in the United States of America

DEDICATION

In memory of my uncle, Marvin Fecher, and my father, Bernard Lecker—
two entrepreneurs whose personal and business iconic code of ethics exceeded
their competition and emulated the virtuous good life; and in memory of my sister,
Laurie Lecker, who inspired me to be the best that I could be as she had done
having Down syndrome and living the most ethical of all lives.

CONTENTS

CHAPTER TWO

CLASSICAL PHILOSOPHERS 33

CHAPTER THREE

EASTERN-WORLD SAGES 79

CHAPTER FIVE

CHAPTER SIX

CHAPTER SEVEN
ETHICAL WORKPLACE ISSUES 203

CHAPTER EIGHT

CHAPTER NINE

CHAPTER TEN

WELCOME

In January 2015, 2.6 million cars and as many as fifty deaths, perhaps even more, were attributed to a defective ignition switch when General Motors executives admitted that the engineers and other employees had known about the problem for more than ten years without recalling the automobiles.[1]

In a National Business Ethics Survey by the Ethics Resource Center, it was reported that 41% of those employees surveyed had observed actions that were either illegal or against their organizations' ethical practices.[2] In an earlier survey by the same organization, one third of those responding to the survey believed that their managers did not display ethical behavior.[3] It is no wonder why a New York City–based law firm found in a survey that 26% of the 500 senior executives polled believed in order to be successful a person had to "engage in unethical or illegal conduct."[4]

This is why so many individuals who conduct business question themselves before deciding on the best course of action to take to enable them to be successful in their career or entrepreneurship without compromising their own moral compass. After all, in the business world there appears to be a set of moral standards that are antithetical to the *just* values instilled in you by your parents, teachers, and religious leaders.

In this textbook, you will learn about different philosophies that may help you to formulate or question your own "moral compass," with a process to apply these philosophies in actual business scenarios.

In Delphi, Greece, an inscription there reads, "know thyself." These words, uttered by Socrates, should be considered as you progress through this course, leading you to ask yourself, "Who am I *really*?" This is why Socrates once said, "the unexamined life is not worth living." Allow yourself to use this course to reflect on your actions in everyday life as well as in the business world.

May you begin this journey!

WORKS CITED

[1] Hilary Stout, "Nearing Cutoff, Victim Claims Pour into G.M. Program," *New York Times*, Late Edition (East Coast), January 30, 2015. *ProQuest.* Web. 31 Jan. 2015.

[2] *House Judiciary Subcommittee on Constitution and Civil Justice Hearing* (Lanham: Federal Information & News Dispatch, Inc, 2014). *ProQuest.* Web. 31 Jan. 2015.

[3] Tammy Cowart, et al., "Ethical Leaders: Trust, Work-Life Balance, and Treating Individuals as Unique," *Journal of Leadership, Accountability and Ethics,* vol. 11, no. 3, 2014, pp. 70-81. *ProQuest.* Web. 31 Jan. 2015.

[4] Noah Plaue, "A Quarter of Wall Street Executives Say You Have To Be Unethical to Succeed," *Business Insider,* July 10, 2012, n.p. Web. 1 Feb. 2015.

A NOTE TO

THE INSTRUCTORS

The primary purpose of this textbook is to introduce some of the classical philosophers and apply their decision making when faced with ethical dilemmas in the business world. Because instructors possess different skills and knowledge in teaching philosophy, and given the pervasiveness of ethics, or the lack of it, in the business world, along with the ever changing issues and situations our society and students are faced with, this textbook is designed to allow instructors to pick and choose which chapters and/or sections meet their needs, their students' needs, and the current times. Therefore, feel free to add or detract as you see fit given that you will have to decide which philosophers or philosophies your students will benefit from, given the limited philosophical exposure the average business student may encounter during their undergraduate education experience.

I would suggest that you include Chapter One to give an overall understanding of the early philosophers, as well as Chapter Two, because it includes a rudimentary method to integrate philosophical thinking with pragmatic case applications. Chapter Six is extremely crucial because it outlines a seven-step method used originally to teach business executives how to make more ethical decisions, but was modified to reflect a more academic, philosophical approach to decision making.

You may decide which philosophers need to be emphasized in Chapters Three, Four, and Five. Chapters Seven through Ten present contemporary issues found in the real business world that enable your students to apply the philosophies learned in the earlier chapters, using the seven-step method introduced in Chapter Six.

PEDAGOGICAL SUGGESTIONS

In my course, students are introduced to the first five chapters and usually complete them around midterm (or within a week or two of it). Regardless of how much of the first five chapters we've covered, usually around the midterm, I introduce Chapter Six, but do not include it in the midterm, since at this point students are expected just to demonstrate that they can select an appropriate philosophy as a rationale for their action or viewpoint; explain the philosophy in their own words and exemplify it with a general example; and finally apply this philosophy by showing how it connects to their action or viewpoint (which is the S.E.A. method introduced in Chapter Two).

After understanding the seven-step method from Chapter Six, students are placed into groups where each group introduces a chapter from Part II (Chapters Seven through Ten) and apply the seven-step method (from Chapter Six) to a case found in one of these aforementioned chapters or a preapproved case. Also, students are free to introduce a preapproved set of contemporary issues not in the textbook. In terms of my final exam, students are required to demonstrate that they can apply the seven-step method to any given case.

In addition, students are required to locate articles from the *New York Times* (since there are some limited copies available for our students free of charge through our Students Activities Division or they can go online at www.nyt.com or www.newyorktimes.com which at the time of this writing is free as long as the article is within two weeks of the date when the article is being accessed) or an approved publications such as the *Wall Street Journal, Harvard Business Review*, etc. and then apply the S.E.A. method (see Chapter Two) after summarizing it. In addition, students must select one of the articles and orally present it to the class on an assigned date. For this reason, this is why the textbook should be considered a "jumping off" point for more experienced instructors who may pick and choose the chapters they want to cover, while less experienced instructors and/or those teaching the course for the first time, may want to teach all the chapters (or as many as possible), and use the text for the semester's course content.

Should you have any questions, suggestions, or wish to provide feedback, email me at mlecker@sunyrockland.edu and in the subject field put in the words "Conducting Business Ethically," so it will receive a high priority in my inbox when I retrieve my emails.

I wish you a successful semester!

ACKNOWLEDGMENTS

To my best friend, soul mate, and wife, Terri Kaye Needle (Lecker), whose professional contributions and moral support gave me the strength to forge on; my children in chronological order of their birth along with their spouses for their input and words of wisdom: Pamela, Adam, Christina, Melissa, Troy, and Isabell; my grandchildren (also in chronological order): Noah, Emily Joshua, Charlotte, and Tyler and Luke, who gave up their "Poppy" for several weekends to complete this project; my parents, Bernard, who passed away and was my "ethical rock and compass" and Ruth Lecker, whose multifaceted support resulted in the letters Ed.D. which follows my name; my two publication "guardian" angels from my first edition, Sue Saad and Katie Riggs, and Lauren Milam and Linda Chapman for this edition, who knew how to encourage me and gently "push me" so this writing project was completed successfully; Dr. Judith Netzer, Profs. Maire Liberace, Deborah Merrigan, Terri Kaye Needle, and Myrna Wulfson, who planted the original seed for this book and handed me the baton to complete the final leg of this long relay race; to my RCC students who provided feedback as well as encouragement throughout the last eighteen years and for whom this textbook has been written; and especially Matthew Hess and Grace Choe, who edited the first edition chapters and my Spring 2015 semester Ethics in Businesses classes who supported me and tested out my new cases.

ABOUT THE AUTHOR

Martin Lecker, EdD, has been a member of the RCC Business faculty since 1985, and a full Professor since 1991. In 2012, the SUNY Board of Trustees conferred him with the highest rank, Distinguished Teaching Professor.

He has co-developed the Ethics in Business course and teaches it online, in the classroom, and as a hybrid course which combines the classroom experience with extensive online student participation. Dr. Lecker had published several national and international articles on ethical business issues and has edited two books on multiculturalism.

Photograph Courtesy Rockland Community College.

CHAPTER 1

LEARNING TO THINK LIKE A PHILOSOPHER

*"Without philosophy we should be little above the animals
that dig or erect their habitations"*

-Voltaire *Antiquity* Sec. V

The Shallow Pond

*Imagine that you are a college professor
and there is a path from the library
at your university to the Humanities
Lecture Hall which passes a shallow
ornamental pond. On your way to give a
lecture, you notice that a small child has
fallen in and is in danger of drowning.
If you wade in and pull the child out, it
will mean getting your clothes muddy*

and either cancelling your lecture or delaying it until you can find something clean and dry to wear. If you pass by the child, so you may give your lecture on time, the child will die.[1a] What would you do? (Refer to questions 1 to 3 at the end of this chapter.)

The Envelope

In your mailbox, there is a letter from the United States Committee for UNICEF, a world organization whose mission is to help less fortunate children from less developed countries. After reading the letter, you researched the organization and know that it is not a "scam" and that 100% of all donations go to their intended "victims." Therefore, you correctly believe that unless you send a $100 check, instead of each child living, over thirty more children will die soon without your contribution. Make no other assumptions; just deal with whether or not you would send the money.[1b] Would you send the $100? (Refer to questions 1 to 4 at the end of this chapter.)

© africa924/Shutterstock, Inc.

Ethics and Values

It has been said that Diogenes of Sinope (c. 400 BCE) roamed the streets with a lantern looking for an honest man.[2] Legend has it that he never found such a person. It is no wonder that there is such cynicism toward business ethics. Just turn to the pages of the *New York Times*, *Los Angeles Times*, or the *Chicago Tribune* and a day will not go by without an article about a business or businessperson who is facing charges or is being questioned about unethical conduct during the course of employment. As a businessperson, will you be able to take the moral high road, or be no different than the Voltaire quote above referring to the metaphorical unethical lower road?

In the first case, "The Shallow Pond," the action you would take may be easier to determine, so at this point you will have passed the litmus test for ethical decision making. Yet, when it meant facing unemployment by missing a class observation, which would result in you losing tenure, did you find your moral compass somewhat shakier? What about the second case, "The Envelope," where there is no clear-cut answer, yet your response will affect the lives of thirty children, not one?

In the business world, you will be faced with a multitude of decisions every day. In each case, the course of action you take and how ethical this course of action is will differ, depending on the situation's complexity and your own moral compass. The famous Greek philosopher Heraclitus once said, "You cannot step into the same river twice, for other waters are continually flowing on." Each day we are faced with a changing river flow of ethical dilemmas and have to determine whether our personal desires or ego will compromise our personal moral compass. But as Aristotle believed, just because we fall down ethically one time, does not mean the next time faced with a similar situation, we cannot make the wiser, ethical choice.

"We only have a few rules around here,
but we really enforce them."

The purpose of this book is to examine your actions and compare them to the standards of morality that we would expect others in our situation would live up to. But, what or who determines these standards and whether we even want to fulfill them, is an even more complex issue. Furthermore, if we decide to follow these moral standards, how can we also satisfy the goals of our business or employer? Throughout this book, various approaches will be used to help answer these questions. Although there may not be any right or wrong answers, by applying some of the philosophies and approaches included in this book, and by reflecting upon your own motives before deciding on a particular course of action, it is expected that the quality of your decisions will be optimized for all parties affected by your decision, including yourself.

For purposes of discussion, I will first refer to a few terms: ethics, ethical dilemma, and values. **Ethics** *is a branch of philosophy that identifies why and if a particular moral standard should be a moral standard.* For example, telling the truth is a moral standard; so is paying one's debts, not cheating one's customers, and not stealing from a business. However, as stated, the study of ethics examines *why* and *if* a particular action should be a moral standard. Whether to miss a class in order to save a drowning child or attend the class and not save the child as discussed in the scenario earlier, is called an ethical dilemma. An **ethical dilemma** *is a situation or decision where there is no obvious solution in terms of what is the right thing to do.* In the study of ethics, the potential actions (such as whether to save the drowning child) are weighed against certain values. **Values** *are those things you believe in and compare to one or more moral standards, which would enable you to make the most ethical choice.* Examples of values include friendship, religion, and money. It has been said that Socrates believed that unexamined life is not worth living.[3] In the following activity, you will be given the opportunity to examine your own values.

ETHICS

is a branch of philosophy that identifies why and if a particular moral standard should be a moral standard.

ETHICAL DILEMMA

a situation or decision affecting others when there may not be an obvious solution in terms of what is the right thing to do.

VALUES

which you believe in and are then compared to one or more moral standards, which would enable you to make the most ethical choice. Examples may be: friendship, religion, money.

The Alligator River Story[4]

© Rudy Umans/Shutterstock, Inc.

Once upon a time there was a woman named Abigail who was in love with a man named Gregory. Gregory lived on the shore of a river. Abigail lived on the opposite shore of the river. The river that separated the two lovers was teeming with man-eating alligators. Abigail wanted to cross the river to be with Gregory. Unfortunately, the bridge had been washed out. So she went to Sinbad, a river boat captain, to take her across. He said he would be glad to if she would consent to go to bed with him preceding the voyage. She promptly refused and went to a friend named Ivan to explain her plight. Ivan did not want to be involved at all in the situation. Abigail felt her only alternative was to accept Sinbad's terms. Sinbad fulfilled his promise to Abigail and delivered her into the arms of Gregory.

When she told Gregory about her amorous escapade in order to cross the river, Gregory cast her aside with disdain. Heartsick and dejected, Abigail turned to Slug for her tale of woe. Slug, feeling compassion for Abigail, sought out Gregory and beat him brutally. Abigail was overjoyed at the sight of Gregory getting his due. As the sun sets on the horizon, we hear Abigail laughing at Gregory.

You may want to discuss this with some of your classmates and friends and see who they believe was the most moral, and rank them to the least moral character. Responding to who you believe was the most or least moral identifies your values. Identifying why these are values reflects the study of ethics. Yet, how do we determine whose values are right or in the case of the Alligator River story, which character was most ethical? (See questions 1 to 3 at the end of the chapter.)

PRECONVEN-
TIONAL LEVEL
*is based upon when
you are making
decisions which the
determining factor
is how you are ben-
efited by that deci-
sion (i.e. motivated
by selfishness).*

CONVENTIONAL
LEVEL
*according to
Kohlberg's model it
is based upon when
you are making
a decision the
deciding factor is
what others think of
your decision (what
will other people
think?). In Gilligan's
model it is based
upon doing what
is best for others
and detrimentally
neglecting yourself.*

POSTCONVEN-
TIONAL LEVEL
*according to the
Kohlberg model, the
determining factor
when making a de-
cision is based upon
a higher level of
development when
you act in a manner
which is for the good
of humankind, and
your motivation is
not for any personal
reward or motivated
by what others
may think. In the
Gilligan model, it
is putting yourself
ahead of others, not
to be selfish but to
be selfless.*

Moral Development

LAWRENCE KOHLBERG

When analyzing what would be the "right" or ethical thing to do, we first need to understand how moral reasoning is developed. According to Piaget and, later on, Kohlberg and Gilligan, moral development is contingent upon the structure of one's thinking over time.[5] One must pass through stages to make an ethical decision, and the higher the stage you are at, the more developed you are. In his landmark study on moral development, using only males, Lawrence Kohlberg developed six stages to identify levels of ethical development of an individual. These six stages were part of three levels: preconventional, conventional, and postconventional. On the **preconventional level,** *your decision making is based on how you will benefit by your decision* (i.e., motivated by selfishness). The **conventional level** *is based upon what others think of your decision*; and the **postconventional level** *is based upon a higher level of development when you act in a manner that is for the good of humankind, and your motivation is not for any personal reward.* The first stage in the preconventional level was based upon punishment and obedience.[6] In this stage, you make a decision based upon whether you will be caught or not. We will use the characters of the "Alligator River Story" to exemplify Kohlberg's theory: If Abigail based her decision on the belief that Gregory would never find out, or if she did not go with Sinbad because Gregory would find out, she would be in the first stage. In the second stage, termed "instrumental-relativist orientation," an action is taken that will benefit another individual only if this person obtains something in return.[6] In this case, Sinbad demonstrated this stage since the only way he would help Abigail get across the river would be if she would return the favor by having sexual relations with him. In other words, I will do something for you, if I can expect eventually you will do something for me.

In the conventional level, we have the third stage, termed "interpersonal concordance," where one does something ethical if he or she believes others will see them as "nice."[7] If Sinbad took Abigail to see Gregory, only because he wanted everyone to see him as a "good guy," but would not have done so if no one else would know that he helped Abigail, this would exemplify the third stage. The fourth stage, "law and order," is based upon rules that society has set up.[8] For example, if Sinbad lacked a license to cross the river and refused Abigail passage, even if it meant "life and death," because he did not want to break the law, Sinbad would be categorized as being in the fourth stage.

© Carlos Yudica/Shutterstock, Inc.

In the postconventional level, the fifth stage appears, called the "social contract" stage. In this stage, there is the view that even though it is a law, it could possibly change given the circumstances (as opposed to not changing in the previous level).[9] Using the example from the fourth stage, if Abigail had to cross the river because Gregory needed a kidney which she could donate, and Sinbad, who lacked a nautical license, took Abigail because he believed even if it was against the law, if he was caught and explained his situation, perhaps he would not be penalized for sailing without the required permit. The last stage, the "universal-ethical principle orientation," is more like a Golden Rule concept of treating others as we would want to be treated and would even be willing to risk something of value to stand up for these rights.[10] In this situation, let us assume the river was very treacherous, but the only way Gregory's life may be saved would be to take Abigail on his boat. If Sinbad did so to save Gregory's life, he would be on the highest stage of moral development according to Kohlberg's theory.

CAROL GILLIGAN

Carol Gilligan, who studied under Kohlberg, also developed a moral development model. However, because Kohlberg's study only involved male subjects, women who were faced with some of Kohlberg's standard decisions found themselves unable to go beyond the third or fourth stage of Kohlberg's model. In her study, Gilligan included females and developed an alternative model, identifying the same three levels that

Kohlberg identified in his study, but differed in terms of the steps, which enabled females to score on the postconventional level, which they could not do under Kohlberg's model. Gilligan found that girls who were faced with some of Kohlberg's ethical dilemmas seldom went beyond the third or fourth stage of Kohlberg's model.

Gilligan's study uncovered a very important point. The reason females scored lower than their male counterparts under Kohlberg's model was because women's construction of a moral problem focuses upon their obligation to care for others and be responsible to maintain good relationships, as opposed to the males whose focus was on rules and justice, where caring for others played little, if any, role in moral decision making.[11] So, those females who were faced with ethical dilemmas, using Gilligan's model of moral development, were found to be on a higher level than if evaluated using Kohlberg's model.

Gilligan's model, like Kohlberg's, had a preconventional level, marked by caring for oneself without regard to others, which she termed "caring for self."[12] However, before moving on to the next level, Gilligan identified a transitional period which she termed "selfishness and responsibility," which recognized an attachment or connection to others. One example may be if Abigail felt it would be too much trouble to see Gregory (preconventional level) but started *to think* about how disappointed Gregory may feel by not seeing her (transitional period). In this transitional period, note how from being selfish, Abigail now weighs her responsibilities to others and may have second thoughts about not seeing Gregory, based upon his feelings.

Now, let us discuss another scenario demonstrating the "caring for others" conventional stage, where Abigail wants to see Gregory because he is so desperate to see her, so she will do anything necessary, in order not to disappoint him. Unfortunately, when she asks Sinbad to take her, he will only do so if she has sexual relations with him. Therefore, even though Abigail believes very strongly in being monogamous to Gregory, at the same time, she does not want Gregory to be disappointed. Complicating the situation more, what If she believes it may take years before the bridge can be rebuilt for her to see Gregory, can her action be seen as a higher level of moral development than Kohlberg's model would show? According to Gilligan, even though it (having relations with Sinbad) might be bad for Abigail, since it is good for Gregory (he will be able to see Abigail), by having sexual relations with Sinbad, Gilligan's model might consider this action to be at the conventional level, as opposed to Kohlberg's model who would consider it preconventional (instrumental relativist).[13] It is at this point that Abigail could be entering the next transitional phase, "goodness to truth."[14] It should also be pointed out that having sexual relations with Sinbad may or may not be accepted by Gregory, but at the time her decision was made, Abigail's thoughts were on doing whatever was necessary to see Gregory and not disappoint him.

This transitional phrase begins with a reconsideration of the relationship between oneself and others, where self-sacrifice in the service of caring for others is being dishonest to oneself.[15] Take the example of a woman with five children who is pregnant by her husband. The husband then announces that he is leaving her and does not want to be married to her anymore. Assuming it is not against her religious beliefs to have an abortion, she realizes that by not having an abortion she would have six children, would not be able to take care of them or herself, but if by having an abortion, she could continue to work and provide a stable home that she could not if she had a sixth child. Using Abigail as an example, let us assume that if she had sexual relations with Sinbad, she would be depressed and would always feel dishonest, even though she knows that Sinbad would never tell Gregory. This awareness may lead her to refuse Sinbad's offer and disappoint Gregory but would enable her to enter into the final level, postconventional, marked by the ethic of care and being responsible to oneself as to others.[16] The best example to substantiate why this is the highest level of moral development hinges upon the belief that being selfless is not the same as being selfish. After all, if you have ever been on an airplane, during the demonstration of what happens if the oxygen mask falls down and you have a young child sitting next to you, the flight attendants always tells you to put the mask on yourself first and then on your child. Why? If you did not put it on yourself first, it is possible that you could pass out and would not be able to help your child and that would be irresponsible or selfish. The same applies with this postconventional level because fully, morally developed individuals take care of themselves so they are able to take care of others.

Comparing the Kohlberg and Gilligan Model

FIGURE 1.1

LEVEL	KOHLBERG	GILLIGAN
Preconventional	**Stage 1:** Punishment and obedience ("If I don't get caught, I will do it.")	**Caring for Self** ("If it is good for me, it was the right choice.")
	Stage 2: Instrumental-relativist orientation ("I will do it for you, if you do something for me.")	**Transitional period:** Selfish to responsibility ("Maybe I should think of others.")
Conventional	**Stage 3:** Interpersonal concordance ("I better do it or others will think I am not nice.")	**Caring for others** ("Even if it is bad for me, since it is good for you, I will do it.")
	Stage 4: Law and order ("If it is a law, it has to be right.")	**Transitional period:** Goodness to truth ("I wonder, if it is good for others, is it also good for me?")
Postconventional	**Stage 5:** Social contract ("It may be against the law, but maybe the law is not right.")	**Ethics of care** ("It is alright to help yourself first, so you are able to help others.")
	Stage 6: Universal-ethical principle orientation ("Despite personal risk, I must do the right thing to help others.")	

The Moral Compass

The following chart (figure 1.2) identifies some of the approaches that may be taken when faced with an ethical dilemma such as the "Alligator River Story." The first approach is *biblical or religious law*. But, can we use religion in all situations to determine which would be the best ethical course to take when faced with a decision such as the one Abigail encountered? To begin with, although most religions may look at Abigail's actions with Sinbad as immoral (sexual relations before marriage), there are other ethical dilemmas that we cannot depend solely on religion to help us steer in the correct moral direction. For example, if Sinbad did not have any preconditions but told Abigail that he could only take her to see Gregory on a Saturday and she was a religious person of the Jewish faith, her action may be considered immoral if she sailed on this day. However, if she was a Roman Catholic, traveling on a Saturday would be permissible and not a breach of ethics from a religious point. Therefore, religion may not be an acceptable moral standard for everyone because with each different religion, there may be a difference in determining whether an act is ethical. Furthermore, if a person is an atheist or agnostic, are they exempt from any moral standards or is their bar of ethics any lower than those who practice their religions?

Perhaps, using *constitutional or state law*, as established and agreed upon by society, could be a potential measurement of morality. After all, if it is constitutionally sound or is statutorily permissible, why wouldn't it be ethical? However, slavery, prohibition of women's rights, and the prohibition of interracial marriages exemplifies why laws do not guarantee ethicality for every given situation.

For the same reason, *moral realism* cannot be deemed an ethical guide either, as there are several practices in business that have been practical because they are acceptable but are not ethical. Examples include: churning a client's portfolio so you earn a commission for doing so; corporate raiding underpriced stocks and after purchasing the company, selling its assets for a profit while letting the firm's employees go; or allowing international child labor in order to keep up with your competitor who also follows this practice.

Instead, maybe we can look at humankind and trust that all people have consciences and thus their *guilt* will prevent them from taking the unethical action. Guilt "is both a cognitive and an emotional experience that occurs when a person believes that he or she has violated a moral standard and is responsible for that violation."[17] After all, "have you ever done something unethical even though you knew it was wrong?" If you or anyone else you know responds affirmatively, it can be strongly argued that you cannot trust guilt (your conscience) to prevent you from conducting an immoral action.

Another approach may be *moral relativism*, which may be defined as "the idea that it is wrong to legislate morality because all morality is subjective."[18] Essentially, this approach may be seen either as each individual determines what constitutes an ethical action *or* society will determine the moral action to take in a given situation. The problem is that individuals may believe they are making moral decisions, when in fact they are not. Look at an individual who steals money from a company so his family may take a well, deserved vacation to Disneyland. Or, what about how certain societies believe a women should not be given the same opportunities as men? Both demonstrate why moral relativism is not an acceptable approach to determine the best ethical course of action when faced with an ethical dilemma.

This then bring us to our final approach, *universal philosophy*. There are certain philosophies that may be used and would be accepted in most societal circles. For example, Immanuel Kant believes that "you never treat humanity as a means but always at the same time an ends."[19] He believed that you do not use people and should their positions be reversed, would anyone want to be used for another's advantage? Would you like to find out that the only reason someone wanted you to take them on a date was so you could drive them to their boyfriend's house only to leave you for him? There are several philosophies that could be applied and still be accepted universally. It is based upon this premise, which we will follow when deciding what the best ethical course of action would be when faced with an ethical dilemma.

The Moral Compass

FIGURE 1.2

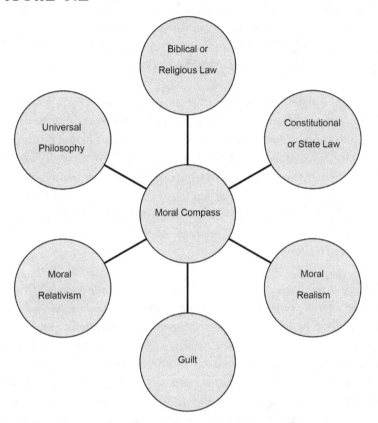

Philosophy and Its Contemporary Branches

What is philosophy? **Philosophy** literally means "lover of wisdom" (*philos*, love; *sophos*, wisdom). However, in his book *First Philosophy*, Andrew Bailey best expressed what it means to be philosophical in the following passage:

> To be philosophical is to continue to question the assumptions behind every claim until we come to our most basic beliefs about reality, and then to critically examine those beliefs. [20]

PHILOSOPHY

means a lover of wisdom and as a philosopher you continue to question the assumptions behind every claim and your most basic beliefs about reality, and then to critically examine those beliefs

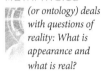
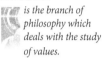
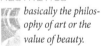
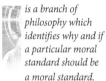

It is believed that the first Western philosophers such as Thales, Xenophanes, Pythagoras, and Heraclitus lived on the banks of the Mediterranean more than 2,500 years ago, while the first Eastern philosophers such as Lao-Tzu were believed to have lived in China around the same time period.[21] But, within the discipline of philosophy there are subdisciplines or branches within the field of knowledge. For purposes of brevity, I will discuss just a few of those branches.

The first is **epistemology,** *which includes questions about knowledge,* such as: What is knowledge? and How do we know what we know? Is something the truth or is it an opinion? A second branch of philosophy is metaphysics or ontology. **Metaphysics** (ontology) *deals with questions of reality*: What is appearance and what is real? What kind of reality does the universe have—it is mind or matter or some kind of spiritual being? What kind of reality do you have as a human being?[22] In addition, it raises questions about our existence, such as: Are our lives predetermined or do we have free will?

Axiology *is the branch of philosophy that deals with the study of values,* which is why we have **political philosophy,** *the examination of social values and the justification of various political institutions and political relations,* as well as **aesthetics,** *which is the philosophy of art or the value of beauty.*[23] This then leads to another form of philosophy, ethics. Whereas morality looks at *what* is right or wrong and focuses upon the standards of morality, **ethics** *is the study of examining these standards and why something may be right or wrong.* So, morality may determine that it is wrong to steal something from another human being. Yet, the study of ethics would look at why it is wrong to steal from another and whether it could be justifiable to steal from another person in a certain situation (e.g., stealing a rowboat to save a child from drowning).

The last branch of philosophy for our purposes of discussion is **logic,** first discovered by Aristotle in the fourth century BCE, *it is a specialized branch of philosophical science that examines the science of valid defense.*[24] One example would be as follows:

All men are mortal.

Socrates is a man.

Therefore, Socrates is mortal. [25]

If the first statements (called premises) are valid, then the final statement is valid (conclusion). Although, this is an elementary example, and the study of logic is more complex, by using logic when determining whether or not an action is moral, the discipline of ethics becomes more plausible. Next, we will explore some of the earlier Greek philosophers.

The First Philosophers

The first or pre-Socratic philosophers were credited with two developments: (1) enabling others to understand the world by their use of reason, without referring to religion and (2) encouraging their followers to use their own reason by thinking for themselves.[26] As a result, they were the first teachers who did not teach dogmatically (unquestioned beliefs) but taught their students to discuss, argue, debate, and put their own ideas forward, in order to be scrutinized by others.[27] Some of these earlier philosophers who will be briefly discussed in this next section are Thales, Anaximander, and Anaximenes of Miletus; Pythagoras of Samos; Heraclitus; and Parmenides. Because most early philosophers were men, following the first six pre-Socratics, we will review three female pre-BCE philosophers: Arignote of Samos, Aesara of Lucania, and Perictione I and II.

PHILOSOPHER

one who looks for a rational explanation of his experience of reality, who tries to grasp the real as a matter of understanding, as opposed...to a magical, mythical, fictional...explanation of things.

THALES OF MILETUS

In ancient history, seven men have been called sages or wise men and Thales was one of the first; he shared this title with Solon, Periander, Cleobulus, Chilon, Bias, and Pittacus.[28] Thales of Miletus (625–545 BCE)[29] was recognized generally as the first in history to define philosophy and did so by defining a **philosopher** as "*one who looks for a rational explanation of his experience of reality, who tries to grasp the real as a matter of understanding,*

as opposed…to a magical, mythical, fictional…explanation of things."[30] The philosophical question that challenged Thales was: "What is the world made of?"[31] Although we now know that all material objects are reduced to energy, Thales believed the world was made of water and that the earth floated on a body of water, which was unbounded (not infinite since the concept had not yet created), and since life depended upon water, the source of all things had to have been water.[32]

It has been said that Thales was the first to believe in the immortality of the soul, as well as being credited for declaring one of the most historical proverbs in philosophy as a response to the question, "What is most difficult?" in which he replied, "to know oneself"[33] Interestingly, some have credited Socrates with the proverb "Know thyself," but many have attributed it to Thales.[34] In addition, according to historical accounts of his life, it has been said that Thales discovered the seasons of the year, divided it into 365 days, and predicted the eclipses of the sun.[35]

Yet, Thales was somewhat of an eccentric. There is one story in which he said that there were three blessings for which he was grateful to *fortune*: "first, that I was born a human being and not one of the brutes; next, that I was born a man and not a woman; thirdly, that I was born a Greek and not a barbarian."[36] There is a tale that once Thales accompanied a woman to observe the stars, but he fell into a ditch because he was not looking around, and his cry for help drew this retort, "How can you expect to know all about the heavens, Thales, when you cannot even see what is before your feet?"[37]

However, it should be pointed out that philosophy is, among other things, "the attempt to find a single intuition of being, a single system of reality, that will synthesize and hold together the many facets of our specialized knowledge and social structure"[38] Although there was never any proof that Thales wrote anything, and his belief that water is what held everything together eventually in time proved wrong, he was the first person to be concerned with looking for explanations in terms of causal relationships between bodies in space and time, rather than solely a subjective association of ideas and will always be remembered for this innovative thinking.[39]

ANAXIMANDER AND ANAXIMENES OF MILETUS

As a pupil of Thales, the Milesian, Anaximander, was born around 611 BCE and is credited with being the first Greek to make a map, develop an instrument in the form of a sundial to measure off the seasons in Sparta, and engineer various types of models to duplicate and study the regularities of nature.[40] This is believed to have led him to the more general idea that nature is regular and predictable, which he believed was natural law.[41] Furthermore, although he had agreed with Thales in thinking that there is a common substance of which all things are composed, it was not water, but a "boundless something" (apeiron) that contained every sort of shape and quality and was without any definition or specific characteristics of its own.[42]

Anaximander believed everything real in matter had definite qualities, where it would be hot in some cases, cold in others, sometimes wet, sometimes dry; however, these qualities were always in pairs.[43] He felt that these opposites were warring with each other such as winter (the moist and cold) against the summer (hot and dry); the cycle of the seasons, and perhaps the day and night.[44] In addition, he believed the earth to be in the center of the universe. However, it is this concept of opposites that had contemporary implications. The following quote epitomizes Anaximander's concept of opposites: "according to necessity; for they pay penalty and retribution to each other for their injustice according to the assessment of Time."[45] This has been used in modern-day tort law where the injury of one individual is compensated by the party responsible for the injury. So, if you steal $1,000 from your employer, you would be responsible for paying back that employer $1,000 (and perhaps the interest lost during the time you possessed the employer's funds). Even if you wanted to apply it to criminal law, suppose someone stole $1,000 and it would take a person a month to earn it, the criminal who stole the money and could not repay it should spend a month in jail, which would be an appropriate penalty in terms of time to compensate for the crime. Oddly enough, this could be classified as an ethical concept.

Another early philosopher, Anaximenes, also from the Ionian region and a citizen of Milesia, was a protégé of Anaximander but believed that all things originated from air.[46] Anaximenes believed that when rarefied (made less dense), air became fire and when condensed it became wind, then cloud, then water, then earth, and then stone; so as condensation was a source of cold, rarefaction was a source of heat and because of his primary focus with the natural world, he was known as a "cosmologist," like Thales and Anaximander.[47] His theory of air was based upon an empirical argument of rarefaction: breath blown through compressed lips is cold, but with the mouth open, it becomes warm."[48] The next philosopher, Pythagoras, finds another solution to the question, What is the world made of?

PYTHAGORAS

Pythagoras believed that the fundamental principles of the universe were derived from mathematical relations (a precursor to Albert Einstein's thinking a millennium later).[49]   Pythagoras is believed to have been born on Samos, an island off Miletus, on the Asia-Minor coast of what is now Turkey around 570 BCE and died in 497 BCE.[50] Although it is agreed that his mother was Pythias, there is a myth that Pythagoras's father was the son of Apollo.[51] However, most believed his father was Mnesarchus, husband to Pythias.[52] Pythagoras is thought to be the first person who invented the term "philosophy" and who first applied the word "cosmos" to the universe.[53]

Pythagoras believed that real things and their relationships are somehow expressible by numbers, if they are not numbers themselves.[54] He believed there was a direct correlation between the unity of numbers and the unity of the universe.[55] To validate this, Pythagoras observed that the interval between notes on the musical scale was expressed numerically, depending on the length of string required to produce these notes or sounds. He reasoned, if the physical length and tone were expressed by numbers, why can't the rest of the universe have this same relationship to numbers? [56]

Pythagoras founded a religious community with a set of ascetic and ceremonial rules, the most famous of which was the prohibition of the eating of beans.[57] He taught the doctrine of transmigration of souls, which is the belief that human beings had souls separable from their bodies, and at death a person's soul enters another body, not necessarily that of a human.[58]

There is an anecdote that Pythagoras intervened in the beating of a dog by saying, "Stop! Cease your beating, because this is really the soul of a man who was my friend: I recognized it as I heard it cry aloud."[59] Pythagoras believed not only in the immortality of the soul but by following these religious rules you are pursuing holiness, which in turn means the pursuit of purification whereby the soul is released from the body.[60] In addition, he contended that final perfection comes when the soul is freed from the body and united or reunited with the One (Unity).[61a]

Pythagoras is known for several quotes, but this one demonstrates the importance of higher level thinking and is found in a book by Diogenes Laërtius: "the soul of a man is divided into three parts, intelligence, reason, and passion. Intelligence and passion are possessed by other animals, but reason by man alone."[61b] Later, in Chapter Four, you may notice how this resembles the thinking of the nineteenth-century philosopher, John Stuart Mill. Basically, this brings reasoning into the discussion of ethics and morals and how humankind is superior to lower level animals, in this respect.

Heraclitus

Heraclitus was born circa 540 BCE in Ephesus and died around 480 BCE.[62] He was considered to be the most famous of the early Ionian philosophers based upon his often quoted statement, "You cannot step into the same river, for other waters are continually flowing on." This statement has been interpreted to mean that everything (e.g., truth, knowledge) is in a constant state of flux.[63] Given this statement is true and all things are in constant motion, Heraclitus then raised two questions: "What is the source of this unified motion?" and "What is the agency (means) where movement is provided?"[64]

His view of the universe focused upon a concept that he termed "logos"—an untranslatable word which means "word"—but has connotations of proportion and measure.[65] Historically, it has also been translated to mean "law, reason, intelligence, and wisdom."[66] But regardless of its exact meaning, according to Heraclitus, the logos was the first principle of *knowledge* to the understanding of the world and represented a structure or pattern of the world, which was concealed from the eyes of an ordinary person.[67] This could be seen as the first seeds of epistemological thought, a branch of philosophy not yet developed.

Heraclitus also believed that the logos was the first principle of *existence* and that the unity of the world as we know it is a process of maintaining a balance between tightening and retracting, much like the shooting of a bow and arrow.[68] His vision of the universe was that enemies sustain their hate through their animosity toward each other much like war, which is inseparable to peace; therefore, we must continue to fight our enemies in order to attain peace.

He also thought the three principal elements of nature were fire, earth, and water. However, of the three, he believed that fire was the primary element controlling and modifying the other two.[69] In Heraclitus's cosmology, fire had the role that water had for Thales and that air had for Anaximenes.[70] Furthermore, he believed that the virtuous soul could survive the death of its physical body and eventually would rejoin the cosmic fire.[71] Curiously, the process of separation and unity (exemplifying Heraclitus's opposites) mirrored the Eastern philosophical concept of the yin and yang and demonstrated that the dynamism between opposites was the driving force for the external conditions of the universe.[72] Is it possible that this was the planting of another seed for a branch in philosophy called metaphysics, which examines the nature of one's existence? The next philosopher we will discuss is considered to be the founder of metaphysics. His name is Parmenides.

PARMENIDES

Although not much is known of Parmenides' life, it is believed that he was born around 510 BCE, died circa 440 BCE, and was originally from Elea, a Greek city on the coast of Italy.[73] Unlike his predecessors, instead of devoting himself to cosmology, Parmenides dedicated his study to metaphysics, or "the study of issues beyond the physical world such as:

the meaning of life, the existence of free will, the nature of the mind, and the possibility of life after death."[74] His works influenced Plato who dedicated one of his writings, *Parmenides*, on his behalf.

Whereas Heraclitus argued that everything changes and denied that anything can stay the same or that permanence exists in the world, Parmenides believed that permanence is the fundamental character of reality.[75] He believed that reality must be eternal and unchanging and therefore the changing world of our experience cannot be real and is actually an illusion.[76] In his poem, "Way of Truth," a goddess reveals to Parmenides that "the unshaken heart of well rounded Truth," is actually reality and that "the opinions of mortals in which is not true belief at all," are the changing untruths.[77] Parmenides' distinction between appearance and reality and between opinion and knowledge led to Plato's doctrine that the sensible world is lower in degree of reality than the world of intelligence.[78]

In the English language just as we tend to use the same word such as "dying" as a verb (he is dying) or as a noun (the dying), the Greeks did the same thing but more often. So, when the Greek philosophers would write "being" as a noun or as a verb "to be," it could be quite confusing especially since there are translations involved as well. To distinguish the difference between the noun and the verb, when discussing Parmenides' topic "being" it will be written with a capital *B* meaning whatever is engaged in being (as opposed to "being" in lowercase letters, which indicates "to be").[79]

Now back to Parmenides, what did he mean by "Being" (for something to be)? When Parmenides refers to Being, he defines it as more than just existing. In the first four lines of his poem, which follows below, Parmenides believes if Being is that of which something is true (be / is), then Unbeing is that of which nothing is true, in other words, cannot exist (cannot be / is not):

> What you can call and think must Being be
> For Being can, and nothing cannot, be.

> Never shall this prevail that Unbeing is;
> Rein in your mind from any thought like this.
>
> Unbeing you won't grasp—it can't be done—
> Nor utter; being thought and being are one. [80]

However, if something does not exist, it must be something or else it cannot be thought of. For example, have you ever been "daydreaming" and someone asks what you have been thinking about and you say nothing or you cannot remember? So, does this mean that because you do not remember what you were thinking it did not exist? And, if it did exist, how can nothing exist?

Where many have accepted the principle "nothing can come from nothing," Parmenides expanded this by believing that Being has no beginning and no end and cannot be subject to change. [81]

Where Heraclitus may have believed that when water boils it changes to air, it is the death of water and the birth of air; while for Parmenides it is not changing from a Being to an Unbeing but changes within Being not changes of Being.[82] Therefore, Being is real or truth which is why one part of his poem is entitled "Way of Truth," while the world of senses or change was reflected in the second part of his poem, "Way of Seeming."[83] The question now facing many philosophers is which of the two theorists were correct, Heraclitus or Parmenides?

In early Greek history, there was a group of sages or wisemen called *Sophos*, who freely gave out their wisdom and would practice what many considered the earlier stages of philosophy throughout each of their wakening moments. Their predecessors, known as *Sophists*, were paid to help their students think philosophically; and since these iterant philosophers traveled from place to place to find students who would pay fees for their services, the word *sophisticated* resulted from them. The next chapter will discuss some of these Sophists.

ARIGNOTE

Women were part of the Pythagorean societies and have been believed to play a major role in the development of early Pythagorean philosophy.[84] Scholars believe that Pythagoras developed much of his philosophical doctrines from Themistoclea, the priestess at Delphi (circa 600 BCE).[85] Arignote, daughter of Pythagoras, describes how mathematical relationships can link what is real with all that exists:

> ..the eternal essence of number is the most providential (n.b. the guardianship of G-d over his creatures) cause of the whole heaven, earth and the region in between. Likewise it is the root of the continued existence of the gods and daimones (demons), as well as that of divine men.[86]

Arignote was born in 500 BCE, and was educated in the Pythagorean School known for the study of mathematics and its role in the order of the universe, which includes astronomy.[87] Not much is known about Arignote except that she believed the numbers 1,2,3, and 4 and their relationships to other numbers support her philosophy that the numbers are central to the origin of all order. She wrote on behalf of her mentor, as did many disciples of the time, which in this case was her father.[88]

AESARA

Aesara was a Pythagorean philosopher born in Lucania, the southern part of Italy, sometime between 425 and 100 BCE, during the time when it was believed that her fragment of work, *On Human Nature*, was written.[89] The passage that appears below describes her philosophy of the tripartite (divided into three parts) of the human soul, which consists of reason or mind, spiritedness, and desire.[90]

> Human nature seems to me to provide a standard of law and justice both for the home and for the city. By following the tracks within himself whoever seeks will make a discovery; law is in him and justice, which is the orderly arrangement of the soul. Being threefold,

it is organized in accordance with triple functions: that which effects judgment and thoughtfulness is (the mind), that which effects strength and ability (high spirit), and that which effects love and kindliness is desire. These are all so disposed relatively to one another that the best part is in command, the most inferior is governed, and the one in between holds a middle place; it both governs and is governed.[91]

Aesara believed that it is important to understand the three parts of the soul. She believed that one part should not dominate another part for harmony to occur for an individual, family, or society. For example, if you need to lease an automobile as transportation to school or work, using *reason*, it would be better to lease a 2015 Jeep Wrangler than a 1999 Jeep Wrangler with over 250,000 miles, with poor brakes and a mechanically unsound transmission. If you would enjoy driving the new Jeep, knowing it was dependable and affordable, your *desire* to work overtime would be a good choice. Your *spirited* part would make sure you lease something you could afford and not let your passion to lease a $1.7 million 2015 Bugatti Veyron 16.4 automobile be dominated by the *desire* part.

PERICTIONE

Many scholars question whether Perictione was Plato's mother or a student of Plato.[92] Although it is believed there were two writings by a Perictione, one called "On the Harmony of Women" (Perictione I) and the other "On Wisdom" (Perictione II), we will concentrate on the first work by Perictione I. The passage below originates from "On the Harmony of Women," written by Periction I:

> One must deem the harmonious woman to be full of wisdom and self control; a soul must be exceedingly conscious of goodness to be just and courageous and wise, embellished with self-sufficiency and hating empty opinion. Worthwhile things come to a woman from these..if..such a woman should govern cities and tribes…

Having mastery over appetite and high feeling she will be righteous and harmonious; no lawless desires will impel her. …Women who eat and drink every costly thing, who dress extravagantly..are ready for the sin of every vice….The woman who seeks these things seeks these things an admirer of feminine weakness. It is beauty that comes from wisdom, not from these things, that gratifies women who are well born.[93]

In this passage, Perictione addresses what a woman must do to be moral and at the same establishes her beliefs that women have the ability to rule their cities as well. It should also be noted that moderation or temperance is included in this philosophy, which was also espoused by Socrates, Plato, and Aristotle. Perictione establishes the philosophy that excess is a vice and wisdom is more important than one's attire. Perhaps one could say, it is the woman who makes the clothes, not the clothes that makes the woman.

"On the Harmony of Woman" was written sometime between 425 and 300 BCE, when some scholars believe her brother (Charmides) and uncle (Critas), both friends of Socrates, were listed as the "Thirty Tyrants" who ruled Athens during the brief oligarchy at the end of the Peloponnesian War. Perictione and her husband Ariston (Plato's father) had four children: Ademantus, Glaucon, Plato, and Potone (their only girl).[94]

Potone became the mother of Speusippus, who eventually took over Plato's Academy upon his death, instead of Plato's best student Aristotle who was not born in Athens.[95]

Although little is known about the other Perictione (II), including her actual name, she is credited with writing "On Wisdom," which discusses the importance of mathematics and its relationship to the world. However, this fragment from her essay below establishes the belief of humankind's contemplation as an avenue to wisdom:

Mankind came into being and exists in order to contemplate the principle of the nature of the whole.

The function of wisdom is to gain this very thing....
It is appropriate to wisdom to be able to see and to
contemplate those attributes which below universally
to all things...wisdom searches for the basic principles
of all things....Therefore...this person seems to be the
wisest and most true and, moreover, to have discovered
a noble height...[96]

Summary

Ethics is a branch of philosophy that examines the reasons why certain
actions are considered moral. However, it first must be determined what
the values are of the decision maker in order to better understand why
one action was taken compared to another action for the same situation.
Values are what are considered to be important to an individual. The
next step is to identify the reasons certain actions or even values would
be categorized in terms of moral development. Two psychologists—
Lawrence Kohlberg and his protégé Carol Gilligan—identified what they
believed to be three different levels of moral development; Kohlberg's
subjects were male and Gilligan's were female. Although the outcome
was different depending upon which model was used, another question
arises: What can you use as a moral standard to determine whether one
individual's value is better than another individual's value?

After assessing some moral standards, such as biblical or religious law,
Constitutional or state law, moral realism, guilt and moral relativism,
and recognizing conflict in all of these standards, the best approach to
decision making is to apply universally accepted philosophies when
measuring whether a particular action would be categorized a being
ethical.

Branches of philosophy include metaphysics, epistemology, axiology,
aesthetics, ethics, and logic, among others. Early male philosophers
helped to shape the modern-day discipline of philosophy. The first
was Thales, considered by many to be one of the seven sages or
wisemen. He questioned what the universe consisted of, and ultimately
came up with the solution that everything was comprised of water.

Anaximander believed that the universe was made up of a "boundless something" (apeiron) which contained every sort of shape and quality and was without any definition or specific characteristics of its own. Anaximenes, a protégé of Anaximander, disagreed with his mentor and believed that all things originated from air. Another philosopher, Pythagoras, believed that the fundamental principles of the universe were derived from mathematical relations. Philosopher Heraclitus raised two questions: What is the source of this unified motion, and what is the agency (means) where movement is provided? He believed that everything changed from earth, fire, and water, but fire was the primary source of change. Parmenides believed that everything, like the truth, did not change and whatever changes would not be real or an illusion. This was the basis for a later known philosopher, by the name of Plato, who used these concepts to further the theories.

In terms of female philosophers, Pythagoras's daughter, Arignote, supported the belief in the importance of numbers and their relationship to the origin of the natural world and causal effects. Aesara of Lucania believed that for harmony to occur between an individual and family or society, the three parts of the soul (reason, desire, and spirit) must be equally applied when making a decision, for allowing one part to dominate another part, could have a detrimental effect on the outcome. Another philosopher, Perictione I, addressed what a woman must do to be moral and at the same established her beliefs that women have the ability to rule their cities as well. Perictione II established the belief of humankind's contemplation as an avenue to wisdom, thus concluding this section on first philosophers.

Key Terms

Aesthetics: basically, the philosophy of art or the value of beauty.

Axiology: the branch of philosophy that deals with the study of values.

Conventional level: according to Kohlberg's model, it is based upon when you are making a decision. The deciding factor is what others think of your decision. (What will other people think?) In Gilligan's model, it is based upon doing what is best for others and detrimentally neglecting yourself.

Epistemology: includes questions about knowledge, such as: What is knowledge? and How do we know what we know?

Ethical dilemma: a situation or decision affecting others when there may not be an obvious solution in terms of what is the right thing to do.

Ethics: a branch of philosophy that identifies why and if a particular moral standard should be a moral standard.

Logic: a specialized branch of philosophical science first discovered by Aristotle in the fourth century BCE which examines the science of valid defenses.

Metaphysics (or ontology): deals with questions of reality: What is appearance? and What is real?

Philosopher: one who looks for a rational explanation of his or her experience of reality, who tries to grasp the real as a matter of understanding, as opposed to a magical, mythical, fictional explanation of things; means a lover of wisdom.

Philosophy: a discipline in which philosophers continue to question the assumptions behind every claim and the most basic beliefs about reality, and then to critically examine those beliefs.

Political philosophy: the examination of social values and the justification of various political institutions and political relations.

Postconventional level: according to the Kohlberg model, the determining factor when making a decision is based upon a higher level of development when you act in a manner for the good of humankind, and your motivation is not for any personal reward or motivated by what others may think. In the Gilligan model, it is putting yourself ahead of others, not to be selfish but to be selfless.

Preconventional level: based upon when you are making decisions in which the determining factor is how you are benefited by that decision (i.e., motivated by selfishness).

Values: ideals you believe in and are then compared to one or more moral standards, which would enable you to make the most ethical choice (e.g., friendship, religion, money).

Chapter Review Questions

1. What is philosophy? How does Andrew Bailey define philosophy in this chapter?
2. What are some of the branches of philosophy? Define at least two of them.
3. Why can we rely more on universal philosophies to use as moral standards than on biblical or religious law, constitutional or state laws, moral realism, guilt, or moral relativism? Explain the advantage of using universal philosophies and give examples of why some of the others may not be used by everyone.
4. How does Kohlberg's theory differ from Gilligan's theory of moral development? Discuss specifically why the female subjects scored lower in their moral development using Kohlberg's model and higher using Gilligan's model.
5. Who are some of the first philosophers and how did their philosophies differ? Respond to this question by describing the philosophies of *at least three* of these philosophers.

Case Review Questions

Answer the following from "The Shallow Pond" found on page 1.
1. Would you save the child or attend the lecture on time? Explain your response.
2. If your weekly lecture was being observed by your Department Chair in order to make a decision on tenure for a Board meeting the following day (a decision on tenure means either you earn a permanent position with the college or you lose your job), would you still save the child? Explain your response.
3. What if the job market was so poor and your were the sole wage earner for your family of four, that being rejected for tenure would lead to unemployment, would you still save the child? Explain your response.

Answer the following from "The Envelope" found on page 2.
1. Would you send the $100 if you had the money? If not, why were you willing to save one child from drowning in a pond but not save the thirty children by donating $100? Explain your responses.
2. Which of your *values* played a role in your decisions?
3. Which of your values played a role in your decisions for the "The Shallow Pond"?
4. Did the values used in "The Shallow Pond" conflict with those from "The Envelope"? If so, how can you justify this conflict?

Answer the following from "The Alligator River Story" found on page 5.

1. Who do you think was the most moral? Why?
2. Who do you think was the least moral? Why?
3. List in order of morality (the most moral first, the next most moral person second) all five of the characters. Then, compare your list with other members in the class. Can you come to a consensus?

Endnotes

[1a] "The Shallow Pond" was found in Peter Unger's *Living High and Letting Die* (New York: Oxford Press, 1996), p. 9.

[1b] Ibid. (modified by author).

[2] Luis E. Navia, *Diogenes of Sinope: The Man in the Tub* (Westport, CT: Greenwood Press, 1998), p. 159.

[3] Plato, *Plato Complete Works*, John Cooper, Ed. (Indianapolis: Hackett Publishing Company, Inc., 1997), p. 33.

[4] Sidney B. Simon, Leland W. Howe, and Howard Kirschenbaum, *Values Clarification: A Handbook of Practical Strategies for Teachers and Students* (New York: Hart Publishing Company, Inc., 1972), pp. 291-292.

[5] Lawrence Kohlberg and Richard H. Hersh, "Moral Development: A Review of Theory," *Theory Into Practice,* Vol. 16, No. 2, April 1977, p. 54.

[6] Ibid., 54-55.

[7] Ibid., 55.

[8] Ibid.

[9] Ibid.

[10] Ibid.

[11] Carol Gilligan, *In a Different Voice* (Cambridge: Harvard University Press, 1982), p. 73.

[12] Ibid., 74.

[13] Ibid.

[14] Ibid., 82.

[15] Ibid., 82-83.

[16] Ibid., 74, 84.

[17] *Encyclopedia of Psychology.* Guilt. 2nd ed. Ed. Bonnie R. Strickland. Gale Group, Inc., 2001.

[18] Michael J. Sandel, *Liberalism and Its Critics: Readings in Political and Social Theory* (New York: New York University Press, 1984), p. 1.

[19] Immanuel Kant, *Groundwork of the Metaphysics of Morals*, H.J. Patton, trans. (New York: Harper & Row Publishers, 1964), p. 96.

[20] Andrew Bailey (Ed.), *First Philosophy* (Ontario: Broadview Press, 2002), p. 3.

[21] Ibid., 1.

[22] T.Z. Lavine, *From Socrates to Sartre: The Philosophical Quest* (New York: Bantam Books, 1984), p. 1.

[23] Donald Palmer, *Does the Center Hold? An Introduction to Western Philosophy* (Boston: McGraw Hill, 2002), p. 21.

[24] Ibid., 20.

[25] Ibid.

[26] Bryan Magee, *The Story of Philosophy* (New York: Dorling Kindersley, 1998), p. 12.

[27] Ibid.

[28] Diogenes Laertius, *Lives of Eminent Philosophers*, R.D. Hicks, trans. (Cambridge: Harvard University Press, 1925/1959), p. 15.

[29] Jonathan Barnes, *Early Greek Philosophy* (New York: Penguin Group, 1987/2001), p. 9.

[30] Albert B. Hakim, *Historical Introduction to Philosophy*, 5th ed. (Upper Saddle River, NJ: Pearson Prentice Hall, 2006), pp. 12-13.

31 Bryan Magee, *The Story of Philosophy* (New York: Dorling Kindersley, 1998), p. 12.

32 Ibid, 2.

33 Ibid, 25, 37.

34 Ibid, 41.

35 Ibid, 25, 28, 29.

36 Ibid., 35.

37 Ibid.

38 Robert S. Brumbaugh, *The Philosophers of Greece* (New York: Thomas Y. Crowell Company, 1964), p. 13.

39 W.K.C. Gutherie, *A History of Greek Philosophy*, Vol. 1 (Cambridge, UK: Cambridge at the University Press, 1967), pp. 53-54.

40 Diogenes Laertus, *Lives of Eminent Philosophers*, R.D. Hicks, trans. (Cambridge: Harvard University Press, 1925/1959), p. 131.

41 Ibid., 23.

42 Ibid., 20.

43 Ibid.

44 Reginald E. Allen, *Greek Philosophy: Thales to Aristotle* (New York: Free Press, 1991), p. 30.

45 Ibid.

46 Anthony Kenny, *A Brief History of Western Philosophy* (Oxford: Blackwell Publishers, 1998), p. 4.

47 Reginald E. Allen (Ed.), Greek Philosophy: Thales to Aristotle, 3rd ed. (New York: The Free Press, 1991), p. 4.

48 Ibid.

49 John Chafee, *The Philosopher's Way: Thinking Critically About Profound Ideas* (Upper Saddle River, NJ: Pearson/Prentice Hall, 2005), p. 48.

50 Bryan Magee, *The Story of Philosophy* (New York: Dorling Kindersley, 1998), p. 15.

51 Kitty Ferguson, *The Music of Pythagoras* (New York: Walker and Company, 2008), pp. 10-11.

52 Ibid., 11.

53 Bryan Magee, *The Story of Philosophy* (New York: Dorling Kindersley, 1998), p. 15.

54 Albert B. Hakim, *Historical Introduction to Philosophy*, 5th ed. (Upper Saddle River, NJ: Pearson/Prentice Hall, 2006), p. 15.

55 Ibid., 13-14.

56 Ibid., 14.

57 Anthony Kenny, *A Brief History of Western Philosophy* (Oxford: Blackwell Publishers, 1998), p. 1.

58 Ibid.

59 Albert B. Hakim, *Historical Introduction to Philosophy*, 5th ed. (Upper Saddle River, NJ: Pearson/Prentice Hall, 2006), p. 14.

60 Ibid.

61a Ibid.

61b Diogenes Laërtius, *Lives and Opinions of Eminent Philosophers*, "Pythagoras", Sect. 30, in the translation of C.D. Yonge (1853). http://www.perseus.tufts.edu/hopper/text?doc=Perseus%3Atext%3A1999.0 1.0258%3Abook%3D8%3Achapter%3D1

62 Op.cit., 48.

63 John Chafee, *The Philosopher's Way: Thinking Critically About Profound Ideas* (Upper Saddle River, NJ: Pearson/Prentice Hall, 2005), p. 420.

64 Albert B. Hakim, *Historical Introduction to Philosophy*, 5th ed. (Upper Saddle River, NJ: Pearson/Prentice Hall, 2006), p. 15.

65 Reginald E. Allen (Ed.), *Greek Philosophy: Thales to Aristotle*, 3rd ed. (New York: The Free Press, 1991), p. 7.

66 Albert B. Hakim, *Historical Introduction to Philosophy*, 5th ed. (Upper Saddle River: Pearson/Prentice Hall, 2006), p. 16.

67 Reginald E. Allen (Ed.), *Greek Philosophy: Thales to Aristotle*, 3rd ed. (New York: The Free Press, 1991), p. 9.

68 Ibid.

69 Philip Stokes, *Philosophy: 100 Essential Thinkers* (New York: Enchanted Lion Books, 2003), p. 15.

70 Anthony Kenny, *A Brief History of Western Philosophy* (Oxford: Blackwell Publishers, 1998), p. 6.

71 Philip Stokes, *Philosophy: 100 Essential Thinkers* (New York: Enchanted Lion Books, 2003), p. 15.

72 Ibid.

73 Ibid., 16.

74 John Chafee, *The Philosopher's Way: Thinking Critically About Profound Ideas* (Upper Saddle River, NJ: Pearson/Prentice Hall, 2005), p. 22.

75 T.Z. Lavine, *From Socrates to Sartre: The Philosophical Quest* (New York: Bantam Books, 1984), p. 24.

76 John Chafee, *The Philosopher's Way: Thinking Critically About Profound Ideas* (Upper Saddle River, NJ: Pearson/Prentice Hall, 2005), p. 22.

77 Reginald E. Allen (Ed.), *Greek Philosophy: Thales to Aristotle*, 3rd ed. (New York: The Free Press, 1991), p. 10.

78 Ibid., 11.

79 Anthony Kenny, *A Brief History of Western Philosophy* (Oxford: Blackwell Publishers, 1998), pp. 8-9.

80 Ibid., 9-10.

81 Ibid., 11.

82 Ibid.

83 Ibid.

84 Mary Ellen Waithe, *A History of Women Philosophers*, vol. 1 / 6000BC-500AD (Hingham, MA: Kluwer Academic Publishers, 1987), p. 11.

85 Ibid., 1, 11.

86 Ibid., 12.

87 "Arignote (fl. 6th c. BCE)," *Women in World History: A Biographical Encyclopedia,* 2002. Encyclopedia.com. 22 Feb. 2015. http://www.encyclopedia.com

88 Ibid.

89 Kate Lindemann, Aesara of Lucania, Society for the Study of Women Philosophers. n.d. Web. 22 Feb. 2015. http://www.societyforthestudyofwomenphilosophers.org/Aesara_Lucania.html

90 Ibid.

91 Mary Ellen Waithe, *A History of Women Philosophers*, vol. 1 / 6000BC-500AD (Hingham, MA: Kluwer Academic Publishers, 1987), p. 20.

92 Ibid., 71.

93 Ibid., 32-33.

94 Op.cit.

95 Ibid.

96 Ibid.

CHAPTER 2

CLASSICAL PHILOSOPHERS

SOPHOS
the original philoso-phers who practiced their craft by raising questions as to the origin of the world and the meaning of a good life.

"The unexamined life is not worth living"

-Socrates in Apology 38a

The Sophists

The **Sophos** *were the original philosophers who practiced their craft by raising questions as to the origin of the world and the meaning of a good life.* Since the majority of Sophos had inheritances, they were able to "philosophize" on a 24/7 basis. The philosophers discussed in the first chapter were examples of these Sophos. However, as the Sophos continued to teach within their small communities, it was the Sophists who took philosophy to another level. The Greek term *sophos* or

© Panos Karas/Shuttrestock.com

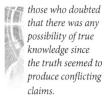

SOPHISTS

those who believed in preparing their students in the art of rhetoric or power of persuasive speech for an usually large fee, unlike their predecessors, the Sophos who did not charge fees.

SKEPTICS

those who doubted that there was any possibility of true knowledge since the truth seemed to produce conflicting claims.

CULTURAL RELATIVISM

the belief that the values of individuals differ from culture to culture, as opposed to being absolute, when values are accepted regardless of cultural background.

sophia means "wise" or "wisdom."[1] The **Sophists** *believed in preparing their students in the art of rhetoric or power of persuasive speech for an usually large fee.*[2] These Sophists who traveled from city to city became the first **skeptics,** *who doubted that there was any possibility of true knowledge since the truth seemed to produce conflicting claims.*[3] Perhaps one reason for this skepticism could be attributed to the inconsistency of philosophical thought from cosmologists, such as Thales, who believed the universe consisted of water; while Heraclitus concluded it was fire; and Anaximander hypothesized it was air.[4] This disagreement among the so-called authorities validated the position of this skeptic school of philosophy.

PROTAGORAS

Probably the most famous of all the Sophists was Protagoras (ca 485-415 BC), born in Abdera in northern Greece and best known for his cultural relativist viewpoint.[5] **Cultural relativism** *is the belief that the values of individuals differ from culture to culture, as opposed to being absolute, when values are accepted regardless of one's cultural background.* Protagoras was one of the first Greeks to earn money in higher education and was known for charging his students exorbitant fees.[6] He taught public speaking, criticism of poetry, citizenship, and grammar but was well paid by his wealthier students because his area of expertise was the art of rhetoric, which included model orations, discussions of the meanings and the correct use of words and the general rules of debating.[7] Given that these skills were necessary to practice law in Athenian society, Protagoras was quite a commodity in his time.

It is believed that Protagoras came to Athens about the middle of the fifth century BCE and was well received by the great statesman, Pericles, who entrusted him to draw up a constitution for the Panhellenic colony of Thurii, which was founded in 444 BCE.[8] Legend has it that Protagoras was indicted for blasphemy because of his book on the gods, but that he escaped from the city before trial and was drowned on the crossing to Sicily, while later on his book was burnt in the marketplace.[9]

Although little of Protagoras's works physically exists, perhaps he is best known for the following sentence from one of his few writings, entitled *Truth*: "Man is the measure of all things, of the existence of what exists, and of the non-existence of what does not exist."[10] What this means is that perception and truth are related to the experience and judgment of the individual as well as the community.[11] For example, if it is acceptable to deny women the right to vote in Country A but unacceptable in Country B, which country is wrong? According to Protagorus, neither, since each country's truth or standards determine what is morally acceptable.

As a point of reference, you may note below that there are notations in parentheses following the passages. *These notations refer to marginal references that describe the corresponding page and section of the relevant volume of the Greek text as edited by the French scholar, Henri Estienne (which in Latin is* Stephanus) *and known as the* **Stephanus numbers**.[12]

STEPHANUS
NUMBERS

These notations refer to marginal references that describe the corresponding page and section of the relevant volume of the Greek text as edited by the French scholar, Henri Estienne (which in Latin is Stephanus)

These Stephanus numbers are commonly used in the works of Plato (and other Greek philosophers); so, regardless of who translated the works, you could still find the particular section identified, such as this passage found below in *Theaetetus* which would be found on 152a-c in the margins of any translation.[13]

In *Theaetetus* (152a-c), written by Plato, the following discussion occurred between the Sophist Theaetetus and Socrates about Protagoras's opening sentence in his work *Truth* (in the boxed area that follows).

SOCRATES: But look here, ...its what Protagoras used to maintain. ...For he says, you know that "Man is the measure of all things: of the things which are, that they are, and of the things which are not, that they are not." You have read this, of course?

THEAETETUS: Yes, very often.

SOCRATES: Then you know that he (referring to Protagoras) puts it something like this, that as each thing appears to me, so it is for me, and as it appears to you, so it is for you—you and I each being a man?

THEAETETUS: Yes, that is what he says.

SOCRATES: Well, it is not likely that a wise man would talk nonsense. So let us follow him up. Now doesn't it sometimes happen that when the same wind is blowing, one of us feels cold and the other not? Or that one of us feels cold and the other very cold?

THEAETETUS: That certainly does happen.

SOCRATES: Well then, in that case are we going to say that the wind itself, by itself, is cold or not cold? Or shall we listen to Protagoras, and say it is cold for the one who feels cold, and for the other not cold?

THEAETETUS: It looks as if we must say that.

SOCRATES: And this is how it appears to each of us?

THEAETETUS: Yes.

SOCRATES: But this expression 'it appears' means 'he perceives it' ?

THEAETETUS: Yes, it does.

SOCRATES: The appearing of things, then, is the same as perception, in the case of hot and things like that. So it results, apparently, that things are for the individual such as he perceives them.

THEAETETUS: Yes, that seems all right.

SOCRATES: Perception, then, is always of what is, and unerring-as benefits knowledge.

THEAETETUS: So it appears.[14]

In the passage above, Socrates and Theaetetus are discussing whether or not perception actually determines a specific situation. Is a person cold because it is cold or because it is cold to him? Socrates was pointing out to Theaetetus that Protagoras's philosophy had a flaw in that respect.

Now let us look at an example to better understand Protagoras's philosophy. In October 2009, Raj Rajaratnam, who managed the Galleon Group hedge fund, was arrested for one of the largest insider trading conspiracies ever, which amounted to almost $63 million and two years later was sentenced to 11 years in federal prison.[15] Insider trading is having confidential knowledge of an action or impending action which can affect the price of stock before the general public. This knowledge enables the individual to purchase or sell a financial security such as stock and financially gain with this confidential information at the expense of others not privy to this information. Even though Rajaratnam was aware of the rules, "cheating became part of his business model."[16] Although insider trading is illegal, since others in their industry engaged in this practice, Rajaratnam considered it to be an industry norm, which personified what Protagoras's philosophy espoused. This is the flaw Socrates finds in Protagoras's philosophy.

Later on in Plato's work *Theaetetus* (166d-167a), Socrates disputes Protagoras's claim. In this statement, Socrates is speaking to Theaetetus:

> SOCRATES: I take my stand on the truth being as I have written it. Each one of us is the measure of both what is and of what is not; but there are countless differences between men for just this very reason, that different things both are and appear to be different subjects.

Socrates then continues after some further explanation about this statement.

> SOCRATES: For instance, …… to the sick man the things he eats both appear and are bitter, while to the healthy man they both appear and are opposite. Now what we have to do is not make one of these two wiser than the other—not even a possibility—nor is it our business to make accusations, calling the sick man ignorant for judging as he does, and the healthy man wise, because he judges differently. What we have to do is to make a change from the one to the other, because the other state is *better*.[17]

In the passage above, Socrates is pointing out that just because others may consider a certain act acceptable, it does not necessarily mean this act is ethical. Just as the sick man believes the food is bitter, when actually it is not, is an unethical action ethical just because the unjust person believes it to be? As in the insider trading example above, just because others in the industry are conducting this practice, and even in their realm it is the norm, it does not deter from the fact that it is an unethical practice. Slavery, women prohibited from voting, and outlawing interracial marriages during and before the early and mid-twentieth century did not change the fact that these culturally accepted practices were still *unjust*, supporting Socrates' claim.

CALLICLES

Another Sophist who Plato made famous by his writings was Callicles, allegedly an Athenian aristocrat, whose history seemed to be nonexistent except when mentioned by Plato in his writing *Gorgias*. Many scholars have debated whether Callicles actually existed; however, it is believed that Plato would not have attributed so much to him in his writings unless he really lived, which most believe was circa 435 BCE.[18] Outside of his dialogue in Plato's *Gorgias*, information about Callicles' life appears to be unknown.[19] Callicles' version of moral realism was known as the **doctrine of the superior individual,** *a theory that justifies why the strong who dominate the weak are constrained by conventional morality*.[20] This could be analogous to a philosophical social Darwinism, where the strongest in a society determine the ethics of its community. For example, according to this philosophy, if an individual such as Bill Gates,

DOCTRINE OF THE SUPERIOR INDIVIDUAL *a social Darwinism theory by Callicles, which justifies why the strong who dominate the weak are constrained by conventional morality.*

who would represent survival of the fittest, has the ability to create a monopolistic organization by his intelligence and business acumen, why should the Department of Justice protect those who are not as talented? Callicles believes that nature, as shown by the strongest or survival of the fittest, should dominate and not by convention as those who are not as strong or knowledgeable (as Bill Gates's weaker competitors).

In the following passage found in Plato's *Gorgias* (483 b-d) Callicles espouses his belief to Socrates that the superior dominate the inferior, just as in the animal world, and that laws are developed to give the inferior more of a share than they are entitled do. After reading this, think about whether you agree with his philosophy or if you can find examples to dispute Callicles' beliefs.

I believe that people who institute our laws are the weak and say that getting more than one's share is "shameful" and "unjust," and that doing what's unjust is nothing but trying to get more than one's share. I think they like getting an equal share, since they are inferior.

These are the reasons why trying to get a greater share than most is said to be unjust and shameful by law and why they call it doing what's unjust. But I believe that nature itself reveals that it's a just thing for the better man and the more capable man to have a greater share than the worse man and the less capable man. Nature shows that this is so in many places; both among the other animals and in whole cities and races of men, it shows that this is what justice has been decided to be: that the superior rule the inferior and have a greater share than they.[21]

In a statement found later on in *Gorgias* (491d), Callicles further supports his views that may be considered somewhat of a social Darwinism (survival of the fittest) philosophy.

But, I've already said that those who are intelligent in the affairs of the city they should be the ones who rule their cities, and what's just is that they, as the rulers, should have a greater share than the others, the ruled.[22]

Callicles' passage above justifies why political dictators such as Fidel Castro and now his brother Raul, who for over 50 years held office, should have more material things than their Cuban constituents. Given what business leaders of Fortune 500 firms like Bill Gates and many others earn in a few hours than many of their employees all year, it would not be surprising that if Callicles was still alive, he would support this disparity of income.

THRASYMACHUS

Another leading Sophist was Socrates' formidable opponent, Thrasymachus (circa 459–400 BCE), whom he described as loud, sarcastic, insulting, and often appeared ready to explode physically.[23] Thrasymachus was born in Chalcedon, a colony of Megara in Bithynia, and he had distinguished himself as a teacher of rhetoric and speechwriter in Athens by the year 427.[24] Other than his memorable place in the first book of Plato's *Republic*, very little is known about this famous Sophist.

Thrasymachus's belief was that justice is defined by the mighty. Whereas Callicles believed that justice would be defined by the strongest over a period of time, Thrasymachus believed that "justice is in the advantage of the stronger," and that individuals are foolish if they are just. However, according to Thrasymachus, if you appear just, but are not just, you are even better off. Perhaps as we mention Machiavelli later, you may wonder if Thrasymachus had any influence on his philosophy. After reading the passage below, do you think this was what Thrasymachus had in mind when "Ponzi schemers" Bernard Madoff and R. Allen Stanford defrauded their investors?

In this passage below, found in Plato's *Republic* (Book One, 338c-339a), Thrasymachus begins his argument with Socrates. In this section, to identify the two interlocutors (speakers taking part in a dialogue), I have followed the passage with (T) to signify Thrasymachus and (S) for Socrates.

"Listen, then. I say that justice is nothing other that the advantage of the stronger. Well why don't you praise me? But then you'd do anything to avoid having to do that." (T)

"I must first understand you, for I don't yet know what you mean. The advantage of the stronger, you say, is just. What do you mean, Thrasymachus? Surely you don't' mean something like this: Polydamus, the pancratist (boxer/wrestler), is stronger than we are; it is to his advantage to eat beef to build up his physical strength; therefore, this food is also advantageous and just for us who are weaker than he is?" (S)

"You disgust me, Socrates. Your trick is to take hold of the argument at the point where you can do it the most harm." (T)

"Not at all, but tell us more clearly what you mean." (S)

"Don't you know that some cities are ruled by tyranny, some by a democracy, and some by aristocracy?" (T)

"Of course." (S)

"And in each city this element is stronger, namely, the ruler?" (T)

"Certainly." (S)

"And each makes laws to its own advantage. Democracy makes democratic laws, tyranny makes tyrannical laws, and so on with the others. And they declare what they have made—what is to be their own advantage—to be just for their subjects and they punish anyone who goes against this as lawless and unjust. This, then, is what I say justice is, the same in all cities, the advantage of the established rule. Since the established rule is surely stronger, anyone who reasons correctly will conclude that *the just is the same everywhere, the advantage of the stronger.*"[25] (T)

Consider our own Supreme Court; whoever is selected will be deciding major issues. So, if the majority of our Justices were against Affirmative Action, it would be considered unjust to favor someone for a position because of their gender or ethnicity. On the other hand, if the majority of our Justices were for Affirmative Action, a qualified female could be hired over a qualified male because of her gender, since it would be considered to be just, or as Thrasymachus said, the advantage of the stronger.

In this next passage, also found in Plato's Republic (Book One, 343d-344a), Thrasymachus explains to Socrates why a just man is foolish for not being unjust.

Socrates, a just man always gets less than an unjust one. First, in their contracts with one another, you'll never find, when the partnership ends, that a just partner has got more than an unjust one, but less. Second, in matters relating to the city, when taxes are to be paid, a just man pays more on the same property, as unjust one less, but when the city is giving out refunds, a just man gets nothing, while an unjust one makes a large profit. Finally, when each of them holds a ruling position in some public office, a just person, even if he isn't penalized in other ways, finds that his private affairs deteriorate because he has to neglect them, that he gains no advantage from the public purse because of his justice, and that he's hated by his relatives and acquaintances when he's unwilling to do them an unjust favor. The opposite is true of an unjust man in every respect. Therefore, I repeat what I said before: A person of great power outdoes everyone else. Consider him if you want to figure out how much more advantageous it is for the individual to be just rather than unjust. You'll understand this most easily if you turn your thoughts to the most complete injustice, the one that makes the doer of injustice happiest and the sufferers of it, who are unwilling to do injustice, most wretched.[26]

In 2015, an article in *Bloomberg Business* reported how the chief executive officer of Target, under whose leadership followed a major credit card data breach, received retirement funds of over $47 million, which is 1,044 times the $45,000 pension balance of the average worker who saved in the company's 401(k) plan.[27a] This illustrates the unbalance of executive compensation, when in 2013, the average CEO was 204 times higher than the pay of the average worker.[27b] Given that the executive compensation is determined by the board of directors, who are affluent, it is precisely what Thrasymachus had in mind by the passage above found in Plato's *Republic*.

SOCRATES

Socrates was the first of the Greek triads, along with Plato and Aristotle, to be considered renowned classical philosophers. It is believed that Socrates was born in 469 BCE. His father, Sophroniscus, was a stonemason; his mother, Phainarete, a midwife. Virtually nothing else is known about the first half of his life.[28] Although some consider him a Sophist, most accounts of his background indicate that he never accepted money for his teachings. It is also

© Marzolino /Shutterstock, Inc.

believed that Socrates came from some sort of wealth, because he served in the heavy infantry, which required supplying your own weapons and armor, yet he possessed remarkable endurance given the extreme cold winter conditions in which he went about wearing ordinary thin clothes and walking barefoot.[29] He married Xanthippe and they had three sons, two of them small children at the time of his death.[30]

Since Socrates never wrote a book, we rely on his protégé, Plato, who used Socrates as a character in his written works, giving Plato the opportunity to describe his mentor's philosophies. However, even though Socrates was still used as a character in Plato's later writings, it has been speculated that it was actually Plato's words and beliefs being mouthed by Socrates toward the latter half of Plato's published works.

Although the words of the Athenian G-d Apollo "know thyself" which was ascribed on the entrance of the temple at Delphi, and some attributed Thales for applying it to philosophy, it was believed that Socrates took it a step further in that by knowing thyself, you then come to know who you really are and can discern between good and evil.[31] This was more apparent when he would raise questions to those who believed they were knowledgeable, only to prove that they were not.

For example, using a contemporary example, he might have asked, What is the meaning of beauty? The respondent might say, "an individual who possesses physical characteristics that are appealing to the eye." So, do you believe that the movie actress Jennifer Aniston is beautiful? But, what about the movie actress Halle Berry—would you say she is beautiful? And, of course the respondent would agree. "But," Socrates might go on, "what if one person thinks Jennifer Aniston is beautiful because she is appealing to his eyes and Halle Berry is not because she is not appealing to his eyes, while another thinks Halle Berry is beautiful and Jennifer Aniston is not for the same reason, then who would be correct?" And, then the respondent would have to change his response or modify his definition.

This is the technique Socrates would use in his search for the truth. By stating, beauty is in the eyes of the beholder, this would be known as the *thesis*. If there was a modification disputing the thesis, that would be the *antithesis*, and if and when there was an agreement as to the definition of beauty, it would be called the *synthesis*. This technique, called the Socratic Method, is used in education frequently, because instead of the student being told what the answer is, the professor continues to question the student's definition until that student develops an acceptable definition. In addition, when Socrates would use this method or technique, it would allow the respondent to be subtly admitting that she did not know the answer and needed to think more profoundly before claiming to do so. For this reason, Socrates considered himself a *gadfly*, which referred to that annoying fly that horses had to use their tails to shake these insects off their bodies. However, Socrates believed unlike being a gadfly to a horse, he was the ethical gadfly to the Athenians.

ETHICAL WISDOM
according to Socrates, "the recognition of the fundamental importance of the ethical in the life of man (humankind) and of doing good as the basic principle of human activity."

Socrates main philosophy was **ethical wisdom**, which he defined according to Seton Hall University Professor Albert Hakim as *"the recognition of the fundamental importance of the ethical in the life of man (humankind) and of doing good as the basic principle of human activity."*[32]

In essence, Socrates believed that virtue is knowledge and that happiness depends upon having this knowledge, which he believed to include courage, piety, and justice; so if individuals choose not to adhere to these virtues, they are really not wise.[33]

Believing that it was his purpose to seek knowledge and help others do the same, Socrates would often go to the marketplace (known in Greece as the *agora*) and become engrossed in these philosophical questions. What irked Socrates most was his disdain for those who had knowledge in one area but believed this knowledge transcended beyond their expertise. It would be the equivalent of a plumber giving stock tips based upon conversations he or she may have had with the customers who had profited in the stock market.

It is for this reason that it would not be uncommon for Socrates to be sent to the market by his wife to pick something up and then return hours later without it because he became engrossed in his philosophical debates and forgot the item.[34] Legend has it that sometimes Socrates' wife, Xanthippe, would hide his clothes, so he could not go out, but he did so anyway; however, not wanting to see their mentor in the nude, his disciples would bring along an extra robe in case Socrates arrived naked.[35]

In 406 BCE, Socrates held an office in the Assembly when several generals were put on trial collectively rather than individually for abandoning the bodies of the dead at the sea-battle of Arginusae, even though it was illegal to prosecute defendants collectively, but Socrates was the only one who voted against it.[36] Furthermore, in 404 BCE, Socrates disobeyed an order to arrest an innocent man when the Spartans replaced the Athenian democracy with an oligarchy called the "Thirty Tyrants," and the Athenians regained control.[37a] In addition, some of his students sided with the Spartans, so Socrates was guilty by association, which led him to be tried by the Assembly for "corrupting the youth" and "impiety to the G-ds." This last charge was because when the Oracle of Delphi announced Socrates as being the wisest, Socrates responded that "I know that I know nothing" (literal Greek translation).

Given the opportunity to cease practicing philosophy and be exiled, Socrates refused and although he was found guilty of the charges referred to above by a narrow margin, during the sentencing phase when Socrates suggested he be given free room and board for life, as well as pay for a minimal penalty, the Assembly voted a death sentence for him with a greater majority than when he was found guilty. Even though he had the opportunity to escape (his friends had arranged to bribe the jailor for his release), as a person of principle, he refused to do so because **he** believed in the Athenian democratic government and just because it was not the outcome that he would have expected, as a lifetime Athenian he would abide by the death sentence, which was carried out sometime around his seventieth birthday. Perhaps when faced with stopping his practice of philosophy or taking hemlock, Socrates realized that an unexamined life was not worth living.

The following quote found in Plato's work, *Protagoras* (358d), shows Socrates espousing his belief that to know the good is to do the good:

"Now, no one goes willingly toward the bad or what he believes to be bad; neither is it in human nature, so it seems, to want to go toward what one believes to be bad instead of to the good. And when he is forced to choose between one of two bad things, no one will choose the greater if he is able to choose the lesser." [37b]

Socrates believes that if you know that something is wrong, you would not do it and if you had to decide whether to do something a little bad or something evil, you would do just what is a little bad. For example, if you had to choose between saving a child in a pond or missing a class as a result of saving the child, not saving the child would be more evil compared to missing a class which would be "a little bad." It should be noted that Socrates would be against any unethical action taken by an individual, who may believe the action was ethical, as the individual's perception of what is evil does not detract from *what actually is evil or unethical.*

In another passage from Plato's *Republic* in Book Two (359d-360a), you will read a description based upon a conversation Socrates had with Plato's brother, Glaucon, about a tale testing Socrates' philosophy "to know the good is to do the good."

The story goes that he (Gyges of Lydia) was a shepherd in the service of the ruler of Lydia. There was a violent thunderstorm, and an earthquake broke open the ground and created a chasm at the place where he was tending his sheep. Seeing this, he was filled with amazement and went down into it. And there, in addition to many other wonders of which we're told, he saw a hollow bronze horse. There were windowlike openings in it, and, peeping in, he saw a corpse, which seemed to be of more than human size, wearing nothing but a gold ring on its finger. He took the ring and came out of the chasm. He wore the ring at the usual monthly meeting that reported to the king on the state of the flocks. And as he was sitting among the others, he happened to turn the setting of the ring towards himself to the inside of his hand. When he did this, he became invisible to those sitting near him, and they went on talking as if he had gone. He wondered at this, and, fingering the ring, he turned the setting outwards again and became visible. So he experimented with the ring to test whether it indeed had this power—and it did. If he turned the setting inward, he became invisible; if he turn it outward, he became visible again. When he realized this, he at once arranged to become one of the messengers sent to report to the king. And when he arrived there, he seduced the king's wife, attacked the king with her help, killed him, and took over the kingdom.[38]

The question now comes up, if you had the ability to be invisible and visible like Gyges, what would you do with this power? Socrates believed a just person would do good and not what Gyges did, because a just person would possess the knowledge of virtue that Gyges did not possess.

PLATO

Plato was born in Athens in 427 or 428 and died in 347 BCE. His father Ariston was believed to have descended from the last king of Athens,

© Everett Historical/Shutterstock, Inc.

while his mother Perictione was a relative of the Athenian statesman, Solon.[39] Plato had two full brothers, Glaucon and Adeimantus, to whom he allots parts in the *Republic* and a half-brother, Antiphon, who is given the role of narrator in another of his works, *Parmedides*.[40] In addition, he had a stepbrother, Demos, who was referred in his work, *Gorgias*.[41] Little is known about Plato's earlier life; however, it is believed that he served in the military service as a member of the Athenian cavalry who saw action against Sparta.[42]

Although he was a student of Socrates for about a year, Plato followed his master's spirit for his entire life.[43] After Socrates' death, and feeling disillusioned with the sentence his mentor was given, Plato spent over ten years traveling throughout Greece, Italy, and Sicily to various centers of intellectual activity.[44] At age forty, after his travels and numerous writings, he founded a school just outside Athens which became known as the *Academy*, a forerunner of the modern university.[45]

Since Plato wrote in a dialogue form and would use Socrates as one of his speakers, it was not known which were Socrates' philosophies and which were his own. However, his earlier works, such as *Apology, Gorgias, Meno,* and *Crito,* were believed to reflect more of Socrates since they were written before founding the Academy.[46] But dialogues such as *Phaedo, Symposium,* and *Republic* or later on in life *Parmenides, Timaeus,* and *Laws,* were believed to be Plato's philosophy rather than those of Socrates.[47] It is believed that two reasons Plato wrote the dialogues and used Socrates as the protagonist were (1) to reassert the teachings of Socrates in spite of their having been officially condemned, and (2) to rehabilitate his beloved mentor's reputation, showing him to have not been a corruptor of young men but their most valued teacher.[48] Of all the Western philosophers, many believe Plato was the best. In fact,

Alfred North Whitehead famously remarked that Western philosophical thought "consists of a series of footnotes to Plato."[49]

Plato's best known work is *Republic* where he identified four cardinal virtues that one needed to lead the Athenian government properly. In this work, Plato demonstrated that those individuals who possessed courage, moderation, wisdom, and justice as well as attended his Academy to further cultivate these skills would eventually become the guardians (philosopher-kings) of Athens. This utopian form of society espoused a system where everyone had a place in it, based upon the virtues they possessed. Plato's society was premised on having an elite class of guardians trained from birth for the task of ruling.[50] The rest of society was divided into soldiers and the common people.[51]

In his famous allegory of the cave found in *Republic*, Plato introduced his theory of Forms used to identify eternal and immutable absolute true definitions of concepts.[52] As an example, take what we consider our knowledge of something blue, such as a shirt. As it is washed, it fades; if washed with something else it could turn orange; and if shredded, it may be a rag rather than a shirt.[53] Since these terms seem to change *the* matter described, they are temporary, as opposed to the Forms which are permanent.[54] Justice is one Form that Plato believed cannot change. Although you may not be able to see Justice, it exists.[55] Relating this to his *Republic,* Plato believed that not everyone had the ability to understand the Form *justice*, and this was why only those who could understand the Forms should lead.

The following passage appears in Plato's *Republic* Book VII (515a-517a), which is the allegory of the cave describing the different levels of metaphysics and epistemology (see Chapter One for these definitions) as discussed above. Since this textbook is not intended to be for an advanced philosophy course, the nuances of the cave will not be discussed in depth, but an overall explanation will follow. Although this was a discussion between Glaucon (Plato's brother) and Socrates, to shorten this dialogue, Glaucon's responses to Socrates were excluded in this allegory, so think of the question posed by Socrates as rhetorical. In the Plato's full literary passage of this allegory, Glaucon either agrees with Socrates or responds in the affirmative.

Imagine human beings living in an underground, cavelike dwelling, with an entrance a long way up, which is both open to the light and wide as the cave itself. They've been there since childhood, fixed in the same place, with their necks and legs fettered, able to see only in front of the, because their bonds prevent them from turning their heads around. Light is provided by a fire burning far above and behind them. Also behind them, but on higher ground, there is a path stretching between them and the fire. Imagine that along this path a low wall has been built, like the screen in front of the puppeteers above which they show their puppets.

Then, also imagine that there are people along the wall, carrying all kinds of artifacts that project above it-statues of people and other animals, made out of stone, wood, and every material. And, as you'd expect, some of the carriers are talking, and some are silent.

They are like use. Do you suppose, first of all, that these prisoners see anything of themselves and one another besides the shadows that the fire casts on the wall in front of them?

What about the things carried along the wall? Isn't the same true of them?

And if they could talk to one another, don't you think they'd suppose that the names they used applied to the things they see passing before them?

And what if their prison also had an echo from wall the facing them? Don't you think they'd believe that the shadows passing in front of them were talking whenever one of the carriers passing along the wall was doing so?

Then the prisoners would in every way believe that the truth is nothing other than the shadows of those artifacts?

Consider, then, what being released from their bonds and cured of their ignorance would naturally be like, if something like this came to pass? When one of them was freed and suddenly compelled to stand up, turn his head, walk, and look up toward the light, he'd be pained and dazzled and unable to see the things whose shadows he'd seen before. What do you think he'd say, if we told him that what he'd seen before was inconsequential, but that now-because he is a bit closer to the things that are and is turned towards things that are more-he sees more correctly? Or to put it another way, if we pointed to each of the things passing by, asked him what each of them is, and compelled him to answer, don't you think he's be at a loss and that he'd believe that the things he saw earlier were truer than the ones he was now being shown?

And if someone compelled him to look at the light itself, wouldn't his eyes hurt, and wouldn't he turn around and flee towards the things he's able to see, believing that they're really clearer than the ones he's being shown?

And if someone dragged him away from there by force, up the rough, steep path, and didn't let him go until he had dragged him into the sunlight, wouldn't he be pained and irritated at being treated that way? And when he came into the light, with the sun filling his eyes, wouldn't he be unable to see a single one of the things now said to be true?

I suppose, then, that he'd need time to get adjusted before he could see things in the world above. At first, he's see shadows most easily, then images of men and other things in water, then the things themselves. Of these, he'd be able to study the things in the sky and the sky itself more easily at night, looking at the light of the stars and the moon, then during the day at the sun and the light of the sun.

Finally, I suppose he'd be able to see the sun, not images of it in water or some alien place, but the sun itself, in its own place, and be able to study it.

And at this point he would infer and conclude that the sun provides the seasons and the years, governs everything in the visible world, and is in some way the cause of all the things that he used to see.

What about when he reminds himself of his first dwelling place, his fellow prisoners, and what passed for wisdom there? Don't you think that he'd count himself happy for the change and pity the others/

And if there had been any honors, praises, or prizes among them for one who was sharpest at identifying the shadows as they passed by and who best remembered which usually came earlier, which later, and which simultaneously, and who could thus best divine the future, do you think that our man would desire these rewards or envy those among the prisoners who were honored and held power? Instead, wouldn't he feel, with Homer, that he'd much prefer to "work the earth as a serf to another, one without possessions," and go through any sufferings, rather than share their opinions and live as they do?

Consider this too. If this man went down into the cave again and sat down in the same seat, wouldn't his eyes-coming suddenly out of the sun like that-be filled with darkness?

And before his eyes had recovered-and the adjustment would not be quick-while his vision was still dim if he had to compete again with the perpetual prisoners in recognizing the shadows, wouldn't he invite ridicule? Wouldn't it be said of him that he'd returned from his upward journey with his eyesight ruined and that it isn't worthwhile even to try to travel upward? And, as for anyone who tried to free them and lead them upward, if the could somehow get their hands on him, wouldn't they kill him? [56]

Plato of course was in this passage (in the words of Socrates) was describing how his fellow Greek citizens condemned Socrates to death for practicing philosophy and questioning the ethics of his fellow citizens. In epistemological terms, Plato's allegory represents from the lowest level to the highest level as follows: imagination as when the prisoners see the shadows; perception when one of the prisoners breaks free and sees that the shadows are actually puppets; reasoning as the prisoner notices the light and begins his travel out of the cave into the light; and understanding, when the freed prisoner finally sees the sun and stars.[57] However, if you wanted to apply this allegory to a contemporary example, let me use the following. Let us assume your parents tell you that one of their friends is developing an online service for college students and is guaranteed to make $1 million each year. If you believe them, this would be the first level which Plato would consider imagination, because you believe the words of your parents without checking it out yourself. This is what the prisoners who believe the shadows to be real, represent. Now, let us assume you read an article in the local newspaper about your parents' friend and the newspaper reporter in this article believes this will be a very lucrative business; this would be the second level, perception. You are reading the information, but you still are accepting it just because it is written. Yet, you did go beyond the images of another, since now it is your perception, just like the freed prisoner who observed the puppeteers speaking and talking for the puppets. The third level of reasoning would be if you used your reasoning through a methodical approach; you read other accounts of other successful businesspersons' internet services who earned $1 million annually and compared it to the business of your parents' friends. Finally, the highest level would be if you were a member of the television show *Shark Tank*, where experienced entrepreneurs analyze the business and intuitively, along with their extensive experience, determine that this will be a successful business and can earn over $1 million a year, just as the freed prisoner saw the sun and the stars. In all honesty, since you may not possess the experience or knowledge at this time (or may never) to be on *Shark Tank*, only those few successful venture capitalists have the ability to make this decision.

The same concept applies to those who understand the Forms or iconic representations of perfection such as justice and beauty. Plato believed that only a few individuals had the ability to understand justice and be a leader, just as only a few people have the ability to analyze a business plan and determine whether a particular business will be successful. This is why Plato's philosophy made it so difficult for the average person to follow a plan for a just life, when not everyone had the ability to do so, in Plato's purist viewpoint. This limitation of having the knowledge to be virtuous or just in the hands of the few may be found in Plato's *Republic* (`518c and 519c), when he states:

"Education isn't what some people declare it to be, namely putting knowledge into souls that lack it, like putting sight into blind eyes....And what about the uneducated who have no experience of truth? Isn't it likely—indeed, does it follow necessarily from what was said before—that they will never adequately govern a city?"

In other words, Plato believed that only a few had the ability to lead since only a few had the knowledge of how to be virtuous. Just having the education is not tantamount to being educated, but understanding what you learned and knowing how to apply it, especially in an ethical manner, is what a good leader should know and practice. Still, even though somewhat of an elitist, Plato was considered to be the most well known and scholarly of philosophers in his time. This is why Sir Alfred Whitehead believed that the history of philosophy is merely a footnote to Plato. Writing until his death, Plato was eighty in 347 BCE at the time of his passing in Athens. [58]

ARISTOTLE

Aristotle was born in Stagira in Macedon (now part of northern Greece) in 384 BCE to Nicomachus, a physician.[59] In 367 BCE, Aristotle came to Athens at age seventeen, and became a member of Plato's Academy until his mentor's death in 347 BCE.[60] Plato's successor was his nephew Speusippus, even though Aristotle was the Academy's best student according to Plato.[61] At that time, Aristotle left Athens, and traveled to Assos (in Asia Minor) where the pro-Macedonian ruler Hermeias was a patron of philosophical studies.[62]

Aritotle married Pythias, a niece of Hermeias, who gave birth to their daughter by the same name.[63] After Hermeias was killed by the Persians, Aristotle moved on to Lesbos, in the eastern Aegean and then to

Macedon, where he became tutor of Alexander.[64] In 334 BCE, he returned to Athens and founded his own school, the Lyceum.[65] The Lyceum duplicated the Academy and since the lecturing and discussion was done by strolling along the garden path, the *peripatos*, the followers of Aristotle were called *Peripatetics*.[66] After the death of his wife, Aristotle had a relationship with Herpyllis and they had a son named Nicomachus.[67]

In 323 BCE, Alexander died as a result of the outbreak of anti-Macedonian feelings in Athens so Aristotle left for Chalcis, on the island of Euboea, where it has been reported that he committed suicide in 322 BCE in order to prevent the Athenians from "sinning twice against philosophy," a reference to the trial and death of Socrates.[68]

Interestingly enough, if you were a Platonist, you favored the abstract, perfect truths of mathematics and logic as a model to be followed by all fields of knowledge including the ideals of moral and political life.[69] So where Plato's theory of Forms explains the nature of things by claiming that abstract forms are only useless copies of actual things and fails to provide any explanation of the existence of concreted things, Aristotelians were more concerned with the practical question of how such knowledge and ideals can relate to more concrete changing actualities of existence.[70]

Plato believed that the intelligible and sensible were dualistic (separate), whereas Aristotle believed they were united and that every individual consisted of formed matter.[71] Aristotle was teleological (*telos* is Greek for "end") in that he believed that in nature, every living thing from its conception is assigned a predestined final end.[72] For example, the end of an acorn is the fully mature oak tree.[73] To Aristotle, the form is the purpose or end which the matter serves, so the oak tree is the purpose or end which the matter of acorn serves.[74]

Aristotle believed that we pursue pleasure, wealth, or honor because it will bring happiness; but in actuality they are only the *means* to happiness.[75] Happiness as the highest good for humankind consists in the fulfillment of an individual's function as a human being in the "activity of soul in accordance with virtue."[76] He believed that there are two kinds of virtue, the first being *moral virtue,* which consists of rationally controlling the irrational desires and appetites of the soul (such as courage, temperance, justice, self-respect) and are developed by practice until they are established as habits.[77] Unlike Socrates who believed that virtue is knowledge and "to know the good is to do the good," Aristotle believed that knowledge of the good can affect our conduct only if it is practiced so that it becomes habit.[78] Furthermore, each of the moral virtues is rationally determined between the extremes of excess and deficiency.[79] So, courage is a mean between the vice of being a coward (excess fear) and the vice of being foolhardy (deficient fear).[80] To determine the mean requires rational judgment based upon considering all the facts in the particular situation.[81]

The second kind of virtue is *intellectual virtue,* and involves the life of contemplation and acknowledges Plato's values that not every individual has the sufficient intellectual ability or leisure to engage in the contemplation of truth and to experience the highest quality of happiness.[82] Therefore, Aristotle's ethics focuses upon the character of the agent as that which is morally good or morally bad and has been termed "virtue ethics."[83] "A good life is one that provides all the necessary conditions and opportunities for a person to become fully himself or herself—and one in which the person has the character to do so."[84] In this passage, Aristotle is not mirroring the more contemporary psychologist, Abraham Maslow, who believed everyone should strive to be the best they could be, because Maslow's focus was on improving oneself generically, whereas Aristotle's focus was on striving to conduct oneself as ethically as possible. Although Aristotle acknowledged, like an acorn, not everyone is born ethical or has been raised to be ethical, however, all individuals can develop their character to become ethical and to conduct their actions as such. In other words, becoming fully oneself, in Aristotle's words, is meant to be, in an ethical sense. To have a good life, one must follow being *just* and conducting oneself in a morally responsible manner.

Aristotle's writings were often based on his lectures and although it has been reported that he wrote five hundred or more "books," only thirty of them survived and were those written intentionally for the use of his pupils within his school.[85] The following passage reflects an example of his philosophy on virtue ethics and originates from his *Nicomachean Ethics* in Book I 109 4a. In this passage Aristotle is explaining that the aim for every philosopher is for "good life."

> Every craft and every investigation, and likewise every action and decision, seems to aim at some good; hence the good has been well described as that which everything aims.[86]

In Book II, 1103a, he discusses the two types of virtue—one of thought and one of character. The first he says may be taught, the second results from practice or habit, which is an instrumental point in his virtue ethics philosophy. In the passage above, Aristotle is stating that everything we do must be measured in ethical terms. Everyone should investigate what good will result from their actions; however, not every action results in some good, unless it will benefit others in a positive way. We should all search and reflect on the question, what can I do to make this world a better place? This is what Aristotle believed should be the aim of all humankind.

> Virtue of character results from habit. A stone, for instance, by nature moves downward, and habitation could not make it move upward. Thus the virtues arise in us neither by nature nor against nature acquire them and reach our complete perfection through habit.
>
> Virtues, we acquire, just as we acquire crafts, by having previously activated them. For we learn a craft by producing the same product that we must produce when we have learned it, becoming builders, for instance, by building and harpists by playing the harp; so also, then, we become just by doing actions, temperate by doing temperate actions, brave by doing brave actions.[87]

You can learn in class how to be ethical, but according to Aristotle, the only way you can become more ethical is by practicing it every day. It is interesting to note that Plato believed to be *just* you needed to have wisdom, practice temperance, and be courageous. As Plato's student, Aristotle seemed to develop these same criteria for describing a *just* person.

Finally, in this last passage, Aristotle discusses the virtue of moderation, which is his golden mean….not being or having too much,…nor acting less than or denying yourself something which would be considered moderate. This final passage is found in Book II, 1106b.

> By virtue I mean virtue of character. We can be afraid, for instance, or be confident, or have appetites but (having these feelings) at the right times, about the right things, toward the right people, for the right end, and in the right way.
>
> Now virtue is concerned with feelings and actions, in which excess and deficiency are in error and incur blame, while the intermediate condition is correct and wins praise, which are both proper features of virtue. Virtue, then is a mean,… It is a mean between two vices, one of excess and one of deficiency.[88]

According to Aristotle, you can be foolish (jump off a ten-foot-high diving board, and then realize there is no water in the pool), you can be cowardly (refuse to jump off, given there is water in the pool), or you can jump off after realizing that you cannot be hurt doing so. In the passage above, Aristotle talks about having feelings at the right time, about the right thing, toward the right people, for the right end, and in the right way is the intermediate condition.

A few years ago, there was a proposal for new faculty to have to pay a part of their health insurance for their first five years. Not being a new faculty member, I would not be affected. I had three choices: one, say nothing (deficiency); two, say that anyone who voted for it was selfish, self-indulging, and an embarrassment to the professoriate (excess); or three, say that we should not support this proposal because it is not fair to new faculty. What if it was reversed, how would we feel and is this not the same thing? (moderate approach). I believe this last choice is what Aristotle was referring to in the passages above.

ST. AUGUSTINE

Another philosopher, Aurelius Augustinus, better known as St. Augustine, was born 354, in Thagaste (currently Souk-Ahras, Algeria), which was part of the Roman Empire. His formal education occurred in Carthage where he studied literary education, the art of rhetoric (persuading others according to formal speaking and writing rules in presentation methods), and philosophy. He lived with a woman, rather than marrying her, which was accepted in those times, and had a son Adeodatus, who died young, just like his father who died when Augustine was 20 years old.[89]

Left with no alternative after his father's death, Augustine turned to teaching and in 383 went to Rome where he became a professor of rhetoric, much like Protagoras in earlier Greek

© Everett Historical/Shutterstock, Inc.]

times, and eventually was appointed a public orator of Milan. Eventually, outside Milan, Augustine established a retreat for himself and friends for the purpose of reflecting, studying, and writing. Although there is much speculation as to why Augustine embraced Christianity, when he did not before, the real reason is unknown. Some of these include the influence of his mother, who later was made a saint (Monica); the influence of the Milan bishop, St. Ambrose; or Augustine's extensive reading of the Christian saints. After his baptism, Augustine left Milan to return to Thagaste, his city of origin, but on the way he visited a church in Hippo, and the parishioners begged him to be their priest, which he did. Later on, he became the bishop of Hippo.[90]

Augustine read about extreme dualism, a doctrine from a third-century Persian, named Mani, which described the relationship between matter and spirit; the former being evil and the latter (spirit) being good. According to Augustine, however, the doctrine espoused the belief that persons would have to either (1) be an aesthetic, and deny all pleasures, avoiding any interaction with the material world, or (2) do whatever they want in this world because it would make no difference in the spiritual world. Augustine rejected this doctrine.[91]

The second doctrine to challenge Augustine was that of the monk Pelagius, who believed the divine gift of grace (virtue from God) was not necessary for salvation; and that bothered him since it takes away from the attainment of salvation from God to the person on earth. As result of these and other Christian doctrines, Augustine began to search out what the characteristics of eternity and immutability were, in order to find the connection between God and the very nature of the truth as to his existence. He wanted to examine the various levels of knowledge and believed it to be reason, which is the path to truth, alongside being something that is unchanging and eternal.[92]

Eventually, Augustine did reconcile the second doctrine by considering the possibility of free will and questioning the extent of how free will could be used. If you cannot attribute that God is the cause of evil, metaphysically there must be some free will on the part of the living, bodily person.[93] In the passage below, of Book One, Chapter 28 of *De Doctrina Christiana*,

Augustine states that you are not expected to help everyone. Because the Bible does not identify every ethical dilemma and what would be the most prudent or wise action to take, especially if faced with helping two people equally in need of your help, with the same connection to you, what you believe the most prudent or wise choice is the one you should take. For example, let us assume you are a stockbroker who has two clients, both who you want to help maximize their portfolio and you know of a stock with a limited amount of shares which will be offered and must be sold within the next few hours. If you know that one client, Jane, is away on a vacation at a remote island and the other client, Tina, may be reached by a cellphone within the local area, the Bible does not tell you who to help. So, you need to make the best choice, which in this case would be Tina, due to her proximity and ability to allow you to execute the stock transaction. This philosophy validates your decision without having to experience guilt or having you feel you did not act ethically. After all, your intentions were to do good without breaching any ethical principles.

Using the same example and assuming that only one client could purchase this stock, but both were in calling distance, another approach that would be supported by this philosophical quote is to leave a phone message to both clients and give the first client to call the opportunity to purchase the stock. Again, the philosophical quote from Augustine is found below.

> *Further, all men are to be loved equally. But since you cannot do good to all, you are to pay special regard to those who, by the accidents of time, or place, or circumstance, are brought into closer connection with you. For, suppose that you had a great deal of some commodity, and felt bound to give it away to somebody who had none, and that it could not be given to more than one person; if two persons presented themselves, neither of whom had either from need or relationship a greater claim upon you than the other, you could do nothing fairer than choose by lot to which you would give what could not be given to both. Just so among men: since you cannot consult for the good of them all, you must take the matter as decided for you by a sort of lot, according as each man happens for the time being to be more closely connected with you.*[94]

In 430, at age seventy-six, Augustine died shortly after the Vandals, who were at war with Rome, reached Hippo.[95]

Major Hedonistic Philosophers

The term **hedonism** originates from the Greek word *hedone* (pleasure) and may be best described as *the philosophy that individuals should maximize pleasure and minimize pain.* Hedonism is a form of consequentialism. There are two major views of this hedonistic philosophy—psychological hedonism and ethical hedonism. **Psychological hedonism** *is the belief that all humans have been developed to desire pleasure, avoid pain, and that it is impossible for humans to pursue anything else.* In contrast, **ethical hedonism** *refers to the view that although it is possible not to seek pleasure and avoid pain, it is morally wrong to do so.* Furthermore, ethical hedonists believe that pleasure is intrinsic (for its own sake) and all other values are a means to pleasure. For example, if you attended a rock concert, the concert itself is merely a means to attain pleasure (intrinsic). Nevertheless, there has been a great philosophical divergence among hedonists (those who believe in hedonism) as to whether pursuing pleasure will guarantee happiness. One of these philosophies is utilitarianism, which advocates for the *collective* pursuit of happiness and minimization of pain. This changes the focus of ethical hedonism from an individual's happiness to the happiness of the society as a whole.[96]

ARISTIPPUS

One of the first hedonists, Aristippus (ca. 435–350 BCE) was born in Cyrene, on the coast of North Africa, and traveled to Athens to become one of Socrates' disciples. Eventually, Aristippus opened his own school of philosophy in Cyrene and taught what is now referred to as **Cyrenaic hedonism**, which was *a belief that there were two states, pleasure and pain, and that one should pursue the former and avoid the latter.* Furthermore, Cyrenaic hedonists believed that all pleasures were good, should be pursued without guilt, and this would lead to happiness. In addition, they believed that bodily pleasures were more intense and more satisfying than mental pleasures. Consequently, avoiding bodily pain was equally paramount in their pursuit of happiness for the same reason.[97]

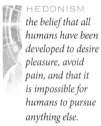

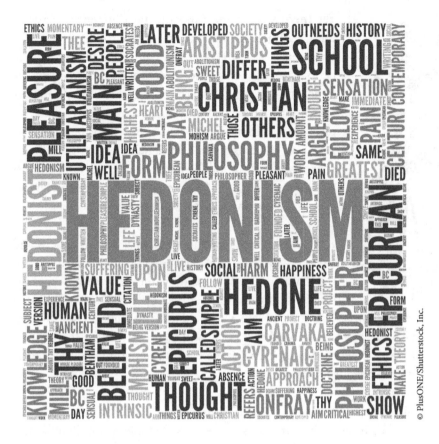

© PlusONE/Shutterstock, Inc.

Interestingly enough, followers of Cyrenaic hedonism did not believe in delaying pleasure just for the sake of receiving more pleasure later, and therefore encouraged pursuing whatever gave one the most immediate pleasure. However, all unrestrained behavior was discouraged because then you would be controlled by your pleasures rather than controlling them.[98]

EPICURUS

Another ethical hedonist philosopher was Epicurus (341–271 BCE), born on the island of Samos and considered the most famous of all hedonists. Oddly enough, Epicurus had been charged by many of plagiarizing Aristippus's teachings as if they were his own. Like Aristippus, Epicurus believed happiness was the highest good and pursuing pleasure and avoiding pain would attain this.[99]

EPICURUS

Yet there were some fundamental differences between these schools. One major difference between the Epicureans and the Cyrenaic philosophies of ethical hedonism was that the **Epicureans** *believed in the importance of mental pleasures.* Another dichotomy was that the Cyrenaic hedonists believed in the quantity of pleasure, while the Epicureans believed in the quality of pleasure. For example, a Cyrenaic hedonist would prefer a larger portion of food, whereas the Epicurean hedonist would prefer the most pleasant of fine dining experiences, even if the portion was not substantive.[100]

At one point in his lifetime, Epicurus visited Athens and studied with Plato's disciples. As a result, Epicurus valued the Platonic virtues of wisdom, temperance, and courage (or the strength of the soul) and believed this would lead to happiness. But, unlike Plato, who held that the highest good was not pleasure but was an ideal form of that which represented the likeness to G-d, Epicurus believed happiness was in the natural world, not the transcended world above.[101]

EPICUREANS

a group who believed in maximizing pleasure and minimizing pain, but also believed in the importance of mental pleasures. In addition, qualitative pleasures were better than quantitative pleasures.

In addition, Epicurus viewed pleasure as the end of life and virtue as the way to do it. Epicurus was of the view that a happy individual was the one who attained wisdom of discrimination and reflection, which would ultimately lead to a blessed existence of painlessness. In his *Letter to Menoeceus*, Epicurus gave special attention to the correct calculation for attaining pleasure. He did not believe in overindulging in alcohol, bodily lusting, or eating, and even supported deferring immediate pleasure if it would avoid pain later on.[102]

"So when we say that pleasure is the end, we do not mean the pleasure of the dissipated (squandered or spread wastefully) and those that consist (stand firm) in having a good time, as some out of ignorance and disagreement or refusal to understand suppose we do, but freedom from pleasant life is not continuous drinking and parties or …womanizing or the enjoyment of fish and the

> other dishes of an expensive table, but sober reasoning which tracks down the causes of every choice and avoidance, and which banishes the opinions that beset (attacks or surrounds) souls with the greatest confusion."[103]

As may be surmised from the passage above (*Letter to Menoeceus* 127-132[5]), although many perceived Epicureans as individuals without any constraints regarding the attainment of pleasure, it was the Epicurean philosophy of reason and reflection that differentiated it from the Cyreniac philosophy of ethical hedonism. In fact, Epicurus leaned more toward asceticism (self-denial of sexual love) than the unrestrained behavior that many attributed to hedonism. This asceticism is also subtly alluded to in Epicurus's *Letter to Menoeceus* passage above, although not to the extreme of self-denial. In fact, this belief is further supported by another of his hedonistic philosophies that the greatest happiness does not originate for the unrestrained enjoyment of physical pleasures but from a life that is free from anxiety (see passage below). Happiness, according to Epicurus, was interrelated with the health of the body and the tranquility of the mind, which would lead to the health of the soul.[104] In the passage below, also found in Epicurus's *Letter to Menoeceus* (127-32[1]), you can see this relationship between the health of the body and soul, as well as aiming to be free from anxiety.

> "We must reckon that some desires are natural and others empty, and of the natural some are necessary, others natural only; and of the necessary some are necessary for happiness, others for the body's freedom from stress, and others for life itself. For the steady observation of these things make it possible to refer every choice and avoidance to the health of the body and the soul's freedom from disturbance, since this is the end belonging to the blessed life. For this is what we aim at in all our actions—to be free from pain and anxiety."[105]

Given the philosophy known as egoism, which is pursuing long-term self-interests, it may be concluded that the Epicurean's were the seeds for this type of philosophy, compared to their counterparts, the Cyrenaic hedonists.

S.E.A. Method: Supporting Ethical Decision Making

As a student of philosophy, it is important to improve your critical thinking skills. In order to do so, you must be able to defend your actions when faced with an ethical dilemma by applying a philosophical concept to your action. An **ethical dilemma** *is when you have to make a decision that is just or not just, even though whatever you decide may be legal.* For example, should you help a colleague in another department, even though it may mean by doing so, she will have a better chance for a promotion over you because of your helpful actions?

Getting back to defending your actions, when faced with an ethical dilemma, there are several steps to take first before you can support successfully your proposed actions. The first step in using this **S.E.A. method** requires you to select (state) a philosophical concept (philosophy) which would support your action or viewpoint. Second, you have to prove your understanding of the philosophical concept beyond just stating, quoting, or vaguely paraphrasing it. Your second step is to demonstrate beyond just quoting or stating the philosophical concept, by explaining it in your own words and giving an example that is not related to your ethical dilemma to further display your comprehension of this philosophy. Finally, you must show that you can apply the philosophy to your selected course of action (or viewpoint) for this ethical dilemma. In order to do this, I have created a guide which enables you to demonstrate the above to me when grading you. It is called the S.E.A. method and is an acronym for **S**tating the philosophy; **E**xplaining/Exemplifying it, and **A**pplying it to your viewpoint (or course of action). A description for each is found below along with a case which applies it. After answering the question in the case (i.e., What would you do?), your next step is to follow the S.E.A. method in qualifying your response.

(**S**) **S**tate the philosophy—write out the entire quote of the philosophy (not just a few words from it).

(**E**) **E**xplain the philosophy in your own words (paraphrase). Remember, many classical philosophies relate to human conduct or behavior; the business world was not the focus in most of these philosophies. Exemplify with an unrelated situation; again, show the intent of the quote in terms of general examples rather than another example similar to your assigned case. Essentially, what does the philosophy mean and what is a general example (i.e., personal)? Make sure your example relates to the quote and its intention. By giving an example of a situation unrelated to the case you are further demonstrating that you understand the philosophy.

(**A**) **A**pply the philosophy to the case. How does your philosophy directly relate to the case, as well as your course of action/viewpoint? Restate the quote or intention of the quote demonstrating its link to your action or viewpoint. Show how the quote directly supports your action or viewpoint.

But it needs to done in paragraph form.

To illustrate this method, I will use "The Shallow Pond" case found in our first chapter with an additional facet. I have identified each part of the S.E.A. method by identifying each part of the S.E.A. method in parenthesis (in boldfaced type), but do not want you to do identify it in this way. Just write your response as if it was a short-answer question on an exam.

The Shallow Pond

Imagine that you are a college professor and there is a path from the library at your university to the Humanities Lecture Hall which passes a shallow ornamental pond. On your way to give a lecture, you notice that a small child has fallen in and is in danger of drowning. If you wade in and pull the child out, it will mean getting your clothes muddy and either cancelling your lecture or delaying it until you can find something clean and dry to wear. If you pass by the child, then, while you'll give your lecture on time, the child will die.[106]

Complicating this case, is the following situation. This is your tenure year, which means that next year you will either have lifetime employment at the college or will be asked not to return. Waiting for your lecture is a Tenure Committee who will observe you and considers your current performance marginal, especially since you cancelled two other observations which they scheduled on your behalf. Furthermore, imagine being a single parent of three children, in a community experiencing an exorbitant rate of unemployment, resulting in you having no possible means of supporting your children. Do not make any assumptions, such as the newspaper lauding you as a hero for saving a child or the Tenure Committee giving you another chance, since the decision must be made on that day, because the Committee will be meeting with the Provost of the College a few hours later, right before the Board of Trustee meeting that night when your tenure or nonrenewal of a contract will be voted upon. By saving the child, you will lose your job and have no way of supporting your family.

DISCUSSION QUESTION

What would you do? Why?

Answer A: I would save the child and if necessary miss the lecture and risk my ability to support my family. (State the full philosophy.) According to Socrates, who I believe would support this action, "Now, no one goes willingly toward the bad or what he believes to be bad; neither is it in human nature, so it seems, to want to go toward what one believes to be bad instead of to the good. And when he is forced to choose between one of two bad things, no one will choose the greater if he is able to choose the lesser." (Explain the quote in your own words.) This means as an individual, one will always do what she believes is right and if faced with two choices, which both can have a negative effect on others, the better, more ethical choice will be selected. It should be noted that Socrates would be opposed to any unethical act conducted by an individual, even if that person believes his/her action was ethical. (Exemplify the quote with a situation not related to the case.) So, if a cashier gave me a $20 bill instead of a $1 (which was due me), I should speak up and not pretend that I did not notice because this is the ethical way to act even if I needed the extra money for food. (Apply your philosophy to your response and the case.) For this reason, by saving the small child instead of letting the child drown so I would not miss my lecture, even though I will be unable to support my family as a result, I am acting in the virtuous, ethical way and would be selecting the good or better choice to save a life over the support of my child. I could never replace a life, but may be able to find a way to support my children, in this community or some other community, if necessary. And, even if I could not support my family, it is better to miss the lecture than not saving the life of a child.

Answer B: I would not save the child since supporting my family is very important to me and hopefully another onlooker will save the child. (State the philosophy.) According to Thrasymachus," This, then, is what I say justice is, the same in all cities, the advantage of the established rule. Since the established rule is surely stronger, anyone who reasons correctly will conclude that *the just is the same everywhere, the advantage of the stronger*." (Explain the quote in your own words.) This means that those who have power over others determine what the law is, in essence what is ethical or just. This power may be a social position, possessing physical strength, or having more influence or finances, to name a few.

(Exemplify the quote with a situation not related to the case.) One example may be a manager who has the power to fire you and then asks you to work overtime on the same night your child is having a concert rehearsal at school. Fearing the loss of your job, you acquiesce and work the overtime, because your manager has the power of your job, potential promotion, and financial security over you. Your manager's word is the law, as Thrasymachus believed. (Apply your philosophy to your response and the case.) In this case, by you not saving the child, you have the advantage of the decision to save or not save the child, to act or not act in helping the less advantaged small child. This is the equivalent of a bully determining what is just. Although this is an extreme example of Thrasymachus's philosophy, it does support your action not to save the child over your ability to save your family financially.

This S.E.A. method will be used throughout this textbook, so you may want to bookmark this section for future reference.

Summary

The Sophos were those who first questioned the universe around them and began philosophy as we know it today. Since they were unpaid in their quest, a new group, called Sophists replaced them. They taught the art of rhetoric or persuasion, and were paid for their services. Traveling around to practice this art, they were named Sophists.

Three well-known Sophists were Protagoras, Callicles, and Thrasymacus. Protagoras believed in ethical relativism, that truth was based upon what the majority believed was correct, or as he put it, "man is the measure of all things." Callicles, a moral realist, believed that time determined truth and that justice was based upon "survival of the fittest," naming this belief, the doctrine of the superior individual. Thrasymachus believed that justice was based upon the "advantage of the stronger," and to be just was foolish.

Socrates, a Sophos, questioned the knowledge of his fellow Athenians, who eventually gave him two choices: either stop philosophizing or you will be condemned to death. He selected the later, stating "the unexamined life is not worth living." His student, Plato, became disillusioned with the democratic process that killed his mentor. He reverted to a government that only those with knowledge, the enlightened, would be permitted to rule, and developed the Academy after completing much soul-searching. One of his prized pupils was Aristotle, who questioned some of his mentor's philosophies, and under the auspices of King Philip of Macedon, created the *Nicomachean Ethics*, a publication depicting how one could be a better individual and build character for a better society.

Another philosopher was St. Augustine who searched for the meaning of truth from a metaphysical approach in his attempt to reconcile his conflict between free will and predestination, and why free will explains how there may be an almighty and omnipotent God, yet evil can still exist.

One of the first hedonists, Aristippus opened his own school of philosophy in Cyrene and taught what is now referred to as Cyrenaic hedonism, which was a belief that there were two states, pleasure and pain, and that one should pursue the former and avoid the latter. Another hedonist philosopher was Epicurus who believed in the importance of mental pleasures over bodily pleasures and in the quality of pleasure over the quantity, which was the opposite of what Aristippus believed.

Finally, in an attempt to bring a connection with philosophy and ethical dilemmas found in business, a model called the S.E.A. method was developed by the author to integrate the two disciplines, business and ethics. The S.E.A. method is an acronym for stating (or quoting) a philosophy to support your viewpoint or proposed action; explaining and exemplifying what you just quoted; and then applying this philosophy to your viewpoint or proposed action.

Key Terms

Cultural relativism: the belief that the values of individuals differ from culture to culture, as opposed to being absolute, when values are accepted regardless of cultural background.

Cyrenaic hedonism: a belief that there two states, pleasure and pain, and that one should pursue the former and avoid the latter.

Doctrine of the superior individual: a social Darwinism theory by Callicles, which justifies why the strong who dominate the weak are constrained by conventional morality.

Epicureans: a group who believed in maximizing pleasure and minimizing pain, but also believed in the importance of mental pleasures. In addition, qualitative pleasures were better than quantitative pleasures.

Ethical dilemma: when an individual is faced with making a decision that involves an ethical situation, such as: Should I receive a full travel reimbursement if an unwritten discount was issued?

Ethical hedonism: refers to the view that although it is possible not to seek pleasure and avoid pain, it is morally wrong to do so.

Ethical wisdom: according to Socrates, "the recognition of the fundamental importance of the ethical in the life of man (humankind) and of doing good as the basic principle of human activity."

Hedonism: originates from the Greek word *hedone* (pleasure) and may be best described as the philosophy that individuals should maximize pleasure and minimize pain.

Psychological hedonism: the belief that all humans have been developed to desire pleasure, avoid pain, and that it is impossible for humans to pursue anything else.

SEA method: a teaching method developed by the author to integrate a philosophy with an action to be taken by an individual in a given case study involving an ethical dilemma (state philosophy, explain and exemplify in general terms the philosophy, apply the philosophy to the case).

Skeptics: those who doubted that there was any possibility of true knowledge since the truth seemed to produce conflicting claims.

Sophists: those who believed in preparing their students in the art of rhetoric or power of persuasive speech for an usually large fee, unlike their predecessors, the Sophos who did not charge fees.

Sophos: the original philosophers who practiced their craft by raising questions as to the origin of the world and the meaning of a good life.

Stephanus numbers: describe the corresponding page and section of the relevant volume of the Greek text as edited by the French scholar, Henri Estienne (which in Latin is *Stephanus*).

Chapter Review Questions

1. How did the Sophos differ from the Sophists?
2. What were some of Protagoras's beliefs? Would he be in favor of restricting immigration in the United States? Defend your viewpoint.
3. How does Callicles and Thrasymachus differ in their philosophies? Are there any similarities?
4. What were some of Socrates' beliefs? Do you agree with them?
5. What were some of Plato's philosophies? Would he be in favor of health care? Defend your viewpoint.
6. What were some of Aristotle's philosophies? Would he be in favor of the compensation currently received by the top officers of our Fortune 500 firms? Defend your viewpoint.
7. In today's business world, could the philosophies of St. Augustine, Aristippus and Epicurus apply?

Cases for Discussion

CASE 2.1 UNPAID INTERNSHIPS: OPPORTUNITY OR EXPLOITATION?[107]

In Australia, there is a test case to determine whether the interns bringing forth the suit were actually unpaid employees, rather than interns. The case involves a sports broadcaster who claims that she was a radio producer and for six months, worked as many as seven out of ten days, and would begin her day at midnight and finish at dawn, without compensation. Another employee at the same firm worked for fifteen months and was paid 2,940 Australian dollars ($2,500 U.S.) but should have been paid seven times that amount. The court paper showed that they should have been paid as casual workers ($18 Australian), not interns.

To differentiate between the two work classifications, unpaid fully supervised work trials to determine whether the applicant possesses the skills are legal, as well as college, short-term placements for course credit, and are internship positions, and generally they do not fall under the paid category of casual worker. To further determine which category a worker falls under, there is a "benefit test" which is based upon whether the worker or the company benefits most from the work relationship. If an employee gains more from the business than the business receives from the worker, it is an internship. This sometimes can be difficult to determine.

In France, for example, if an intern works longer than two months, the employer must offer the intern payments. In the United States, the Labor Department uses six criteria, which primarily determines whether the intern is being trained or is doing the work of a regular employee.

DISCUSSION QUESTION

What do you believe should be the standards to determine whether the worker should be an unpaid intern or paid employee?

Defend your response, using the full S.E.A. method discussed in this chapter (state the philosophy, explain the philosophy in your own words, give a general example, and apply the philosophy to your action). Use any philosopher discussed in this chapter or in Chapter One.

Case 2.2 Let Them Eat Beef, or Not?[108]

The slaughtering of cows in India is sacrosanct given the country's vast population of Hindus. Therefore, a Big Mac in India may be an unrealistic expectation when frequenting a McDonald's franchise. Yet, beef can be eaten in Mumbai restaurants such as a hamburger at the Leopold Café or marrowbone curry at some Muslim neighborhood eating establishments, to reflect India's diversity of religion, culture, and wealth. This was before the March 2015 Maharashtra ban on the slaughtering of cows, which also was extended to bulls and oxen. Maharashtra is India's second most populated state, where the state of Haryana passed a similar legislation a few weeks later.

These laws have affected restaurants, thousands of butchers and vendors, whose businesses came to a screeching halt, joined by those in the leather industry. Since beef is not only consumed by Indian Muslims and Christians, many lower income Hindus depend on eating beef for protein, looking the other way in terms of their own religious beliefs. However, as a result of this ban, three Muslim men have been arrested and accused of calf slaughtering, and may face up to five years in prison as a result of this newly legislated crime. Should this ban be fully exercised throughout the country, one fear is the expense of unwanted cattle if they are not to waste away. The only practical reason supporting this ban is that in difficult economic times, if the farmers hold on to their cattle, instead of selling them for slaughter, they may be used to plow fields, provide dung for fertilizer, and produce calves to stock their herds. Historically, those who kept their cattle were the only ones to survive during a poor economy.

At the crust of this controversy is the personal freedom of those who are not Hindu, given India's long secular constitution. The government must decide how to balance the majority Hindu sentiments with the minority needs of those who do not practice the Hindu religion.

DISCUSSION QUESTION

Using one full philosophy from this chapter, identify whether you believe India should continue the ban on beef by applying the full S.E.A. method (state the philosophy, explain the philosophy in your own words, give a general example, and apply the philosophy to your action) to your philosophy.

Case 2.3 Living the High Life or Low Life?

You are the owner of Joe's Plumbing, a local plumbing company and you just hired your main competitor's (ACE Plumbing) sales agent, Fred Sanford. Mr. Sanford informs you that if you give the purchasing agent of Barkley Condominiums, Jack Ward, World Series tickets to his favorite team, you will gain a minimum of $1 million a year in plumbing supplies sales. After computing the potential sales, you calculate that as a result of these plumbing supplies sales, you and your family will now be living in a higher lifestyle, while at the same time, Fred will receive 10% in sales commissions, which is $100,000.

In addition, Fred tells you that ACE Plumbing has a strict policy of "no gift giving to purchasing agents" (you do not have any policies on gift giving).

Barkley Condominiums is ACE's number one client and if this client is lost, ACE Plumbing will be forced out of business, which will result in his twenty-five employees losing their jobs. These employees are the sole financial providers for their families. Furthermore, you have no plans to help these twenty-five employees, since the additional labor costs of their hiring would not be profitable.

DISCUSSION QUESTION

What will you do? Use one philosopher from this chapter or Chapter One, and apply the S.E.A. method to your decision.

Endnotes

[1] Ian P. McGreal (Ed.), "Protagoras of Abdera," *Great Thinkers of the Western World* (New York: Harper Collins Publishers, 1992), p. 12.

[2] T.Z. Lavine, *From Socrates to Sartre: The Philosophical Quest* (New York: Bantam Books, 1984), p. 24.

[3] Ibid.

[4] Ibid., 24-25.

[5] David Roochnik, *Retrieving the Ancients: An Introduction to Greek Philosophy* (Malden, MA: Blackwell Publishing, 2004), p. 68.

[6] "Protagoras," *The Internet Encyclopedia of Philosophy*. 20 Jan. 2007. http://www.utm.edu/research/iep/p/protagor.htm

[7] Ibid.

[8] Frederick Copleston, *A History of Philosophy: Volume I: Greece and Rome* (New York: Battam Doubleday Dell Publishing Company, 1993), p. 87.

[9] Ibid.

[10] J.V. Luce, *An Introduction to Greek Philosophy* (London: Thames and Hudson, 1992), pp. 81-82.

[11] Ian McGreal, P. (Ed.), "Protagoras of Abdera," *Great Thinkers of the Western World* (New York: Harper Collins Publishers, 1992), p. 12.

[12] John M. Cooper (Ed.), *Plato: Complete Works* (Indianapolis: Hackett Publishing Company, 1997), p. xxvii.

[13] Ibid.

[14] Ibid., 169.

[15] Peter Lattman and Azam Ahmed, "Hedge Fund Billionaire Is Guilty of Insider Trading," *New York Times*, May 11, 2011. www.nytimes.com and Reuters; "Charges Upheld in Another Galleon Trading Case," *New York Times*, April 18, 2014. www.nytimes.com

[16] Ibid.

[17] John M. Cooper (Ed.), *Plato: Complete Works* (Indianapolis: Hackett Publishing Company, 1997), p. 185.

[18] Douglas J. Soccio, *Archetypes of Wisdom: An Introduction to Philosophy* (Belmont, CA: Wadsworth/Cengage Learning, 2010), p. 79

[19] John M. Cooper (Ed.), *Plato: Complete Works* (Indianapolis: Hackett Publishing Company, 1997), p. 791.

[20] Douglas J. Soccio, *Archetypes of Wisdom: An Introduction to Philosophy* (Belmont, CA: Wadsworth/Cengage Learning, 2010), p. 79.

[21] John M. Cooper (Ed.), *Plato: Complete Works*. (Indianapolis: Hackett Publishing Company, 1997), pp. 827-828.

[22] Ibid., 835.

[23] John Chaffee, *The Philosopher's Way: Thinking Critically About Profound Ideas* (Upper Saddle River, NJ: Pearson/Prentice Hall, 2005), p. 53.

[24] Nils Rauhut, "Thrasymachus," *The Internet Encyclopedia of Philosophy*, Ed. James Fieser, 2006. 29 June 2009. http://www.iep.utm.edu/t/thrasymachus.htm

[25] John. M. Cooper (Ed.), *Plato: Complete Works* (Indianapolis: Hackett Publishing Company, 1997), p. 983.

[26] Ibid., 988.

[27] Frank Rich, "Bernie Madoff Is No John Dillinger," *The New York Times*, This Week in Review, p. 8.

[27a and 27b] "A Retirement Toast," *Bloomberg BusinessWeek,* Jan. 12-18, 2015, pp. 19-20.

[28] C.C.W. Taylor, *Socrates: A Very Short Introduction* (Oxford: Oxford Press, 2000), pp. 4-5.

[29] Ibid.

[30] Ibid., 5.

[31] Reginald E. Allen (Ed.), *Greek Philosophy: Thales to Aristotle*, 3rd ed. (New York: The Free Press, 1991), pp. 17-18.

[32] Albert B. Hakim, *Historical Introduction to Philosophy*, 5th ed. (Upper Saddle River, NJ: Pearson/Prentice Hall, 2006), p. 32.

[33] Ibid.

[34] Donald Palmer, *Does the Center Hold? An Introduction to Western Philosophy* (Boston: McGraw Hill, 2002), p. 29.

[35] Ibid.

[36] Anthony Kenny, *A Brief History of Western Philosophy* (Oxford: Blackwell Publishers, 1998), p. 23.

[37a] Ibid.

[37b] John M. Cooper (Ed.), *Plato: Complete Works.* (Indianapolis: Hackett Publishing Company, 1997), p. 787.

[38] Ibid., 1000.

[39] Jeremy Stangroom and James Garvey, *The Great Philosophers: From Socrates to Foucault* (New York: Metro Books, 2005), p. 12.

[40] Julia Annas, *Plato: A Very Short Introduction* (Oxford: Oxford University Press, 2003), p. 13.

[41] Ibid.

[42] Ibid., 12.

[43] Albert B. Hakim, *Historical Introduction to Philosophy*, 5th ed. (Upper Saddle River, NJ: Pearson, Prentice Hall, 2006), p. 54.

[44] Ibid.

[45] Ibid., 55.

[46] Ibid., 54.

[47] Ibid.

[48] Bryan Magee, *The Story of Philosophy* (New York: D.K. Publishing, Inc., 2001), p. 24.

[49] Jeremy Stangroom and James Garvey, *The Great Philosophers: From Socrates to Foucault* (New York: Metro Books, 2005), p. 15.

[50] Philip Stokes, *Philosophy: 100 Essential Thinkers* (New York: Enchanted Lion Books, 2003), p. 15 .

[51] Ibid.

[52] T.Z. Lavine, *From Socrates to Sartre: The Philosophical Quest* (New York: Bantam Books, 1984), p. 38.

[53] Jeremy Stangroom and James Garvey, *The Great Philosophers: From Socrates to Foucault* (New York: Metro Books, 2005), p. 14.

[54] Ibid.

[55] Ibid.

[56] John M. Cooper (Ed.), *Plato: Complete Works.* (Indianapolis: Hackett Publishing Company, 1997), pp. 1132-1134.

[57] Douglas J. Soccio, *Archetypes of Wisdom: An Introduction to Philosophy.* (Belmont, CA: Wadsworth/Cengage Learning, 2010), p. 147.

[58] Reginald E. Allen (Ed.), *Greek Philosophy: Thales to Aristotle*, 3rd ed. (New York: The Free Press, 1991), p. 20.

[59] *Aristotle: Selections*, Terrance Irwin and Gail Fine, trans. (Indianapolis: Hackett Publishing Incorporated, 1995), p. xiii.

[60] Ibid.

[61] Ibid.

[62] Ibid.

[63] Ibid.

[64] Ibid.

[65] Ibid.

[66] Ibid.

[67] Ibid.

[68] Paul Cartledge, *The Greeks: Crucible of Civilization* (New York: Atlantic Productions, 2000), p. 210.

[69] T.Z. Lavine, *From Socrates to Sartre: The Philosophical Quest* (New York: Bantam Books, 1984), p. 70.

[70] Ibid.

[71] Ibid., 71.

[72] Paul Cartledge, *The Greeks: Crucible of Civilization* (New York: Atlantic Productions, 2000), p. 201.

[73] Ibid.

[74] T.Z. Lavine, *From Socrates to Sartre: The Philosophical Quest* (New York: Bantam Books, 1984), p. 71.

[75] Ibid., 73.

[76] Ibid., 73.

[77] Ibid., 74.

78 Ibid.

79 Ibid.

80 Ibid.

81 Ibid.

82 Ibid., 75.

83 Philip Stokes, *Philosophy: 100 Essential Thinkers* (New York: Enchanted Lion Books, 2003), p. 75.

84 Douglas J. Soccio, *Archetypes of Wisdom: An Introduction to Philosophy* (Belmont, CA: Wadsworth/Cengage Learning, 2010), p. 181.

85 Paul Cartledge, *The Greeks: Crucible of Civilization* (New York: Atlantic Productions, 2000), p. 204.

86 *Aristotle: Selections*, Terrance Irwin and Gail Fine, trans. (Indianapolis: Hackett Publishing Incorporated, 1995), p. 347.

87 Ibid., 366.

88 Ibid., 372.

89 Albert B. Hakim, *Historical Introduction to Philosophy* (Upper Saddle River, NJ: Pearson Prentice Hall, 2006), p. 153.

90 Ibid., 154.

91 Ibid., 155.

92 Ibid., 156.

93 Ibid., 159.

94 Saint Augustine. *On Christian Doctrine,* book 1, chap. 28, Ed. D.W. Robertson, Jr. (New York: The Bobbs-Merrill Company, Inc., 1958), pp. 23-24.

95 Douglas J. Soccio, *Archetypes of Wisdom: An Introduction to Philosophy*. (Belmont, CA: Wadsworth/Cengage Learning, 2010), p. 232.

96 Martin J. Lecker, "Ethical Hedonism," *Encyclopedia of Business and Society,* vol. 3: H-N, Ed. Robert W. Kolb (Thousands Oaks, CA: Sage Publications, 2008), p. 1062.

97 Ibid.

98 Ibid.

99 Ibid.

100 Ibid.

101 Ibid.

102 Ibid.

103 A.L. Long and D.N. Sedley, *The Hellenistic Philosophers* (New York: Cambridge University Press, 1987), p. 114.

104 Martin J. Lecker, "Ethical Hedonism," *Encyclopedia of Business and Society,* vol. 3: H-N, Ed. Robert W. Kolb (Thousands Oaks, CA: Sage Publications, 2008), pp. 1062-1063.

105 A.L. Long and D.N. Sedley, *The Hellenistic Philosophers* (New York: Cambridge University Press, 1987), p. 113.

106 Peter Unger, *Living High & Letting Die: Our Illusion of Innocence* (New York: Oxford University Press, 1996), p. 9.

107 This case was rewritten based upon the following article: Michelle Innis, "Australia Challenges Use of Unpaid Internship," *The New York Times*, November 10, 2014, p. B4.

108 This case was rewritten based upon the following article: Manil Surl, "Ancient Laws, Modern Problems," *The New York Times*, Sunday Review, April 19, 2015, p. SR5.

CHAPTER 3

EASTERN-WORLD SAGES

"He who never acts with the motivation of personal desire, whose (ego-binding) karma has been burned up in the fire of wisdom: such a one (alone) may be considered wise."

—The Essence of the Bhagavad Gita, Chapter 4, verse 19

© saiko3p/Shutterstock, Inc.

Although we eliminated the study of religion as a moral standard due to its ethical relativist nature, I would be remiss not to acknowledge the philosophical contributions of such Eastern philosophers as Lao Tzu, Confucius's *Analects,* and Siddhartha Gautama; or works such as the *Tao Te Ching, Diamond Sutra*, and *Bhagavad Gita,* as well as the antithesis of these aforementioned philosophies written by Sun-tzu called the *Art of War.* For this reason, this chapter will explore some of the philosophies of these sages, where in some cases religion has centered around them.

Lao Tzu

There has been much controversy over who Lao Tzu really was, when he lived, and whether he wrote the *Tao Te Ching* on his own. The *Tao Te Ching* is a small collection of reflections on the meaning of a good life from a Chinese perspective. Tao means "the way" and by some accounts, Lao Tzu wrote the book on his own, around 600 BCE.[1] Lao Tzu means "old master," and according to some historians, a revered sage. Confucius sought his advice, but Lao Tzu left only to be detained by a gatekeeper at Hsien Ku Pass, as he traveled westward and asked him to write a treatise on the way (tao) and virtue (te), which he did.[2] After writing the *Tao Te Ching* in two sections of 5,000 words for each section, he wandered off, never to be heard from again.[3] Recently, some scholars believed that the text was written by several people around 300 BCE.[4] Regardless of when it was written, or even by whom, as a result of its writing, a religion (Taoism) developed by practicing Lao Tzu's *Tao Te Ching* philosophy. *Tao Te Ching* means the Book (Ching) of How (Tao) Things Happen or Work (Te) and consists of three topics: (1) natural law—how things happen; (2) how to live in harmony with this law; and (3) a method to lead, govern, or educate others in accordance with this natural law.[5] In order to exemplify the teachings of Lao Tzu, some of the *Tao Te Ching* passages will follow to exemplify the three sections depicted above. This first passage is found in Chapter 22.

Yield and become whole
Bend and remain straight
Be low and become filled
Be worn out and become renewed
Have little and receive
Have much and be confused
Therefore sages hold to the one as an example for the world
Without flaunting themselves-and so are seen clearly
Without presuming themselves-and so are distinguished
Without passing themselves-and so have merit
Without boasting about themselves-and so are lasting

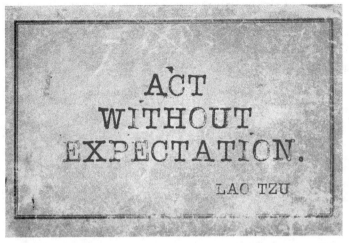

ACT WITHOUT EXPECTATION.

LAO TZU

© YuryZap/Shutterstock, Inc.

This passage (Chapter 22) epitomizes the Taoist philosophy of having an open heart, being humble, not showing off, or being highly visible— even though some may see these characteristics as a sign of weakness; and not being on the defensive because you cannot be attacked if there is nothing to attack; by being defensive, it is a waste of energy where you can direct it to something more constructive.[7] When Ben Cohen and Jerry Greenfield first created Ben and Jerry's, the famous ice cream corporation, their goal was to develop a socially responsible business. To commemorate their first day of business, when the lines were too long to serve the unexpectedly large crowd, every year they give free ice cream on the anniversary of that first day. In addition, they wanted to give 12% of their pretax profits to charitable organizations but their board of directors pushed for only 5%, so they agreed on 7.5%. When they created the ice cream, they exceeded the legal percentage of cream (much of ice cream is air filled). They even made sure that the highest paid employee would not receive more than seven times the amount of the lowest paid employee. They did so with an open heart, not to receive praise, and were not known to be on the defensive because their actions were honor based.

In the next passage, found in Chapter 45, it discussed the love of material things and what happens when this love takes over one's judgment.

Fame of the self, which is dearer?
The self or wealth, which is greater?
Gain or loss, which is more painful?

Thus excessive love must lead to great spending
Excessive hoarding must lead to heavy loss

Knowing contentment avoids disgrace
Knowing when to stop avoids danger
Thus one can endure indefinitely.[8]

In this passage, there are questions that we are faced with all the time. Which are more important, material possessions or spiritual enlightenment? If our love of material worth is so great, what price eventually must be paid? Gain can bring our lives complications while loss can yield us freedom.[9]

For a practical example of the above, think of the many Americans who purchased homes that they could not afford at sub-prime rates, only to watch their homes drop in value, when many lost their jobs due to a poor economy, which lead them to losing their homes, and in some cases resulting in homelessness. Of course, this was then compounded by many financial institutions purchasing these sub-prime mortgages from these homeowners' banks, watching the value of the homes and ultimately the banks' assets devalue, and having others who invested in these financial institutions watch their investments decrease. According to the Tao, if the chase for material gains was replaced by accepting what was given to them, perhaps these financial losses would not have expanded exponentially throughout our economy.

How many times have you observed others who have purchased or leased an automobile above their income in order to fit in with the neighbors or fellow employees or business partners? Then, they are worried if the automobile is damaged, stolen, or they do not earn the bonus they expected which would enable them to make the next car payments.

This next passage (Chapter 66) looks at individuals in high positions and their relationships and actions with those in lower positions.

> Rivers and oceans can be the kings of a hundred valleys
> Because of their goodness in staying low
> So they can be the kings of a hundred valleys
> Thus if sages wish to be over people
> They must speak humbly to them
> If they wish to be in front of people
> They must place themselves behind them
> Thus the sages are positioned above
> But the people do not feel burdened
> They are positioned in front
> But the people do not feel harmed
> Thus the world is glad to push them forward
> without resentment[10]

In Chapter 66, the message is simple: If you want to influence others and have friends, you need to be humble; rivers and oceans receive water from streams; the Tao emphasizes rather than force you attain cooperation through harmony, quite the opposite of Thrasymachus's philosophy of "might makes right."[11]

In research with a colleague, Prof. Terri Kaye Needle, at the 10th International Conference Promoting Business Ethics, after surveying over 100 employees, most had been victimized by a form of discrimination termed workplace rankism (coined by Robert Fuller, author of *Somebodies and Nobodies*). Essentially, workplace rankism occurs when you are bullied by superiors, either when they ask you to do something they would not be asked to do if they were in the same hierarchical position as you, or when you are spoken to in a disrespectful manner, which would not be done if they reported to you. Workplace rankism is an example of not following the Tao as discussed in Chapter 66.

The final three lines come from a section of Chapter 81 and are self-explanatory. Perhaps, once again we can refer to Socrates' statement that "wealth does not make excellence but excellence makes wealth."

Sages do not accumulate
The more they assist others, the more they possess
The more they give to others, the more they gain.[12]

© aphotostory/Shutterstock, Inc.

Confucius

Although it cannot be proved, it is believed that Confucius, the Latinized form of the name Kong Fuzi, Master Fong, was born 551 BCE and died in 479 BCE.[13] Confucius lived in Lu, China and grew up without a father; and since he was impoverished, he would hold various odd jobs to support himself.[14] At age fifteen, he discovered a love for classical learning, when four years later he was married and they produced two children, a boy and a girl.[15] At around age twenty-three, Confucius worked as a teacher and studied ancient government structures with a scholar known as the master of Tan.[16] With a shifting in government, Confucius traveled to a northern state, Qi, but eventually returned to Lu when the political climate changed.[17] While in his fifties, Confucius was made the first governor of a city and later was made the constabulary of Lu.[18] During this time period, again there were shifts in the government philosophy and Confucius spent the next fourteen years teaching students and seeking to spread his message of social regeneration among the holders of political power.[19]

At age seventy, he returned to Lu (484 BCE), the same year that his son died and his greatest disciple, Yan Hui, also passed away.[20] Three years later at age seventy-three, Confucius died. For two thousand years, Confucius has been canonized as China's first and supreme teacher and even today on September 28, his birthday is still celebrated as Teachers Day in China.[21]

Some believe that there was an analogy of Confucius to Socrates, in that they shared the same vocation as teacher and who attracted themselves to a host of disciples.[22] The *Analects* are extremely controversial because not only do they contain the sayings of Confucius, but like Socrates and Plato, it is difficult to discern where the master's work ends and his disciples' works begin.[23]

The *Analects* is a text consisting of a series of anecdotes, brief statements, and dialogues written by Confucius and his disciples approximately seventy-five years after his death, which historians place around 400 BCE.[24] What follows are selected passages from the *Analects*, for which further interest on the part of the reader may be satisfied by referring to them directly. Please note after each passage, the first number identifies the chapter, while the second number represents the verse.

> Confucius said, "Wealth and rank are desired by people, but they do not stay if they are not gotten in the right way. Poverty and lowliness are disliked by people, but they do not leave if this is not accomplished in the right way. If exemplary people departed from humanness, how could they be worthy of the name? Ideal people do not deviate from humaneness at any time; they are at it even when in a rush, they are at it even in the midst of turmoil."[25] (4:5)

Confucius said, "Don't worry about having no position; worry about that whereby you may effectively become established. Don't worry that no one recognizes you; seek to be worthy of recognition." [26] (4:14)

The Master said: "A gentleman seeks virtue; a small man seeks land. A gentleman seeks justice; a small man seeks favors."[27] (4:11)

The master said, "A gentleman eats without stuffing his belly; chooses a dwelling without demanding comfort; is diligent in his office and prudent in his speech; seeks the company of the virtuous in order to straighten his own ways. Of such a man, one may truly say that his is fond of learning."[28] (1:14)

The passages above refer to the fact that one's material status in life does not really reflect one's ethical character. This parallels Socrates' statement from the *Apology* that "wealth does not make excellence but excellence makes wealth." According to Confucius, regardless of the circumstances, you should always act in an ethical manner and not be concerned whether you are receiving outside praise for these virtuous actions. In the last passage, you may notice shades of Socrates' belief in moderation which his disciple Aristotle uses in his golden mean of virtue.

In the next passage found below in the *Analects*, another parallel between Socrates and Confucius may be noted. In this Confucian passage, does it not seem to resonate Socrates' quote, "the unexamined life if not worth living"?

Master Zeng, one of the pupils of Confucius,said, "I examine myself three times a day; have I been unfaithful in planning for others? Have I been unreliable in conversation with friends? Am I preaching what I haven't practices myself?"[29] (1:4)

Immanuel Kant, famous Prussian philosopher who we will discuss in the next passage, is known for his quote, "treating humanity as an ends not a means," with shades of the golden rule, "do unto others, as you would want others to do unto you." Notice the following statement which resembles both quotes:

Zigeng, one of the pupils of Confucius, said, "What I don't want others to do to me, I do not want to do to others."[30] (5:12)

This last selection is a description of how Confucius sees establishing one's character.

Confucius said, "Cultivated people have nine thoughts. When they look, they think of how to see clearly. When they listen, they think of how to hear keenly. In regard to their appearance, they think of how to be warm. In their demeanor, they think of how to be respectful. In their speech, they think of how to be truthful. In their work, they think of how to be serious. When in doubt, they think of how to pose questions. When angry, they think of trouble. When they see gain to be had, they think of justice." [31] (16:10)

© Irafael/Shutterstock, Inc.

Siddhartha Gautama

Siddhartha Gautama was an Indian philosopher born in Kapilavastu, India (now Nepal), April 8, 563 BCE, and died on February 25, 483 BCE in Kusinagra, India, at the age of eighty. [32]

It is believed that when first born, his father, a prince, summoned fortunetellers to find out what the future held in store for his son and was told that Siddhartha would become a king if he remained within his father's world, but a world redeemer if he left the monarchy.[33] Wanting his son to be a national leader, Siddhartha's father shielded him from all contact with the outside world and all its evils and ailments. At age sixteen, he married a princess from another close village whose name was Yasodhara, and who bore him a child, Rahula.[34] Eventually, he ventured out on his own, outside of his father's castle, where he had contact with an old man, a sick man, a corpse, and an **ascetic** (*one who denies himself basic ordinary pleasures*).[35] His charioteer explained that each represented the following: just as a man is born, he grows old; in time he becomes sick, and eventually this leads to death; while the ascetic seeks to end life's suffering and with it, continues rebirth in an *endless cycle* which is called **samsara.**[36]

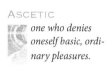
It was shortly after these experiences that Siddhartha, at age twenty-nine, renounced his worldly possessions and birthright as a prince.[37] For the next six years, he joined five ascetics who practiced an extreme form of self-mortification, but after almost dying as a result of this lifestyle, he recovered and realized that his fasts and penances had been useless, and began begging for food, while at the same time these five ascetic disciples left him.[38] One day, at age forty-nine, he sat beneath a tree and after forty-nine days, he found the truth and believed to understand what must be done to solve suffering and unhappiness of all kinds, so he journeyed to the Deer Park near Banaras (the modern Sarnath) and preached his first sermon to these five former disciples, which he said "set in motion the Wheel of the Law."[39] He regained them as disciples and a few days later a band of sixty ascetics became his disciples; and had them disperse geographically to preach the Buddhist Dharma (doctrine), which he did as well until his death at age eighty.[40] At the end of his life, he asked his disciples not to look for a new leader, but to look to the Dharma which he preached and would lead them, so in essence, he was asking them to rely on themselves to carry on their work.[41]

The **Buddha's Dharma**, *the doctrine depicting the true way of life*, consists of four basic truths. They are: (1) life entails suffering; (2) the cause of suffering is desire; (3) the way to escape suffering is to rid oneself of desire; and (4) to be free from desire you must follow the eightfold

88

path.[42] The eightfold path is: (1) right understanding, (2) right resolve, (3) right speech; (4) right conduct; (5) right livelihood; (6) right effort; (7) right attention; and (8) right concentration.[43]

Since the Buddha's Dharma was passed down by word of mouth and the religion of Buddhism has many braches, the next facet of this section will address the **Diamond Sutra**, *a written record of a teaching given by the Buddha over 2,500 years ago, which had been passed down from generation to generation.* [44] The original *Diamond Sutra* was taught by the Buddha in Sanskrit, the ancient language of India about 4,000 years ago, but 3,000 years later was translated into Tibetan, and eventually Chinese after Tibet was invaded by Communist China in 1950.[45] The *Diamond Sutra,* original teachings of the Buddha, is cloaked in mystical language that can be revealed only by a learned teacher using explanations that were written over several centuries.[46] The original title is the *Diamond Prajnaparamita Sutra,* where *sutra* denotes an ancient book,[47] **prajnaparamita** loosely interpreted refers to *the ability to understand the way* (*Tao* or *dharma*), and since the diamond is one of the hardest materials know to humankind, the *sutra* metaphorically can penetrate all *dharmas,* as well as establish all *dharmas.*[48] As a result, the *Diamond Sutra* (shortened title) is to the Buddhists what the *Tao Te Ching* is to those following Taoism.

It is believed that everyone has the potential which, if harnessed, can lead to success, both spiritually and professionally; and if they follow the *Diamond Sutra,* they will realize this potential.[49] The *Diamond Sutra* is based upon the teachings of Siddhartha who was discussed earlier, and whose disciples recounted his quest for prajnaparamita, which they then wrote down creating the *Diamond Sutra* as it is known today.[50] The *Diamond Sutra* was first initiated by a disciple, Subhuti, who asked the Buddha a question, leading to many other questions and responses which made up this work.[51]

One of the teachings found in Section 3 of the *Diamond Sutra* is:

DIAMOND SUTRA
a written record of a teaching given by the Buddha over 2,500 years ago, which had been passed down from generation to generation.

PRAJNAPARAMITA
loosely interpreted refers to the ability to understand the way (Tao or dharma).

The Buddha then said, "Subhuti, all the Bodhisattvas and Mahasattvas should quell their minds in this way: All kinds of sentient beings-whether egg born, womb born, moisture born, or transformation born, having form or not having form, having thought or not having thought-through my reaching nirvana are saved. Yet when immeasurable, innumerable and unlimited numbers of beings have been liberated, verily, no beings have been liberated. And why is this Subhuti? If a Bodhisattva retains the notion of ego, a personality, a being and a life, he is not a true Bodhisattva." [52]

BODHISATTVA
(OR MAHA-
SATTVAS)
*one who wants to
be enlightened and
helps others to be
so as well.*

Subhuti is one of the eldest disciples and asks questions to the Buddha, who will not respond with an answer but with another question. A **Bodhisattva** or **Mahasattvas** *is one who wants to be enlightened and help others to be so as well.*[53] In the passage above, you will notice that all beings humans, bears, or cockroaches have the right to be enlightened. On a personal level, I once watched an ant crawl on the bare foot of a yogi who did not flinch or attempt to kill the ant, he just let the ant walk off his foot. Charitable actions are not to be enacted for any other reason other than to help the person to whom it was enacted for, not to take pride in doing the charitable act.[54] You should have an open heart and should think of others as part of the community or humanity, but actions are not intended to benefit the individual's ego.

This philosophy is also found in Section 4.

"Furthermore, Suhuti, a Bodhisattva ought to practice charity without dwelling. That is to say, a Bodhisattva should also practice charity without dwelling in form, sound, smell, taste, touch, or even dharma. Subhuti, Bodhisattvas ought to practice charity without dwelling in form, the blessings will be inestimable and inconceivable." [55]

Basically, you should be living to help others for no rewards including feeling better about yourself for doing the right action. Teaching others to do the right thing is also part of this philosophy.

In this passage found in section 23, virtue is discussed in terms of why a few ethical actions do not mean you are virtuous. Again, it involves your intention.

> "Furthermore, Subhuti, this Dharma is without differentiation or degree, and is therefore called anuttara-samyaksambodhi. The practice of all good virtues, free from the conception of an ego, a being, a personality, and a life will result in the attainment of Supreme Enlightenment, Subhuti, these so called virtues, the Tathagata says are not really virtues, but are nevertheless called good virtues."[56]

In section 23 above, Subhuti (a disciple of Buddha) is being told by the Buddha that if you want to become a Buddha (the term **anuttara-samyaksambodhi** *refers to a person who wants to become a Buddhist*), you must practice the Dharma, or way of life, by being virtuous all the time and should do so because that is the way (Dharma) and not to seek merit or fortune for doing so.[57] According to the **Tathagata** (*sage or Buddha*), virtues are not really virtues unless they satisfy the essence of being Buddhist, and for no other reason.[58]

In the last sentence of section 28, the same philosophy is repeated below.

> "Bodhisattvas should not have any longing for fortune and merit which they have created, and so do not obtain fortune and merit."[59]

This seems to resonate from similar beliefs found in the *Tao Te Ching* of putting others or purpose before self. In a 1994 Northridge, California, earthquake where two stores were so badly damaged they could not

ANUTTARA-SAMYAKSAM-BODHI
refers to a person who wants to practice Buddhism.

TATHAGATA
a sage or Buddha.

be open, the store manager used the payroll system to quickly deliver cash to employees whose homes were destroyed and gave $1,000 cash advances to these employees, so they could use these funds for food, shelter, and whatever else was needed for their families.[60] This type of a virtuous action is what the Buddha had in mind.

Bhagavad Gita

BHAGAVAD GITA

the equivalent of a Hindu bible, written around 3000 BCE.

The **Bhagavad Gita** *is the equivalent of a Hindu bible, taken to be have written around 3000 BCE according to some scholars*; and like the *Diamond Sutra* repeating the words of wisdom of Siddhartha Gautama, the Indian Buddhist, this represents some of the philosophies of Krishna, the sage who was Hindu.[61] The *Bhagavad Gita* is part of the *Mahabharata*, which involves two main characters, a general named Arjuna and a charioteer called Krishna, who was invited by the general to observe two armies fighting.[62] However, unknown to Arjuna, Krishna was actually a "Divine Presence" and in time unfolded the guiding principles which will lead one to a higher, spiritual existence.

GUNAS

it is believed there are three possessed by all individuals; even though one dominates over the others.

Through these teachings by Krishna, Arjuna learned of *three qualities* (called **gunas**) *possessed by all individuals; even though one dominates*

© Kailash K Soni, 2010. Used under license from Shutterstock, Inc.

over the others. [64]The highest guna or quality is **sattwic** described by Krishna as *an individual who is honest, compassionate, competent, intelligent, courageous, and trustworthy.*[65] A sattwic deed is one offered without personal gain from the deed which is in accordance with the teachings of the scripture and its firm belief in righteousness, according to a passage found in Chapter 17, verse 11 of the *Bhagavad Gita* below.[66]

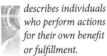

SATTWIC
one who acts without personal gain in accordance with the teachings of the scripture and its firm belief in righteousness.

> That yagya (sacrificial rite, or performance of duty) is sattwic which is offered without any desire for (personal) gain from the deed, which is performed in accordance with (the teaching of) scripture, and with firm belief in it rightness.[67]

It is interesting to note, how the Lao Tzu, Confucius, Siddhartha Gautama, and the Krishna's *Bhagavad Gita* all focus on being virtuous for, as Aristotle would have said, the sake of virtuousness, not for the instrumentality of it, as Plato had said when referring the personal rewards or outcome you may derive from your action. The second quality, **rajasic**, *describes individuals who perform actions for their own benefit or fulfillment.* This is best described in the Chapter 14, verse 12 below. [68]

RAJASIC
describes individuals who perform actions for their own benefit or fulfillment.

> When a person shows greed, restless activity, and selfish motivation, rajas predominates in his nature.[69]

The third and lowest guna, **tamasic**, *is demonic, corrupt, driven by personal interests or prejudices, and will not hesitate to put people in pain to achieve a selfish goal.* [70] Below see one description of a tamasic found in Chapter 7, verse 15.

TAMAS
one who is not compassionate, will put people in pain to achieve selfish goals, bring discomfort to their organizations, and are demonic or corrupt.

> Evildoers (in whom tamas predominates), lowest of human beings, dull witted and bereft of understanding by the power of *maya*, failing to take shelter in Me, partake of the nature of demons.[71]

In this passage, *maya* refers to a delusion as part of the description of the guna, tamas, an individual who is uncompassionate, will put people in pain to achieve selfish goals, will bring discomfort to their organizations, and is demonic or corrupt. [72]

At the beginning of the story found in the *Bhagavad Gita*, Arjuna is reluctant to join in the battle against other members of his family, because he believes it is morally wrong to go against his own kinsmen.[73] However, toward the end of his discourses, Krishna encourages Arjuna to rise and fight the battle against his cousins.[74] In actuality, we find that this battle is merely a metaphor of good fighting evil, a battle faced by all executives… profits versus people and the planet. The message of the *Bhagavad Gita*, according to Pujan Roka, is that we are constantly struggling between "any force of good or evil. It could be a battle of ethics and morality that brews in our hearts and minds. Or it could be a battle between the virtuous and the corrupt. ..We expect our leaders to have a high degree of morality and ethics; we expect our leaders to be sattvic." [75]

Sun-tzu

© Christopher Poliquin, 2010. Used under license from Shutterstock, Inc.

In the Western world, many look at Prince Niccolo Machiavelli as the anti-sattvic. However, the Eastern world has its share as well. One well-known militarist whose military philosophy has been emulated in our contemporary world is that of China's Sun-tzu. Although not a philosopher, his philosophies are quite well known.

Sun-tzu's *Art of War* has been reportedly used by Napoleon and individuals in the Nazi High Command.[76] The *Art of War*, recognized as China's oldest and most profound military treatise, was written by Sun-tzu, an effective military strategist, who wrote sections of this book each time he was summoned to create a military strategy for the King of Wu.[77] Sun-tzu's work was better known in the late eighteenth century and was not translated correctly until the twentieth century.[78] His approach was to use psychological warfare more than physical force (in fact, the Chinese character li signifying force is mentioned only nine times in the thirteen chapters of his work).[79] Some of his strategies included: change the enemy's leadership and society from a condition of harmony to chaos, splitting alliances, evading battle, attacking by surprise, using secret agents, and attacking the enemy's strategy.[80] Much controversy has evolved on the dates of Sun-tzu's birth and death, believed to have taken place some time in the sixth century BCE, and in some cases whether he existed at all, although most are in agreement with his existence.

However, some of these strategies are used today by unethical individuals. The passages that follow will demonstrate Sun-tzu's military philosophies on defeating the enemy (which in business is called competition). The first passage comes from Chapter One:

"Display profits to entice them. Create disorder (in their forces) and take them.
If they are substantial, prepare for them; if they are strong, avoid them.
If they are angry, perturb them; be deferential to foster their arrogance.
If they are rested, force them to exert themselves.
If they are united, cause them to be separated.
Attack where they are unprepared.
Go forth where they will not expect it.
These are the ways military strategists are victorious. They cannot be spoken in advance." [81]

In the beginning of the U.S. industrial revolution, with the "robber barons" of capitalism, this was considered business as usual. Today, you can equate these strategies with **hostile takeovers**, which many corporations have experienced by *corporate raiders (those who purchase a business with the intention of selling its assets for a profit at the expense of jobs, local economies, etc.).*

HOSTILE
TAKEOVERS
those who purchase a business with the intention of selling its assets for a profit at the expense of jobs, local economies, etc., who are sometimes called corporate raiders.

In the 1980s, IBM had a stronghold market in personal computers (PCs), but their target market was primarily businesses. Apple Computers saw a niche that IBM missed, which was the educational institution market, and took full advantage when it created software that was more user friendly than its competitor. Read the following passage and observe if you find any similarities to Sun-tzu's strategy and Apple Computers.

> "It is the nature of the army to stress to speed; to take advantage of the enemy's absence; to travel unanticipated roads; and to attack when they are not alert."[82]

Apple Computer took advantage of its competition's lack of insight into the computer user target market of educational institutions and created a product to meet the needs of this previously unrecognized consumer. On the other hand, in the next passage found in Chapter 11 of *Art of War:*

> "If the enemy opens the door, you must race in. Attack what they love first."[83]

This is the rationale for executive recruiters who "woo" the competition's managerial personnel from one company to another, who will pay them more. This is quite similar to baseball, where one team will offer another player more money to leave their competition's team and join theirs where they can do more damage. The same strategy is used for patent infringements, especially when taken from a foreign country where enforcement of the patents is more difficult. These Sun-tzu military strategies are all part of a philosophy called **predatory capitalism,** *defined as developing strategies where your intention is to drive the competitors out of business.* This is exactly what happened in late 1980s to the textile industry when foreign competitors, who paid their employees unconscionable low wages, drove many American textile companies out of business.

Mencius

Mencius or "Master Meng" ("Mengzi" in Chinese) was born in the state of Zou in 372 BCE, and was a disciple of Confucius who believed that all human beings were innately good, which could be acquired by education and self-discipline, or lost through neglect and negative influences, but always had the opportunity to return to the righteous path.[84] He was born only eighteen miles from Confucius' birthplace and was named Meng Ke or Ko, who belonged to the ruling Meng-sun family. Mencius was brought up primarily by his mother, since his father passed away at a young age. He was trained as a scholar and teacher based upon his education which many believed was received from Confucian schools which he attended. In 324 (age forty-eight), he moved from Ch'I, north of Lu, where he was a teacher, and visited the states of Sung and Hsueh from the funding of these states' respective leaders, only to return back to his home state as an advisor to the court of Duke Wen of T'eng.[85]

Being resented by those around the duke, because of his influence on him and the duke's policies, Mencius moved to Liang, the state of Wei's capital, to advise King Hui. However, after the king's death, his successor also resented Mencius, so he returned to Ch'I, where he became king in 319 BCE. Following a three-year hiatus after his mother's death, Mencius once again became an advisor, this time to King Hsuan, until the Ch'I army was overthrown by the Yen. Mencius returned back to his home state and for the remainder of his life (289 BCE) studied Confucian texts. His teachings were eventually written in a book titled *Meng-tzu* (*Mengzi*).[86]

One of Mencius' philosophies was his list of four cardinal virtues: benevolence, righteousness, wisdom, and propriety. Benevolence was the compassion one had for family, as well as for the suffering of all humans and non-humans. So, a benevolent ruler will be cognizant of how policies affect those being ruled. Righteousness is not being disrespectful to others and serving one's parents. Sexual harassment in today's world, along with sending parents to a nursing home rather than having them live in your own home, would not be virtuous, and one would not be considered to be righteous. Propriety is respecting your elders and legitimate authority figures. In the Asian culture, touching another man's wife is prohibited, but if your sister-in-law passed out in the middle of a busy highway, carrying her to safety would be permissible since a higher obligation (saving a life) takes priority over the custom of not touching the body of a married woman, especially one's sister-in-law. The last virtue is wisdom, which involves the commitment to the other virtues. It is very much like Socrates' justice, which consisted of moderation, courage, wisdom, and justice, which was possessing the first three. In Mencius' virtual philosophy, possessing benevolence, righteousness, and propriety results in wisdom. One metaphorical example of his philosophy is being in the shoes of the person who's the recipient of your action. For example, you should not discharge a subordinate who has more expertise than you and could surpass you for a promotion as a result.[87]

The philosophical quote discussed above may be found in the boxed area below and originates from his works, entitled *Mengzi* from his sixth book, part A, chapter 6. *Mangzi's* text consists of seven books, parts A and B and then divided into chapters, much like the Stephanus number in Plato's (and Socrates') works.

> "The feeling of compassion is *benevolence*. The feeling of disdain is *righteousness*. The feeling of respect is *propriety*. The feeling of approval and disapproval is *wisdom*."[88]

© Bill Perry/Shutterstock, Inc.

In an article written by Pete Engardio, entitled "Karma Capitalism," he compared the philosophies of Sun-tzu's *The Art of War* with the Hindu text, *The Bhagavad Gita*, and developed the business philosophy he termed **karma capitalism**, *defined as "good leaders (who are) selfless, take initiative, and focus on their duty rather than obsessing over outcomes or financial gain."*[89] Unfortunately, too many businesses do not follow the "karma capitalistic" philosophy, and appear more entrenched in following principles similar to those of Sun-tzu.

Summary

In this chapter, the focus is on the Eastern philosophers and included Lao Tzu's *Tao Te Ching*, Confucius' *Analects*, Prince Siddhartha Gautama's *Diamond Sutra*, Krishna's *Bhagavad Gita*, Sun-tzu's *The Art of War*, and Mencius. China's Lao Tzu's philosophy centered around the Taoist philosophy of having an open heart, being humble, not showing off or being highly visible even though some may see these characteristics as a sign of weakness; and not being on the defensive because you cannot be attacked if there is nothing to attack; by being defensive, it is a waste of energy where you can direct it to something more constructive. Confucius, also from China, wrote the *Analects* wherein his philosophy is summarized as follows: Regardless of the circumstances, you should always act in an ethical manner and not be concerned whether you are receiving outside praise for these virtuous actions.

Another philosopher, from India, Siddhartha Gautama, wrote the *Diamond Sutra*, also called the Buddha's Dharma or the true way of life, which consists of four basic truths. They are: (1) life entails suffering; (2) the cause of suffering is desire; (3) the way to escape suffering is to rid oneself of desire; and (4) to be free from desire you must follow the eightfold path.[42] The eightfold path is: (1) right understanding, (2) right resolve, (3) right speech, (4) right conduct, (5) right livelihood, (6) right effort, (7) right attention, and (8) right concentration.

Also from India is the *Bhagavad Gita*, which is the equivalent of a Hindu bible, written around 3000 BCE and represents some of the philosophies of Krishna, the Hindu sage believed to have written it. Through these teachings by Krishna, three qualities (called gunas) are addressed and believed to be possessed by all individuals; even though one guna will dominate over the others. The highest guna or quality is sattwic, described as an individual who is honest, compassionate, competent, intelligent, courageous, and trustworthy. The second quality, rajasic, describes someone who performs actions for his or her own benefit or fulfillment. The third and lowest guna, tamasic, is demonic, corrupt, driven by personal interests or prejudices, and will not hesitate to put people in pain to achieve a selfish goal.

The *Art of War*, recognized as China's oldest and most profound military treatise was written by Sun-tzu, an effective military strategist, who wrote sections of this book each time he was summoned to create a military strategy for the King of Wu. His approach was to use psychological warfare more than physical force. Some of his strategies included: change the enemy's leadership and society from a condition of harmony to chaos, splitting alliances, evading battle, attacking by surprise, using secret agents, and attacking the enemy's strategy.

Mencius, a disciple of Confucius, believed that all human beings were innately good, which could be acquired by education and self-discipline, or lost through neglect and negative influences, but always had the opportunity to return to the righteous path. In order to find this path of good one had to attain four cardinal virtues: benevolence, righteousness, wisdom, and propriety. Benevolence was having compassion for others; righteousness is respecting others; propriety is respecting other authority figures; and wisdom is integrating and attaining all three virtues in one's life.

In an article written by Pete Engardio, entitled "Karma Capitalism," he compared the philosophies of Sun-tzu's *The Art of War* with the Hindu text, *Bhagavad Gita*, and developed a business philosophy which he termed karma capitalism, defined as "good leaders (who are) selfless, take initiative, and focus on their duty rather than obsessing over outcomes or financial gain."[84] Unfortunately, too many businesses do not follow the "karma capitalistic" philosophy and appear more entrenched in following principles similar to those of Sun-tzu.

Key Terms

Anuttara-samyaksambodhi: refers to a person who wants to practice Buddhism.

Ascetic: one who denies oneself basic, ordinary pleasures.

Bhagavad Gita: the equivalent of a Hindu bible, written around 3000 BCE.

Bodhisattva (or Mahasattvas): one who wants to be enlightened and helps others to be so as well.

Buddha's Dharma: a doctrine depicting the way of life.

Diamond Sutra: a written record of a teaching given by the Buddha over 2,500 years ago, which had been passed down from generation to generation.

Gunas: it is believed there are three possessed by all individuals; even though one dominates over the others.

Hostile takeovers: those who purchase a business with the intention of selling its assets for a profit at the expense of jobs, local economies, etc., who are sometimes called corporate raiders.

Karma capitalism: when good leaders who are selfless take initiative and focus on their duty rather than obsessing over outcomes or financial gain.

Prajnaparamita: loosely interpreted refers to the ability to understand the way (*Tao* or *dharma*).

Predatory capitalism: where your intention is to drive competitors out of business.

Rajasic: describes individuals who perform actions for their own benefit or fulfillment.

Samsara: endless cycle of rebirth.

Sattwic: one who acts without personal gain in accordance with the teachings of the scripture and its firm belief in righteousness.

Tamas: one who is not compassionate, will put people in pain to achieve selfish goals, bring discomfort to their organizations, and are demonic or corrupt.

Tathagata: a sage or Buddha.

Chapter Review Questions

1. Who was Lao Tzu and what were some of his philosophies? Can they be applied in the business world currently? Explain.
2. Who was Confucius? What were some of the philosophies found in the *Analects*?
3. What is the *Diamond Sutra* and what philosophies did it reflect?
4. What is the *Bhagavad Gita* and what are some businesses following it?
5. How are the philosophies of Sun-tzu being used in the financial world today?
6. Could Mencius' philosophy be applied to current leaders or leadership programs?

Cases for Discussion

CASE 3.1 MATERNITY LEAVES: PAID OR UNPAID?[90]

The United States is the only developed country not requiring employers to pay their employees for maternity leaves. The Family and Medical Leave Act (FMLA) permits employees to take some time off without pay. According to the National Partnership for Women and Family, almost 50% of those workers eligible to take off under the FMLA cannot afford to do so. For example, according to the Community Service Society, a New York nonprofit research center, those earning minimum wages are able to take off eight days off without pay before losing his or her life savings. As a result, two congresswomen are pushing to introduce legislation that would require twelve weeks of paid leaves for employees to care for a newborn or seriously ill relative. There would be a minimal cost by employees of about $1.50 each week, along with some funding from Social Security to reduce the cost for the employers.

Two points of contention raised by small businesses, as well as larger ones, are the costs attributed to these proposed bills and the right of an employer to determine what, if any, benefits to her employer may be required through governmental intervention. The sponsors of the bill believe that it would give economic security for workers with family responsibilities, improve health outcomes for children and senior-aged relatives (will improve long-term health care by making it easier to take newborns for health checkups or senior-aged relatives to physicians reducing hospital readmissions), and improve lower employee turnover, since employees will be allowed to return to work after their family or health leave.

DISCUSSION QUESTION

Would you support this bill? You may think of yourself as an employer or employee.
Defend your response, using the full S.E.A. method discussed in Chapter Two (state the philosophy, explain the philosophy in your own words, give a general example, and apply the philosophy to your action). Use any philosopher discussed in this chapter.

Case 3.2 Higher Wages for Employees or Company Profits?[91]

Based upon the research of some economists, the United States has one of the largest pay gaps with chief executives earning nearly 300 times what the average employee does. Therefore, when the founder, Dan Price, of the Gravity Payments, a credit card payment processing firm, heard from his friends how earning salaries way above the minimum $7.25 an hour minimum wage resulted in meeting their nondiscretionary financial obligations, he decided to do something about it in his own company. While he, the owner, was earning a little less than $1 million annually, his employees earned an average $48,000 a year, making it difficult to support a family in Seattle, Washington.

This epiphany resulted in Price making a radical policy change; within the next three years, all employees, himself included, would earn $70,000 a year. Out of the 120 employees on staff, about 70 of their salaries will grow as a result of this increase, with 30 of them having their salaries doubled. Price followed suit, but in the opposite direction, and will give himself a salary decrease so he too will be earning $70,000 along with the lowest ranking employee. Also contributing to this salary increase will be 75% to 80% of the $2.2 million in profits from this first year earned by his company. In addition, Price pledges that he does not plan on charging higher prices or cutting back any services, so his customers will not be indirectly participating in this salary change. He believes as a result of this action, his employees will be able to purchase their own homes and pay for their children's education.

DISCUSSION QUESTION

What do you think of this policy change? You may think of yourself as Mr. Price or an employee of his company and respond from either perspective (owner or employee).
Defend your response, using the full S.E.A. method discussed in Chapter Two (state the philosophy, explain the philosophy in your own words, give a general example, and apply the philosophy to your action). Use any philosopher discussed in this chapter.

Case 3.3 The Friend

Envision working for a software company and you have just been promoted to a sales district manager of the Northeast Marketing Division of your firm. You are responsible for increasing the sales of this territory which has been number one until recently, because of the poor performance of the salesperson assigned to the Boston area. This person was reassigned to the Omaha division and will be on probation there. Your first task is to hire a salesperson for this territory who can regain the lost sales and turn it around for your territory, because currently it is the lowest in your entire firm. After interviewing several candidates, you have narrowed it down to two. One candidate, Jane, has an extensive record with her former employer whose product is similar to yours and is looking to locate to the Boston area where her husband has just recently relocated. The other person is your best friend, who lacks the software selling experience for your particular product and sometimes has motivational issues. However, his wife is pregnant and working for this firm would give him paid health insurance, which he lacks, as well as a substantial increase in his salary. Your reputation and job depend upon whether the candidate you select will be able to increase the sales in your Boston territory.

DISCUSSION QUESTION

Would you hire Jane or your friend?

Defend your response, using the full S.E.A. method discussed in Chapter Two (state the philosophy, explain the philosophy in your own words, give a general example, and apply the philosophy to your action). Use any philosopher discussed in this chapter.

Endnotes

1. *Tao Te Ching*, James Legge, trans. (Mineola: Dover Publications Inc., 1997), p. i.
2. Ibid.
3. Ibid.
4. Ibid.
5. John Heider, *The Tao of Leadership: Leadership Strategies for a New Age* (New York, Bantam Books, 1985), pp. 1-2.
6. Derek Lin, *Tao Te Ching* (Woodstock, VT: Skylight Press, 2006), p. 45.
7. Ibid., 44.
8. Ibid., 89.
9. Ibid., 88
10. Ibid., 133.
11. Ibid., 132.
12. Ibid., 163.
13. Zinzhong Yao, *An Introduction to Confucianism* (Cambridge, UK: Cambridge University Press, 2000), pp. 21-22.
14. Thomas Cleary, *The Essential Confucius* (San Francisco: Harper Collins Publishers, 1992), p. 9.
15. Ibid., 10.
16. Ibid.
17. Ibid.
18. Ibid.
19. Ibid.
20. Ibid.
21. Simon Leys, *The Analects of Confucius* (New York: W.W. Norton and Company Inc., 1997), pp. xxii-xxiii.
22. Benjamin I. Schwartz, *The World of Thought in Ancient China* (Cambridge: Harvard University Press, 1985), p. 60.
23. Ibid., 61.
24. Simon Leys, *The Analects of Confucius* (New York: W.W. Norton and Company Inc., 1997), p. xix.
25. Thomas Cleary, *The Essential Confucius* (San Francisco: Harper Collins Publishers, 1992), p. 43.
26. Simon Leys, *The Analects of Confucius* (New York: W.W. Norton and Company Inc., 1997), p. 16.
27. Ibid.
28. Ibid., 5.
29. Thomas Cleary, *The Essential Confucius* (San Francisco: Harper Collins Publishers, 1992), p. 43.
30. Ibid., 83.
31. Ibid., 93.
32. "Buddha," *The Encyclopedia of World Biography*, 2nd ed., 17 vols. (Farmington Hills, MI: Gale Research, 1998). Reproduced in *Biography Resource Center* (Farmington Hills, MI: Gale, 2009). 28 Oct. 2009. http://galenet.galegroup.com/servlet/BioRC
33. "Siddhartha," *Historic World Leaders* (Farmington Hills, MI: Gale Research, 1994). Reproduced in *Biography Resource Center* (Farmington Hills, MI: Gale, 2009). 28 Oct. 2009. http://galenet.galegroup.com/servlet/BioRC
34. Ibid.
35. Wade Clark (Ed.), *Contemporary American Religion* (New York: Macmillan Reference, USA, 1999), p. 85.
36. Ibid.
37. "Siddhartha," *Historic World Leaders* (Farmington Hills, MI: Gale Research, 1994). Reproduced in *Biography Resource Center* (Farmington Hills, MI: Gale, 2009). 28 Oct. 2009. http://galenet.galegroup.com/servlet/BioRC
38. Arthur L. Basham, *The Wonder That Was India: A Survey of the Culture of the Indian Sub-Continent Before the Coming of the Muslims* (New York: Grove Publishers, 1959), p. 258.
39. Ibid., 258-259.
40. Ibid., 259-260.
41. Ibid., 260.

42 J. Gordon Melton (Ed.), "Eastern Family Part II: Buddhism, Shintoism, Japanese New Religions," *Encyclopedia of American Religions,* 7th ed. (Detroit: Gale Publishing, 2003), p. 201.

43 Ibid.

44 Geshe Michael Roach, *The Diamond Cutter: The Buddha on Managing Your Business and Your Life* (New York: Doubleday, 2000), p. 10.

45 Ibid., 10-11.

46 Ibid., 11.

47 Ibid., 13.

48 Master Nan Huai-Chin, *Diamond Sutra Explained,* Pia Giammasi, trans. (Florham Park, NJ: Primordia Press, 2004), pp. 2, 9.

49 Geshe Michael Roach, *The Diamond Cutter: The Buddha on Managing Your Business and Your Life* (New York: Doubleday, 2000), p. 15.

50 Ibid., 21.

51 Master Nan Huai-Chin, *Diamond Sutra Explained*, Pia Giammasi, trans. (Florham Park, NJ: Primordia Press, 2004), p. 26.

52 Ibid., 45.

53 Ibid., 25, 29.

54 Ibid., 55.

55 Ibid., 65.

56 Ibid., 239.

57 Ibid., 35, 239, 240.

58 Ibid., 27.

59 Ibid., 269.

60 Jane E. Dutton, et al., "Leading in Times of Trauma," *Harvard Business Review*, Vol. 80, No. 1, January 2002, p. 60.

61 Pujan Roka, *Bhagavad Gita on Effective Leadership: Timeless Wisdom for Leaders* (New York: iUniverse Incorporated, 2006), p. 3.

62 Swami Kriyananda, *The Essence of the Bhagavad Gita* (Nevada City, CA: Crystal Clarity, 2006), pp. 9-10.

63 Ibid., 9-13, 64.

64 Ibid., 455.

65 Pujan Roka, *Bhagavad Gita on Effective Leadership: Timeless Wisdom for Leaders* (New York: iUniverse Incorporated, 2006), p. 65.

66 Swami Kriyananda, *The Essence of the Bhagavad Gita* (Nevada City, CA: Crystal Clarity, 2006), p. 512.

67 Ibid.

68 Ibid., 457.

69 Ibid.

70 Pujan Roka, *Bhagavad Gita on Effective Leadership: Timeless Wisdom for Leaders* (New York: iUniverse Incorporated, 2006), p. 70.

71 Swami Kriyananda, *The Essence of the Bhagavad Gita* (Nevada City, CA: Crystal Clarity, 2006), p. 320.

72 Pujan Roka, *Bhagavad Gita on Effective Leadership: Timeless Wisdom for Leaders* (New York: iUniverse Incorporated, 2006), p. 67.

73 Swami Kriyananda, *The Essence of the Bhagavad Gita* (Nevada City, CA: Crystal Clarity, 2006), p. 10.

74 Ibid., 545.

75 Pujan Roka, *Bhagavad Gita on Effective Leadership: Timeless Wisdom for Leaders* (New York: iUniverse Incorporated, 2006), p. 157.

76 Sun-tzu, *The Art of War*, R.D. Sawyer, trans. (New York: Barnes and Noble, 1994), p. 79.

77 Ibid., 80.

78 Sun-tzu, *The Reader's Companion to Military History*, Biography Reference Database, 1996. 2 Nov. 2009. http://vnweb.hwwilsonweb.com/

79 Ibid.

80 Ibid.

81 Sun-tzu, *The Art of War*, R.D. Sawyer, trans. (New York: Barnes and Noble, 1994), p. 168.

82 Ibid., 220.

83 Ibid., 224.

84 Jeffrey Richey, "Mencius," *Internet Encyclopedia of Philosophy*, James Fieser (ed.), n.d. Web. www.ied.utm.edu/mencius

85 "Mencius," Society for Recognition of Famous People Website. www.thefamouspeople.com/profiles/mencius

86 Ibid.

87 Bryan van Norden, "Mencius," *The Stanford Encyclopedia of Philosophy*, Edward N. Zalta (ed.), Winter 2014 Edition. http://plato.stanford.edu/archives/win2014/entries/mencius/

88 Ibid.

89 Pete Engardio, "Karma Capitalism," *Business Week*, October 30, 2006, p. 86.

90 This case was rewritten based upon the following articles: Lauren Sandler, "How to Love Paid Family Leave," *Bloomberg Businessweek*, July 21-27, 2014, pp. 8-9; and "Family and Medical Insurance Leave Act," National Partnership Fact Sheet, March, 2015. www.nationalpartnership.org

91 This case was rewritten based upon the following article: Patricia Cohen, "Owner of Credit Card Processor Is Setting a New Minimum Wage: $70,000 a Year," *The New York Times*, April 14, 2015, p. B3.

CHAPTER 4

SOCIAL AND POLITICAL PHILOSOPHERS

"The power of man is his present means, to obtain some future apparent Good."

-Thomas Hobbes in Leviathan, Chapter 10, Part One[1]

Courtland Kelley worked for General Motors for thirty years, and when as a safety inspector, he reported a flaw in the ignition of the Chevrolet Cobalt, which could easily shift into the "off" position, resulting in the automobile stalling and not disabling the airbags so it would not open up and protect the passenger in a collision, just when it was designed to engage upon such an impact. Consistently reporting to his colleagues and supervisors, no action was taken even though Kelley threatened to report it to the National Highway Traffic Safety Administration.[2]

In 2001, Kelley came across a problem involving the Chevrolet Trailblazer SUV, which leaked fuel because the fuel line disconnected at the filter. Discovering from police reports that if a spark occurred, it could ignite the fuel resulting in a severe injury for the driver and any of the passengers. Approaching his product investigator, her reaction was, "Well, what do you want us to do, recall all the cars?"[3]

A year later, Kelley, believing he had no other alternative, sued General Motors under a Michigan whistle-blower law, but the case was dismissed, and Kelley was reassigned to another part of the company and the production of the Chevrolet Cobalt continued. In 2005, a sixteen-year-old driver was killed when her airbag did not deploy when her 2005 Cobalt crashed into a tree. Although many other reports surfaced, the company waited until February 2014 to issue a recall. At the time of the investigation, thirteen deaths were attributed to this defect.[4]

If put in Kelley's position, what would you do? If you, like the other employees, believed in not changing anything, so the company would not have to recall the faulty automobiles, and therefore save GM costs and a

potential decrease in goodwill or confidence in the company and their automobiles, you believe in **consequentialism** (or sometimes called the teleological approach) *in which the ends justify the means.* In other words, the focus of moral decision making is on the results, not the process or the intentions of the decision maker. For example, if an automobile salesperson convinces a potential buyer to purchase additional warranty insurance, which he knows is not necessary, but does so for a higher commission as a result, this personifies consequentialism. The potential commission justifies the process of not pointing out to the client the limitations of purchasing such a warranty.

The **non-consequentialist** (or one who takes a deontological approach— *deon* is a Greek root word meaning "from duty") *believes that the means is more important than the ends.* It is not the results that should be taken into account when faced with a moral dilemma, but the process. Courtland Kelley was a non-consequentialist because he believed that the safety of the passengers (process or means) was more important than the profits (outcome or ends),

In this chapter will we look at some of the earlier social and political philosophers who have shaped the moral standards of our society as we know it in today's world. This chapter will focus on consequentialism, non-consequentialism, capitalism, and communism. Before we discuss these concepts, however, we turn our attention to philosopher Thomas Hobbes.

CONSEQUENTIAL-ISM
(or the teleological approach): the ends justify the means— in other words, the focus of moral decision making is on the results not the process.

NON-CONSEQUEN-TIALIST
(or deontological thinker): believes that the means is more important than the ends. It is not the results that should be taken into account when faced with a moral dilemma, but the process.

Thomas Hobbes

Thomas Hobbes was a philosopher born in Westport, England, on April 5, 1588, and the author of *Leviathan* in 1651, which many believe was his best written work. His early years were marked by his father, who abandoned his family. As a troubled youth, Hobbes fought the vicar in front of his own parish, so his uncle stepped in and sent Hobbes (then fourteen) to Magdalen Hall in Oxford to study. It was there that Hobbes proved himself to be a student of classical languages. In 1608, he left Oxford to become a private tutor for Lord Cavendish of Harwick's older

son, William. Lord Cavendish later became the first Earl of Devonshire. This connection paid off as two years later when traveling with him to France, Italy, and Germany, Hobbes met leading scholars, including Francis Bacon and Ben Jonson.[5]

Studying on his own, Hobbes gained enough knowledge to research the field of optics, and was considered somewhat of a pioneer. Being somewhat of a Renaissance man, he was an expert in mathematics, translating the classics and law. He stood out for his writing and disputes on religious subjects and was a member of a theologian's circle (Marin Mersenne) in Paris, which was part of an elite group of ethical and political theorists. While part of this group, Hobbes was asked to critique Descartes' work, which eventually led him to expand his writing by publishing his first book, *De Cive*, on political philosophy. Its purpose was to present the civil unrest occurring during this time period.[6]

Nine years later (1651) Hobbes wrote the Leviathan, also known as *Leviathan, The Matter, Forme and Power of a Commonwealth Ecclesiasticall and Civil*. In it, Hobbes advocated for a social contract whereby citizens agree to follow common laws and accept the duties that go along with these laws. In addition, he believed that in order to maintain a civil society, one has to give up some individual rights to a sovereign power, to prevent the chaos, which he termed a "state of nature."[7] In Chapter 13 of the *Leviathan*, Hobbes espoused the belief that left to themselves, humankind would attack each other, because if left alone, without government "the life of man (would be) solitary, poore, nasty, brutish, and short" (i.e., state of nature).[8] So, given this state of nature, the only solution would be to have a powerful government, as strong as the biblical sea creature Leviathan, to protect humankind from their own selfishness and prevent as he termed, "Bellum omnium contra omnes" ("the war of all against all.").[9]

In addition, Hobbes believed that *individuals have been created by nature to maximize pleasure and minimize pain and could not do anything for another person unless it benefited them.* This belief is sometimes known as **psychological egoism.** For example, if you donate money to a charitable organization or your time to help those in need, according to Hobbes, it is not because you are a philanthropist or are altruistic, it is because you personally derive some satisfaction from it and would not do it otherwise. Hobbes continued to write and authored *De Corpore* (1655) and *De Homine* (1658), which completed his trilogy. Then, he reverted to his passion as a boy: classics and published translations of Homer's *The Odyssey* and *The Illiad.* On December 4, 1679, Hobbes died.[10]

The following passages are from Chapter 13 of the Leviathan:

"Nature hath made men so equall, in the faculties of body, and mind; as that though there be found one man sometimes manifestly stronger in body, or of quicker mind then another; yet when all is reckoned together, the difference between man and man, is not so considerable, as that one man can thereupon claim to himself any benefit, to which another may not pretend as well as he. For as to the strength of body, the weakest has strength enough to kill the strongest, either by secret machinations, or by confederacy with others, that are in the same danger with himself."[11]

In the passage above, Hobbes stated that everyone is given equality, in one form or another. One person may have more strength than another, but that person can compensate either by being more intelligent, using something to enable him to overpower the other person, such as a gun, or have others join him, so the group becomes stronger than the one person. In business, this may be exemplified by protectionism for a country economically threatened by a potentially more powerful foreign industry (e.g., Irish beef imports). The United States, fearing beef imports would affect the U.S. beef market, instituted a quota on the amount of beef from Ireland that could be imported (brought into the United States).

> "From this equality of ability, ariseth equality of hope in the attainment of our Ends. And therefore if any two men desire the same thing, which nevertheless they cannot both enjoy, they become enemies; and in the way to their End, endeavor to destroy, or subdue on another."[12]

In the passage above, Hobbes is referring to his "state of nature" philosophy. It is here where he believes since humankind may not be satisfied as being equal, one individual will always want more than another individual and will do whatever is necessary to take it. This may be best exemplified when a company like Wal-Mart or Home Depot enters a community and drives out local businesses.

The next passage justifies why Hobbes believes we need common law and a strong government to protect its citizens:

> "To this warre of every man against every man, this is also consequent; that nothing can be Unjust. The notions of Right and Wrong, Justice and Injustice have there no place. Where there is no common Power, there is no law."[13]

For this reason, Hobbes' quote above calls for a strong government that will protect its citizens from each other, since the state of nature of humankind is to do whatever is necessary to attain its material desires, even if unjustly. In today's world, Hobbes would want the government to intervene to protect its citizens from the business world and businesses from each other.

The Consequentialist Utilitarians

When the Industrial Revolution emerged, the focus of pursuing pleasure for an individual's happiness was replaced with the happiness of society as a whole. This ethical hedonistic philosophy was termed **utilitarianism**, *which advocated pursuing the greatest amount of pleasure for the greatest amount of people and was also a consequentialist philosophy.*

UTILITARIANISM *advocates pursuing the greatest amount of pleasure for the greatest amount of people, also a consequentialist philosophy.*

JEREMY BENTHAM

One of these utilitarians was Jeremy Bentham (1748–1832), born in London and credited with coining the term *utilitarian* from a letter he wrote to a friend in 1781. This term was based upon the notion of the greatest happiness for the greatest number, which he found from a copy of Joseph Priestly's *Essay on Government*, thirteen years earlier. Bentham was influenced by Thomas Hobbes, who was considered to be a psychological hedonist and although Bentham agreed with his maximizing pleasure and minimizing pain philosophy, Bentham believed that it was possible to seek pleasure for another person for altruistic reasons.[14]

In 1785, Bentham left England for Russia, but did not return to England until persuaded by friends to publish a book on moral and political philosophy, which was published a year later in 1789 when completing his most famous work, *Introduction to the Principles of Morals and Legislation*.[15] In 1808, Bentham met James Mill, who under his influence became more a political and social activist.[16] This friendship and influence led to Bentham's training of his friend, James Mill's son, John Stuart, when Mills moved near Bentham in London.[17] In 1822, he published a codification of laws which greatly influenced the Great Reform Bill passed in 1832, shortly before his death.[18] Upon his death, as he instructed, his body was dissected at the Webb School Street of Academy and his skeleton is still in the library of University College in London.[19] Even more strange is the fact that once a year his body is rolled out for the annual meeting of their Board where his attendance is noted.

Furthermore, Bentham believed that he could create a hedonic calculus, which could be used in computing the pleasure or pain that would be the result of a certain action. In his essay, *An Introduction to the Principles of Morals and Legislation*, Bentham identified four measurement values of pleasure or pain endured by an individual: intensity, duration, certainty or uncertainty, and propinquity or remoteness. Intensity referred to the strength or the pleasure, duration was how long the pleasure would last, certainty or uncertainty was the likelihood that the pleasure occurred, and propinquity or remoteness related to how soon the pleasure occurred. This was the first section of his utilitarian theory.[20]

The second section of Bentham's hedonic calculus was based on the number of persons affected by given actions, with reference to each of their values of pleasure or pain. It consisted of the four measurement values discussed above and the addition of three others: fecundity, purity, and extent. Fecundity meant the likelihood that the action would produce more pleasure, purity referred to the pain that would accompany the action, and extent was the number of individuals who would be affected by the action. Bentham believed that we all use a hedonic calculus when faced with making a decision to maximize our pleasure and minimize our pain. Therefore, he developed this hedonic calculus of seven values to add a scientific aspect to his theory, which also has been called the greatest happiness principle of utility or felicity of expression.[21]

The passages below describes his overall philosophy of utilitarianism and was taken from Chapter One of his book, *An Introduction to the Principles of Morals and Legislation.*

"By the principle of utility is meant that principle which approves every action whatsoever, according to the tendency which it appears to have to augment or diminish the happiness of the party whose interest is in question: or, what is the same thing in other words, to promote or to oppose that happiness. I say of every action whatsoever; and therefore not only of every action of a private individual, but of every measure of government.

An action then may be said to be conformable (similar) to the principle of utility, or , for shortness sake, to utility, (meaning with respect to the community at large) when the tendency it has to augment the happiness of the community is greater than any it has to diminish it."[22]

JOHN STUART MILL

Another utilitarian, and a friend of Bentham's family, John Stuart Mill (1806–1873) disagreed with Bentham's approach to a hedonic calculus and believed it to be too narrow. Mill met Bentham at age two, and was believed to have learned Greek from his father at age three or four; arithmetic and Latin at age eight, logic at twelve, and political economy at thirteen.[23] It was not until he was age fourteen when he had contact with children his own age, since most of this time he would mix with only his father's utilitarian friends.[24] Unfortunately, this intensity of home teaching from his father resulted in a nervous breakdown at age twenty, but while recovering, he read the poet Wordsworth.[25]

© Everett Historical/Shutterstock, Inc.

In 1830, he had a love affair with a married woman, Harriet Taylor, who he eventually married after her husband's death in 1851 and stay married until her death seven years later.[26] After her death, he was a member of the Parliament from 1865-68, until he was defeated and then retired to Avignon, France, with his stepdaughter, Helen Taylor, near where his wife Harriet was buried.[27] In May 1873, he returned to England, where he died suddenly of a local fever.[28]

Mill was credited with coining the term *utilitarianism* and was unaware of Bentham's term, *utilitarian*. Nevertheless, the dichotomy in their theories mirrored the difference between Aristippus and Epicurus. Bentham, like Aristippus, believed in the quantity of satisfaction and that all pleasures were the same. Mill, like Epicurus, believed that all pleasures were not the same.[29]

In his work, *Utilitarianism*, Mill stated that some kinds of pleasures were more desirable and more valuable than others were. However, one of his fears was that a decision maker might not have experienced all the pleasures, which would be relevant when judging which one pleasure would be more desirable. For example, a child who has played a game may believe that she will receive more satisfaction from it than if she attended a poetry reading. Mill believed that many individuals, like this child who may not understand poetry or has never experienced poetry, were unable to evaluate the difference in quality between two different actions. As a result, they would not be able to determine which of these actions would yield the most satisfaction to the majority affected by them.[30]

This is apparent in the passage found below from *Utilitarianism* where he describes his differences with his predecessor, Jeremy Bentham.

"If I am asked, what I mean by difference of quality in pleasures, or what makes one pleasure more valuable than another, merely as a pleasure, except its being greater in amount, there is but one possible answer. Of two pleasures, if there be one to which all or almost all who have experience of both give a decided preference."[31]

Mill criticized Bentham's quantity of pleasure theory and proposed a quality of pleasure theory, where he contended that there were two types of desires: a higher level and a lower level. The lower level desires were like those of an animal, while the higher level desires were more valuable and could only be appreciated by a cultured person. Therefore, Mill was actually concerned that if given a choice between funding a symphony concert hall or a bowling alley, those not familiar with the arts would not fund the symphony hall, which he believed ought to be funded. This passage resonates this point.[32]

"It is better to be a human being dissatisfied than a pig satisfied; better to be Socrates dissatisfied than a fool satisfied. And if the fool, or the pig, is of a different opinion, it is because they only know their own side of the question. The other party to the comparison knows both sides."[33,34]

Mill's utilitarianism supports the belief that decisions should be formulated only after taking into consideration which action would result in attaining the greatest good for the greatest number of people, not the greatest good for the individual, as his critics erroneously believe. However, some of these critics believed in making decisions not based upon the results, ignoring how these results were attained, but rather by looking at the process or intention of how the results will be derived.

The Non-Consequentialist Deontologists

In this section, we will look at two non-consequentialists who do not believe in the ends justifying the means, but rather focusing in on the means. One of these two is Immanuel Kant representing the late eighteenth to early nineteen century, while the other represents the late nineteenth to early twentieth century, William David Ross.

IMMANUEL KANT

Immanuel Kant was born in Königsberg, East Prussia, on April 22, 1724, to a family of Pietists, a Lutheran sect whose beliefs deemphasized theological dogmatism, but possessed a strong ethical orientation.[35] After attending the University of Königsberg, Kant served as a tutor for several aristocratic families, and then a lecturer with the title of Privatdozent (a rank which entitled him to charge more for his tutoring) at the university, which he held for fifteen years, lecturing and writing on metaphysics, logic, ethics, mathematics, and the natural sciences.[36] The three works Kant is best known for are the *Critique of Pure Reason* (1781), *Critique of Practical Reason* (1790), and the *Critique of the Faculty of Judgment* (1793).[37]

Immanuel Kant.

Kant's daily routine was so precise that each day he would wake up, drink coffee, prepare for his lectures, and have lunch at the same time;

and for this reason, the German poet, Heinrich Heine once wrote, "neighbors knew that it was exactly half past three when Immanuel Kant in his grey coat, with his bamboo cane in his hand, left his house door and went to the Lime tree avenue, which is still called in his memory of him, the 'Philosopher's Walk.'"[38] He was so regimented that one day he was scheduled to meet a friend for his midday meal at a local inn, when his friend running late, did not show up, Kant ate his lunch, and proceeded to take his hat, and left as his friend was leaving, walking by him and not stopping.[39] Rumor has it that the housewives of Königsberg set their clocks by his afternoon walks.[40] In fact, it is believed that Kant missed his walk only once, when he became so absorbed in reading Rousseau's *Émile* that he forgot to take it.[41] Kant never married and died in Königsberg on February 12, 1804, at age seventy-nine.[42]

Kant's works are very difficult to read and for this reason, only a few of his philosophies will be discussed with brief excerpts from his publications. Generally, Kant believed that decisions should be made *by reason* (**a priori**) not sensual experience. The first of these philosophies is key to those who are non-consequentialists, and that is a good will, which in essence is doing something out of duty rather than doing something to benefit oneself. The passages below describe this good will which is found in the first section of Kant's *Groundwork of the Metaphysic of Morals*.

A PRIORI

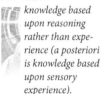

knowledge based upon reasoning rather than experience (a posteriori is knowledge based upon sensory experience).

> "Nothing in the world—indeed nothing even beyond the world—can possibly be conceived which could be called good without qualification except a GOOD WILL."
>
> "The good will is not good because of what it effects or accomplishes or because of its competence to achieve some intended end; it is good only because of its willing (i.e. it is good in itself)."[43]

For example, a high school class collected money from students to purchase a gift, a bicycle, for a disadvantaged twelve-year-old boy living in a third-world country. By donating the money, there was no other

CONDUCTING BUSINESS ETHICALLY

ulterior motive than helping out a less fortunate person, which Kant would have considered a good will. Unfortunately, the boy fractured his arm while riding the bicycle. The good will of giving a gift Kant would consider good, even though the unforeseen outcome resulted in something bad, the fractured arm. Ironically, when the high school class received the thank-you letter from the boy, who fractured his arm, he was still appreciative of the students' gesture, since the intention was recognized by him to be conducted out of a positive sense of moral duty or good will. In other words, there was not benefit to the donors nor any intention of malice against this recipient.

A second philosophy espoused by Kant is his categorical imperative, which means that a rule (maxim) cannot be universally accepted unless it is unconditional, not based upon any condition. For example, the maxim you shall never lie, according to Kant, cannot have any exceptions. So, if a friend asks you if his girlfriend is attractive, and you do not think so, Kant would expect you to tell your friend that you do not believe that his girlfriend is beautiful. Now, obviously, this will probably jeopardize most friendships, but Kant believed that if you "lied" to your friend, where would you draw the line from truthfulness to falsehoods? If you can lie about the beauty (or lack of beauty) of his girlfriend, can you lie about other things more serious? (For example, "I will always pay back money loaned to me...unless it is not convenient to me or I need to use the money for something more important.") If you can lie about more serious things, then who determines where this line is to be drawn? Kant merely believed that if there are not exceptions, the maxim can be followed. The passage below is found from his second section of the *Groundwork of the Metaphysic of Morals.*

"Finally, there is one imperative which directly commands certain conduct without making its condition some purpose to be reached by it. This imperative is categorical. It concerns not the material of the action and its intended results, but the form and principle from which it originates."

> "The categorical imperative, on the other hand, is restricted by no condition. As absolutely, though practically, necessary it can be called a command in the strictest sense."[44]

This second philosophy which Kant termed the **categorical imperative** *is the belief that a rule cannot be accepted unless there are no conditions or exceptions to that rule.* From this, we find another philosophy in which rules should not be developed unless they can be accepted everywhere as stated, also in his second section of the *Groundwork of the Metaphysic of Morals*.

> "There is, therefore, only one categorical imperative. It is: Act only according to the maxim by which you can at the same time will that it should become a universal law."[45]

This may not be as easy as it reads, because if you develop a rule or law without any exceptions, what would it be? Never lie? This would mean always telling the truth even if it means losing friends because you think their significant others may be unattractive. Never kill? If a robber was about to attack your mother with a knife and the only way you could save her life would be to shoot the assailant, would you, even if it meant that it could kill him? If so, this would be an exception and could not be a universal law, since all categorical imperatives cannot have any exceptions attached to them.

Another philosophy by Kant was his belief that individuals should never be used as a means to someone's ends. For example, let us say that you are a New York Yankees baseball fan and know someone whose father has season tickets in the front row of the stadium. This person likes you, even though you do not like her. If you pretended to like her, just so you could get to see the Yankees and planned on breaking up with her at the end of the baseball season, this would be an example of what Kant believed was unethical. This is also found in the second section of Kant's work:

> "Man, however, is not a thing, and thus not something to be used merely as a means; he must always be regarded in all his actions as an end in himself." [46]

In this final passage, Kant repeats his philosophy of not treating an individual as a means to an ends, but in addition includes shades of the golden rule (in boldface type):

> "**Act in such a way that you always treat humanity, whether in your own person or in the person of another**, never simply as a means, but always at the same time as an end."[47]

In essence the first part of this passage could be interpreted as, treat others the way you want others to treat you. And, we conclude with a sampling of some of Kant's non-consequentialist philosophies.

WILLIAM DAVID ROSS

William David Ross was born in Thurso, Scotland, on April 15, 1877, but lived in India until age six, when his father became the Principal of Maharajah's College.[48] He attended the Royal High School in Edinburgh, the University of Edinburgh, and Balliol College (Oxford University) which led him to a lecturing position at Oriel College (Oxford University) in 1900, and was elected fellow at Merton College, also part of Oxford, which he held until 1929.[49] However, Ross's career was not only in academe, since in 1915 he joined the army and three years later was promoted to the rank of major where he was honored as an Officer of the Order of the British Empire, served as the Deputy Assistant Secretary in the Ministry of Munitions, and even was recognized Knight of the Order of the British Empire.[50] In terms of his academic career, Ross served as the President of the British Academy (1936–1940), nine years

© iDesign/Shutterstock, Inc.

after being made a fellow, and throughout his illustrious career received numerous honorary degrees.[51]

Ross was influenced by G.E. Moore, H.A. Prichard, Aristotle, and Kant, and believed in ethical intuitionism which is that we determine what is right or wrong based upon the situation and intuitively determine what prima facie duties will result in us acting dutifully so that certain duties can be overridden by stronger duties.[52] So, for example using the example of the "The Shallow Pond" opening vignette found in Chapter One, where you are on the way to give a lecture and see a child drowning in a pond, although you have a duty to be at the lecture on time, there is a greater duty to save the life of a child. *The duty to save a life, a primary duty* which Ross terms a **prima facie duty**, takes precedence over the lesser duty, to be on time. This is in opposition to Kant's categorical imperative which was the belief that there was no lesser duty that could be overridden by a greater duty. According to Kant, if it was a duty, there could be no exceptions to fulfilling it.

In his book, *The Right and the Good*, Ross states:

PRIMA FACIE DUTY
according to W.D. Ross, when one more important duty (such as saving a life) becomes more important than a lesser duty (being on time for a date).

"There are two theories that offer a solution of such cases of conscience. One is the view of Kant, there are certain duties of perfect obligation, such as those of fulfilling promises, that there is only the duty of producing good, and that all 'conflicts of duties' should be resolved by asking 'by which action will most good be produced?' ......

I suggest 'prima facie duty' or 'conditional duty' of referring to the characteristic (quite distinct from that of being a duty proper) which an act has in virtue of being of a certain kind (e.g. the keeping of a promise), of being an act which would be a duty proper if it were not at the same time of another kind which is morally significant. Whether an act is a duty proper or actual duty depends on all the morally significant kinds it is an instance of." [53]

Ross categorized the following as prima facie duties: explicit and implicit promises (such as not telling lies) which he called duties of fidelity; duties of reparation (those resting on a previous wrongful act); duties of justice; duties of gratitude (promises to fulfill certain services, pay a debt back rather than use money to purchase a new pair of designer jeans); those whose conditions would be made better in respect of virtue or pleasure (killing is wrong, but to engage in war in order to save others from being killed even though war includes killing others may be right); self-improvement (improve our own condition of virtue of intelligence); and the duties not to injure others.[54]

The greatest challenge to Ross's philosophy was determining when a particular duty takes precedence over another and how an individual can make the correct choice. He addresses this in his book as follows:

"Where a possible act is seen to have two characteristics, in virtue of one of which it is a *prima facie* right, and in virtue of the other *prima facie* wrong, we are taking a moral risk.

In this respect the judgement as to the rightness of a particular act is just like the judgement as to the beauty of a particular object or work of art....Both in this and the moral case we have opinions which are not logically justified conclusions from the general principles that are recognized as self-evident."[55]

In this case, I would consider Ross a pragmatic deontologist, in that like Kant, he believed that certain universal principles or duties must always be adhered to and satisfied. But unlike Kant, Ross believed that sometimes there were exceptions when these duties would not be moral if they were satisfied, and in this respect, he believed that the intention of the individual wanting to do the right thing was not only just as important a factor in determining which duty to fulfill, but was even more important.

Political Philosophers

This section will examine three of the most influential political philosophers in their time. From the seventeenth and eighteenth century, was John Locke; from the nineteenth century, Adam Smith; and from the twentieth century, Karl Marx. John Locke was a social contractarian; Adam Smith, a capitalist; and Karl Marx, a communist.

JOHN LOCKE

© Everett Historical/Shutterstock, Inc.

SOCIAL CONTRAC-
TARIAN
an individual who believes that individual citizens have a bilateral contract with the government in terms of how much control and restraint it has over its societal members.

John Locke was a **social contractarian,** *which is the belief that individual citizens have a bilateral contract with the government in terms of how much control and restraint it has over its societal members.* John Locke was born in the western part of England (near Bristol) in 1632 to an upper-middle-class family, whose father was a landowner and an attorney.[56] Locke's philosophies have been credited as sources for the English Revolution of 1688 and the American Revolution of 1776.[57] Locke was educated in his early childhood by his father whose religious background was Puritan, and political sympathies towards the Parliament led his father to fight on its behalf during the Civil War.[58] After spending six years at the Westminster School, Locke entered Christ Church, Oxford (1652) who he had an association of thirty years, even though he was extremely critical of his education both at the school and university.[59]

Under the patronage of the Earl of Shaftesbury, Locke read Descartes, and although he disagreed with much of his principles, it sparked his pursuit of intellectual interests.[60] Due to the uncertainty of his future of his patron, and for health reasons, Locke went for several years (1675-79) to Montpellier, France, where he was able to complete writing his *Essay Concerning Human Understanding* in 1690 as well as the *Two Treatises of Government.*[61] He returned to England to renew his relationship with Shaftesbury from 1679 to 1683, but due to his liberal attitudes he ran into some problems at Oxford, and went to Holland as a political exile.[62]

Locke returned to England in 1689 and lived mostly in the country except when his official duties demanded his presence in the capital.[63] His chief position during this time was commissioner with the Board of Trade and Plantations, at a salary of £1,000 a year, a post he held from 1696 to 1700, when illness forced him to resign, and passed away four years later on October 28, 1704.[64]

One major philosophy of Locke was the belief that we are all entitled to life, health, liberty, and our possessions, which he considered real property (land, etc.). In the second chapter of "The Second Treatise of Government," Locke begins as follows:

> "The state of nature has a law of nature to govern it, which obliges every one; and reason, which is that law, teaches all mankind who will but consult it that, being all equal and independent, no one ought to harm another in his life, health, liberty or possessions...."[65]

Concurring with these rights, in Chapter 16, Locke continues:

> "Every man is born with a double right: first, a right of freedom to his person, which no other man has a power over, but the free disposal of it lies in himself; secondly, a right, before any other man, to inherit with his brethren his father's goods."[66]

In fact, not only does Locke believe in these natural rights, which he terms the state of nature, as opposed to Hobbes' interpretation, but Locke believes that these rights need to be protected against any breaches, and the punishment should be in proportion to these breaches. This passage from the seventh chapter of his work describes this ideology:

> "Man has by nature a power not only to preserve his property—that is, his life, liberty, and estate—against the injuries and attempts of other men, but to judge of and punish the breaches of law in others as he is persuaded the offense deserves, even with death itself in crimes where the heinousness of the fact requires it."[67]

You will notice by the passage above that although Locke believed in personal freedom for all individuals, if the social contract not to interfere with another's freedom is broken, it would be justifiable to punish (therefore limiting) the personal freedom of the party whose actions took away the personal freedom (i.e., property) of another innocent party, even if it meant death. From this, it would appear that Locke would support capital punishment in certain situations (death for committing the murder of another).

What you may find interesting is that Locke treasured the labor of individuals and would not support those who idly would sit and watch his land remain uncultivated. He believed this type of laziness was a waste and a right of owning property was applying your labor towards it, or you should lose your rights. In chapter five, Locke states:

> "It is labor, which puts the greatest part of the value upon land, without it would be scarcely worth anything.
>
> The extent of ground is of so little value without labor that I have heard it affirmed that in Spain itself a man may be permitted to plough, sow, and reap, without being disturbed upon land he has no other title to but only his making use of it.
>
> As much land as a man tills, plants, improves, cultivates, and can use the product of, so much is his property."[68]

Such a "use it or lose it" philosophy reflects the times, where in an agrarian society, food was necessary and was the primary source of economic growth and sustenance. So, by allowing its potential to remain idle and virtually useless for the society at large, it was justifiable to reward the industrious person to take over the property of one who was not.

However, money would be treated by Locke differently since it cannot be wasted over time like a bushel of berries and justifies having an overabundance.

In other words, unlike food which can spoil, since money can remain for an infinite amount of time, as long as you do not infringe upon the laws of nature, or harm anyone else, you are free to accumulate as much wealth as you want. Yet, Locke was not the only one who believed the "least governed is the best governed." Adam Smith, a capitalist philosopher, believed that the market (law of supply and demand) should determine the laws of business and not the government.

ADAM SMITH

Adam Smith was born on June 5, 1723, in Kirkcaldy, Scotland to a father who was the local comptroller of customs and had died several months before Smith's birth, and a strong mother who he lived with most of his adult life, outliving her by only six years. Smith studied at Glasgow University and at Oxford University's Balliol College under a scholarship for six years.[71] He returned to Edinburgh where he gave a successful series of lectures; and in 1751, he was appointed professor of logic at Glasgow University, and was appointed chair of moral philosophy a year later.[72]

© Everett Historical/Shutterstock, Inc.

In 1759, Smith wrote *The Theory of Moral Sentiments*, in which he espoused his beliefs that individuals were conflicted with a tension created by having self-interests as well as a tendency to do the right things for others; and then concluded that moral judgments were formulated by being an impartial spectator.[73] In other words, we all want to do what is best for us, as individuals, but would also like to do what is best for others, and feel conflicted as to what action to take when faced with an ethical dilemma. Smith's theory was that ethical decision making should be made from an objective perspective, which he called being an impartial spectator, and this perspective would lead to a better moral decision.

As a result of Smith's *Theory* book, Charles Townsend, an English politician, offered Smith a lucrative position to tutor his eighteen-year-old stepson, the Duke of Buccleauch, which he did for three years. This position involved traveling to France and Switzerland, where Smith also studied and discussed contemporary political and economic issues with the leading intellectuals of the time, and compiled information which led to his next book, *The Wealth of Nations*, written in 1776.[74] In this work, Smith believed that the government should not allow monopolies which created poverty for those not benefiting from these monopolies and instead maintained that all citizens should possess the freedom to pursue their own economic interests as long as they did not harm others in the process and the sole duty of the government was to provide a national defense, a system of justice, public works, and education.[75] Smith spent the remainder of his years revising both books, serving as the commissioner on the Customs Board of Edinburgh, where he addressed various local economic issues, and writing the manuscripts for two other books—one on jurisprudence and the other on the philosophical history of literature, which he destroyed shortly before his death on July 17, 1790.[76]

Yet, perhaps with all his writing, Adam Smith is best known for his belief of laissez-faire in which the government should play a minor role in the world of business and let the market decide which businesses will prosper or fail, how many goods or services will be provided, and what price will be acceptable for adequate enough consumption so the providers of these goods or services will want to continue to do so. He states this philosophy in *The Wealth of Nations* in Book IV, Chapter II as follows:

"As every individual, therefore, endeavours as much as he can both to employ his capital in the support of domestic industry, and so to direct that industry that its to produce may be of the greatest value; every individual necessarily labours to render the annual revenue of the society as great as he can. He generally, indeed, neither intends to promote the public interest, nor knows how much he is promoting it. By preferring the support of domestic to that of foreign industry, he intends only his own security; and by directing that industry in such a manner as its produce may be of the greatest value, he intends only his gain, and his in this, as in many other cases, led by an invisible hand to promote an end which was no part of his intention. Nor is it always the worse for the society that it was no part of it. By pursuing his own interest he frequently promotes that of the society more effectually than when he really intends to promote it. I have never known much good done by those who affected to trade for the public good. It is an affection, indeed, not very common among merchants, and very few words need be employed in dissuading them from it."[77]

In this passage, Smith's thesis is basically that if individuals pursue what is best for them, then they will actually be doing what is best for society, since if their product is inferior, their price too high, their wages too low, or their business practices unfair, eventually the market (consumers) will reject it and select individual businesses whose product, price, wages, or practices are acceptable to society, and therefore in the long run society will be best served by this free market, or invisible hand, as Smith termed it.

KARL MARX

Karl Marx was a **communist** *who believed that economic resources should be shared by all members of society, by any means necessary, and not just the owners who possessed the abundance of society's wealth at the expense of those workers who actually created it.* Born May 5, 1818, at Trier,

COMMUNISM
(MARXIST)
those who believe that economic resources should be shared by all members of society, by any means necessary, and not just the owners who possessed the abundance of society's wealth at the expense of those workers who actually created it.

© Everett Historical/Shutterstock, Inc.

Germany, his father was a solicitor (attorney) and came from a family of rabbis, who adopted Christianity a year before Karl's birth.[78] Influenced by his father and State Counselor Ludwig von Westphalen to read the Greek poets and Shakespeare, while attending a Lutheran grammar school, Marx was intellectually challenged.[79] From 1835 to 1841, Marx attended Bonn University (for two terms) and then Berlin University, where he earned a doctoral degree, and in 1836 became engaged to Jenny von Westphelan, who he eventually married in 1843.[80] In 1843 he and his wife moved to Paris, and met Frederick Engels whom he began collaborating with on various writing projects, but due to Marx's radical ideologies, he was expelled from France in 1845, and moved to Brussels, beginning a string of financial woes which plagued him for the rest of his life. [81]

ALIENATION
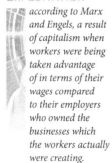
the separation of a worker as an individual from his job and self, as well as from his family, which according to Marx and Engels was a result of capitalism's demands on the proletariat working class.

From December 1847 to February 1848, in collaboration with Frederick Engels, Karl Marx wrote the *Manifesto of the Communist Party*, popularly called the *Communist Manifesto*.[82] Accused of inciting an armed rebellion even though he was acquitted by a Cologne jury, Marx was expelled as a "stateless person," and was exiled to London in 1849 and continued to write for several publications including the *New York Tribune*.[83] From 1864 on, he organized various labor unions and conferences, was elected to various political positions, and continued to write until his death on March 14, 1883, less than two years after his wife Jenny died.[84]

EXPLOITATION
according to Marx and Engels, a result of capitalism when workers were being taken advantage of in terms of their wages compared to their employers who owned the businesses which the workers actually were creating.

Karl Marx believed that workers were being alienated and exploited. To Marx, **alienation** *was being separated from who you really are.* For example, if you were a creative artist but your job required you to paint houses the same ivory white color daily, this would be an example of alienation according to Marx. On the other hand, **exploitation** *was when workers were being taken advantage of.* So, if you worked as a house painter for $10 an hour and your employer, the owner of the painting business, received $100 an hour, and due to your superior performance, your employer now receives $200 an hour, but you still are earning $10 an hour, Marx would consider this worker as one who has been exploited.

This is best described in his first section of the *Communist Manifesto* passage which follows:

> "The proportion as the bourgeoisie, i.e. capital, is developed, in the same proportion as the proletariat, the modern working class, developed—a class of labourers, who live only so long as they find work, and who find work only so long as their labour increases capital. These labourers, who must sell themselves piecemeal, are a commodity, like every other article of commerce, and are consequently exposed to the vicissitudes of competition, to all the fluctuations of the market.
>
> Owing to the extensive use of machinery and to division of labour, the work of the proletarians *has lost all individual character, and, consequently, all charm for the workman.* He becomes an appendage of the machine, and it is only the most simple, most monotonous, and most easily acquired knack, that is required of him. In proportion, therefore, as the repulsiveness of the work increases, the wage decreases.
>
> Not only are they slaves of the bourgeois class, they are enslaved by the machine, the overlooker, and, the individual bourgeoisie manufacturer."[85]

You will note in the passage above, there is a reference to the loss of *all individual character, and, consequently, all charm for the workman,* which is what alienation is—workers' individuality is separated from their work, and eventually who they are (character).

> "No sooner is the *exploitation of the labourer* by the manufacturer, so far, at an end, and he receives his wages in cash, than he is set upon the other portions of the bourgeoisie, the landlord, the shopkeeper, the pawnbroker, etc."[86]

In this passage above, the term *exploitation* is manifested by not only the employer, but also the landowner, shopkeeper, pawnbroker, who could also be termed members of the bourgeoisie, but who Marx and Engels later on include as those who will be replaced eventually by technology and other methods infused in the capitalistic system developed by the bourgeoisie, and will become members of the proletariat as well.

> "The bourgeoisie has stripped of its halo every occupation hitherto honoured and looked up to with reverent awe. It has converted the physician, the lawyer, the priest, the poet, the man of science, into its paid wage-labourers."[87]

In this last passage above, it is being demonstrated how capitalism is reducing even professionals to a proletariat worker-status. Once again, the bourgeoisie has exploited another class of individuals, according to Marx and Engels, those representing the professionals.

This chapter presented a brief description of some of the consequentialist, non-consequentialist, social, and political philosophers who led the way for the upcoming twentieth- and twenty-first-century contemporary philosophers, many who are still living today. Although William David Ross's philosophy was primarily introduced in the twentieth century, his first twenty-three years were spent in the nineteenth century, so he was included in this chapter; also because he was a perfect example of a non-consequentialist philosopher. The next chapter will depict a sampling of thoughts of our more contemporary philosophers.

Summary

There were two major philosophies discussed in this chapter: consequentialism, which is making decisions based solely on the results of your actions, and non-consequentialism, which is determining actions not by their results but by their intention.

Thomas Hobbes was a social contractarian who espoused the belief that left to themselves, humans would attack each other, because if left alone, "the life of man (would be) solitary, poore, nasty, brutish, and short" (i.e., state of nature). So, given this state of nature, the only solution would be to have a powerful government, to protect humankind from their own selfishness.

Utilitarianism is another consequentialist theory, which advocates pursuing the greatest amount of pleasure for the greatest amount of people. One such utilitarian was Jeremy Bentham, who developed a hedonic calculus of seven values which added up would determine what action taken would yield the greatest satisfaction. Bentham believed that satisfaction was quantitative since all experiences were the same. His protégé, John Stuart Mill, believed that some kinds of pleasures were more desirable and more valuable than others were. He was more like Epicurus (quality over quantity), while Bentham was more like Aristippus (quantity over quality).

One well-known non-consequentialist was Immanuel Kant, who believed decisions must always be made based upon duty or sense of obligation rather than doing something for expected (sometimes selfish) outcomes or results; rules should be developed only if there are no exceptions (categorical imperatives) and they would be accepted everywhere (universal maxim); individuals should never be used as a means to someone's ends; and individuals should always treat other individuals with humanity, whether in one's own person or in the person of another (the golden rule).

However, opposing some of Kant's philosophy was another non-consequentialist, Scottish philosopher William David Ross, who agreed that rules should be followed, and there were certain situations when one duty would necessitate the breaking of the rule because the duty to keep it would actually be less moral than not keeping it. For example, if a friend needed to be rushed to the emergency room in a hospital and you promised to be at a restaurant at a given time and had to choose between keeping your promise to be on time or saving a friend's life, your duty to save your friend's life is more important than being on time for another friend. This overriding or more important duty was termed by Ross, a prima facie duty, and was a pragmatic solution to Kant's categorical imperative, which was unyielding regardless of the situation.

In terms of political and social theorists, one well-known social contractarian discussed in this chapter is John Locke, who believed that we are all entitled to life, health, liberty, and our possessions, which he considered real property (land, etc.). As a social contractarian, his philosophy centered around the social contract that society had with the government and that the role of the government should be limited to protecting the life, liberty, and possessions of its citizens so they are free to do what they want, as long as they do not interfere with the same rights as others.

Another political theorist was Scottish economist Adam Smith who believed that the government should play a minimal role in interfering with business activities and believed if left alone, businesses would be guided by the market, which he termed the invisible hand, to make the best decisions for their interests and would also be best for society in the long run.

Finally, the last political theorist discussed, who opposed Adam Smith, was a German political activist, Karl Marx, who along with his friend and colleague, Frederick Engels, developed an anti-capitalistic movement which they believed would eliminate the alienation and exploitation of the lower, working-class experienced at the hands of the proletariat who were from the upper class, also known as the bourgeoisie. This movement was the beginning of Communism.

Key Terms

Alienation: the separation of a worker as an individual from his job and self, as well as from his family, which according to Marx and Engels was a result of capitalism's demands on the proletariat working class.

A priori: knowledge based upon reasoning rather than experience (a posteriori is knowledge based upon sensory experience).

Categorical imperative: the belief that a rule cannot be accepted unless there are no conditions or exceptions to that rule.

Communism (Marxist): those who believe that economic resources should be shared by all members of society, by any means necessary, and not just the owners who possessed the abundance of society's wealth at the expense of those workers who actually created it.

Consequentialism (or the teleological approach): the ends justify the means—in other words, the focus of moral decision making is on the results not the process.

Exploitation: according to Marx and Engels, a result of capitalism when workers were being taken advantage of in terms of their wages compared to their employers who owned the businesses which the workers actually were creating.

Non-consequentialist (or deontological thinker): believes that the means is more important than the ends. It is not the results that should be taken into account when faced with a moral dilemma, but the process.

Prima facie duty: according to W.D. Ross, when one more important duty (such as saving a life) becomes more important than a lesser duty (being on time for a date).

Psychological egoism: individuals have been created by nature to maximize pleasure and minimize pain and could not do anything for another person unless it benefited them.

Social contractarian: an individual who believes that individual citizens have a bilateral contract with the government in terms of how much control and restraint it has over its societal members.

Utilitarianism: advocates pursuing the greatest amount of pleasure for the greatest amount of people, also a consequentialist philosophy.

Chapter Review Questions

1. Do you believe that Hobbes is correct and we are not capable of doing anything unless we have a powerful government, limiting our freedom? List some examples to prove your viewpoint.
2. Imagine that you are faced with a decision. Either you go with your friends to a trip to the Bahamas for your spring break or you work during the spring break so you can afford to pay for your next tuition payment due when you return. What will you do? Now, using all seven measurements from Bentham's hedonic calculus, determine your decision. Was it the same? Do you believe this would be a good model to use when faced with a decision? Discuss your responses.
3. Can you create a universal law that would include Kant's maxim of the categorical imperative?
4. Which philosophy do you seem to favor, John Locke, Adam Smith, or Karl Marx? Explain why.
5. Of all the philosophers discussed in this chapter, if you owned a small business, which philosopher would you favor? Explain your response.

Cases for Discussion

CASE 4.1 HACKERS FOR HIRE [88]

In New Zealand, a teenager was arrested for infecting more than 1.3 million computers and stealing millions of pounds (the equivalent of U.S. dollars). The eighteen-year-old was released and not charged but had to help the police with their investigations of other computer-related crimes.

Hiring former hackers is not an uncommon practice. For example, FireEye Incorporated hired more than 100 ex-government hackers since 2013; while Symantec employed 500 former hackers, in 2013, increasing its division by one third.

Today, many businesses employ former hackers to find ways to strengthen their firewall from others who may attempt to commit crimes by illegally gaining entrance into the company's private software programs. Although quite a different situation, it is not an uncommon occurrence for government authorities to use convicted "cyber-thieves" or hackers for their projects, instead of prosecuting them to the full extent of the law.

DISCUSSION QUESTIONS

(a) Do you believe individuals responsible for committing a crime should be released if in return they use their skills to capture others who are doing the same thing but on a large scale? Defend your response, using the full S.E.A. method discussed in Chapter Two (state the philosophy, explain the philosophy in your own words, give a general example, and apply the philosophy to your action). Use any philosopher discussed in this chapter.

(b) There are some cyber-thieves who purposely hack into a company's private software and then ask to be hired in order to work with them on how to protect their programs from unwarranted cyber-theft. Would you hire such a person?

Defend your response, using the full S.E.A. method discussed in Chapter Two (state the philosophy, explain the philosophy in your own words, give a general example, and apply the philosophy to your action). Use any philosopher discussed in this chapter.

CASE 4.2 FREE SPEECH OR LICENSING RACIAL DISCRIMINATION?[89]

There are nine states that allow drivers to choose specialty license plates displaying the Confederate flag and honoring the Sons of Confederate Veterans, who claim enables them to celebrate their southern heritage. When the Texas Board of Motor Vehicles met, they said the plates were too offensive to permit their display and refused to issue them. However, to some, such as Sherrilyn Ifill, president of the NAACP Legal Defense and Educational Fund, "It's a powerful symbol of the oppression of black people." Another critic of African American descent, eighty-two-year-old Reverend George V. Clark, agreed with Ifill by stating that for him to "see something that represents hate and…made people feel less than human" was intolerable.

Yet, with approximately 30,000, representing those who served honorably in the Confederate Army and whose membership includes people of African American, Jewish, Hispanic, and Native American descent, to Ben Jones, national spokesperson for the group, this ban breaches their right of free speech if they cannot display the flag on their license plates. Many federal appeals courts have ruled that specialty license plates are "mobile billboards" for those who have like-minded beliefs. Some even charge Texas with hypocrisy since they celebrate Confederate Heroes Day and have erected monuments to Confederate soldiers.

DISCUSSION QUESTION

If you were sitting on the Texas State Supreme Court, would you allow the Department of Motor Vehicles to issue specialty plates with the Confederate flag honoring the Sons of Confederate Veterans?

Defend your response, using the full S.E.A. method discussed in Chapter Two (state the philosophy, explain the philosophy in your own words, give a general example, and apply the philosophy to your action). Use any philosopher discussed in this chapter.

Endnotes

1. Thomas Hobbes, *Leviathan,* C.B. MacPherson, Ed. (New York: Penguin Putnam: 1651/1968), p. 150.

2. Tim Higgins and Nick Summers, "If Only They Had Listened…," *Bloomberg Businessweek,* June 23-30, 2014, p. 50.

3. Ibid., 51-52.

4. Ibid., 50

5. Thomas Hobbes, The Biography.com website, 26 April 2015. http://www.biography.com/people/thomas-hobbes-9340461

6. Ibid.

7. Ibid.

8. Thomas Hobbes, *Leviathan*, C.B. MacPherson, Ed. (London: Penguin Books, 1651/1968).

9. Thomas Hobbes, The Biography.com website, 26 April 2015. http://www.biography.com/people/thomas-hobbes-9340461

10. Ibid.

11. Thomas Hobbes, *Leviathan*, Richard Tuck, Ed. (New York: Cambridge University Press, 1991), pp. 86-87.

12. Ibid., 87.

13. Ibid., 90.

14. John Stuart Mill, *Utilitarianism,* Mary Warnock, Ed. (New York: New American Library, 1974), p. 7.

15. Ibid.

16. Ibid., 8.

17. Ibid.

18. Ibid., 9.

19. Ibid.

20. Ibid.

21. Ibid.

22. Ibid., 34-35.

23. Ibid., 9.

24. Ibid.

25. J.S. Mill, *Utilitarianism,* Roger Crisp, Ed. (New York: Oxford University Press, 1998), p. 8.

26. Ibid.

27. Ibid., 8-9; and John Stuart Mill, *Utilitarianism,* Mary Warnock, Ed. (New York: New American Library, 1974), p. 11.

28. John Stuart Mill, *Utilitarianism,* Mary Warnock, Ed. (New York: New American Library, 1974), p. 1.

29. Martin J. Lecker, "Ethical Hedonism," *Encyclopedia of Business and Society,* vol. 3: H-N, Robert W. Kolb, Ed. (Thousand Oaks, CA: Sage Publications, 2008), p. 1063.

30. Ibid.

31. J.S. Mill, *Utilitarianism,* Roger Crisp, Ed. (New York: Oxford University Press, 1998), p. 56.

32. Martin J. Lecker, "Ethical Hedonism," *Encyclopedia of Business and Society,* vol. 3: H-N, Robert W. Kolb, Ed. (Thousand Oaks, CA: Sage Publications, 2008), p. 1063.

33. J.S. Mill, *Utilitarianism,* Roger Crisp, Ed. (New York: Oxford University Press, 1998), p. 57.

34. Ibid., p. 64.

35. Immanuel Kant, *Foundations of the Metaphysics of Morals*, 2d ed., Lewis White Beck, Ed. (Upper Saddle River, NJ: Prentice Hall Inc., 1990), p. xxv.

36. Albert B. Hakim, *Historical Introduction to Philosophy*, 5th ed. (Upper Saddle River, NJ: Pearson Prentice Hall, 2006), p. 391.

37. Ibid.

38. Ibid., 391-392.

39. Ibid., 392.

40. Ibid.

41. Douglas J. Soccio, *Archetypes of Wisdom: An Introduction to Philosophy*, 7th ed. (Belmont, CA: Wadsworth Cengage Learning, 2010), p. 313.

42. Immanuel Kant, *Foundations of the Metaphysics of Morals*, 2nd ed., Lewis White Beck, Ed. (Upper Saddle River, NJ: Prentice Hall Inc., 1990), p. xxv.

43. Ibid., 9-10.

44. Ibid., 32-33.

45. Ibid., 38.

46 Ibid., 45-46.

47 Immanuel Kant, *Groundwork of the Metaphysic of Morals,* H.J. Paton, trans. (New York: Harper and Row Publishers, 1964), p. 96.

48 "William David Ross," Gifford Lectures, 02 Jan. 2010. http://www.giffordlectures.org/Author.asp?AuthorID=146

49 Ibid.

50 Ibid.

51 Ibid.

52 Ibid.; and David Ross, *The Right and the Good,* Philip Stratton-Lake, Ed. (Oxford: Claredon Press, 1930/2009), p. xiii.

53 David Ross, *The Right and the Good,* Philip Stratton-Lake, Ed. Oxford: Claredon Press, 1930/2009), pp. 18-20.

54 Ibid., 21-22.

55 Ibid., 30-31.

56 John Locke, *The Second Treatise of Government,* Thomas P. Peardon, Ed. (Indianapolis: The Bobbs-Merrill Company, Inc., 1690/1952), p. vii.

57 Ibid.

58 Ibid.

59 Ibid.

60 Albert B. Hakim, *Historical Introduction to Philosophy,* 5th ed. (Upper Saddle River, NJ: Pearson Prentice Hall, 2006), p. 319.

61 Ibid.

62 John Locke, *The Second Treatise of Government,* Thomas P. Peardon, Ed. (Indianapolis: The Bobbs-Merrill Company, Inc., 1690/1952), p. viii.

63 Ibid.

64 Ibid.

65 Ibid., 4-5.

66 Ibid., 107.

67 Ibid., 48.

68 Ibid., 20, 22, 26.

69 Ibid., 28.

70 Ibid., 29.

71 Adam Smith, *An Inquiry into the Nature and Causes of the Wealth of Nations,* Edwin Cannan, Ed. (New York: Random House Incorporated, 1994), p. vii.

72 Ibid.

73 Denis Collins, "Adam Smith," *Encyclopedia of Business and Society,* vol. 4: O-S, Robert W. Kolb, Ed. (Thousand Oaks, CA: Sage Publications, 2008), p. 1940.

74 Ibid.

75 Ibid.

76 Ibid.

77 Adam Smith, *An Inquiry into the Nature and Causes of the Wealth of Nations,* Edwin Cannan, Ed. (New York: Random House Incorporated, 1994), pp. 484-485.

78 Ernst Fischer (Ed.), *The Essential Marx,* Anna Bostock, trans. (New York: Herder and Herder, 1970), p. 7.

79 Ibid.

80 Ibid., 7-8.

81 Ibid., 8.

82 Karl Marx, *The Communist Manifesto,* Frederic L. Bender, Ed. (New York: Norton and Company, 1988), p. 1.

83 Ernst Fischer (Ed.), *The Essential Marx,* Anna Bostock, trans. (New York: Herder and Herder, 1970), p. 9.

84 Ibid., 9-10.

85 Karl Marx, *The Communist Manifesto,* Frederic L. Bender, Ed. (New York: Norton and Company, 1988), pp. 61-62.

86 Ibid.

87 Ibid., 58.

88 This case was rewritten based upon the following articles: "Global Snapshots," *SC Magazine for IT Professionals,* January 8, 2008, p. 9; and Jordan Robertson, "Security Companies Hire Hackers, Ex-Spies to Fight Cyber Attacks," *BloombergBusiness Inc.,* April 14, 2015. www.Bloombergbusiness.com

89 This case was rewritten based upon the following article: Adam Liptak, "A Test of Free Speech and Bias, Served to Court on a Plate from Texas," *The New York Times,* March 23, 2015, p. A14.

CHAPTER 5

CONTEMPORARY PHILOSOPHICAL THINKERS

"A free market never loses sight of the question:
Of value to whom?"

-Ayn Rand in Capitalism: The Unknown Ideal[1]

Management theorist Peter Drucker believed individuals could measure their ethical actions based upon a "mirror test," in which you ask yourself, "What kind of person do I want to see when I shave myself in the morning, or put on my lipstick in the morning?" [2] Although being ethical is an individual value, it should be a business world value as well, which is not always the case. The selected contemporary philosophers who represent the twentieth- and twenty-first-century thinking have wrestled throughout their careers with several issues including how freedom for you and freedom for others may be interpreted. Some philosophers such as Ayn Rand, Milton Friedman, and Robert Nozick believe more in self-interest and less in how it affects others, compared to philosophers, John Rawls, Peter Singer, Michael Sandel, and Martha Nussbaum, whose focus is less on self-interest and more on utilitarianism. Sissela Bok's philosophy was more over the debate about private and public morality which seemed to be a common theme throughout her writings. Another leading philosopher, Robert Solomon, is also included in this chapter because his philosophy called the "Three C's" enabled decision makers to determine whether a company or their actions were ethical. In this chapter, the philosophers just referred to will be discussed in terms of their beliefs with some excerpts from their philosophical works and will be introduced based upon the order of their birth.

Ayn Rand

Allisa Rosenbaum was born February 2, 1905, in St. Petersburg, Russia, to Fronz Rosenbaum, a chemist of Jewish descent and a self-made merchant, and Ann, her mother. She was the oldest of their three daughters.[3] Rand taught herself to read at a very young age and by age nine decided to become a writer fascinated by her greatest hero, Victor Hugo.[4] During World War I, because her family had to endure the financial and psychological effects of the siege of St. Petersburg, the Russian Revolution, and the new communist doctrine, Rand became so embittered that she vowed to devote the rest of her life to criticizing communism and lauding capitalism.[5] In 1921, Rand entered the University of Petrograd where she studied philosophy and history believing that by learning history it would enable her to write better on social issues integrated with her philosophical knowledge and when she graduated from the University, decided to further diversify her education by entering the State Institute for Cinema Arts where she studied screenwriting.[6]

© catwalker/Shutterstock, Inc.

Resentful about how her family was devastated by the new Communist Party, and rejecting its economic and social ideologies, but not its opposition to religion, Rand abandoned her own religious heritage for secular agnosticism and later for atheism, left the Soviet Union in 1926 to live with relatives in Chicago, moved to California to work as an extra (actress) and then as scriptwriter and eventually met her husband Frank O'Connor, an actor who she married in 1929 until his death fifty years later.[7] Concerned that she would be deported to Russia, Alissa Rosenbaum changed her first name to Ayn (rhymes with "mine"), a Finnish writer and last name to Rand (for the Remington-Rand typewriter that she brought with her).[8] Rand wrote her first major novel, *The Fountainhead*, in 1935, which examined an architect's struggle to maintain his own integrity against those who would compromised it and used her own philosophy of rational self-interest to demonstrate the application of her thesis which compared individualism to collectivism, and why the latter was best for society in the long run.[9] From 1943 to its publication date in 1957, Rand worked on her masterpiece, *Atlas Shrugged*, a novel about how a genius named John Galt grew wary of supporting a society of "ungrateful parasites" and rebels by just shrugging it off and walking away, inspiring other men and women do the same thing until called back by society to continue their role of being responsible and respectful.[10] From 1961 to her death, she published numerous philosophical books, including *The New Intellectual* (1961), *The Virtue of Selfishness* (1964), *Capitalism: The Unknown Ideal* (1966), *Introduction to Objectivist Epistemology* (1967), and *Philosophy: Who Needs It?* (1982), to name a few.[11] She died three years after her husband, the same year (1982) her book *Philosophy Who Needs It?* was published.

On a personal level, in 1950, Rand received a letter from a fan, Nathaniel Blumenthal (who later changed his name to Brandon), who along with his wife were students at UCLA, and she became not only his mentor, but his lover for over thirteen years, until she learned he had another lover, despite the fact that both Blumenthal and Rand were married to two other individuals.[12] One definitely could conclude that Ayn Rand "beat to another drummer," and used her novels for her **objectivist philosophy,** *which endorsed individualism by stressing "rational self-interest" over charity and the welfare state.*[13]

In her book, *Capitalism: The Unknown Ideal*, Rand demonstrates her objectivist philosophy as follows:

OBJECTIVIST PHILOSOPHY *which endorsed individualism by stressing "rational self-interest" over charity and the welfare state.*

"When 'the common good' of a society is regarded as something apart from and superior to the individual good of its members, it means that the good of *some* men takes precedence over the good of others, with those others consigned to the status of sacrificial animals. It is tacitly (implied) assumed, in such cases, that the 'common good' means 'the good of the majority' as against the minority or the individual. Observe the significant fact that that assumption is *tacit*: even the most collectivized mentalities seem to seem to sense the impossibility of justifying it morally. But 'the good of the majority,' too, is only a pretense and a delusion: since, in fact, the violation of an individual's rights means the abrogation of all rights, it delivers the helpless majority into the power of any gang that proclaims itself to be 'the voice of society' and proceeds to rule by means of physical force, until deposed by another gang employing the same means.

If one begins by defining the good of individual men, one will accept as proper only a society in which that good is achieved and *achievable*. But if one begins by accepting 'the common good,' as an axiom and regarding individual good as its possible but not necessary consequence (not necessary in any particular case), one ends up with such a gruesome absurdity as Soviet Russia, a country professedly dedicated to 'the common good' where, with the exception of a minuscule clique of rulers, the entire population has existed in subhuman misery for over two generations."[14]

Basically, you can observe her disgust for the communistic collectivism and support the freedom capitalism is purported to possess for individuals. Therefore, if you ascribe to her beliefs, it does demonstrate that utilitarianism rips individual freedom away for others to prosper. In modern political terms. Rand's philosophy best follows the Conservative front found in the early twenty-first century and their opposition to a universal health care system for all U.S. citizens.

Milton Friedman

Believed by many to be the twentieth century's most prominent advocate of the free market system, Milton Friedman was born in New York City to Jewish immigrants in 1912. He attended Rutgers University, where at age twenty earned his B.A. degree, attended the University of Chicago in 1933 where he earned an M.A., and in 1946, earned a Ph.D. from Columbia University.[15] As a coauthor with Simon

Kuznets, in their 1945 book, *Income from Independent Professional Practice*, he was recognized for his belief that state licensing procedures limited entry into the medical profession, which resulted in higher fees than if there was more competition which would lead to lower fees, which many believe catapulted him to fame as an economist.[16] From 1946 to 1976, Friedman taught economics at the University of Chicago and was awarded the Paul Snowden Russell Distinguished Service Professor Emeritus of Economics, while concurrently serving from 1937 to 1981 as a member of the research staff of the prestigious National Bureau of Economic Research.[17]

In his 1962 landmark book, *Capitalism and Freedom*, Friedman argued for relatively free markets and in addition for a volunteer army, freely floating exchange rates, abolition of physician licenses, a negative income tax, and education vouchers (i.e., charter schools competing with private schools using taxpayer monies).[18] In 1976, he was the recipient of the Nobel Memorial Prize for economic science, and was a senior research fellow at Stanford University's Hoover Institution from 1977 to 2006, when he died on November 16, 2006.[19]

What follows is an excerpt from *Capitalism and Freedom*, where Friedman espouses his belief that the sole responsibility of a business is to the stockholders in the form of profits.

> "The view has been gaining widespread acceptance that corporate officials and labor leaders have a 'social responsibility' that goes beyond serving the interest of their stockholders or their members. This view shows a fundamental misconception of the character and nature of a free economy. In such an economy there is one and only social responsibility of business—to use its resources and engage in activities designed to increase its profits so long as it stays within the rules of the game, which is to say, engages in open and free competition, without deception or fraud....
>
> Few trends could so thoroughly undermine the very foundation of our free society as the acceptance by corporate officials of a social responsibility other than to make as much money for their stockholders as possible. This is a fundamentally subversive doctrine. If businessmen do have a social responsibility other than making maximum profits for stockholders, how are they to know what it is?"[20]

It is important to note that although Friedman is a staunch supporter of businesses only pursuing their best interests in the name of profits, it must be done so fairly. He also makes the point that if the sole responsibility of a business is to expand beyond the organization's borders, how can we trust that business owners will know what is best for society? In essence he is raising the question of expertise; after all, do physicians know what is best for selecting lumber, or can construction workers select the most exquisite artwork? Then, how would businesses know what is best for society?

In this next passage, also from *Capitalism and Freedom*, Friedman poses another issue and that is, It is the responsibility of businesses to donate their stockholders' profits to charities? Before doing so, should they not first obtain the stockholders' permission, since after all, is it not the shareholders' investments to begin with?

> "One topic in the area of social responsibility that I feel duty-bound to touch on, because it affects my own personal interests has been the claim that business should contribute to the support of charitable activities and especially universities. Such by giving by corporations is an inappropriate use of corporate funds in a free-enterprise society."[21]

When Ben Cohen and Jerry Greenfield first formed Ben and Jerry's they wanted to donate 12% of their pretax profits to charitable organizations; however, their board of directors wanted them to donate only 5% of their pretax profits. Eventually, they compromised and donated 7.5% of their pretax profits to charities. It is highly probable that Milton Friedman would have been against this practice since he believed the donation of profits to a charitable organization was not the responsibility of a business, Furthermore, as stated above, he would have believed Ben and Jerry's actions were an inappropriate use of corporate funds.

John Rawls

John Rawls was born February 21, 1921, to William and Anna Rawls, in Baltimore. William, without any formal training working for a law firm, studied on his own and passed the bar exam only to be accepted to the most famous law firm in Baltimore, the Marbury Law Firm, where John was subsequently born.[22] Both John's parents were involved in politics; his father was approached to run for senator, which he declined due to health reasons, and his mother was the chapter president of the Women's League of Voters.[23] John attended a private school except when his father was on the Board of Education in Baltimore, so to show support of the public school system, John's father required him to attend public school for two years, which eventually led to his attending Princeton University, where he majored in philosophy summa cum laude.[24]

After graduation, Rawls spent two years in the army where he won a Bronze Star as a radio work behind enemy lines and was promoted to sergeant, only to be demoted to private when he refused to punish

© FikMik/Shutterstock, Inc.

a soldier who had insulted the first lieutenant.[25]   Rawls returned to Princeton University under the G.I. Bill and after spending one year at Cornell University as a fellow, he completed his dissertation, earning a doctorate and meeting his wife who he married a year after she graduated with her baccalaureate at Brown University in 1949.[26] Rawls taught at Princeton, Cornell University, MIT, and eventually at Harvard where he taught from 1962 to 1991, when he was forced to retire, but received special permission from the president of Harvard to continue to teach for a nominal fee, until a series of strokes forced him to permanently retire in 1991.[27] Rawls died in 2002 as a result of these earlier strokes.

ORIGINAL POSITION *developed by John Rawls as part of a thought experiment where you imagine being in a new society free to create whatever rules you wish.*

Best known for his book *Theory of Justice,* written in 1971 and revised in 1999, Rawls developed a theory using a modern alternative to utilitarianism by taking into consideration the moral quality of individuals. He first began by using what he called the **original position,** *a thought experiment where you imagine being in a new society free to create whatever rules you wish.* At this point, self-interest plays a major role in the creation of these rules. Rawls recognized that given this assumption, justice may be interpreted as what is fair to the individual as opposed what is fair to all members of society. He defines the original position as:

> "the principles that free and rational persons concerned to further their own interests would accept in an initial position of equality as defining the fundamental terms of their association......Among the essential features of this situation is that no one knows his place in society, his class position or social status, nor does any one know his fortune in the distribution of natural assets and abilities, (etc.)...The principles of justice are chosen behind a veil of ignorance."[28]

However, in the second phase of this experiment because *you do no know your place in society nor what abilities you may possess*, you will have to modify these rules since you are under a **veil of ignorance** to what advantages or disadvantages you will have when entering this new society.

> "For example, if a man knew that he was wealthy, he might find it rational to advance the principle that various taxes for welfare measures be counted unjust. To represent the desired restrictions one imagines a situation in which everyone is deprived of this sort of information. One excludes the knowledge of those contingencies which sets men at odds and allows them to be guided by their prejudices. In this manner the veil of ignorance is arrived in a natural way."[29]

In his original position, Rawls believed that individuals would still include personal freedoms such as the right to select one's religion, freedom of the press, freedom of speech, right to petition, etc. Under the veil of ignorance, some of the societal rules would be modified since individuals would not know how they would be affected if the rules change on them. For example, if the male population stated that only men can run for political office and not knowing the gender requirement, if the next day it changed to only women being eligible, now excluding men, it is highly unlikely that the men of this new society would be willing to take the chance of not ever being able to run for

VEIL OF IGNORANCE *developed by Rawls where after creating societal rules under his original position you modify them since you will not know anything (be ignorant) about what your own circumstances or background will be (e.g., poor, wealthy, old, young).*

a political leadership position. You can see some of Immanuel Kant's philosophy infused in Rawls's thoughts (treat individuals the same way as you would want to be treated).

Rawls's theory of justice could be divided into two principles as he stated in his book:

First Principle
"Each person is to have an equal right to the most extensive total system of equal basic liberties compatible with a similar system of liberty for all."

Second Principle
"Social and economic inequalities are to be arranged so that they are both:
(a) to the greatest benefit of the least advantaged, consistent with the just savings principle, and
(b) attached to offices and positions open to all under conditions of fair equality of opportunity."[30]

In this First Principle, which Rawls called "the priority of liberty," he was referring to the personal freedoms under the "original position" previously discussed (freedom of religion, speech, etc.) which all individuals would initially ascribe to. The Second Principle referred to the priority of justice over efficiency and welfare, which the "veil of ignorance" would most likely address, such as being able to hold political office regardless of your gender.

LEAST ADVANTAGED *endorses individualism by stressing "rational self-interest" over charity and the welfare state, as espoused by Ayn Rand.*

However, in the Second Principle, two philosophical concepts need to be further explained: what Rawls meant by the "least advantaged" and the "just savings principle." The **least advantaged** *are those who are least favored by categories such as family and class origins (those who are from an upper aristocratic family or an impoverished one), natural endowments (such as the famous world-class Olympian sprinter Usain Bolt of Jamaica), or situational events (fortune or luck, such as winning the lottery).*[31] As an example of the least advantaged rule, let us assume that employees will be required to pay 15% more in income taxes next year, but owners of a business will only have to pay 10% more in business taxes. If those who own a business had to pay only 10% in business taxes and as a result of this new tax structure now would have more money for capital expenditures which would increase their profits so they could offer free health insurance to their employees, the least advantaged individuals (the employees) are now in a better financial position than they were before (free health insurance). In other words, if all parties are in a better position than before an action is taken, it is a *just action*.

The Second Principle is justified through a combination of the difference principle with fair equality of opportunity. Basically, although it recognizes that individuals have different opportunities, they must be fair. For example, if those in society starting out as members of the entrepreneurial class in a property-owning democracy have a better prospect than those who begin in the class of unskilled laborers, it is only justifiable according to the **difference principle** *if the differences in expectations are to the advantage of the representative person who is worse off* (in this case the representative unskilled worker).[32] Exemplifying this further, if an individual works as a custodian and lives in a one-bedroom apartment and another employee is in the sales department and has a two-bedroom apartment, and both receive salary increases, if the custodian now moves into a two-bedroom apartment (it could have even been the salesperson's apartment) and the salesperson moves out of her two-bedroom apartment into a five-bedroom home, although the salesperson has three more bedrooms compared to the custodian who gained only one bedroom, the custodian is still in a better position than he was before the salary increases. As a result, under the difference principle, the least advantaged individual (custodian) is still in a better position than before and therefore Rawls would consider these salary increases to be acceptable (just). Rawls's philosophy is an alternate approach to utilitarianism because under his approach, everyone can be in a better position than before, just as long as those with the most advantages do not take away anything from those with the least advantages or put them in a worse off position prior to the policy, decision, action, etc.

DIFFERENCE PRINCIPLE
when expectations are to the advantage of the representative person who is worse off, it is just.

Sissela Bok

Sissela Myrdal Bok was born December 2, 1934 in Stockholm, Sweden, to her parents, Gunnar and Alva Myrdal, social reformers who were the only husband and wife to have been awarded the Nobel Prize in two different fields—Economics (1974) and Peace (1982).[33] After studying in Europe, she came to the United States and concentrated in clinical philosophy, earned a B.A. and M.A. from George Washington University, and a Ph.D. in philosophy from Harvard in 1970. She married Derek Bok in 1950, who became the president of Harvard years later, and had three children together.[34] She was a Professor of Philosophy at Brandeis University, Radcliffe Institute, Simmons College, Tufts University, the John F. Kennedy School of Government, and is currently a Senior Visiting Fellow at Harvard's Center for Population and Development Studies.[35] Bok has written several books, which include the third edition of her book *Lying: Moral Choice in Private and Public Life* (1978) reissued in 1999 with a new preface; *Secrets: On the Ethics of Concealment and Revelation* (1982, 1989); *A Strategy for Peace: Human Values and the Threat of War* (1989); *Alva Myrdal: A Daughter's Memoir* (1991); *Common Values* (1996, reissued in 2002 with a new preface); and

© 244405033/Shutterstock, Inc.

Mayhem: Violence as Public Entertainment (1998).[36] With John Behnke, Bok has co-edited *The Dilemmas of Euthanasia* (1975) and, with Daniel Callahan, *Ethics Teaching in Higher Education* (1980). With Gerald Dworkin and R. G. Frey, she has coauthored *Euthanasia and Physician-Assisted Suicide* (1998).[37] In each of her books, Bok contributed to modern philosophical thought; however, her book, *Lying: Moral Choice in Public and Private Life* was one of the most significant books written in the twentieth century as is established her as a world renowned moral philosopher who advocated that the medical profession should tell the truth about a patient's condition and prognosis.[38]

Yet, her book *Secrets: On the Ethics of Concealment and Revelation*, continued the discussion of moral issues begun in *Lying* and looks at moral situations when keeping a secret is important (i.e., national security) and when it is controlling others (i.e., need-to-know basis as in business). In the passage below, which appears in *Secrets*, she gives an example of when a psychotherapist has a moral obligation to keep a secret (patient confidentiality) and when this confidentiality has to be breached. It is based on an actual case, which is quite disturbing.

"The conflicts that psychotherapists face in this respect (when a professional owes confidentiality to a patient) were brought to public attention by the murder in 1969 of a young woman, Tatiana Tarasoff. The young man who killed her had earlier told his psychotherapist that he wanted to do so (kill Tatiana). The psychotherapist had alerted the police, who detained the student briefly, then released him after determining that he seemed 'rational' and asking him to promise to leave Miss Tarasoff alone. When the police reported the matter back to the director of psychiatry, he asked that the matter be dropped and that the correspondence with the police be destroyed. The student did not return for further treatment, and no effort was made to get in touch with him. Two months later, he went to Miss Tarasoff's home and shot and stabbed her to death. Her parents then brought suit against the university, the campus police, and the therapists for negligence in failing to warn either their daughter or themselves.

The California Supreme Court concluded that the psychotherapists had breached a duty overriding that of confidentiality: the duty to use reasonable care when they determine that a patient presents a serious danger of violence to another, to protect the intended victim against such danger. 'The privilege ends,' the courts held, 'when the public peril begins.'"[39]

In her research, Bok looks at keeping secrets as both necessary and unnecessary depending upon the situation and defines the conflict in her book.

Bok's works have brought forth into the limelight issues concerning patient confidentiality, whistleblowing, trade secrets, undercover journalistic reporting, euthanasia, deception, and other situations which have been prevalent but not addressed using such well-presented philosophical arguments and reasoning.

Robert Nozick

Robert Nozick was born in Brooklyn, New York, on November 16, 1938, to Eastern European Jewish immigrant parents, earned a B.A. from Columbia in 1959, and a M.A. (1961) and Ph.D. (1963) from Princeton.[41] Nozick was an instructor and assistant professor of philosophy at Princeton from 1962 to 1965 but left for Harvard for an assistant professorship in 1967-1969 when at age thirty, became one of the youngest full professor's in the university's history.[42] Best known for his first book, *Anarchy, State and Utopia* (1974), which was a critique of John Rawls's *Theory of Justice*, he argued that the rights of an individual are primary and that a minimal state was sufficient enough to protect against violence, theft, fraud, and to ensure that the enforcement of contracts were justified.[43]

In addition to his 1974 landmark book, Nozick wrote other books, including *Philosophical Explanations* (1981), *The Nature of Rationality*

(1993), and *Invariances: The Structure of the Objective World* (2001).[44] Nozick's writing was lively and unorthodox, much as his teaching when he would speak without notes, pace restlessly back and forth, with a can of diet cola (Tab) in his hand, drawing his students into a free ranging discussion of the topic at hand, and claiming never to have taught the same course twice.[45] Succumbing to an eight-year bout with stomach cancer on January 23, 2002, Nozick was scheduled to teach at Harvard that spring, and even was critiquing and talking to his colleagues a week before his death.[46]

Of Nozick's philosophy, the **entitlement theory**, based upon libertarians such as Locke, was stated in his book, *Anarchy, State, and Utopia* as follows:

1. A person who acquires a holding in accordance with the principle of justice in acquisition is entitled to that holding.
2. A person who acquires a holding in accordance with the principles of justice in transfer, from someone else entitled to the holding, is entitled to the holding.
3. No one is entitled to a holding except by (repeated) applications of 1 and 2.[47]

Therefore, if Jane purchases land from a family who lost the home because they could not pay their mortgage and the sole wage earner lost her job, if then Jane neglects to maintain the house properly and does not even have anyone living in it, she has that right. And, if she gives it to her child, who decides he wants to level it and leave it as a "junk yard," it is the child's right to do so, since he acquired it legally from his mother, who obtained it justly. Furthermore, in his book, Nozick espouses his belief that some want the government to be involved only when it has to protect its citizens against violence, theft, fraud, and the enforcement of contracts, which was termed the minimal state, but even this is too much involvement and there should be more of an **ultraminimum state** *where all use of force should be suspended except for self-defense and only by those who purchased its protection*.[48] In essence, this is the opposite of the welfare state, where if a person is unemployed, the police will protect them. Under Nozick's philosophy, if you do not pay, you are not entitled to the service, because otherwise, those who are working are supporting those who are not.

In contrast to Rawls, who believed that you do not institute any policy unless the least advantaged individuals will benefit as well, under Nozick's entitlement theory, Rawls's philosophy was not plausible because society when left to their own state of nature will still redistribute their resources from the least advantaged to the most advantaged members of the society. For his example, he uses the late but great basketball player, Wilt Chamberlain, to demonstrate that if consumers were left on their own they would still be willing to place talented individuals over those who were less talented which would negate Rawls's difference theory favoring the least advantaged. In his book, Nozick explained why his entitlement theory was more plausible than Rawls's difference theory.

"Now suppose that Wilt Chamberlain signs the following sort of contract with a team: In each home game, twenty-five cents from the price of each ticket of admission goes to him. The season starts and people buy their tickets, each time dropping a separate twenty-five cents of their admission price into a special box with Chamberlain's name on it. They are excited about seeing him play; it is worth the total admission price to them. Let us suppose that one million persons attend his home games, and Wilt Chamberlain winds up with the $250,000, a much larger sum than anyone else has. Is he entitled to his income? Is this new distribution..unjust?

.... Each of these persons chose to give twenty-five cents of their money to Chamberlain. If the people were entitled to dispose of the resources to which they were entitled, didn't this include their being entitled to give it, or exchange it with, Wilt Chamberlain? Can anyone else complain on grounds of justice?"[49]

What Nozick is demonstrating is as a **libertarian** (*one who believes that individuals are free to do what they please, without any government intervention, as long as they do not interfere with the rights of others*) if it is the right of everyone to spend their resources as they see fit, those who are not "the least advantaged," which I will call the "most advantaged," will receive more benefits than the least advantaged since they are entitled to it. This directly refuted Rawls's philosophy.

Robert Solomon

Born September 14, 1942, in Detroit, but growing up in Philadelphia with two brothers, with his father (an attorney) and mother (an artist), Robert Solomon received a B.A. in microbiology (1963) from the University of Pennsylvania and a Ph.D. in philosophy from the University of Michigan, even though he initially

© Zerbor/Shutterstock, Inc.

intended to earn an M.D. there until walking into a graduate philosophy class by chance, which changed his life forever.[50] After he received his doctorate in 1967, he taught at several universities, including Princeton, the University of Pittsburgh, Queens College, and the University of Auckland, where he visited on and off for thirty-eight years.[51] However, in 1973, he accepted a position at the University of Texas where he was named Quincy Lee Centennial Professor and Distinguished Teaching Professor and taught for thirty-four years until his death on January 2, 2007 (on his way to changing planes) of pulmonary hypertension, due to a congenital heart defect.[52]

At Texas, he met and married fellow philosopher Kathleen Higgins, who frequently collaborated with him on the 160+ articles, 28 original books, 13 edited books, and 11 textbooks which were published in several editions and many languages.[53] His first book, *From Rationalism to Existentialism*, was published in 1972, but his second book, *The Passions*, four years later demonstrated a philosophical interest in the emotions and their place in art, life, politics, and business, which led in time to help found the International Society for Research on Emotions.[54]

As a teacher, he overloaded his classes and even appeared in a movie, Richard Linklater's philosophical *Waking*, where he appeared as himself. [55] In the year of his death, he was elected president of the Society of Business Ethics.[56]

In 1985, Solomon published his first business ethics book, *It's Good Business*, which was followed up with his wife to be, Kristine, by a 1994 *The New World of Business,* which included the essay, "It's Good Business."[57] This passage found below describes Solomon's "Three C's" theory which may be used to determine whether a business or action is ethical.

"Business ethics is nothing less than the full awareness of what one is doing, its consequences and complications. Thinking about ethics in business is no more than acknowledging that one has taken these into account and is willing to be responsible for them. It is being aware of

1. the need for *compliance* with the rules, including the laws of the land, the principles of morality, the customs and expectations, the policies of the company and such general concerns as fairness;

2. the ***contributions*** business can make to society, through the value and quality of one's products or services, by way of the jobs one provides for workers and managers, through the prosperity and usefulness of one's activities to the surrounding community;

3. the ***consequences*** of business activity, both inside and outsider the company, both intended and unintended, including the reputation of one's own company and industry...."[58]

THREE C'S THEORY *consists of three components: compliance to laws and principles of morality; contributions to society; and consequences of actions. In order for a business or one's actions to be ethical all three must be satisfied, according to Robert Solomon.*

Basically Solomon's **Three C's theory** *consisted of three components; compliance to laws and principles of morality; contributions to society;*

© Dirk Ercken/Shutterstock, Inc.

and consequences *of your actions*. In order for a business or one's actions to be ethical all three must be satisfied. When Bernie Madoff was found imprisoned for his fraudulent Ponzi scheme (taking funds from one set of investors to give to other investors, so they will continue to invest even though no real profits are being generated) he did not satisfy any of Solomon's three criteria. He broke the law (non-compliance), many non-profit organizations lost millions of dollars (did not positively contribute to society), and was imprisoned as a result of his actions (negative consequences). Solomon's theory proved to be an excellent tool as a measurement for assessing the ethicality of a particular business decision.

Peter Singer

Born on July 6, 1946, to Jewish Austrian refugees, Peter A.D. Singer's father, Ernst, worked in the tea and coffee importing business while his mother, Cora Renata (Oppenheim), was a doctor who practiced medicine until they were forced to escape the Nazi persecution of Jews, by moving to Australia in 1938 where they found a sponsorship, unlike three of his grandparents who died in the Holocaust.[59] Singer attended Scotch

College in Melbourne for his secondary school education excelling in swimming and chess outside of his academic studies, but majored in history and philosophy at the University of Melbourne where he earned his B.A. with honors in 1967, and continued on there earning his M.A. degree in philosophy after writing his thesis "Why Should I Be Moral?" which he received in 1969, and then continued at Oxford University to earn a B.Phil. in 1971.[60]

Writing hundreds of books and articles, his best known writing was *Animal Liberation*, a work that gave its name to a worldwide movement and created the term **speciesism,** *the discrimination against any species that has sentience or the ability to feel (pleasure or pain).*[61] In this book, Singer documented the systematic horrors of factory farming and even advocated any measures, legal or illegal, to raid animal laboratories, when results could not be obtained by any other means to stop animal suffering, but stood vehemently against violence that harmed other people and advocated the use of mental reasoning over physical force.[62] Singer considers his philosophy a form of preferential utilitarianism in that he approaches each issue by seeking the solution that has the best consequences for all affected, satisfying the most preferences, weighted in accordance with the strength of preferences over the long run.[63] When appointed to Princeton University, hundreds of protestors were present when he first came on campus because of his utilitarian belief in infanticide, killing deformed babies if they are not expected to have a fulfilling life. A married father of three daughters, Singer eats no meat and avoids using products made from animals, believes that the rich have an ethical obligation to the poor, and personally routinely donates between 10% and 20% of his salary to such organizations as Community Aid Abroad, even though he admits that when he takes his family out to a restaurant and spends $80 for his family of four, this is "ethically dubious"

© Oko Laa/Shutterstock, Inc.

since he should have donated that money to Community Aid Abroad.[64]

In his article, "The Singer Solution to World Poverty," in the *New York Times Magazine* section, he further expounds on this point of donations in the passage below:

"In the world as it is now, I can see no escape from the conclusion that each one of us with wealth surplus to his or her essential needs should be giving most of it to help people suffering from poverty so dire as to be life-threatening. That's right: I'm saying that you shouldn't buy that new car, take that cruise, redecorate the house or get that pricey new suit. After all, a $1,000 suit could save five children's lives.

So how does my philosophy break down in dollars and cents? An American household with an income of $50,000 spends around $30,000 annually on necessities, according to the Conference Board, a nonprofit economic research organization. Therefore, for a household bringing in $50,000 a year, donations to help the world's poor should be as close as possible to $20,000. The $30,000 required for necessities holds for higher incomes as well. So a household making $100,000 could cut a yearly check for $70,000. Again, the formula is simple: whatever money you're spending on luxuries, not necessities, should be given away."[65]

Although Singer's article was written in 1999, with inflation, the amount for necessities is higher, yet as a utilitarian, his point is, how much do you need for necessities and why can't you donate the remainder? The Princeton professor continues to lecture and write extensively on his utilitarian philosophical viewpoint.

Martha Nussbaum

Martha Nussbaum was born May 6, 1947, to an "aristocratic" family on her mother's side which extends back to the Mayflower, and to her father, George Craven, a conservative southerner who became a prosperous lawyer in trusts and estates at a large Philadelphia law firm.[66] At a young age, Nussbaum rebelled, once inviting a black girl over to play, only to hear her father scold her by saying, "Don't you ever bring a black person into our home again!"; it is no wonder she became involved in civil rights.[67] Nussbaum received her B.A. in 1969 from N.Y.U. and her M.A. in 1971 along with her Ph.D. in 1975 from Harvard.[68] Brought up in a strict Protestant family, her father was shocked when she married a Jewish man and then converted to Judaism.[69]

Yet Nussbaum's career was followed by controversy in one form or another. While attending Harvard as a classics graduate student, as the first woman ever elected to the prestigious Society of Fellows, which guaranteed a member three years of financing, her male classmates did not think it "proper" to call her a "fellow," in Greek ("hetairos"), so instead they called her "hetaera," which in Greek meant "prostitute."[70] Once in an interview, Nussbaum when asked about her experiences as a student at Harvard, she replied, "I didn't like Harvard. I disapproved of the classicists. They were anti-Semites, racists, and sexists and had a real thuggishness about them."[71] Although Harvard had appointed her to teach classics and philosophy in 1975, as a writer who demonstrated breadth in a diversity of topics, Harvard's response to this style of intellectual pursuit was to deny her tenure in 1982, which devastated her, and for a while even contemplated initiating a lawsuit against them, but instead taught at Brown until the University of Chicago hired her in 1995 with appointments in the law and divinity school, as well as in the departments of philosophy, classics, and Southern Asian studies.[72]

Believing in rights-based universalism (rights for all), in 1993 she was asked to be a prosecution witness in *Romer v. Evans*; the case that challenged a Colorado amendment to reverse the local laws that protected homosexuals from discrimination and even used the dialogues of Plato to prove her point resulting in the Supreme Court ruling in favor of

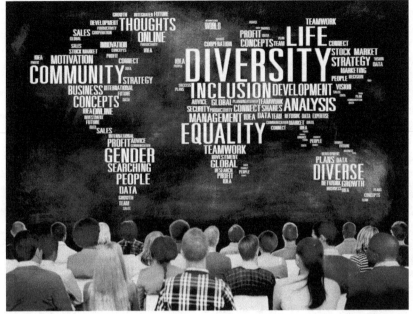

protecting the rights of gays/lesbians, but also created a stir among several conservative scholars who accused her of distorting Plato's words.[73] She has published over fifteen books, including *From Disgust to Humanity: Sexual Orientation and Constitutional Law* (2010), has edited thirteen books, and is working on several others to be published in the near future. In 2009, Nussbaum won the ASK award from the German Social Science Research Council for her contributions to "social system reform" and the American Philosophical Society's Henry Ml. Phillips Prize in Jurisprudence, among many other awards during her career.[74] At the time of this writing, Nussbaum was teaching at the University of Chicago as the Ernst Freund Distinguished Service Professor of Law and Ethics.[75]

In the introduction to her book, *The Therapy of Desire*, Nussbaum discusses why she believes it is up to every philosopher to not only analyze philosophy and its relationship to the "good life," but also to make a positive difference for humanity.

"The idea of practical and compassionate philosophy—a philosophy that exists for the sake of human beings, in order to address their deepest needs, confront their most urgent perplexities, and bring them from misery to some greater measure of flourishing—this idea makes the student of Hellenistic ethics riveting for a philosopher who wonders what philosophy has to do with the world. The writer and teacher of philosophy is a lucky person, fortunate, as few human beings are, to be able to spend her life expressing her most serious thoughts and feelings about the problems that have moved and fascinated most. But his exhilarating and wonderful life is also part of the world as a whole, a world in which hunger, illiteracy, and disease are the daily lot of a large proportion of the human beings who still exist, as well as causes of death for many who do not still exist. A life of leisured self-expression is, for most of the world's people, a dream so distant that it can rarely even be formed. The contrast between these two images of human life gives rise to a question: what business does anyone have living in the happy and self-expressive world, so long as the other world exists and one is a part of it?

One answer to this question may certainly be to use some portion of one's time and material resources to support relevant types of political action and social service. On the other hand, it seems possible that philosophy itself, while remaining itself, can perform social and political functions, making a difference in the world by using its own distinctive methods and skills.

The Hellenistic philosophical schools in Greece and Rome—Epicureans, Skeptics, and Stoics—all conceived of philosophy as a way of addressing the most painful problems of human life. They saw the philosopher as a compassionate physician whose arts could heal many pervasive types of human suffering. They practiced philosophy not as a detached intellectual technique dedicated to the display of cleverness but as an immersed and worldly art of grappling with human misery. They focused their attention, in consequence, on issues of daily and urgent human significance---the fear of death, love and sexuality, anger and aggression—issues that are sometimes avoided as embarrassingly messy and personal by the more detached varieties of philosophy. They confronted these issues as they arose in ordinary human lives, with a keen attention to the vicissitudes of those lives, and to what would be necessary and sufficient to make them better....In the process they forge new conceptions of what philosophical rigor and precision required. In these ways Hellenistic ethics is unlike the more detached and academic moral philosophy that has sometimes been practiced in the Western tradition."[76]

COMMUNITARIAN
commonly believed to be when individual rights are superseded by community rights, but Sandel believes this term refers to all groups who should be considered before deciding on what is the best action to take when faced with an ethical public policy decision.

Michael Sandel

Michael Sandel was born March 5, 1953, in Minneapolis, Minnesota. At age thirteen, his family moved to Los Angeles, where he was elected president of his senior class. In 1975, he graduated from Brandeis University as a member of Phi Beta Kappa. He earned his doctorate from Balliol College, which was part of Oxford University as a Rhodes Scholar. Although he does not like the label **communitarian** (*when individual rights are superseded by community rights*), perhaps since some may think of this "community more" philosophy as socialism or, many put Sandel's philosophical beliefs in this category. Sandel's view is that Rawls's veil of ignorance, discussed earlier in this chapter, missed an important point: you cannot disconnect totally from your veil of ignorance, since it may be unconsciously embedded in your mind. Furthermore, all groups

© Michele Paccione/Shutterstock, Inc.

should be considered before deciding on what is the best action for a good or better life (decision).[79]

In 1980, he began teaching political philosophy at Harvard University, where at the time of this writing he was the Anne T. and Robert M. Bass Professor of Government.[80] In 2002, he was elected a Fellow of the American Academy of Arts and Sciences.[81] Sandel has written many books, including *Justice: What's the Right Thing to Do?* (2009) and *What Money Can't Buy: The Moral Limits of Markets* (2013), in which asks what the role of money is in our society.[82]

"A just society can't be achieved simply by maximizing utility or by securing freedom of choice. To achieve a *just* society we have to reason together about the meaning of the good life, and to create a public culture hospitable to the disagreements that will inevitably arise.

A politics of moral engagement is not only a more inspiring ideal than a politics of avoidance. It is also a more promising basis for a *just* society."[83]

In the above passage, the first approach (utilitarian) maximizes the greatest happiness for the greatest number of individuals affected by the selected decision. The second approach is more libertarian, but according to Sandel, those ascribing to this approach may agree that certain rights must be respected since they are fundamental, but does not develop any basis as to which rights are important enough to override the utilitarian rights. His approach is to reason together with a conversation, or how he terms it a "public discourse" on what is or determines the good life. For example, a civic education should not be learning only facts or concepts, but when young people from different socioeconomic classes, religious backgrounds, and ethnicities come together in common institutions there's much to be gleaned. With many public institutions in peril financially and educationally, and a small fraction of individuals serving in the military, perhaps requiring a national service in exchange for a reduced college tuition may be one potential approach. Other questions that would exemplify his philosophy include: Should students be given cash incentives to improve their standardized test scores if they are in an underperforming school? Why are private health clubs replacing municipal recreation centers and swimming pools (gentrification)? Just because we have different moral and religious convictions from our neighbors, is ignoring them by leaving them to practice these convictions enough, or should we include them in our decision-making process?[84] If we consider this as communitarian, perhaps Sandel would be more comfortable with this label of his beliefs.

It is quite fitting that Martha Nussbaum and Michael Sandel are the last contemporary philosophers of this chapter. After all, Nussbaum's proactive, pragmatic approach to philosophy connects the Hellenistic Age of Philosophy to the more modern era of twenty-first-century philosophy. As Nussbaum pointed out, the philosopher needs to do more than just analyze, synthesize, meditate, and debate; action is also expected to be a prerequisite if one wants to consider herself a full philosopher not only seeking the good life, but making changes so our world is a better place to live. On the other hand, Sandel's philosophy is requiring an ongoing public discourse as to what is the good life and how we collectively may determine it by including individuals from all walks of life.

Summary

This chapter involved nine contemporary philosophers: Ayn Rand, Milton Friedman, John Rawls, Sissela Bok, Robert Nozick, Robert Solomon, Peter Singer, Martha Nussbaum, and Michael Sandel. Ayn Rand, a novelist and a philosopher, wrote about how capitalism was superior to communism, after watching her father lose his business to the communists, as a young child. By using her novels to demonstrate her objectivist philosophy, which endorsed individualism by stressing "rational self-interest" over charity and the welfare state, Rand would compare individualism to collectivism in her writings, and why the former was best for society in the long run.

Another individual who would agree with this was Milton Friedman, although an economist, he philosophically believed that the sole purpose of a business's social responsibility was to create a profit for its stockholders as long as it was not obtained with deception or fraud. Furthermore, he believed that any corporation who donated any profits to a charitable organization was misappropriating funds. Milton Friedman, like Adam Smith, believed in the "invisible hand" of the marketplace. John Rawls, a modern utilitarian created a philosophy in which everyone starts out with equal freedoms and can have more advantages than others if everyone has an equal chance to have these advantages (no gender or ethnic discrimination) and for those who have advantages over others (i.e., economic class) if those in the worse off position are in a better position than they were before (due to circumstances) it is justifiable. In other words, the affluent can be more affluent just as long as those in the lower class are better off than before (so the affluent cannot be wealthier at the expense of the lower class).

Sissela Bok was the next philosopher whose works have brought forth into the limelight issues concerning patient confidentiality, whistleblowing, trade secrets, undercover journalistic reporting, euthanasia, deception, and other situations that have been prevalent but not addressed using such well-presented philosophical arguments and reasoning. Bok wrote several books including *Lying: Moral Choice in Public and Private Life,* which many consider to be one of the most significant books written in the twentieth century and established her as a world renowned moral philosopher who advocated that the medical profession should tell the truth about a patient's condition and prognosis (in certain situations), and should not be withholding information from the patient.

A libertarian, Robert Nozick's philosophy developed the entitlement theory, which was based upon other libertarians such as John Locke. This entitlement theory was discussed in his book, *Anarchy, State, and Utopia,* as follows: a person who acquires a holding in accordance with the principle of justice in acquisition is entitled to that holding; a person who acquires a holding in accordance with the principles of justice in transfer, from someone else entitled to the holding, is entitled to the holding; and no one is entitled to a holding except by the two applications just mentioned.

Robert Solomon was a prolific writer in the philosophical area of emotions and their place in art, life, and politics. However, a very useful theory which he created was the Three C's theory, consisting of three components: *compliance* to laws and principles of morality; *contributions* to society; and *consequences* of your actions. In order for a business or one's actions to be ethical all three must be satisfied, according to Solomon's theory.

Princeton University's bioethics professor, Peter Singer, another prolific writer, considers his philosophy a form of preferential utilitarianism in that he approaches each issue by seeking the solution that has the best consequences for all affected, satisfying the most preferences, weighted in accordance with the strength of preferences over the long run. Best known for his philosophy to prevent speciesism, discriminating against any living thing that feels pleasure or pain, Singer continues to lecture and write on a diversity of topics applying his utilitarian philosophy.

Martha Nussbaum believes the scope of a philosopher is beyond academics. Nussbaum believes in rights-based universalism, where all individuals should be given equal rights and that philosophers should be involved in making the world a better place by using their philosophical knowledge and skills and applying them to make changes. In her own career, Nussbaum has advocated for gay rights, feminist rights, and civil right6s; she has opposed all forms of discrimination. Still teaching at the University of Chicago, Nussbaum continues to write books for her causes.

Our final philosopher is Michael Sandel, a political philosopher who teaches at Harvard University, when at the time of this writing was the Anne T. and Robert M. Bass Professor of Government. Sandel has written several books, including his well-known *Justice: What Is the Right Thing to Do?*, where he espouses using reason together with a conversation, or how he terms it a "public discourse" on what is or determines the good life. This philosophy includes taking into consideration all groups or factions before deciding on what is the best action to take when faced with an ethical public policy decision.

Key Terms

Communitarian: commonly believed to be when individual rights are superseded by community rights, but Sandel believes this term refers to all groups who should be considered before deciding on what is the best action to take when faced with an ethical public policy decision.

Difference principle: when expectations are to the advantage of the representative person who is worse off, it is just.

Entitlement theory: where individuals are entitled to their holdings as long as they have been obtained fairly and may not be taken by anyone else including the government.

Least advantaged: those who are least favored by categories such as family and class origins, natural endowments, or situational events (such as entrepreneur Donald Trump).

Libertarian: one who believes that individuals are free to do what they please, without any government intervention, as long as they do not interfere with the rights of others.

Objectivist philosophy: endorses individualism by stressing "rational self-interest" over charity and the welfare state, as espoused by Ayn Rand.

Original position: developed by John Rawls as part of a thought experiment where you imagine being in a new society free to create whatever rules you wish.

Speciesism: discrimination against any species that has sentience or the ability to feel (pleasure or pain), as created by Peter Singer.

Three C's theory: consists of three components: *compliance* to laws and principles of morality; *contributions* to society; and *consequences* of actions. In order for a business or one's actions to be ethical all three must be satisfied, according to Robert Solomon.

Ultraminimum state: where all use of force is suspended except for self-defense and only by those who purchase its protection, as believed by Robert Nozick.

Veil of ignorance: developed by Rawls where after creating societal rules under his original position you modify them since you will not know anything (be ignorant) about what your own circumstances or background will be (e.g., poor, wealthy, old, young).

Chapter Review Questions

1. Do you agree with Friedman that the sole responsibility of the business is to its stockholders or should it be extended beyond to other stakeholders? Justify your response.
2. As discussed in this chapter, the founders of Ben and Jerry donated their pretax profits to charitable organizations. Milton Friedman believed doing so was an inappropriate use of

corporate funds. As a utilitarian, how would Peter Singer view this action? Do you agree with Friedman or Singer? Explain your response.

3. (a) John Rawls's "original position" is based upon rules individuals would create for society and would probably include some rules where self-interest would be a factor. List some rules you believe society should follow.

(b) Now, using Rawls's veil of ignorance, where you do not know what gender, ethnicity, income, etc. you will possess, determine if you would modify your original societal rules listed in the original position. For example, if you created a rule that college students should not have to pay for tuition, if the only way that could occur is if senior citizens must pay higher taxes, if you were a senior citizen, would you still agree to that rule? Eliminate the rules that would not survive the "veil of ignorance" factor. Which rules remain?

4. Do you agree with Nozick's philosophy or Rawls's philosophy? Explain your reason from a business owner's viewpoint.

5. Do you agree with the California Supreme Court in finding the psychotherapist guilty of neglect for not revealing his patient's confidentiality? What would you do? Which philosopher would support your viewpoint?

6. Do you agree with Sandel's philosophy? How can it apply in the business world today?

7. Of all the philosophers presented in this chapter, which do you agree with the most? The least? Explain your responses.

Cases for Discussion

CASE 5.1 MEDICAL MARIJUANA: WHICH LAW? [85]

Charles Lynch opened a medical marijuana dispensary in Morro Bay, California, in accordance with state law. The requirements for selling the medical marijuana included prohibiting its sale to anyone under the legal state law age of eighteen. Two years later, Mr. Lynch found himself in a quagmire between the state and the federal government for selling marijuana to some of his customers who were over the age of eighteen but under the federal law of twenty-one. As a result, he was convicted of multiple felonies under the federal law, which puts marijuana in the same class as heroin, with no medical sales exceptions.

At the time, Washington, D.C., and twenty-three states permitted medical marijuana, while four of them legalized recreational sales, too. Since his case is awaiting an appeal, his five-year sentence is currently stayed, and after a nine-month house arrest along with being unable to seek work due to his conviction, he now has changed his career to that of a one-person musician, playing the electric guitar accompanied by a computer-controlled bass, drums, and flashing lights. However, seeking the opportunity to play at local bars has been problematic because some of these tavern owners will not allow him to play in their establishment as a result of his record as a "convicted drug felon."

DISCUSSION QUESTIONS

(a) If you were the owner of one of those local bars, would you hire Charles Lynch? Defend your response, using the full S.E.A. method discussed in Chapter Two (state the philosophy, explain the philosophy in your own words, give a general example, and apply the philosophy to your action). Use any philosopher discussed in this chapter.

(b) Should Lynch be prosecuted, given the disparity between the federal laws which supersede the state laws? If not, should he be allowed to have a medical marijuana business? Defend your response, using the full S.E.A. method discussed in Chapter Two (state the philosophy, explain the philosophy in your own words, give a general example, and apply the philosophy to your action). Use any philosopher discussed in this chapter.

CASE 5.2 CHECKING APPLICANTS' CREDIT: EMPLOYER'S RIGHT OR INVASION OF PRIVACY?[86]

A study conducted by the Society for Human Resource Management reported that 60% of the firms relied on credit checks before hiring a potential employee. In New York City, for example, credit checks were sometimes used for potential dog walkers and custodial staff members. Employers believe that where cybercrimes and theft are increasing, using the credit worthiness of a prospective employee is warranted and can act as a safeguard against such criminal acts. Critics, on the other hand, cited the disproportionate number of African Americans and Latinos who may be adversely affected by these credit checks. In addition, those who are in the lower income bracket, or others who have experienced personal, health, or economic setbacks, also would lose the opportunity for employment, which could reverse their credit scores. In addition, credit scores may not accurately predict poor job performance, fraud, or any other type of potential theft.

In New York City, there was a bill prohibiting employers from denying applicants with poor credit histories with the exceptions of police officers, fire marshals, or an employee who has the signatory power over assets totaling $10,000 or more.

DISCUSSION QUESTION

Should employers have the right to check the credit of potential employees prior to hiring? When considering this question, think of Rawls's "veil of ignorance," where you can either be an employee or an employer? Defend your response, using the full S.E.A. method discussed in Chapter Two (state the philosophy, explain the philosophy in your own words, give a general example, and apply the philosophy to your action). Use any philosopher discussed in this chapter.

Endnotes

[1] Ayn Rand, *Capitalism: The Unknown Ideal* (New York: Signet, 1966), p. 24.

[2] Peter Drucker, *Management Challenges for the 21st Century* (New York: Harper Business, 1999), p. 176.

[3] "Ayn Rand," *Gale Encyclopedia of U.S. Economic History*, vol. 2 (Detroit: Gale, 2000), p. 857; and James T. Baker, "Rand, Ayn," *American National Biography Online*, American Council of Learned Societies, published by Oxford University Press, Feb. 2000. 30 Jan. 2010. http://www.anb.org/articles/16/16-01341.html

[4] "Ayn Rand," *Gale Encyclopedia of U.S. Economic History*, vol. 2 (Detroit: Gale, 2000), p. 857.

[5] Ibid.

[6] "Ayn Rand," *Encyclopedia of World Biography*, 2d ed., vol. 20 (Detroit: Gale, 2004), p. 307.

[7] James T. Baker, "Rand, Ayn," *American National Biography Online*, American Council of Learned Societies, published by Oxford University Press, Feb. 2000. 30 Jan. 2010. http://www.anb.org/articles/16/16-01341.html

[8] "Ayn Rand," *Encyclopedia of World Biography*, 2d ed., vol. 20 (Detroit: Gale, 2004) p. 307; and James T. Baker, "Rand, Ayn," *American National Biography Online*, American Council of Learned Societies, published by Oxford University Press, Feb. 2000. 30 Jan. 2010. http://www.anb.org/articles/16/16-01341.html

[9] "Ayn Rand," *Encyclopedia of World Biography*, 2d ed., vol. 20 (Detroit: Gale, 2004), p. 308.

[10] James T. Baker, "Rand, Ayn," *American National Biography Online*, American Council of Learned Societies, published by Oxford University Press, Feb. 2000. 30 Jan. 2010. http://www.anb.org/articles/16/16-01341.html

[11] Ibid.

[12] "Ayn Rand," *Encyclopedia of World Biography*, 2d ed., vol. 20 (Detroit: Gale, 2004), p. 308; and James T. Baker, "Rand, Ayn," *American National Biography Online*, American Council of Learned Societies, published by Oxford University Press, Feb. 2000. 30 Jan. 2010. http://www.anb.org/articles/16/16-01341.html

[13] "Ayn Rand," *Gale Encyclopedia of U.S. Economic History*, vol. 2 (Detroit: Gale, 2000), p. 857.

[14] Ayn Rand, *Capitalism: An Unknown Ideal* (New York: Signet, 1966), p. 21.

[15] "Milton Friedman," *The Concise Encyclopedia of Economics Library*. Library of Economics and Liberty. 05 Jan. 2010. www.econlib.org/library/Enc/bios/Friedman.html

[16] Ibid.

[17] "Milton Friedman: Expertise: Monetary and Price Theory, Monetary History," Hoover Institution, Stanford University. 05 Jan. 2010. www.hoover.org/bios/friedman.html

18 "Milton Friedman," *The Concise Encyclopedia of Economics Library*. Library of Economics and Liberty. 05 Jan. 2010. www.econlib.org/library/Enc/bios/Friedman.html

19 "Milton Friedman: Expertise: Monetary and Price Theory, Monetary History," Hoover Institution,   Stanford University. 05 Jan. 2010. www.hoover.org/bios/friedman.html

20 Milton Friedman (with assistance of Rose Friedman), *Capitalism and Freedom* (Chicago: The University of Chicago Press, 1962/1982), p. 133.

21 Ibid., 135.

22 Thomas Pogge, *John Rawls: His Life and Theory of Justice* (New York: Oxford Press, 2007), pp. 4-5.

23 Ibid., 5.

24 Ibid., 7-11.

25 Ibid., 12.

26 Ibid., 14-15.

27 Ibid., 16-18.

28 John Rawls, *A Theory of Justice* (Cambridge: Harvard University Press, 1971/1999), pp. 10-11.

29 Ibid., 17.

30 Ibid., 266.

31 Ibid., 83.

32 Ibid., 67-68.

33 Denise K. Magner, "Sissela Bok and the 'Socially Useful' Study of Philosophy," *The Chronicle of Higher Education,* vol. 36, no. 9, 1989, p. A 3. Academic OneFile. 30 Jan. 2010. http://find.galegroup.com/gtx/start.do?prodld=AONE&userGroupName=rocklandcc

34 "Sissela Ann Bok," *Encyclopedia of World Biography*, 2d ed., vol. 2 (Detroit: Gale, 2004), p. 372.

35 Ibid.; and Website: Harvard Center for Population and Development Studies: Researchers/Affiliates. 30 Jan. 2010. www.hsph.harvard.edu/centers-institutes/population-development/ people/researchersaffiliates/

36 Website: Harvard Center for Population and Development Studies: Researchers/Affiliates. 30 Jan. 2010. www.hsph.harvard.edu/centers-institutes/population-development/ people/researchersaffiliates/

37 Ibid.

38 Ibid.

39 Sissela Bok, *Secrets: On the Ethics of Concealment and Revelation* (New York: Pantheon Books, 1982), pp. 127-128.

40 Ibid., 282.

41 *Encyclopedia of World Biography on Robert Nozick.* 27 Jan. 2010.   http://www.bookrags.com/biography/robert-nozick/

42 *Encyclopedia of World Biography on Robert Nozick and* Robert Nozick, Bio.True Story. 27 Jan. 2010. http://www.biography.com/articles/Robert-Nozick-9425767

43 Ken Gewertz, "Philosopher Nozick Dies at 63," *Harvard Gazette Archives.* 27 Jan. 2010. http://www.news.harvard.edu/gazette/2002/01.17/99-nozick.html

44 Robert Nozick, Bio.True Story. 27 Jan. 2010. http://www.biography.com/articles/Robert-Nozick-9425767

45 Ken Gewertz, "Philosopher Nozick Dies at 63," *Harvard Gazette Archives.* 27 Jan. 2010. http://www.news.harvard.edu/gazette/2002/01.17/99-nozick.html

46 Ibid.

47 Robert Nozick, *Anarchy, State, and Utopia* (New York: Basic Books, 1974), p. 151.

48 Ibid., 26.

49 Ibid., 161.

50 Joanna B. Ciulla, "The Man with a Hole in His Heart," *Business Ethics Quarterly*, vol. 17, no. 2, April 2007, p. 185.

51 Ibid.

52 Ibid.

53 Ibid.

54 Ronnie de Sousa, "Robert Solomon Remembered, Aesthetics online." 01 Feb. 2010. http://www.aesthetics-online.org/memorials/index.php?memorialsid=16.

55 Ibid.

56 Joanna B. Ciulla, "The Man with a Hole in His Heart," *Business Ethics Quarterly*, vol. 17, no. 2, April 2007, p. 185.

57 Ibid., 185-186; and William H. Shaw and Vincent Barry, *Moral Issues in Business* (Belmont, CA: Wadsworth Cengage Learning, 2010), p. 36.

58 William H. Shaw and Vincent Barry, *Moral Issues in Business* (Belmont, CA: Wadsworth Cengage Learning, 2010), p. 39.

59 "Peter Singer," *Current Biography* (New York: The H.W. Wilson Company, 1991). Biography Reference Bank Database. 1 Feb. 2010. http://vnweb.hwwilsonweb.com

60 Ibid.

61 "Peter Singer," *World Authors 1985-1990* (New York: The H.W. Wilson Company, 1995). Biography Reference Bank Database. 1 Feb. 2010. http://vnweb.hwwilsonweb.com

62 "Peter Singer," *Current Biography* (New York: The H.W. Wilson Company, 1991). Biography Reference Bank Database. 1 Feb. 2010. http://vnweb.hwwilsonweb.com; and "Peter Singer," *World Authors 1985-1990* (New York: The H.W. Wilson Company, 1995). Biography Reference Bank Database. 1 Feb. 2010. http://vnweb.hwwilsonweb.com

63 "Peter Singer," *World Authors 1985-1990* (New York: The H.W. Wilson Company, 1995). Biography Reference Bank Database. 1 Feb. 2010. http://vnweb.hwwilsonweb.com

64 Ibid.

65 Peter Singer, "The Singer Solution to World Poverty," *The New York Times Magazine*, September 5, 1999, p. 63.

66 McLemee, Scott. "What Makes Martha Nussbaum Run?" *The Chronicle of Higher Education* 48.06 (2001). Academic OneFile. 3 Feb. 2010. http://find.galegroup.com/gtx/start.do?prodId=AONE&userGroupName=rocklandcc

67 Robert Boynton, "Who Needs Philosophy?: A Profile of Martha Nussbaum," *The New York Times Magazine*, November 21, 1999. 03 Feb. 2010. http:/www.robertboynton.com

68 "Martha Nussbaum," The Department of Philosophy, University of Chicago Website. 01 Feb. 2010. http://philosophy.uchicago.edu/faculty//nussbaum.html

69 Robert Boynton, "Who Needs Philosophy?: A Profile of Martha Nussbaum," *The New York Times Magazine*, November 21, 1999. 03 Feb. 2010. http://www.robertboynton.com

70 Ibid.

71 Ibid.

72 Ibid.

73 Ibid.

74 "Martha Nussbaum," The Department of Philosophy, University of Chicago Website. 01 Feb. 2010. http://philosophy.uchicago.edu/faculty//nussbaum.html

75 Ibid.

76 Martin C. Nussbaum, *The Therapy of Desire: Theory and Practice in Hellenistic Ethics*. (Princeton: Princeton University Press, 1994), pp. 3-4.

79 Michael Sandel-Biography, Jewage Website. n.d. 26 April 2015. www.jewage.org/wiki/en/Article:Michael_Sandel_-_Biography

80 "About Michael Sandel," Harvard University's Justice with Michael Sandel. www.justiceharvard.org/about/michael-sandel/

81 Michael Sandel-Biography, Jewage Website. n.d. 26 April 2015. www.jewage.org/wiki/en/Article:Michael_Sandel_-_Biography

82 "About Michael Sandel," Harvard University's Justice with Michael Sandel.

www.justiceharvard.org/about/michael-sandel/

[83] Michael J. Sandel, What's the Right Thing to Do? (New York: Farrar, Straus and Giroux, 2009), pp. 261, 269.

[84] Ibid., 261-268.

[85] This case was rewritten based upon the following article: Erik Eckholm, "Federal Law, State Law and Medical Marijuana Law," *The New York Times*, April 9, 2015, pp. A14 and A22.

[86] This case was rewritten based upon the following article: Rachel L. Swarns, "Unexpected Fight on Bill Banning Employer Credit Checks," *The New York Times*, March 30, 2015, p. A14.

CHAPTER 6

THE MODIFIED VELASQUEZ MODEL OF DECISION MAKING

"If we can prevent something bad without sacrificing anything of comparable significance, we ought to do it."

-Peter Singer, Practice of Ethics

In the business world, executives are faced with many moral dilemmas. Traditionally, most decisions follow the **Harvard Case Method**, *which includes:*
(1) identifying the opportunity or problem, (2) identifying the alternative actions that may be taken, (3) developing a list of criteria to screen out the least desirable alternative actions, (4) comparing each alternative to each criterion, (5) selecting the optimum alternative, (6) implementing the selected optimum alternative, and (7) following its progress

to ensure that the alternative selected resolved the problem or realized the desired opportunity (and modify it if not). Yet, this method neglects to consider whether any of the alternatives selected would be an ethical one and how this decision would affect all of the stakeholders as a result of this decision.

However, in 1992, Dr. Manuel Velasquez developed a seven-step model for moral decision making in compliance with an initiative by Arthur Andersen and Company. With some modifications, which are noted, this will be the model that shall be followed throughout this textbook. This chapter will focus on this model and will use the Ford Pinto case to demonstrate its application.

INTRODUCTION: THE FORD PINTO CASE

In 1970, the Ford Motor Company introduced the Pinto, a small automobile that was developed to compete with the European and Japanese manufacturers. The Pinto was manufactured from inception to production in the record time of approximately 25 months (compared to the industry average of 43 months). In addition to the time pressure, the engineering and development teams were required to adhere to the production "limits of 2,000"; its costs could not exceed $2,000 nor weight be more than 2,000 pounds. Any decisions that threatened these targets or the timing of the car's introduction into the market were discouraged. As a consequence, retooling was already under way when a routine crash testing revealed that the Pinto's fuel tank often ruptured when struck from the rear at a relatively low speed (31 miles per hour in crash tests).[1]

Reports indicated that fuel tank failures were the result of some rather marginal design features. The tank was positioned between the rear bumper and the rear axle and during an impact, several studs protruding from the rear of the axle housing would puncture holes in the tank and spilled gasoline then could be ignited by sparks. During these crash tests, eight of the vehicles suffered potentially catastrophic gas tank ruptures. The only three automobiles that survived intact had each been modified in some way to protect the tank.[2]

In the meantime, Ford conducted a cost-benefit analysis, which indicated the following:

PRODUCTION COSTS: $137,000,000
(Estimated production costs to fix the gas tanks for the 12,500,000 vehicles at a cost of $11 per vehicle)

POTENTIAL LAWSUITS: $49,530,000

(Estimated as the costs of lawsuits based upon actuarial studies for 180 projected deaths @$200,000 per death = **$36,000,000** + 180 projected burn injuries @ $67,000 per injury = **$12,060,000** + 2,100 projected burned cars @ $700 per car = **$1,470,000**).[3]

As the Chief Executive Officer who must meet the needs of the stockholders as well as to society, what would you do? Why did you decide this (i.e., what did you use as your standards in your decision)?

TRADITIONAL BUSINESS ETHICAL APPROACHES

In an article entitled, "*Thinking Ethically: A Framework for Moral Decision Making*," Manuel Velazquez, along with Clair Andre, Thomas Shanks, and Michael J. Meyer identified five ethical approaches in moral decision making. These approaches described below are: (1) Utilitarian Approach; (2) Rights Approach; (3) Fairness or Justice Approach; (4) Common Goods Approach; and (5) Virtue Approach.[4]

THE UTILITARIAN APPROACH

According to nineteenth-century philosophers Jeremy Bentham and John Stuart Mill (see Chapter 4), **utilitarianism** *was the approach of selecting*

UTILITARIANISM
selecting actions that produced the greatest good over evil for the majority of those affected by these actions.

STAKEHOLDERS
those parties who influence the organization or are influenced by the organization (e.g., stockholders, employees, clients, society, government agencies).

actions which were those that produced the greatest good over evil for the majority of those affected by these actions.[5] However, when the **utilitarian approach** is applied, there is an emphasis on the effect that it will have primarily on the stockholders (or owners), while the other stakeholders may be considered as secondary. **Stakeholders** *are those parties who influence the organization or are influenced by the organization.*

Therefore, in this Ford Pinto case, the utilitarian approach could be to manufacture the vehicles *as is.* After all, from an economic viewpoint, the savings for not modifying the vehicle would be greater than the potential lawsuits that may result from the damage caused in an automobile accident, whereby the gas tank may explode upon impact in a rear-end collision. Because economics was at one time a branch of philosophy, the utilitarian would most likely make a decision based upon the most profitable action, which would lead to the satisfaction of the majority affected by this decided action.

THE RIGHTS APPROACH

RIGHTS APPROACH
the right for an individual to choose for oneself (right of privacy, freedom of speech, freedom of religion, etc.).

Using eighteenth-century philosopher Immanuel Kant's view (see Chapter 4), this **rights approach** *focused upon the right for an individual to choose for oneself.*[6] Individual rights include the right to the truth and be informed about matters that affect our choices; of privacy; not to be injured; and to what has been agreed upon by those entering into a contract or agreement.[7] Although these are some rights, you may also add the right to speech, to assemble, and have freedom of religion (i.e., The Bill of Rights). Basically, as sentient beings, there are some unalienable rights that we all must have.

Regarding the Pinto case, an individual who follows the rights approach of Kant would modify the vehicle because every individual has the right to safety. Furthermore, because of the implied contract that any vehicle manufactured would not be sold if a defect existed that could lead to the death or injury of a passenger or driver, the economic facets of this decision would be secondary and safety of the passenger primary.

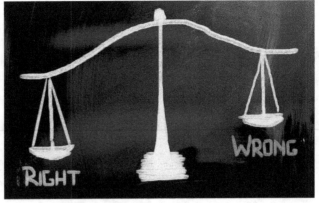

© Krasimira Nevenova/Shutterstock, Inc.

THE FAIRNESS OR JUSTICE APPROACH

Ancient Greek philosopher Socrates (see Chapter 2) said, "Equals should be treated equally." [8] The **fairness or justice approach** *seeks equality for all individuals and answers questions such as: How fair is an action? Does it treat everyone in the same way, or does it show favoritism and discrimination?*[9] Favoritism benefits some individuals, while discrimination places burdens on them, without any moral justification for doing so.[10] In essence, this approach advocates equal treatment for all individuals.

FAIRNESS/JUSTICE APPROACH *seeks equality for all individuals and asks questions such as: How fair is an action? Does it treat everyone in the same way, or does it show favoritism and discrimination?*

John Rawls (see Chapter 5) believed that all individuals should be treated equally without knowing their place in the outcome of the decision. For example, in our case study, if you did not know whether you would be a stockholder or a passenger in a collision with this potentially dangerous vehicle (the Ford Pinto), how would you decide? Most likely, you would want to make sure that the vehicle was safe, since according to Rawls's philosophy, you would be under what he termed a **veil of ignorance**, and would not want to take a chance of being a passenger in an unsafe automobile.

© Ivelin Radkov/Shutterstock, Inc.

© Rawpixel/Shutterstock, Inc.

THE COMMON GOODS APPROACH

In this approach, society is perceived as "a community whose members are joined in the shared pursuit of values and goals they hold in common."[11] In the **common goods approach**, *all members of society are ensured agreed upon common goods such as affordable health care, effective public safety, peace among nations, a just legal system, and unpolluted environment.*[12] In terms effective public safety, using the common goods approach, the only viable decision would be to retool the automobile or not sell it at all, since it would be a safety hazard otherwise.

THE VIRTUE APPROACH

The **virtue approach** *assumes that there are certain ideals toward which we should all strive for, in order to develop us as better human beings.*[13] Honesty, courage, compassion, generosity, self-control, and integrity are some examples of these ideals

© iQoncept/Shutterstock, Inc.

or virtues.[14] When faced with an ethical problem, questions that may arise are: What kind of person should I be? What will promote the development of character within my community and me?

Management theorist Peter Drucker calls this character building a mirror test, when one asks oneself, "What kind of person do I want to see when I shave myself in the morning or put on my lipstick in the morning?"[15]

An individual facing the decision as to whether or not to manufacture and sell an unsafe automobile would neither produce nor sell it, unless it was proven to be safe. You could argue that by deferring profits now, in order to produce a safe automobile, would be a virtuous act and character builder.

THE SEVEN-STEP APPROACH TO MORAL DECISION MAKING[16]

Returning back to the original case, as the Chief Executive Office of Ford Motor Company, which approach will you use? And, what course of action will you take? Evidently, this is not an easy task and complicating it even more is that by selecting one business ethical approach over another, your final decision on what course of action to take can differ with each approach. So, what approach will you take?

In 1988, Dr. Manuel Velasquez, an ethics professor at Santa Clara University, developed the **Velasquez Model of Decision Making**, *which is a seven-step method to decision making that considers the ethical consequences for all the stakeholders affected by the decision.* He developed this moral reasoning model in conjunction with the Andersen Business Ethics program of Arthur Andersen and Company, SC. It should be noted that there are many other models and even this one was modified after implementing it in my classes. However, the purpose of this course is twofold: first to learn philosophical theories, and second to apply these philosophical theories to actual case studies. With this in mind,

VELASQUEZ MODEL OF DECISION MAKING
a seven-step method to decision making that considers the ethical consequences for all the stakeholders affected by the decision.

there is an academic component that may not be applied in the real business world. Nonetheless, by integrating the theoretical component with a pragmatic one, you should find this seven-step approach raises the bar in determining what ethical action could be taken. Then it will be up to you as to whether or not after making your choice, you will be able to look at yourself in the mirror the next morning.

STEP ONE: WHAT ARE THE FACTS?

In this step you identify the facts of the case. Your task is to be able to separate facts from irrelevant information, as well as eliminating any assumptions or personal interpretations. In addition, no decisions should be made at this point. You should be able to limit the facts to a paragraph; otherwise you will be just rewriting the case.

Example of Step One

Facing a competitive market, Ford Motor Company manufactured an automobile that had to cost less than $2,000 and weigh less than 2,000 pounds, as well as be produced in a record time of 25 months (compared to the industry average of 43 months) in order to be more competitive with the European and Japanese manufacturers.   As a consequence of its quick production, when routine crash tests of it vehicles resulted in

© Rawpixel/Shutterstock, Inc.

catastrophic gas tank ruptures which ignited in eight of the eleven tested vehicles, while the other three were modified so the gas tanks did not ignite, Ford conducted a cost-benefit analysis to determine the course of action it could take. The analysis found that if the vehicle was to be retooled and the gas tanks repaired so they were safe, it would cost $137 million; if not, the potential lawsuits would result in losses amounting to approximately $49.5 million.

STEP TWO: WHAT ARE THE ETHICAL ISSUES?

Define the ethical issues and separate them from other non-ethical issues. Ethical issues are points of debate or questions about what ought to be done about a particular situation and raise questions whether a past or proposed course of action is consistent with one's moral standards or the moral standards of one's society. Generally, these ethical issues involve parties that have interests in a moral conflict.

© Iliana Mihaleva/Shutterstock, Inc.

When identifying the one or two ethical issues in the case, you should consider its *effects upon the individual parties, the organization as a whole*, or as a **systemic** (as Velasquez terms it) facet. Examples of a systemic ethical issue would be developing affirmative action policies affecting an entire industry, encouraging insider trading, refusing to approve paternity leaves, fostering a glass ceiling, etc. *Systemic issues involve more than one system (or organization) with global ramifications.*

SYSTEMIC
more than one organization (or its global ramifications). In the case of a systematic ethical issue, it refers to the ethical issue that affects many organizations, such as affirmative action, insider trading, etc.

Sometimes an ethical issue may have elements of all three facets: individual, organizational, and systemic. For example, as a Human Resource Manager, you have a proposed policy to extend maternity leave to fathers (paternity leave). It will have an effect on the individual who may be eligible for such a leave, the future of anyone in the organization seeking a paternity leave, and possibly other organizations who may use your organization as an industry benchmark (or icon).

Example of Step Two

There are two ethical issues facing the Ford Pinto Company: (1) Should Ford continue to manufacture an automobile that appears to be unsafe due to a gas tank defect (to what extent is a company responsible for the safety of its societal members)? (2) Should Ford Motor Company jeopardize profits and/or its position in the market (to what extent are a company's profits more important than the safety of others)?

There are many other sub-problems as well (i.e., When does "whistle blowing" supersede job security? Is there a social contract between a corporation and its societal members? Should an organization jeopardize profits to remedy unethical behavior, as opposed to only illegal behavior?). However, for demonstration purposes only these two issues will be addressed and could actually be boiled down to one ethical issue: Should Ford Motor Company sell the Pinto, even though it may be unsafe at the expense of profits?

STEP THREE: WHAT ARE SOME ALTERNATIVES?

In this step you consider your possible courses of action. Remember, if you decide not to do anything, this is an alternative as well. In most

© MB-O/Shutterstock, Inc.

cases, it might behoove you to identify at least three alternatives, instead of just x (to do it) or y (not to do it).

However, an alternative that delegates the decision-making aspect of this step is not a viable alternative (i.e., refer it to a committee or your superior), since you do not gain the experience of applying the seven-step method to your case, plus you cannot always delegate every decision to another individual.

It should be noted that at this point, no judgments should be made about the alternatives. This is merely the "brainstorming" step, where the alternatives are generated, without any evaluation of these alternatives occurring at this time.

Example of Step Three

One alternative is to sell the Ford Pinto without any modifications and risk any lawsuits that occur due to the malfunctioning of the gas tank which may explode upon a rear-end collision impact. The cost for this alternative would be $49,530,000 in potential lawsuits.

A second alternative is to modify the vehicle, which was estimated to cost approximately $11 per vehicle. The total cost for this alternative would have been $137,000,000. This would be done by positioning the gas tank over the rear axle of the vehicle.[17]

A third alternative would be to line the gas tank with a rubber bladder which would have cost only $5.08 per automobile, and would have reduced the risk for bodily injury and property damage, as well as the number of potential lawsuits associated with these consequences.[18] The total cost for this alternative would have been approximately $63.5 million.

Two other potential alternatives are to place a piece of steel between the gas tank and the bumper or to insert a plastic protective device between the gas tank and the bolts on the differential housing.[19] Both of these alternatives would have cost less than the $11 per vehicle, required to position the gas tank over the rear axle (alternative number two), but could have reduced the bodily injury and property damages risks associated with not modifying the vehicle at all.

STEP FOUR: WHO ARE SOME OF THE STAKEHOLDERS?

"No person is an island," and everyone may be affected by the actions of others. When faced with a business decision, the chances are strong that they will affect someone else other than just the decision maker (you). So, who are the stakeholders affected by your decision?

Stakeholders are those influenced by the organization or who can influence the organization. In this case, there are many stakeholders. The purpose of this step is to begin the evaluation process which takes into account who will be affected by your decision. The *how* step will be examined in the next three steps (i.e., how will the stakeholders be affected by your decision?).

Example of Step Four

Although there are many stakeholders affected by this decision, I will narrow it down to five stakeholders: customers, stockholders, drivers and their passengers (potential victims in other vehicles), executives, and employees. However, other stakeholders who could be considered include the National Highway Traffic Safety Administration, attorneys, families of the potential victims, Ford Motor Company's Board of Directors, news media, suppliers of gas tanks, insurance companies, and labor unions. It is important to realize that stakeholders may be organizations consisting of many individuals (i.e., news media, labor union) or those who are not direct parties of the decision but will be affected indirectly (such as the families of the victims). The more inclusive you are with the list of stakeholders, the better will be your chances for making a more informed decision. However, for academic purposes, narrowing the number to five enables most of the major stakeholders to be considered.

STEP FIVE: WHAT IS THE MOST ETHICAL AMONG ALL OF YOUR ALTERNATIVES?

In this step, you select the most ethical or as Socrates would say, the most *virtuous* alternative. Although any alternative selected may result in a decision, where some individuals benefit and others will not, the key question is whether the *process* was just or virtuous.

In selecting the most ethical alternative, your focus should be based upon the *stakeholders affected by your decision, who may benefit least from your decision.* The late Harvard University ethicist John Rawls termed these stakeholders the **least advantaged**.[20]

LEAST

ADVANTAGED
the stakeholders who benefit the least from the alternative that could be selected by the decision maker in an ethical dilemma.

In order to complete this step, there are several substeps. First, you identify each alternative listed in step three. Next, identify each stakeholder listed in step four. Then, compare each alternative and its affect on each stakeholder.

Of the alternatives identified, which one would benefit the least advantaged stakeholder? In most cases, by using this approach, you will then be able to identify the most ethical alternative. Finally, you must identify the philosophy, which would support your choice and validate that your alternative would be the most ethical for the least advantaged

stakeholder and use the full S.E.A. method introduced in Chapter Two. In the full S.E.A. method, you state the philosophy that would support what you believe would be the most virtuous alternative, by stating (not just labeling) the entire philosophy, explaining what the philosophy means in your own words, giving a general example unrelated to the case, and then applying the philosophy by directly linking the philosophy with the ethical alternative, which you selected.

© iQoncept/Shutterstock, Inc.

Example of Step Five

For example, in this case, by comparing the three alternatives identified in step three, to the effects it would have on the stakeholders in step four, the stakeholders—who would be identified as the least advantaged individuals—would be the drivers and their passengers (including potential passengers in other vehicles). Of the three alternatives, the second alternative would be to the benefit of the least advantaged stakeholder and would therefore be selected as the most ethical. This second alternative is to position the gas tank over the rear axle of the vehicle. By modifying the vehicle, which was estimated to cost approximately $11 per vehicle or $137,000,000 for a total cost, it would save the most lives and reduce potential injuries to the passengers and damage to their cars. This would be done by repositioning the gas tank over the rear axle of the vehicle (here the most ethical action is identified).

The final substep in this fifth step is to identify a philosophy to validate your most ethical alternative.[21] (After identifying your most ethical alternative, you now STATE the full philosophical quote and identify the philosopher.) In this case, I will demonstrate using this substep by citing Immanuel Kant's philosophy from his book, *Groundwork of the Metaphysics of Morals*, *"There is, therefore, only one categorical imperative. It is: Act only on that maxim through which you can at the same time will that it become a universal law."*[22] (Now you EXPLAIN the quote in your own words.) According to Immanuel Kant, every action should be performed only if it could be followed in every situation without any exceptions. In addition, Kant believed that the maxim (rule, principle) has to be one that would be accepted everywhere. This means that when we want to create a policy or take action, it has to be one that would be followed without any deviation, regardless of the situation. (Next, you give a general example of the quote without using an example related to the case.) For example, one maxim that could be accepted universally is that adultery is not permitted by a person who is married. A second example is murdering a defenseless person who is not physically threatening you or another individual from immediate harm, is not justifiable and anyone who does murder another under these conditions should be tried as a criminal act. (Finally, you then

APPLY the quote to your action.) Therefore, would anyone knowingly want to allow the sale of an unsafe vehicle? Would a law ever be passed that would enable an automobile manufacturer to produce unsafe vehicles? Would that manufacturer want his family in such a vehicle? Since the answer to this would be unequivocally "no," Kant's philosophy would support our decision because our universal law is that one should never manufacture an automobile that is unsafe and could cause bodily injury to its passengers.

Of the three alternatives, the second alternative would satisfy Kant's philosophy and result in being the safest for any of the drivers and their passengers (least advantaged) who are affected by the manufacturing of this vehicle. For this reason, using Kant's philosophy (which was discussed more fully in Chapter Four of this text) would support the second alternative of positioning the gas tank over the rear axle of the vehicle because it is the most ethical.

STEP SIX: WHAT ARE THE TRADEOFFS FOR SELECTING THE MOST ETHICAL ALTERNATIVE?

In this step, after you identified the most ethical alternative in step five, you must view it from the perspective of the other stakeholders and how it will affect them, as well as the organization responsible for implementing the decision. Basically, you are asking, what will be the tradeoffs, disadvantages, downsides, or consequences for the implementation (putting into action) of the most ethical decision? In other words, to take the ethical action, how will your stakeholders be negatively affected?

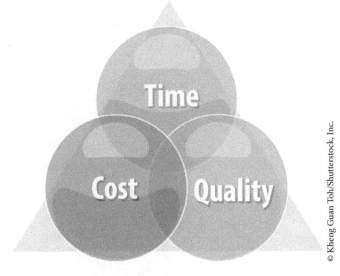

© Kheng Guan Toh/Shutterstock, Inc.

Your concerns should include the cost, the profits, the goodwill, the continued existence of the organization, the effects on jobs, and other factors that may be more concerned with "the bottom line," rather than the ethical choice.

Example of Step Six

If positioning the gas tank over the rear axle of the vehicle is selected, what will it cost? In this case, it was estimated that the cost would be $11 per vehicle for a total cost of $137 million for the 12,500,000 vehicles requiring the repositioning of the gas tanks. Compared to the potential lawsuits of approximately $49.5 million, it would save the company approximately $87.5 million not to reposition the gas tanks. Therefore, for making the ethical decision, the tradeoffs would be the $137 million cost incurred for the gas tank repositioning, the delay to have the vehicles available on the market (and dealer's lots), potential job losses, decreased value of the stock to its owners, and the loss to the foreign competition for not having the vehicles available for sale.

STEP SEVEN: WHAT ACTION WILL YOU TAKE?

In this final step, you will select the action you will take. As in the real world, any alternative may be selected, including none of the ones you

© tomertu/Shutterstock, Inc.

may have identified yet. For example, you can decide to manufacture the automobile with a warning that extra care must be taken when driving (impractical choice) or quietly recall some models after manufacturing the automobile and earning some profit to cover the cost of repositioning the gas tank. However, regardless of what action you take, in this step, you must once again identify a philosophy to support your decision.

Even though you have completed these seven steps, and still may select the "most unethical alternative," this method required you to at least examine the possibility of selecting the most ethical alternative, as well as justifying philosophically why you selected what you believed was the best alternative for the case. If nothing else, by following this method when faced with an ethical dilemma, you will be required to view all aspects of the situation, examine how it will affect all of the stakeholders, and to justify your final decision.

In this step, like in step five, you will follow the full S.E.A. method, but will use another philosopher to demonstrate your vast knowledge in applying multiple philosophers to an ethical dilemma or situation. Also, use another philosopher (not the same one used in step five), even if you select the same action. This requirement is for pedagogical purposes to demonstrate your understanding of more than one philosopher.

Example of Step Seven
Even though any of the three alternatives may now be selected (or even a new alternative), a justification for the selection must be made. For demonstrative purposes, I will select the second alternative, and will STATE Aristotle's quote, *"Every craft and every investigation, and likewise every action and decision, seems to aim at some good; hence the good has well described as that at which everything aims."* According to this quote by Aristotle, every action an individual takes must always be directed for the good of society, rather than just the individual. The just action or the moral action is the only course of action to be taken after reflecting (investigating) upon all the possible alternatives. (This previous step satisfied the EXPLAIN facet of the SEA method.) For example, if you are faced with a decision to report a colleague who has stolen money, it is the most moral or just action to report him, then look the other way because

you do not want to be involved. (This satisfied the EXAMPLE phase of the SEA method.) Therefore, the most moral action to take in this case is to repair the gas tank because the good that could come from saving lives would outweigh the loss of time or profits for looking the other way and not fixing the gas tank's placement. After all, if the Ford Motor executives did not know whether they would be in the passenger seats or in the executive suite making the decision, the chances are fairly strong that they would want to ensure that the automobiles were safe. In other words, the costs to reposition the gas tanks would not outweigh the costs to their own lives, if the automobiles were unsafe. This action to ensure the safety of all passengers is the good for what we as individuals strive or aim for as a society. (This satisfied the APPLY section of the SEA method).

CONCLUSION

After understanding how to apply this model to the Ford Pinto case, you should be able to apply it to other ethical decisions that you may be faced with either in the business world or even personally. This model does not guarantee that the most ethical decision will be selected, but it does enable the decision maker to examine how the final decision will affect all of the stakeholders. Perhaps, as a final thought, you can always ask yourself after making the decision, as Peter Drucker alluded, "Will you be able to look at yourself in the mirror the next morning?"

SUMMARY

Traditionally, decisions are made using the traditional Harvard Case Method approach consisting of (1) identifying the opportunity/problem; (2) identifying the alternative actions that may be taken; (3) developing a list of criteria to screen out the least desirable alternative actions; (4) comparing each alternative to each criterion; (5) selecting the optimum alternative; (6) implementing the selected alternative, and (7) following its progress to ensure that the alternative selected resolved the problem or realized the desired opportunity (and modify it if not).

Based upon the research of Manuel Velasquez and his colleagues, five ethical approaches were identified in decision making. The five approaches are (1) selecting the action producing the greatest good over evil for the majority affected by the action (utilitarianism); (2) selecting actions that give individuals basic unalienable rights, such as the right to speech (rights approach); (3) actions that are equitable for all individuals (fairness/justice approach); (4) ensuring actions only if all members of society are given basic rights, such as affordable health care (common goods approach); and (5) assuming that there are certain ideals that all individuals accept and strive for, such as honesty (virtue approach). However, when Velasquez developed a seven-step method, he incorporated only three of these approaches; utilitarian, rights, and fairness/justice.

In 1992, Velasquez developed a seven-step moral reasoning model, which was modified to integrate a multitude of classical and contemporary philosophies, as reflected in his fifth step (where he used only three ethical philosophies). In addition, step five reflects another modification whereby the most ethical of all the alternatives is identified (as opposed to testing the ethicality of each alternative with each stakeholder) as is a philosopher who would support the most ethical action to be taken in a given situation. The last modification is in step seven, which now requires you to identify a philosophy to support the action to be taken after the ethical and practical aspects of the ethical dilemma have been analyzed in the previous steps.

Therefore, the modified seven-step method to be practiced throughout this text is as follows:

STEP ONE: **WHAT ARE THE FACTS?**
STEP TWO: **WHAT ARE THE ETHICAL ISSUES?**
STEP THREE: **WHAT ARE SOME ALTERNATIVES?**
STEP FOUR: **WHO ARE SOME OF THE STAKEHOLDERS?**
STEP FIVE: **WHAT IS THE MOST ETHICAL AMONG ALL YOUR ALTERNATIVES? (full SEA method)**
STEP SIX: **WHAT ARE THE TRADEOFFS FOR SELECTING THE MOST ETHICAL ALTERNATIVE?**
STEP SEVEN: **WHAT ACTION WILL YOU TAKE? (full SEA method)**

KEY TERMS

Common goods approach: an approach where all members of society are ensured agreed upon common goods such as affordable health care, effective public safety, peace among nations, a just legal system, and unpolluted environment.

Fairness/justice approach: seeks equality for all individuals and asks questions such as: How fair is an action? Does it treat everyone in the same way, or does it show favoritism and discrimination?

Harvard Case Method: a seven-step approach that identifies the optimum alternative for a specific problem or opportunity faced by an organization, without taking into consideration any ethical consequences to all the stakeholders affected by the selected alternative.

Least advantaged: the stakeholders who benefit the least from the alternative that could be selected by the decision maker in an ethical dilemma.

Rights approach: the right for an individual to choose for oneself (right of privacy, freedom of speech, freedom of religion, etc.).

Stakeholders: those parties who influence the organization or are influenced by the organization (e.g., stockholders, employees, clients, society, government agencies).

Systemic: more than one organization (or its global ramifications). In the case of a systematic ethical issue, it refers to the ethical issue that affects many organizations, such as affirmative action, insider trading, etc.

Utilitarian approach / utilitarianism: selecting actions that produced the greatest good over evil for the majority of those affected by these actions.

Veil of ignorance: presupposes that the parties who will be developing a policy or course of action will have no knowledge in terms of their place in that decision (e.g., whether they would be the executives making the decision or the customers affected by the decision).

Velasquez Model of Decision Making: a seven-step method to decision making that considers the ethical consequences for all the stakeholders affected by the decision.

Virtue approach: assumes there are certain virtues or ideals that we should all strive for in order to develop us as better human beings (e.g., honesty, self-control, integrity).

CHAPTER REVIEW QUESTIONS

1. What are the basic steps in the Harvard Case Method?
2. Describe the following five ethical approaches identified by Dr. Velasquez and his colleagues: utilitarian, rights, fairness or justice, common goods, and virtue approach.
3. What are the seven steps in moral decision making developed by Dr. Velasquez and his colleagues, and modified by the author of this text?

4. How is the Harvard Case Method different from the Velasquez Method?
5. Do you agree with the author that the Velasquez Method is better than the Harvard Case Method for the purposes of this course? For approaching an ethical dilemma in the real business world? Defend your viewpoint.

CASES FOR DISCUSSION

CASE 6.1 PROMOTION OR TERMINATION?[24]

In 2014, David Tovar, Walmart Vice President for Corporate Communications was slated for a promotion to senior vice president, after eight successful years there, until it was revealed that he had not earned a degree from the University of Delaware which he listed on his original resume. This was a result of a more rigorous background check, which was routinely given for employees who were being vetted for promotions.

Although Tovar did participate in his graduation ceremony, he claims that he discovered that he was a "couple of credits short" after. In his defense, he said it was more of an error of omission, because when asked by others about his academic background, he would only admit that he attended the university and not that he graduated, and had no memory of what he disclosed on his original resume. Upon being told of this discovery by Walmart, Tovar stated that he contacted the University of Delaware to determine what he was missing and planned on completing his course requirements to satisfy the requirements for the baccalaureate degree that he originally claimed to have earned.

In 2012, Yahoo's chief executive, Scott Thompson, claimed to have earned a computer science degree, which he had not, and was forced to resign under pressure from Yahoo.

DISCUSSION QUESTION

If you were a member of Walmart's Board of Directors what would you do? Using the seven-step Velasquez Model, and numbering each step, apply this method to your decision-making process.

CASE 6.2 RELIGIOUS FREEDOM OR CIVIL RIGHTS?[25]

Chick-fil-A is an American fast food company selling fried chicken whose founder, S. Truett Cathy, and family members have very strong Christian values. The founder's son, in the position of President, was interviewed in the media and stated his Christian beliefs that a marriage is only between a man and a woman, not same sex partners. In an effort to expand his restaurants in Chicago, New York, Boston, and other areas, the younger Cathy found resistance by the mayors of Chicago, Boston, and San Francisco who announced their pledge to block any of these establishments the ability to conduct business in their respective cities.

In 2015, the Indiana and Arkansas governors supported legislation to allow businesses the right to refuse to serve clients, if it breached their religious beliefs. For example, if a gay couple wanted a wedding planner or cake bakery establishment for their wedding, these businesses could refuse to do so on religious freedom grounds. As a result of this legislation, companies such as Angie's list cited it would cancel its plans to expand its facilities in Indianapolis. In another case, several days before the N.C.A.A. men's basketball's Final Four were scheduled to play in Indianapolis, one of the college teams scheduled to play threatened to boycott attending the championship.

Additional facts for the case:
Assume a number of key players on your team threatened to boycott playing in the championship game and you are the President of the University. In addition, what if the Board of Trustees, who you report to, wants the team to attend since the prestige and potential increase in enrollment could lead to a major monetary boost for the college currently experiencing a financial crisis. In addition, presume further that the majority of the student population believes the boycott is warranted since it is a violation of civil rights. Complicating this matter is, many members of your Student Alumni Association, who give heavy donations to the college and have strong Christian beliefs, agree with the legislation, which they see as protecting one's religious beliefs.

DISCUSSION QUESTION

As the President of the University, what would you do? Using the seven-step Velasquez Model, and numbering each step, apply this method to your decision-making process.

ENDNOTES

[1] Douglas Birsch and John H. Fiedler (Eds.), *The Ford Pinto Case: A Study in Applied Ethics, Business, and Technology* (Albany: State University of New York, 1994), pp. 99, 100.

[2] Ibid., 100.

[3] Ibid., 101.

[4] Manuel Velasquez, Claire Andre, Thomas Shanks, S.J., and Michael J. Meyer, "Thinking Ethically: A Framework for Moral Decision Making," *Annual Editions: Business Ethics 2002/2003*, 14th ed., John E. Richardson, Ed. (Guilford, CT: McGraw-Hill/Dushkin, 2002), p. 2.

[5] Ibid.

[6] Ibid.

[7] Ibid., 2, 3.

[8] Ibid., 2.

[9] Ibid., 2, 3.

[10] Ibid., 4.

[11] Ibid.

[12] Ibid.

[13] Ibid.

[14] Ibid.

[15] Peter F. Drucker, *Management Challenges for the 21st Century* (New York: HarperCollins Publishers Inc., 1999), p. 176.

[16] *Business Ethics Program: Ethics Foundation Presentation* (St. Charles, IL:
Arthur Andersen and Company, SC, 1992), pp. 70-81.

[17] Francis Cullen, *Corporate Crime Under Attack: The Ford Pinto Case and
Beyond* (Cincinnati: Andersen, 1987), p. 161.

[18] Ibid.

[19] Ibid.

[20] John Rawls, *A Theory of Justice* (Cambridge, MA: Harvard University Press, 1999), p. 83.

[21] Manuel Velasquez, Claire Andre, Thomas Shanks, S.J., and Michael J. Meyer, "Thinking Ethically: A Framework for Moral Decision Making," *Annual Editions: Business Ethics 2002/2003*, 14th ed., John E. Richardson, Ed. (Guilford, CT: McGraw-Hill/Dushkin, 2002), pp. 77-78.

Please note: In the original Velasquez model, three ethical perspectives were applied, utilitarian, rights, and justice. The *utilitarian perspective* selects the alternative that produces the greatest good for the greatest number of individuals affected by the decision. The *rights perspective* chooses the alternative, which respects the most rights and duties of the individual stakeholders (as opposed to the aggregate) with the focus upon the present, not estimates of what they may occur in the future. The final ethical perspective, *justice*, examines the distributive consequences in terms of being fair and just. This step has been modified to emphasize the classical philosophers and the modern ethical philosophical theories that will require the decision maker to select the alternative that will benefit the *least advantaged* stakeholder affected by the final decision.

[22] Immanuel Kant, *The Metaphysics of Morals*, H.J. Patton, trans. (New York, Harper and Row, 1964), p. 88.

[23] Terrance Irwin and Gail Fine, trans*., Aristotle: Selections* (Indianapolis: Hackett Publishing Incorporated, 1995), p. 347.

[24] This case was rewritten based upon the following article: Rachel Abrams, "Walmart Vice President Forces Out for Lying About Degree," *The New York Times* , September 17, 2014, p. B3.

[25] This case was rewritten based upon the following articles: "Deep Fried Civil War: The Christian Values of Chick-fil-A's Founding Family Have Triggered a Backlash. They're also the Fast-Food Chain's Secret Sauce," *Business Week New York*, 4291, 2012, pp. 62-66, British Library Document Supply Centre Inside Serials & Conference Proceedings, EBSCO*host*, viewed 18 April; and Campbell Robertson and Richard Perez-Pena, "Bills on 'Religious Freedom' Upset Capitols in Two States," *The New York Times*, April 1, 2015, p. A14.

CHAPTER 7

ETHICAL WORKPLACE ISSUES

Outback waitress Megan Geller was fired for wearing a brightly colored bracelet with the motto, "Don't Tread On Me," affiliated with the Republican Tea Party, purchased by her mother; in Michigan four workers were fired for refusing to quit smoking during their off hours; a hotel in Atlantic City threatened to discharge any cocktail waitress who gained 10% over her baseline body weight; Google fired a worker for chronicling his daily life at the search-engine with too many details; and a CEO was fired for having consensual sex with his female subordinate.[1] Each of these situations brings up the question: Where do the rights of private citizens begin and the rights of employees end? On the other hand, when does an employer have the right to monitor employees' computers, determine when a manufacturing plant should be closed, or expect loyalty from employees? This chapter investigates the ethical issues in

the workplace from the viewpoints of employees and employers and will cover topics such as job discrimination in the workplace; privacy issues in the workplace; safety and health issues; abuses by employees; abuses by employers; unions and whistleblowing.

Job Discrimination in the Workplace

As an owner, there is the belief that the decision to hire, fire, promote, and determine compensation is an unalienable employer right. Yet, employees have rights as well, but when the rights of the employer conflict with the rights of the employee, it can become a legal or an ethical matter. This section will review some of these rights from the perspective of the employer and employee on issues such as hiring, terminating an employee, affirmative action, sexual harassment, comparable worth, the Americans with Disabilities Act, and workplace rankism.

HIRING POLICIES

As a general rule, employers have the right to hire employees who they believe are the best for their businesses. However, in certain cases if discrimination against a particular group appears to exist when hiring a given employee, the law may intervene. Under the law, employers do

© ProStockStudio/Shutterstock, Inc.

not have the right to discriminate against a particular race, age, gender, physical challenge, etc. if the individual is qualified to perform the duties required of the position. However, certain jobs allow employers to hire someone based upon looks (such as a modeling agency) or gender (hiring a female as a locker attendant at a health club in a women's locker room) since it is a bona fide occupational qualification which under the law allows employers the ability to discriminate against a potential applicant based upon the operation of the business or the essence of its business. As an aside, Hooters was sued by a group of men claiming gender discrimination because only women were hired; the case was unsuccessful.

Still, not every group is protected. For example, in 2015, thirty-two states still did not have laws protecting gays and lesbians from being discriminated against when applying for a job.[2] For example, Marty Edwards, a Texas Bank employee was fired, not because of his job performance but because of his sexual orientation. Comments by his employer included, "a guy who has three kids, a wife and white picket fence was a better fit for the image we are looking for," "I don't care if you are seeing Billy Graham as your counselor," and "You obviously have some things messed up in your head."[3] Even more disturbing was that Edwards needed the assistance of the American Civil Liberties Union, as no local attorney wanted to take the case.

Another type of discrimination is known as **lookism**, *discriminating against individuals because of their physical appearance*. Because only four jurisdictions nationwide—the state of Michigan, the District of Columbia, and the California cities of San Francisco and Santa Cruz—have ordinances against discrimination based on weight or appearance, applicants have few or no options if they are not hired because the employer discriminates against their physical appearance.[4] But, what if a candidate is not hired because of his weight? There have been some cases where applicants claimed they were discriminated against because their obesity was considered a physical disability and were protected under the Americans with Disabilities Act, although these types of cases were more of an exception than a rule.

LOOKISM
discriminating against an individual because of physical appearance.

Having a foreign accent is also another example of discrimination but applicants are protected under the Civil Rights Act which outlaws discrimination based upon an individual's national origin, even though one study found that 19% of employers surveyed discriminated against individuals who speak with an accent or appear "foreign."[5] Even religion plays a role in discrimination. Under the Civil Rights Act it is illegal to discriminate against hiring someone based upon their religion, including if they wear a religious headdress. There were two cases when a Chicago-based law firm and security firm would not hire Muslims because they wore a headdress, so they filed a complaint with the Equal Employment Opportunity Commission who in both cases ruled in their favor.[6] However, it should be pointed out that when it comes to accommodating an employee for religious reasons, employers are under less an obligation than if they were hiring someone under the Americans with Disabilities Act (which will be discussed later on in this chapter). Even though Title VII of the Civil Rights of 1964 bans religious discrimination in the workplace and requires employers to accommodate strictly held religious beliefs by the employees, it cannot overly burden the employer, which is why religious discrimination charges have gone to a record 2,880 in 2007 most likely due to the ambiguity of the law.[7]

The latest discrimination, which is due to scientific technology, revolved around genetic testing where employers are trying to claim that knowing a potential applicant has a predisposition for a certain illness, will affect their cost for providing health insurance to employees. However, the Genetic Information Nondiscrimination Act prohibits employers from asking for genetic tests or taking into account an employee's genetic background when hiring, firing, or promoting an employee.[8]

In a survey conducted by the Bureau of National Affairs, it was found that 52% of employers use medical or physical exams for screening purposes (but can experience potential legal problems under the Americans with Disabilities Act); 26% use drug testing; and 6% administer polygraph testing, which is illegal under the Polygraph Protection Act of 1988, although exceptions for polygraph testing include private employers who provide security services or employers of nuclear facilities, public water facilities, public transportation, shipment or storage of radioactive or toxic waste materials, or federal, state, and local governments, to name a few.[9] This becomes problematic when certain tests or requirements are used to discriminate against a certain group of people. This occurred in the 1971 *Griggs vs. Duke Power Company* Supreme Court case, when a high school diploma was required of all applicants but was shown during the court proceedings that this power company used the educational requirement purposely to eliminate the hiring of African Americans, many who at the time had not possessed such a diploma and did not need one to perform the job.

TERMINATIONS

Since the same laws that protect potential applicants from not being hired cover the same basic situations for terminations and promotions, only those cases that are more prevalent in the firing or termination of an employee will be discuss in this section. The first situation is the charge of pregnancy discrimination, even though it is protected under the Pregnancy Discrimination Act of 1978. Examples of companies accused of breaching this law include Wal-Mart for rejecting a pregnant job applicant; Verizon for terminating benefits for thousands of female workers during their maternity leaves; Delta Airlines for firing a pregnant ramp attendant and forcing another to take an unpaid leave; Spelling Entertainment, producer of the "Melrose Place," television series when they fired pregnant actress Hunter Tyler because they felt that she would be unable to play the role of a seductress. In one case, an Oregon woman sued her former employer for $400,000 when during her pregnancy, her employer felt that she was taking too many bathroom breaks.[10]

AGEISM *discrimination against an individual based upon age.*

Although discriminating against one's age is also illegal and is protected under the Age Discrimination in Employment Act (1967), **ageism** (*discrimination against an individual based upon age*) continues to exist. In Los Angeles, a sixty-six-year-old man successfully sued the office supply chain Staples for $26

© plkon_Grafix/Shutterstock, Inc.

million based upon the harassment and unwarranted firing due to ageism. For nine years, since being hired by Corporate Express, which was acquired by Staples, Bobby Dean Nickel received positive reviews and as a result, was on a higher pay scale than many of his younger fellow employees. In the lawsuit, Nickels claimed that he was called "old coot" and "old goat" and when approached to resign by a manager, he refused. Shortly after that, he was suspended for allegedly stealing a $0.68 bell pepper. Later on, a receptionist told Nickel that she was ordered by management to provide a false statement about Nickel's conduct but refused to do so. When he was fired, he took the case to court winning the largest verdict of its type in Los Angeles County's history.[11]

Although unethical, some companies will "layoff" their senior managers claiming new reorganization or downsizing, which often is difficult to prove since the real reason for discharging these "older" workers is due to ageism discrimination. Still it would behoove the company in the long run not to let go their senior executives since many are extremely knowledgeable and possess the experiential skills that their younger former colleagues may lack.

Another example of an alleged unethical firing was when Starbucks fired a barista, Daniel Gross, who was in the process of organizing a union on behalf of six Manhattan Starbucks but his employer claimed that he made a threatening remark to a district manager at a union rally.[12] Firing an employee for attempting to start a union is illegal under the Wagner Act of 1935, which will be discussed later in this chapter; however, it is up to the fired employee to prove that he was unjustly fired.

Yet, this is not the only time that a business fired an employee for activities outside of their employment. In 2005, Weyco Incorporated fired four employees for smoking, even though it was off the premises and not during their work hours, since Michigan is one of the twenty states that does not prohibit an employer for **lifestyle discrimination** (*discrimination against employees because of their personal leisure activities outside the work environment, which may include smoking or skydiving*).[13] But recently the courts seem to be reviewing when an employer has the right to fire an employee. Historically, businesses were protected under the common law known as **employment at will**, *where "the company may terminate any employee at any time for any reason,"* but there have been several cases when employees have claimed they were being discharged because they were members of a protected group (age, gender, race, etc.) and the onus was on the employer to prove otherwise.[14] It appears that the scales of justice are teetering between both the employer and employee contingent upon the case and that employers may not be as free to discharge employees as easily as they once had.

PROMOTIONS

Just as employees have been protected under the Civil Rights Acts from being unjustly fired or denied being hired, the laws concur with cases involving promotions, as well. But, although laws were established to prevent the unjust hiring and firing of employees, there have been some cases that were not as consistent when dealing with the denial of employees' promotions. In 2009, the Supreme Court ruled 5-4 against the City of New Haven when it discarded the rights of the promotion exams of the white firefighters who outscored their minority counterparts, and ordered the results to be valid.[15] Under Title VII of the Civil Rights Act, which bars discriminatory treatment, especially if it may be demonstrated that a particular test results in a discriminatory impact, the Supreme Court ruled that by using the original scores of the white firefighters, this was not acting against the intention of the law to protect minorities.[16] But the law does protect those who have been discriminated against as was the case of a former Queens-Midtown Tunnel employee who proved that due to his Jewish background, he was denied a promotion and was awarded $735,000 for emotional pain and punitive damages.[17] In another case, a female thirteen-year veteran of the

© The Cute Design Studio/Shutterstock, Inc.

Pennsylvania State Police scored sixth out of 2,000 test takers, was a member of MENSA, and despite an exemplary record, she was passed over for a promotion and filed a lawsuit where she had evidence of sexual harassment, as well.[18]

Even internationally, the law protects the physically challenged. For example, in 2009 Abercrombie and Fitch in London was ordered by a United Kingdom court to pay 9,000 British pounds to an employee, who as also a law student, with a prosthetic arm, who was placed in the stockroom because she did not fit its "look" policy.[19] Whether it be an unjust hiring, firing, or refusal to promote a qualified employee, employers must learn to follow the law and act as Kant stated, "in such a way that you always treat humanity, whether in your own person or in the person of another."[20]

AFFIRMATIVE ACTION

Affirmative Action *consists of policies that require the protection of certain groups (African American, Latinos, etc.) to be given a special opportunity to be hired or promoted in an effort to reverse past discriminatory practices which will now result in minorities being hired or promoted fairly.* Affirmative Action itself, began under President John F.

© iQoncept/Shutterstock, Inc.

Kennedy's 1961 Executive Order 10925, which created the President's Commission on Equal Employment Opportunity and progressed under President Lyndon B. Johnson who demanded that based upon flexible goals and timetables, Affirmative Action towards equal employment opportunity must be implemented after he signed the Civil Rights Act of 1964 and the Voting Rights Act of 1965.[21] As time passed, pressure was placed on any contractor who wanted to do business with the federal government if and only if they had a greater representation of African Americans in their labor pools. Later on this was extended to protected groups such as women, Latinos, etc.

However, some viewed this legislation as discrimination in reverse. In June 1978, Caucasian student Alan Bakke was denied admission to the University of California's Medical School at its Davis campus since there were some slots left open for minorities and he was denied admission because he was not a minority. Believing that he should have been admitted based upon his credentials, he sued, which led to his case being argued before the Supreme Court

© Iliana Mihaleva/Shutterstock, Inc.

who in a 5-4 majority vote found in favor of Alan Bakke, who was later admitted to the school because his rejection was proven to be race based.[22] In 2003, after being rejected six years earlier, a white Michigan resident, Barbara Grutter, who was denied from the University of Michigan's Law School, had her case argued before the Supreme Court which ruled in the law school's favor by a 5-4 vote, since race was not a primary factor in their selection of candidates; yet the undergraduate school who use raced as a factor, was found to be guilty of reverse discrimination against the plaintiff, Gratz. The Supreme Court ruled against the undergraduate school but not the law school for reverse discrimination (actually the president of the college, Lee Bollinger, was the defendant in both cases).[23] In a 2009 survey released by the Pew Research Center, only 31% believed that "we should make every effort to improve the position of African Americans and other minorities," while 65% were against such preferential treatment.

For the previous twenty-two years, during the time the survey was given, the response had minor fluctuations in the responses. Racially, those supporting Affirmative Action or similar type policies were as follows: African Americans (58%); Latinos (53%); and Caucasians (whites, 22%).[24] Given the dichotomy of public opinion, Affirmative Action policies will be contested for a while, yet if those hiring or promoting individuals did so based upon their qualifications and performance and had done so historically, perhaps there would be no need for Affirmative Action policies in the future.

Sexual Harassment

According to the Equal Employment Opportunity Commission, sexual harassment is defined as "unwelcome sexual advances, requests for sexual favors and other verbal and physical conduct of a sexual nature when: (1) submission to such conduct is made either explicitly or implicitly a term or condition of an individual's employment; (2) submission to or rejection of such conduct by an individual is used as a basis for employment decisions affecting such individual; or (3) such conduct has the purpose or effect of unreasonably interfering with an individual's work performance or creating an intimidating, hostile or offensive environment."[25]

© Photographee.eu/Shutterstock, Inc.

In 1996, one of the largest sexual harassment lawsuits recorded under the 1991 Civil Rights Act was against Mitsubishi Motor Manufacturing of America where as many as 700 women were subjected to sexual remarks, as well as groping and having sexual graffiti placed on the wall which had created a hostile and abusive work environment, and had not been rectified by upper management for years. A year later, Mitsubishi Motors Corporation settled the lawsuit with twenty-seven women promising to donate $100,000 to women's causes in the Bloomington-Normal area, and would pay $9.5 million to the plaintiffs where some were to have reported receiving as much as $500,000 individually.[26] This settlement was second to Del Laboratories of Farmingdale, Long Island (New York) when $1.85 million was paid out to plaintiffs for the behavior of their chief executive officer accused of engaging in lewd and abusive behavior (for years).[27]

In another case, Ellen Pao, a Harvard School graduate from the venture capitalist firm of Kleiner Perkins Caufield & Byers brought forth a lawsuit when fired for what she called was sexual harassment. Feeling pressured to intimately date a married co-worker, Pao found herself, after breaking off the relationship, being accused of poor performance, after experiencing a hostile environment where she was excluded from certain meetings and company trips. Pao alleged that the men in the firm treated her differently and although lost the case, exposed the double standard experienced by her and many of her colleagues.[28]

However, women are not the only victims of sexual harassment; in 1993, a California Superior Court awarded a former male manager of a spa manufacturing company more than $1 million when he sued his former female supervisor claiming that she had sexually harassed him daily on the job for six years.[29] Although it has been estimated that approximately less than 10% of all sexual harassment complaints are filed by men, and most involve males harassing other males, with more females entering the executive suite, men can be subjected to sexual harassment as well.

In order to prevent sexual harassment, most companies now have anti-sexual harassment company policies in their employee handbooks, which also reduce most liabilities in case they are sued. In addition, companies have ongoing sexual harassment workshops as part of their training and development programs. Given some of the ambiguities of the requirements of employers to prevent exposure from potential sexual harassment lawsuits, in 1998 the Supreme Court ruled that if a company had an anti-sexual harassment policy with a set of procedures for an individual who is being sexually harassed, if the (victim) employee does not follow this policy, the employer may not be liable.[30] Furthermore, it found that if an employee resists the advances of a supervisor, that person does not have to suffer any tangible job detriment, such as being discharged or passed over for a promotion, to be able to institute a lawsuit against the company.[31] For this reason, employers must make sure that they do everything possible to establish a sexually hostile–free environment for their employees.

COMPARABLE WORTH

Comparable worth, *also known as pay equity, is a broad term for a range of policies developed to reduce the pay gap between occupations traditionally filled by women.*[32] Under the Equal Pay Act of 1963, and later under Title VII of the Civil Rights Act of 1964, Congress prohibited pay inequities for equal work, which included any attempt by an employer to circumvent this law by assigning different job titles to male and female

COMPARABLE WORTH
also known as pay equity, a broad term for a range of policies developed to reduce the pay gap between occupations traditionally filled by women.

© PathDoc/Shutterstock, Inc.

employees for the same work.[33] In 1970, the American Can Company was found to have discriminated against its female machine operators, by paying them $0.20 an hour less than their male counterparts who were operating the same machinery under the landmark case *Shultz v. Wheaton Glass*.[34]

In 1992, Teresa Ellison of the United States Marshall Service issued a claim that she was denied a promotion that would have enabled her to earn the same salary as her male co-workers only because of her gender and this was an attempt to deny her equitable pay resulting in the court finding in her favor.[35] This was one example of a breach of comparable worth which appears to discriminate primarily against women in the workplace. One of the greater challenges is proving that an individual is not receiving comparable worth, since the burden of proof is generally on the plaintiff, who must prove that he or she was denied the same pay for equivalent work. Unfortunately, there are so many nuances in job responsibilities, activities, and even hours worked, that it is very difficult to prove an organization is not complying with the comparable worth doctrine.

However, there have been several cases in which female plaintiffs have been extremely successful. In 2004, Boeing Company agreed to a pay $72.5 million settlement to 29,000 current and former female employees who proved that they were paid $1,000 to $2,000 less than their fellow male workers and that men were more likely to be promoted than women.[36] In fact, in that same year, Morgan Stanley, an investment securities firm, settled a case by paying $54 million to a few hundred female employees for a sex discrimination case, seven years after Home Depot settled a sex discrimination class action for $104 million, all based upon comparable worth situations.[37] Besides being unethical, not complying with equal pay rates for the equivalent work is costly to the business in terms of finances and reputation.

As a result of this pay inequity, women find themselves being plagued by a **glass ceiling**, *a term defining the inability of women to be promoted into the executive suite compared to their male co-workers*. In 2015, there were twenty-five female CEOs listed in the Standard and Poor's (S&P) 500 Companies, representing 5.0% of all chief executives. In terms of women in other executive positions in the S&P 500 of the total positions, women represent: 19.6% of the Board of Director positions; 25.1% senior level positions; 36.8% midlevel positions; but 45% of the entire workforce.[38] In addition, women have earned less than eighty cents for every dollar a man has earned, which also demonstrates a breach of comparable worth in the business world against women. Efforts must be made by businesses to rectify these inequities.

AMERICANS WITH DISABILITIES ACT

In 2009, Sears Roebuck agreed to settle a case under the Americans with Disabilities Act for $6.2 million for allegedly firing employees instead of providing reasonable accommodations.[39] Four years earlier, in a 5-4 decision, the United States Supreme Court expanded the landmark Americans with Disabilities Act to apply to cruise lines including foreign cruise lines sailing in U.S. waters and ordered them to provide better access for passengers in wheelchairs, even though it costs the cruise lines millions of dollars.[40] In that same year, a federal jury found that Wal-Mart had discriminated against a Long Island, New York, man who had cerebral palsy and applied for a position in their pharmacy department, but when his job responsibilities were changed to do activities such as collecting garbage and shopping carts from the parking lot, he quit.[41] As a

result of a federal court decision, the plaintiff, Patrick Brady, was awarded $7.5 million because the jury believed Wal-Mart created a "hostile environment," and discriminated against him because of his physical challenge.[42]

With the advent of the American Disabilities Act of 1992 which requires all public buildings to be accessible to handicapped people, with wider doorways, restrooms,

© Francesco83/Shutterstock, Inc.

telephones, drinking fountains, elevators, and full access for wheelchairs, in addition to reasonably accommodating employees in the workplace, employers have been faced with many new challenges in order to comply with this federal law.[43] Complicating these challenges further is that the courts seem to be unclear as to the intention of the Americans with Disabilities Act. In 2002, a New Jersey Supreme Court found that Regina Viscik, weighing nearly 400 pounds, was disabled under the state's Law Against Discrimination, which extended the definition of disability beyond the federal guidelines, and ruled that because she was dismissed as if she had a physical disability, which her physician claimed was a metabolic disorder, she was protected under the state's discrimination laws.[44] Although this was a state ruling there have been many documented cases where out-of-court settlements have resulted for individuals using the Americans with Disabilities Act for overweight individuals because they have been discriminated against. If employers would not discriminate against individuals because of their weight, in the same way they should not discriminate against others because of their race, gender, age, etc., less time would be spent in court or with attorneys.

Privacy Issues in the Workplace

As discussed in the chapter's opening paragraph, employees believe that under the Fourth Amendment of the Constitution, they are protected against any illegal searches, which guarantees privacy in the workplace. However, this may or may not be true given the courts have not quite caught up with modern technology. For example, does an employee expect a degree of privacy when on the computer at work? Can an employer be fired for her actions when not at the workplace? May an employer use technology to predict your character or physical deficiencies prior to your hiring?

© JoeBakal/Shutterstock, Inc.

These questions challenge the moral fiber of an employee's right in the workplace, but also the rights of employers to monitor their employees to ensure that they will be acting in an ethical and productive manner.

The law generally follows the "employment at will" philosophy in many cases, despite the Fourteenth Amendment of legal searches, which means employers usually have the right to monitor their employees. For example, in 2006, there were over 6,000 companies with a ban on hiring smokers, including Turner Broadcasting System, Union Pacific, Alaska Airlines, and Schweitzer Engineering Laboratories.[45] More than thirty states prohibit an employer from discriminating against employees or applicants if they smoke. In some states, the law prohibits making it illegal for an employer to fire an employee for "lifestyle discrimination" for activities conducted away from the workplace, such as smoking, political activities, etc. One such state is New York where under Labor Law Section 201-d it is illegal to fire someone based upon lifestyle discrimination. Yet, in states such as Michigan, they are free to even fire their current employees from smoking, as discussed at the beginning of this chapter.

In 1996, a grocery store worker in Dallas was fired for wearing a Green Bay Packers t-shirt to work on the day before a Dallas Cowboys–Green Bay Packers football game, because in Texas at that time it was legal for an employer to do so.[46] Although this ruling was an extreme, the law does favor employers when it deals with employees using company equipment, including computers. Generally, the courts have ruled that employers have the right to monitor employees' email communications on company time.[47] For example, in 2006 and 2007, a NASA employee in Houston was found using his government email account for organizing activities for a political group, and made blog postings from work to promote his candidate and was suspended for 180 days without pay when his employer used a 1939 law (Hatch Act) which limited government workers from political activities, especially on the job.[48] In another case, *Hernandez v. Hillsides* (No.S147552, Supreme Court of California, 2009), the California Supreme Court ruled with regards to video camera surveillance, that although employees have an expectation of privacy in the workplace, the employer has the right under limited circumstances to breach those rights.[49] The courts found that in this case, an employee had used the company's computer to visit a pornographic website at a residential non-profit center for abused and neglected children, and the video surveillance was used to protect the rights of these children, which superseded the privacy of the employees.

But, the courts will also protect employees. In 1987, New York State's Court of Appeals, the highest court in the state, ruled that it was illegal to require its public school teachers to take random drug tests unless there was a "reasonable suspicion" that the test was warranted.[50] Another example of employee privacy rights is with genetic information that identifies certain predispositions to a particular disease or propensity for a particular mental disorder. However, some companies feel that although this may be legal, since the courts have not yet concurred given that this process is fairly new, it may be an invasion of privacy. Yet, International Business Machines (IBM), is promising not to use any genetic information in hiring or in determining eligibility for an employee's health care or benefits plan nor will it use this genetic data when hiring potential employees.[51] It is believed that IBM is the first by any major corporation to make such a pledge, which will affect more than 300,000 of its employees worldwide.[52]

From an ethical viewpoint, employers should protect the privacy rights of their employees but also must be protective of their businesses, as well as their clients, in case they have some unscrupulous employees. One way of clarifying the expectations of the employers and at the same time informing their employees of the privacy rights which they may or may not expect at the workplace is by including these employee privacy rights in their employee handbooks. By doing this, although it may not guarantee being exempt from any lawsuit as a result of an employee who believes his or her privacy rights have been invaded, it will clarify these rights for the employees and may possibly diminish lawsuits.

Safety and Health Issues

Although every employee has the right to safe working conditions, to what extent should the responsibility be placed on the worker, as well

as the employer? In one study by DuPont Company it was found that 96% of the accidents that occurred were the result of employee negligence rather than unsafe working conditions.[53] For example, workers would lift more than they were capable of doing or not use proper techniques for doing so. Still, the number of situations where employers breach safety regulations appears to be greater than the employees who are negligent of the job.

For example, the Occupational Safety and Health Administration (OSHA) found in their annual studies that employers underreport work-related injuries and illnesses to avoid increased workers' compensation costs.[54] Also, workers would not report job-related injuries to avoid losing rewards like bonuses or steak dinners as part of safety-based incentive programs, which some companies found in their research.[55] Evidently, employers may be just as responsible for the accidents as their employees, or more so.

One situation that demonstrates the employer's responsibility for unsafe working conditions is the abuse of foreign or illegal immigrants, by some employers who threaten their employees with deportation or firing, which will result in these workers to be less likely to file any safety infractions experienced on the job. Taking advantage of the undocumented or immigrants who have newly arrived to the United States, is a prevalent practice by some employers. But, these immigrants are not the only ones working in unsafe conditions.

In one nationwide study of over 117,000 people and 500 working sites, 73% were placed in hazardous conditions when digging ditches, working with chemicals, or roofing work, with little if any safety training.[56] In this same study, researcher professors Nik Theodore from the University from the Illinois in Chicago and Able Valenzuela Jr. from the University of California in Los Angeles found that one fifth interviewed had suffered injuries requiring medical attention, where 60% missed more than one week of work as a result of these injuries.[57]

Unfortunately, there have been several examples of tragedies occurring as a result of unsafe working conditions. In 2008, there was a fire at a sugar refinery, the Imperial Sugar Company near Savannah, Georgia, which resulted in fourteen deaths and thirty-six injuries.[58] The Chemical Safety Board blamed inadequate equipment design, poor maintenance, and ineffective housekeeping for the explosion, which if rectified may have averted this tragedy.[59] In 2009, the Occupational Safety and Health Administration fined BP (oil company) $87 million for a 2005 explosion, which killed fifteen workers, and was linked to extreme cost-cutting on safety, antiquated equipment, and undue production pressures.[60] Some employees worked twelve hours a day for twenty-nine straight days.[61] It is the responsibility of each employer to safeguard employees from being exposed to unsanitary or unsafe working conditions. Unfortunately, since not every employer is motivated by the safety of the employees, but rather profits yielded from these employees, there is a governmental agency established to protect employees from unsafe working conditions, called the Occupational Safety and Health Administration (OSHA).

OSHA was established in 1970, under the Occupational Safety and Health Act within the Department of Labor to ensure safe working conditions for every employee in the country except for those who work in mines since they are covered under the Mine Safety and Health Act of 1977.[62] **OSHA**'s *purpose is develop standards, issue regulations, conduct inspections, and issue citations to ensure the safety and health of all workers.* As a result of OSHA, work-related accidents have decreased markedly and the health conditions of workers have been improved since its inception.

The last health-related issue to be discussed is the rights of gays and lesbians to have domestic partnership benefits. **Domestic partnership benefits** *are when gay or lesbians have long-term partnerships, are living together, and can have health insurance for their partners through their partner's company.* Although many companies provide coverage for the spouses of married couples, or give the employees an option of paying for their spouses' premiums, there are no federal laws mandating that gays or lesbians have the same rights as heterosexuals. In 2008, the

OSHA
under the Occupational Safety and Health Act of 1970, OSHA's purpose is to develop standards, issue regulations, conduct inspections, and issue citations to ensure the safety and health of all workers.

DOMESTIC PARTNERSHIP BENEFITS: *are when primarily gay or lesbians have long-term partnerships, are living together, and can have health insurance for their partners through their partner's company.*

Human Rights Campaign, a non-profit organization dedicated to gays, lesbians, bisexuals, and transgenders, studied 590 corporations finding that almost 94% offered domestic partnership benefits, but since it was not required by law, firms such as ExxonMobil did not extend these benefits to their employees.[63]

Abuses by Employees

Up to this point the topics presented were largely concentrated on the unethical practices of employers with regard to discrimination and health and safety conditions; however, in all fairness, employees can also conduct business in an unethical manner. The main areas to be discussed in this section are trade secrets, misuse of funds, insider trading, executive compensation, and bribes.

TRADE SECRETS

One obligation as an employee is not to give proprietary information (trade secrets) to any other competitor. However, not all employees abide by this ethical obligation, even if most employers require their employees to sign statements that prohibit the revelation of trade secrets to another employer or to use personally. For example, in 2006, a former Ford Motor Company engineer was charged with stealing trade secrets after accepting a job in China and was found also having access to a protected computer from his former employer when arrested at Chicago's O'Hare Airport after traveling to the United States from China.[64] In another case, an advisor from Tourakji Capital Management was being sued by Amaranith for $350 million for breach of contract, fraud, and misappropriation of trade secrets when he allegedly used confidential information about the company's trading strategy and its financial position, despite signing a confidentiality contract.[65] Although the suit eventually was dropped, the ethics of the defendant brings up another ethical obligation by an employee—and this is being loyal to the client.

Yet, this not only happens for product trade secrets, but it can also extend to using databases containing customers and vendor lists. A former employee of Gibraltar Metals was hired by its competitor, Spectrum

Metals Incorporated, and was concerned that this employee would use confidential information including customer and vendor database lists and trade secrets against him (Gibraltar) that it petitioned for an injunction to prevent this information from being used.[66] Employees have an obligation to be loyal to their employers even if they no longer work for them. Included in this obligation is that it should be understood that if an employee uses company time or property to develop a patent, copyright, etc., if it is not agreed to by the employer, generally it can become the property of that employer.

MISUSE OF FUNDS

Although using the funds of the business personally is illegal, there appears not only to be lower level employees being accused of this action, but also upper level executives. In 2006, the president and CEO of Amtel Corporation, who was its founder, and the executive vice president were fired after an internal investigation found that they misused corporate travel funds.[67] A year earlier, Tom Coughlin, former Vice Chairman of Wal-Mart Stores, was under investigation by a federal grand jury for the misuse of company cards and fake expense accounts which covered the purchase of "snake boots, an XM radio, truck accessories, and airplane tickets."[68] He resigned after finding out about the impending investigation.

Yet, even if a subordinate is not the one who may be using the funds, an executive is still responsible for the actions of his subordinates, as was the case of Germany's Peter Hartz, VW's Director of Personnel. Hartz stepped down after it was found that while under his command, workers' representatives misused funds when they "procured prostitutes" and had arranged luxury foreign travel for employees who were member of VW's supervisory board.[69] But, perhaps the most famous case was that of former Tyco International Ltd. Chief Executive Dennis Kozlowski and Finance Chief Mark Swartz who were found guilty and faced 25 years in prison for stealing more than $150 million by secretly taking loans and unauthorized bonuses from the company.[70]

Even small businesses are not immune from unscrupulous behavior of their employees. Many years ago, in New Haven, Connecticut, at a small family business jewelry store, the bookkeeper noticed a few irregularities between the cash receipts and accounts receivables (cash due the business from customers who did not pay cash but charged their purchases on account). After her son, who earned an M.B.A. in Finance from the Wharton School of Business (University of Pennsylvania) conducted an audit, it was revealed that their accountant had been embezzling funds from their company over several years in the neighborhood over $100,000 which was a large amount at that time. The results were that this accountant, in order to avoid criminal prosecution, had to sell his home as well as lose his job.

INSIDER TRADING

Insider trading is *"illegal trading in securities by individuals or firms possessing non-public information."*[71] As an example of this type of transaction, suppose a stockbroker tells her spouse that a company will be merging tomorrow, which will result in a higher market price for the stock, which currently is selling at $100 for each share. If the spouse buys it at $100, and then sells it the following week for a $150, the person who it was sold to is paying $50 more because he lacked this type of inside information. From an ethical viewpoint, this can be seen as an unfair advantage for the unsuspecting buyer. Conversely, if someone owns stock and has inside information that an impending lawsuit will be settled causing the stock price to drop, an individual having this information can sell it before the price drops to someone lacking this knowledge resulting in the possession of stock which has lost its value, and who did not have the advantage of selling the stock before the price dropped, like the inside trader.

© ary yim/Shutterstock, Inc.

Perhaps the most well-publicized insider trading case was Martha Stewart. She sold stock from ImClone Systems as a result of allegedly obtaining non-public information from her stock broker, which she denied. In 2006, Martha Stewart agreed to pay $195,000 in fines and penalties and will not serve as a director or chief executive officer for any public company for a five-year period.[72] Martha Stewart was sentenced to five months in prison and five months of home confinement for lying to federal investigators about her alleged insider trading actions, which were never proven.[73] It was believed that information to be publicly announced the following day, which would have resulted in the lowering of the stock, immediately was told indirectly to Stewart who sold her stock before the official announcement was to be released.

EXECUTIVE COMPENSATION

Several studies have shown that incentives to remove moral decision making results in its citizens asking, What is in my best interest?[74] For example, in one study by two college professors it was revealed that at one Israeli day care center, if parents were fined for being late, the frequency of lateness increased.[75] Executives find themselves in the same position. They ask, What must be done to give the impression that my company's stock price is higher or profits greater than they actually are, so I may be compensated as a result of this perception? In essence, many executives will do whatever is necessary to justify their compensation.

One such situation that angered most taxpayers occurred in 2009, when the American International Group, which received more than $170 billion in taxpayer bailout money from the Treasury and Federal Reserve, planned to pay out about $165 million in bonuses to 400 of its executives.[76] In another case, former Chief Executive John Thain of Bank of America was forced out after lavishly spending on renovations to his office and giving several huge bonuses to his Merrill employees after his company lost billions of dollars.[77] Yet in 2010, he was appointed the Chairperson and CEO of CIT Group earning $500,000 in base salary and $5.5+ million worth of restricted stock which is less than he has made in many years.[78]

In 2010, Congress passed legislation, the Dodd-Frank Act, whereby a company must publically disclose its CEO ratio (comparing what a CEO is paid to a typical employee). This was based upon the median compensation of all employees at the point where half of them earn more and half earn less, and then compared this median with the amount awarded to the chief executive officer. For example, in March 2015, Disney's Robert Iger earned 2,238 times the median compensation for all employees with his

$43.7 million paid compensation; Starbucks' Howard Schultz's $21.5 million resulted in a 1,073 to 1 pay ratio; and Oracle's Lawrence Ellison earned $67 million which was a 1,183 to 1 pay ratio.[79].

When Ben and Jerry began their ice cream business they believed that no one in the company in the highest position should earn more than seven times the amount of anyone in the lowest position. Although the management has changed hands, and this no longer applies, it brings up the question, When is an executive's compensation too much? If we return to Aristotle's virtue of character and "mean," which denoted having neither excess nor deficiency, would he not agree that our contemporary executives are being overly compensated based upon their performance?

BRIBERY

Robert Watson, a Kraft Foods purchaser, needed $20,000 to pay his taxes so he called a California tomato processor who had been paying Watson bribes for years, as a way to get his products into Kraft's plants.[80] A few days later, federal agents arrested him and other purchasing agents.[81] One question to consider would be, If *bribery* was a factor in selecting a supplier, could it compromise the health and safety of consumers who are purchasing these foods?

© Alexander Raths/Shutterstock, Inc.

According to the *Bloomsbury Business Library Business and Management Dictionary*, **bribery** *is the act of persuading somebody to exercise his or her business judgment in one's favor by offering cash or a gift and thereby gaining an unfair advantage.* The reason this is considered unethical is because the motivation to make a decision may be based upon the gift or cash received as opposed to selecting the action that would best benefit the organization represented by the individual taking the bribe.[82]

BRIBERY

the act of persuading somebody to exercise his or her business judgment in one's favor by offering cash or a gift and thereby gaining an unfair advantage.

One of the most controversial bribery cases involved the Justice Department's investigation into whether Blackwater Worldwide tried to bribe Iraqi government officials in order to retain the firm's security work in Iraq. According to the *New York Times*, top executives authorized secret payments of about $1 million to Iraqi officials to buy support after Blackwater security guards fatally shot seventeen Iraqi civilians.[83] In 2010, the Justice Department was considering prosecuting the individual executives rather than getting companies to pay large fines, which could potentially result in jail time, even though it was not established at the time that the Iraq actually accepted any bribes.[84] This new legal strategy on behalf of the courts to prosecute employees personally both civilly and criminally demonstrated the gravity of bribery and why consumers are directly affected by this unethical behavior.

Abuses by Employers

In a 2010 study by the U.S. Conference Board, it was reported that only 45% of the employees surveyed were satisfied with their job compared to 61% in 1987, when it was first conducted.[85] Although it is believed that the uncertainty of the economy at the time the survey was conducted could be attributed to this sentiment, there may be other factors worth examining which just as equally may be a factor in this revelation. This section will examine some of the abuses conducted by employers which may also have led to this job dissatisfaction. They include outsourcing, plant closings, independent contractors, workplace rankism, and nepotism.

OUTSOURCING

INFORMATICS
optically scanned paper transferred to computer screens where a distance away the relevant information is keyed in and then digitized material speedily returned to the home office.

Between 2006 and 2007, IBM added 10,000 jobs in India.[86] In 1997, one person in fifty living in Barbados was working in the field of **informatics,** *where optically scanned paper is transferred to computer screens a distance away, the relevant information is keyed in, and then digitized material is speedily returned to the home office.*[87] However, the distance away may be hundreds or thousands of miles in countries such as Barbados, Grenada, Mexico, and China. In terms of hourly wages, workers are compensated between $2-$2.88 in Barbados; $1.26-$2.10 in Grenada, Mexico, and China; and by outsourcing, the informatics

© ChristianChan/Shutterstock, Inc.

pay scales in these developing countries range from one half to less than a tenth of the rates earned in the United States.[88] Hewitt Associates had conducted research on this topic and found that more than one half of the Fortune 500 companies are outsourcing their work.[89] Given the pressure of businesses to reduce costs, especially salaries, health benefits, and other perks, the number of outsourced employees is likely to increase in the future, as well.

Yet, many ethical questions have arisen as a result of companies outsourcing their work. First, in terms of national support, to what extent should business owners have to consider allegiance to their countries and maintain a domestic employment base? Are companies more responsible to their stockholders to cut costs or increasing the national unemployment, if they elect outsourcing as an option? By paying lower than minimum wages to foreign employees are they not exploiting the outsourced workers? These questions have several facets and cannot be answered easily, but do bring up issues that executives should consider before outsourcing their work.

In addition, to the issues raised above, outsourced workers due to the workload demanded upon them by their employers, have been found to be suffering from obesity, sleep disorders, depression, broken relationship problems, and other stress-related conditions in countries where public health care systems may be minimal and in the long run could result in a health crisis in the country where the outsourced workers are employed.[90] On the other hand, opponents against those criticizing outsourcing point out that in a capitalistic society, where competition is a characteristic of such an economic system, if U.S. employees would accept lower wages and were just as productive, these positions would not be outsourced. Although this debate will not likely be settled in the near future, it does behoove business owners and corporate executives to weigh all these factors before making the final decision to outsource their work.

PLANT CLOSINGS

On July 8, 2009 a temporary worker was killed after he slipped and fell into an eight-foot deep vat of liquid chocolate in Camden, New Jersey, working there for only two weeks, as a result of a layoff by Hershey Company who outsourced all of its production to new facilities in Mexico, after closing its Pennsylvania plant.[91] This tragic death demonstrated the desperation that this employee must have experienced in order to take a temporary position which involved using machinery that he was unfamiliar with, just to be employed. Yet, many analysts believe as technology and globalization have accelerated, workers have experienced permanent job losses due to plant closings, automation, and outsourcing.[92]

However, not all employers will shut down their plants, even if it is the easiest action to take. After a fire burned down his plant, one

© ChristianChan/Shutterstock, Inc.

Massachusetts owner decided to pay his employees for the three months it would take to rebuild his factory rather than outsourcing the work or just retiring with the insurance money which he would have received for the fire.[93] This owner demonstrated how considering people before profits was his priority.

Sometimes, an owner does not have a choice. Such was the case of a business called Jabil Circuit Incorporated in which the owner had to close his plant and lay off more than 300 workers in 2009. However, the owner set up a state career center at his plant, donated computers and printers, and assisted the employees to be laid off in finding jobs before closing the plant.[94] In one plant closing planned for June 2010, it was estimated that for every $10,000 a person earned in salary, it will take that long to find a new job.[95] So, if a person is earning $50,000, it can take five months before being hired. One general rule of the economy is that for every $1 a person earns for payroll, it goes through an area (business community) seven times, which economists term the multiplier effect.[96] So, this person may no longer go to Starbucks for a $3 cup of coffee, Starbucks will order $1 less in coffee cups from its supplier, who may cut back on purchasing $2 of electricity, etc. until $7 is reached. Collectively if an individual loses a salary of $100,000, the business community may lose the equivalent of $700,000. For this reason, it may behoove an owner to consider the adverse financial effects on the community, and not just the personal profits of the owner. Many stakeholders are affected by a decision to close a business and therefore the effects beyond the owners should be heavily weighed.

INDEPENDENT CONTRACTORS

A recent trend to avoid costs attributed to health and other employee benefits is for firms not to hire employees permanently but to assign them roles as independent contractors. One example of this is FedEx who now treats 12,000 package deliverers as independent contractors.[97] As a result of this action, the attorney generals of New York, New Jersey, and Montana threatened to sue FedEx unless they would reclassify them, so the states can then collect millions of dollars due them in payroll taxes, besides the fact that these independent contractors deserve fringe benefits

which they would have received if they were full-time employees.[98] Although the government has not released any figures, the U.S. Government Accounting Office estimates that misclassification resulted in the underpayment of over $2.5 billion in Social Security taxes, unemployment insurance, and income taxes annually.[99] In one case, Microsoft reached a settlement with the Internal Revenue Service for approximately $96.9 million for misclassifying its workers as independent contractors.[100] However, it should be pointed out that employers can save as much as 30% on payroll costs which allows them to undercut their competition. [103]

INDEPENDENT CONTRACTORS *individuals who work for themselves and are exempt from overtime, fringe benefits, ability to join a union, and are responsible for paying any required taxes which normally are paid by employers, such as Social Security taxes.*

A definition of an **independent contractor** *is, anyone who is "in business for themselves. They cannot unionize and are exempt from overtime and minimum-wage protections. If they are injured on the job, they pay their own bills if they have not paid their own workers' compensation premiums. They are hired to carry out specific tasks. Their work is closely supervised, they cannot take other jobs and the boss decides where, when and for long they work."*[102] Employers appear to have been left with determining whether classifying an employee as an independent contractor is an exploitation of a potential employee and an obfuscation of abiding with the required taxes traditionally paid by employers or whether they are being fiscally responsible by reducing the costs attached to a larger, permanent workforce.

WORKPLACE RANKISM

WORKPLACE RANKISM *when a superior abuses his/her power at the expense of subordinates.*

Rankism according to former Oberlin President Robert Fuller is "abuse of power associated with rank."[103] **Workplace rankism** *is when a superior abuses his/her power at the expense of subordinates.* Whether it is subtle or overt, the effects on its workers leads to depression, increased absences, loss of productivity, low self-esteem, and low employee moral, which are just a few negative consequences.

© Antonmaria Galante/Shutterstock, Inc.

Britain's Trade Union Congress conducted a survey in 2000 of 5,300 public, private, and voluntary sector employees, and discovered that workplace bullying (a more overt form of workplace rankism) contributed to the loss of 18 million working days annually; bullied workers take an average of seven days a week off more than those not bullied; more than 47% of British employees reported that they witnessed bullying at their workplace; and 10.5% claimed that they had been bullied within the last six months of the survey.[104] In Sweden, there were even reports that bullying led to 10% to 15% of all suicides and that in Japan in an effort to force employees to resign during the downsizing of several firms, superiors bullied their subordinates to voluntarily leaver their companies which resulted in record levels of suicide, as well.[105]

According to the Washington State Department of Labor and Industries sometimes *"bullying is entrenched in an organization and becomes accepted as part of the workplace culture,"* which has been termed **institutional or corporate bullying**.[106] What makes bullying so prevalent is that although it is a form of discrimination, unless the discrimination is against an employee because of age, race, religion, gender, etc., workplace rankism is not illegal. Therefore, it is up to the employer to ensure that bullying and workplace rankism in the workplace are not tolerated and

INSTITUTIONAL OR CORPORATE BULLYING *when bullying is entrenched in an organization and becomes accepted as part of the workplace culture.*

that the institutional or the corporate culture objects to such behavior. If bullying or workplace rankism is shown to be unacceptable as practiced by management from the top down, and if an anti-bullying or anti-rankism at work was a corporate policy found in the mission of the organization as well as the employee manual, it could be reduced or perhaps even eliminated from the workplace. Robert Fuller, who coined the term *rankism*, stated, "great companies have CEOs who demand all their subordinates treat their subordinates with dignity."[107] Perhaps this should be worth noting for all CEOs.

NEPOTISM

From 1994 to 2008, a Manhattan real estate company owned by Stephen Green gave millions of dollars in business to various companies owned by his chairman, Gary, who was his son; in that same year Michael Dell spent $155 million to buy MessageOne, a company owned by his brother, Adam Dell, and from 2005 to 2008, Best Buy purchased almost $80 million in fixtures from a company owned by the brother of a former Best Buy CEO and chairperson.[108] *This process of favoritism to relatives, especially in appointments to desirable positions, is called* **nepotism**.

NEPOTISM
the process of favoritism to relatives, especially in appointments to desirable positions.

However, there are two sides of the question—Is nepotism bad for business? Sometimes, knowing an individual will result in competence and loyalty beyond that of an individual who is not a family member or friend. Family members or friends will many times work beyond the required hours or may be asked to accept lower wages during difficult economic times or take on responsibilities or tasks beyond the scope of their position. On the other hand, friends and family can take advantage of the owners since they have the advantage of lineage or friendship over the other employees, or there may be a perception of favoritism, even if it does not exist, by other employees which can reduce the morale of the workplace. The most grievous situation

© lculig/Shutterstock, Inc.

is when only friends or family members are promoted, which gives the message to others that neither their (non family members') productivity nor loyalty matters. Perhaps, the best approach is to either have an anti-nepotism policy or have a balance in hiring or promoting friends or family members and "outsiders," as well.

Unions

Although there were several attempts to organize unions, ruthless corporate owners made it extremely difficult for employees to demand fair wages, safe working conditions, and benefits. The first act supporting unions was the Norris-La Guardia Act of 1932, which limited the use of court injunctions to stop strikes, allowed unions to organize, and made it easier to picket, which is "the act of patrolling a place of work affected by a strike in order to discourage its patronage, to make the public the workers' grievances, and in some cases to prevent strikebreakers from taking the strikers' jobs."[109] The second act supporting unions was the Wagner Act of 1935, also known as the National Labor Relations Act. Its provisions entitled all workers employed in industries engaged in interstate commerce to have the right to select their own union to bargain

Raise?

© Imilian/Shutterstock, Inc.

on their behalf (called collective bargaining); the union that won as a result of a secret ballot was to be given sole bargaining privileges in that industry; employers to be required to recognize the elected union and bargain in good faith, and lastly, the National Labor Relations Board to be granted the power to ensure fair practices and gave them the status as an independent agency to ensure that the provisions of this act would be followed.[110]

In 1947, the Taft-Hartley Act was signed which limited some of the provisions of the Wagner Act. These included: the government could obtain an eighty-day injunction against a strike if it believed that the national health or safety would be compromised; prohibiting strikes if two unions were in dispute over who should act as the bargaining agent; outlawing the closed shop; permitting only the union shop if the majority of employees voted for it; and outlawing striking just because another union had a dispute (secondary boycott).[111] A closed shop means that only union members can be hired, as opposed to a union shop that refers to a company where a union exists and requires that new employees must join, if hired.

The last major act was the Landrum-Griffin Act (1959), also known as the Labor-Management Reporting and Disclosure Act. Basically, it regulated the internal union affairs such as control of the union funds; outlawed union members who were communists (or former members of the Communist Party unless they resigned five years before) or former convicts (unless they were released from prison five years before) from holding office; restricted secondary boycotts more stringently; and ensured union members freedom of speech and secret elections.[112]

However, employers do not always follow the letter of the law. In a 2009 study of 1,004 union organizing drives, Cornell University Director of Labor Education Kate Bronfenbrenner found that during these campaign attempts, employers would threaten to close down the plant (57%); cut wages (47%); individually interrogate workers (63%), or actually would fire the organizers (34%).[113] On the other hand, unions are also guilty of not following the union labor laws. For example, there is a practice known as "pink sheeting," named after the color of paper where the private details of potential union members were recorded on; so, those seeking support for the union would use these private details against those who might not vote the union in, as a way to convince them for their union vote.[114] The purpose of the pink sheets was to record information about the organizers such as they had an illness and were not covered by health insurance or they were single parents and due to low wages needed a second job, but in several cases this information was being recorded on computer databases and not being used for its intended purpose other than to use against an individual who would not comply with the demands of the union.[115] Although labor union laws have been established to ensure that employers and their employees who are represented by their union would be treated in a just manner, it did not always happen, but would behoove both parties if they did take on a supererogatory (more than duty requires) approach when dealing with each other.

Whistleblowing

In August 2001, Sherron Watkins, a midlevel executive wrote a letter to Enron Chairman, Kenneth Lay, about serious accounting inconsistencies, while J. Clifford Baxter, former Enron vice chairman, who committed suicide (and some believed it happened as a result of his whistleblowing), fought with the CEO at the time about the inappropriateness of his firm's accounting practices.[116] In two other cases, Noreen Harrington, a former executive with the billionaire Stern family, contacted the state attorney general when she overheard hedge fund traders doing business over cocktails after the stock market closed; and Cynthia Cooper, an internal auditor at WorldCom, exposed the company's strategy of disguising expenses as profits.[117] What

© Elnur/Shutterstock, Inc.

do all of these individuals have in common? They are what is termed **whistleblowers,**_which involves "the act of reporting wrongdoing to internal or external parties."_[118] These individuals have risked their careers and in some cases reputations, just to bring notice of the injustices they observed and in most cases tried to resolve when approaching the "perpetrators," but were turned away. Out of a sense of justice and frustration, feeling left with no other choice, they went to the next level; either the top executives in the organization or the authorities out of the organization, since no one else within their organization would rectify the unethical situation.

How important are whistleblowers in catching fraudulent parties? According to Stephen Obie, acting director of the division of enforcement at the Commodity Futures Trading Commission, "over 50% of Ponzi schemes and other frauds he investigates came to him through whistleblowers and investor complaints."[119] Yet, in a 2006 Supreme Court case, _Garcetti v. Ceballos_, it was ruled that public employees may be denied constitutional protection when performing whistleblower duties.[120] The logic for this decision is more for national security purposes, but is quite troubling for an individual whose knowledge may not pose a security risk and still may be exempt from being protected by the freedom of speech laws which generally apply to all individuals.

Ethical organizations should have a process, whether it be an ethics officer, ethics committee, and/or policy which encourages whistleblowers to come forward without any recrimination for doing so. However, the other facet of the issue is whether the whistleblower has any ulterior motives, such as a personal vendetta or increased opportunity for promotion. In her book _Secrets: On the Ethics of Concealment and Revelation_, Harvard Professor Sissela Bok points out the importance of whistleblowing to our society in general and the issues that are raised as to why the individual is a whistleblower. Thomas Aquinas is reported to have said, "business is a necessary evil"; perhaps, it could also be stated that "whistleblowing is a necessary evil," as well.

Summary

In the business world, there have been many instances where job discrimination has taken place. Some examples include discriminatory hiring practices against protected groups such as African Americans, or unprotected groups such as gays and lesbians. In some cases, discrimination occurs due to one's physical appearance which has been termed "lookism," and includes weight discrimination. However, some job applicants who have been rejected due to their weight have used the Americans with Disabilities Act, if their physical challenge is found to be a reason for not being hired and the condition can be documented such as a metabolic condition, for example. Having a "foreign accent" has also been a form of discrimination, but the courts have not specifically addressed this unless it is found to be a form of religious or ethnic discrimination which is protected under the Civil Rights Act. Even more challenging has been technology such as polygraph testing or testing an individual's genetic code which the courts and laws are defining.

Several cases involving ageism in terminations have occurred especially during an economic recession. Even lifestyle discrimination has been inconsistent with the courts' rulings; for example in some states, such as Michigan, even if you smoke outside of the workplace, a company can terminate you legally.

Affirmative Action policies have still been inconclusive in terms of their ability to eradicate discrimination. In some cases, without these policies, those protected, such as women and minorities, would still be excluded from employment and promotions. Yet, there have been cases where "reverse discrimination" has been the cry of those not protected under these affirmative action policies such the University of Michigan where the undergraduate school was found to be discriminating against white candidates, but their law school was not.

Sexual harassment has found to still be a problem in the workplace and companies have instituted workshops and policies to reduce their incidences. Comparable worth, which is an unethical way of classifying the same jobs differently so gender wage and salary disparities can occur, still exist and may be indicative of why the glass ceiling continues as evidenced by the Fortune 500 companies who have only 5% female CEOs representing their gender. The Americans with Disabilities Act has seemed to improve since its inception in 1992, yet many major firms are still being sued because they are not complying with its provisions.

Privacy in the workplace is another issue employers are faced with as well as employees. Due to its ambiguity, many disagreements have been referred to the courts, which are not always consistent. Safety and health issues have also been problematic with some instances where employees are rewarded for not following the laws or threatened if they attempt to report an infraction. However, OSHA has tried to rectify many of these unsafe conditions.

Yet, employees also abuse the system. Some employees breach the trade secret agreement they have signed with their employers, others misuse funds, some may profit from non-public information such as insider trading, while others demand excessive executive compensation while their firms are losing profits or consider bribery as a perk of the job.

Employers are also faced with breaching their moral compasses. Examples include outsourcing while exploiting foreign workers who take the positions of now downsized domestic employees; closing plants at the detriment of the community; using independent contractors to avoid payroll taxes and fringe benefits to employees who should be classified as "full time"; using their superior power to demean their subordinates (workplace rankism); and hiring or promoting only their friends and family (nepotism).

Unions are another area in the workplace where controversy occurs and even though federal laws are to ensure that both the employers and union members will be treated fairly, there appears to be several examples of unethical and illegal behavior by both parties. Finally, the whistleblower is discussed and when it is and is not appropriate to report unethical company actions to superiors or outsiders. The workplace must be conducive to productivity, but also harmony and justness.

KEY TERMS

Affirmative Action: policies that require protected groups (African American, Latinos, etc.) be given a special opportunity to be hired or promoted in an effort to reverse past discriminatory practices which now will result in minorities being hired or promoted fairly.

Ageism: discrimination against an individual based upon age.

Bribery: the act of persuading somebody to exercise his or her business judgment in one's favor by offering cash or a gift and thereby gaining an unfair advantage.

Comparable worth: also known as pay equity, a broad term for a range of policies developed to reduce the pay gap between occupations traditionally filled by women.

Domestic partnership benefits: are when primarily gay or lesbians have long-term partnerships, are living together, and can have health insurance for their partners through their partner's company.

Employment at will: when employers have the right to terminate any employee at their discretion.

Glass ceiling: a term defining the inability of women to be promoted into the executive suite compared their male co-workers.

Independent contractors: individuals who work for themselves and are exempt from overtime, fringe benefits, ability to join a union, and are responsible for paying any required taxes which normally are paid by employers, such as Social Security taxes.

Informatics: optically scanned paper transferred to computer screens where a distance away the relevant information is keyed in and then digitized material speedily returned to the home office.

Insider trading: illegal trading in securities by individuals or firms who possess non-public information.

Institutional or corporate bullying: when bullying is entrenched in an organization and becomes accepted as part of the workplace culture.

Lifestyle discrimination: discrimination against employees because of their activities outside the work environment, which may include smoking or skydiving.

Lookism: discriminating against an individual because of physical appearance.

Nepotism: the process of favoritism to relatives, especially in appointments to desirable positions.

OSHA: under the Occupational Safety and Health Act of 1970, OSHA's purpose is to develop standards, issue regulations, conduct inspections, and issue citations to ensure the safety and health of all workers.

Whistleblower: involves the act of reporting wrongdoing to internal or external parties.

Workplace rankism: when a superior abuses his/her power at the expense of subordinates.

CHAPTER REVIEW QUESTIONS

1. What are some specific examples of job discrimination experienced by potential applicants or employees?
2. Do employees have the right to privacy in the workplace? Prove your response with examples from this chapter.
3. What are some examples of how employees have been unethical in the workplace? Use examples found in this chapter.
4. What are examples of unethical practices by employers? Use examples found in this chapter.
5. Are you in favor of unions? Explain why or why not using one example from this chapter.
6. Should whistleblowing be encouraged? Explain your response using material from this chapter.

CASES FOR DISCUSSION

CASE 7.1 BROKEN PIPE OR BROKEN CAREER?[121]

Newly hired John Hendrix was trained to field customer complaints and determine why the pipes manufactured by his employer ruptured. After discovering the cause was due to purchasing lower grade materials and manipulated quality test results, he contacted his supervisor, who responded, "this is a normal business risk."

DISCUSSION QUESTIONS

(a) If this was your first job with equally lucrative employment opportunities in the area should you have to leave this position, and you found out that the rupturing of pipes would emit toxic chemicals into the land and water in the surrounding area, causing potential harm to the members of your community, would you "blow the whistle" (be a whistle blower)? Defend your response, using the full S.E.A. method (state the philosophy, explain the philosophy in your own words with a general example, and apply the philosophy to your response).

(b) *If in part (a) you responded* that you would be a "whistleblower," would you still be a whistleblower if you were a single parent with two children who could not find work for a year as a result of losing your job for being a whistleblower? Defend your response, using the full S.E.A. method (state the philosophy, explain the philosophy in your own words, give a general example, and apply the philosophy to your response).

(Supplemental question c) Apply the seven-step Velasquez decision-making model found in Chapter 6.

CASE 7.2 MORAL HAZARDS OR GOOD BUSINESS?[122]

In 2015, the UNI Global Union (UNI), a union with 20 million employees in 150 countries, was looking to extend its membership to the United States, where only 1.6% of its unions represent the financial industry. At the height of the controversy, is the imposing of sales quotas in which banks pressure their personnel to sell to customers various financial products, which these customers don't need nor are given enough information to understand the risks involved with their purchase. The bank employees do not want to be placed in this position and as a result, European and South American employees are looking to join unions to protect them from this unethical practice and this is why UNI believes it can make its mark in the United States.

UNI is seeking the bank employees to provide adequate advice to their customers, rather than selling as many products as they can, to reduce their sales quotas, more protection for whistleblowers, and better training in terms of responsible, more ethical selling techniques. In essence, the bank workers are trying to prevent being in a moral hazard. "Moral hazard is a situation in which one party gets involved in a risky event knowing that it is protected against the risk and the other party will incur the cost." Basically, if a person knows the action will not be a risk because the risk will be on someone else, that person will act in a riskier way. Therefore, by the financial sales agent convincing his potential client, the customer, to purchase a risky money market instrument or insurance which he does not need, the financial risk or responsibility is on the customer so the sales agent can be as aggressive as possible.

DISCUSSION QUESTIONS

If you were the Chief Executive Officer, would you keep or reduce your sales quotas for your sales agents (employees)?
(a) Defend your response, using the full S.E.A. method (state the philosophy, explain the philosophy in your own words, give a general example, and apply the philosophy to your response).
(Supplemental question b) Apply the seven-step Velasquez decision-making model found in Chapter 6.

CASE 7.3 ROMANCE IN THE OFFICE?[123]

On March 5, 2005, Boeing Company's CEO Harry C. Stonecipher was asked to resign because he refused to end his romantic relationship with his subordinate. Several studies have indicated that up to 80% of Americans have experienced some type of relationship at work either through personal experience or by observation. In some research it was found that being involved with a co-worker may lead to a more inspired, creative individual, as well as enrich personal relationships. On the other hand, a preponderance of the literature suggests that there are several detrimental consequences associated with a workplace romance.

In her landmark book, *Office Romance: Love, Power & Sex in the Workplace*, Lisa Mainiero identified several potential negative outcomes, including jeopardizing career advancement; negatively impacting professional relationships; enduring other colleagues; observing the relationship as if it was in a fishbowl; reducing a couple's work performance; exacerbating potential office gossip; developing a potential conflict of interest; and being vulnerable for sexual harassment charges.

More recently, in 2015, an unsuccessful lawsuit by Ellen Pao, a junior partner of Kleiner, Perkins, Caufield and Byers, who earned a law and business degree from Harvard, admitted "succumbing" to the advances of another junior partner, who she had sexual relations with. According to Pao, when she ended the relationship, for the next five years, this junior partner, along with the support of the company retaliated against her. Her firm said it was a consensual affair and after they fired her for poor job performance. However, the issue still remains, should office romances be permitted and, if so, within what guidelines?

DISCUSSION QUESTION

If you were the CEO of your company, what would you do regarding a policy on office romances (e.g., create a policy against co-workers dating, sometimes called a "no-fraternization" policy, not have a policy, etc.)? Be specific. Defend your response, using the full S.E.A. method (state the philosophy, explain the philosophy in your own words, give a general example, and apply the philosophy to your response).

(Supplemental question) Apply the seven-step Velasquez decision-making model found in Chapter 6.

ENDNOTES

1 Les Christie, "New Ways to Get Fired," CNNMoney.com, March 15, 2005. 12 Feb. 2010. http://money.cnn/2005/03/11/pr/companiescrackdown/index.htm; and Alina Tugend, "Speaking Freely About Politics Can Lose Your Job," *The New York Times*, February 21, 2015, p. B4.

2 Luke Malone, "There are 32 States Where You Can Be Fired For Being LGBT," *HuffPost Gay Voices*, February 15, 2015. http://www.huffingtonpost.com/2015/02/15/lgbt-fired-32-states_n_6669842.html

3 David Taffet, "Gay Man's EEOC Complaint Against Granbury Bank Heads to Mediation," *Dallas Voice.com*, February 11, 2013. 28 April 2015. http://www.dallasvoice.com/bank-discrimination-case-headed-mediation-10139083.html

4 "A Weighty Battle in the Workplace," *Chicago Tribune*, September 23, 2003. 15 Feb. 2010. http://www.proquest.com

5 Iris Yokoi, "Legal Center Targets Race Discrimination in Hiring," *Los Angeles Times*, November 7, 1993. 15 Feb. 2010. http://www.proquest.com

6 "Two Religious-Bias Suits Are Filed by the EEOC," *Wall Street Journal*, September 30, 1998. 15 Feb. 2010. http://www.proquest.com

7 Lois K. Solomon, "Jews Must Make Tough Choice Between Work, School and Religion: With Midweek Holidays, Jews Face Tough Choices at Work and School," *McClatchy - Tribune Business News*, September 29, 2008. 15 Feb. 2010. http://www.proquest.com

8 "A Ban on Genetic Discrimination," Editorial, This Week in Review, *The New York Times*, November 22, 2009, p. 9.

9 David E. Terpstra, R. Bryan Kethley, Richard T. Foley, and Wanthanee Limpaphayom, "The Nature of Litigation Surrounding Five Screening Devices," *Public Personnel Management*, vol. 29, no. 1, April 1, 2000, pp. 45-46. 15 Feb. 2010. http://www.proquest.com

10 Sharon Linstedt, "U.S. Agency Finds Rising Frequency of Illegal Bias Related to Pregnancy," *Knight Ridder Tribune Business News*, January 26, 2004, p. 1. 15 Feb. 2010. http://www.proquest.com; and "Lawsuit: Pregnant Woman Fired for Restroom Breaks," *The New York Times*, December 4, 2014. www.nyt.com

11 City News Service, "**66-Year**-Old Man Awarded $26 million in Age Discrimination Lawsuit Against Staples," *Los Angeles Daily News*, February 27, 2014. www.dailynews.com

12 "Starbucks Fires Barista Who Organized NYC Union," *FinancialWire*, August 8, 2006, p. 1. 15 Feb. 2010. http://www.proquest.com

13 Amy Joyce, "So Much for 'Personal' Habits,'" Tech News, *Washington Post*, October 15, 2006, p. F01. LexisNexis Academic, SUNY Rockland, Suffern, NY. 16 Feb. 2010.

14 Michael Orey, "How the Threat of Litigation Is Making Companies Skittish About Axing Problem Workers," *Business Week*, vol. 4031, April 23, 2007, p. 52. LexisNexis Academic, SUNY Rockland, Suffern, NY. 16 Feb. 2010.

15 Joan Bikupic, "Ruling Impact on Hiring Weighted: High Court Reverses Sotomayor's Panel," *USA Today*, June 30, 2009, p. 1A. LexisNexis Academic, SUNY Rockland, Suffern, NY. Accessed 16 Feb. 10.

16 Ibid.

17 John Eligonm, "Jury Awards Former Tunnel Worker $735,000 in Discrimination Case," *The New York Times*, Metropolitan Section, July 30, 2008, p. 2. LexisNexis Academic, SUNY Rockland, Suffern, NY. 16 Feb. 2010.

18 Dana Defilippo, "Pennsylvania Female Trooper Alleges Sex Bias and More," *Philadelphia*

Daily News, November 12, 2009. EBSCO Host, SUNY Rockland, Suffern, NY. 17 Feb 2010. http://ezproxy.sunyrockland.edu:2048/login?url=http://search.ebscohost.com/login.aspx?direct=true&db=n5h&AN=2W6355947354&site=ehost-live

[19] Frank Urquhart, "Fashion Giant's Desire for Only Cool and Good-Looking Staff Branded Plain Ugly," *The Scotsman*, February 6, 2010, p. 17. LexisNexis Academic, SUNY Rockland, Suffern, NY. 13 Feb. 2010.

[20] Immanuel Kant, *Groundwork of the Metaphysic of Morals,* H.J. Paton, trans. (New York: Harper and Row Publishers, 1964), p. 96.

[21] Hilary O. Shelton, "Society Needs Affirmative Action," *At Issue: Affirmative Action,* Ed. Bryan J. Grapes (San Diego: Greenhaven Press, 2000). Opposing Viewpoints Resource Center. Gale. Rockland Community College - SUNY. 17 Feb 2010. http://find.galegroup.com/ovrc/infomark.do?&contentSet=GSRC&type=retrieve&tabID=T010&prodId=OVRC&docId=EJ3010001204&source=gale&srcprod=OVRC&userGroupName=rocklandcc&version=1.0

[22] Stephen G. Christianson, "Bakke v. University of California, Appeal, 1978," *Great American Trials,* 2003, p. 672. EBSCO Host, SUNY Rockland, Suffern, NY. 22 Feb. 2010. http://ezproxy.sunyrockland.edu:2048/login?url=http://search.ebscohost.com/login.as

[23] Sandra Day O'Connor, et al., The Supreme Court: Excerpts from Justices' Opinions on Michigan Affirmative Action Cases, *New York Times*, June 24, 2003, p. A24. 22 Feb. 2010. http://www.nyt.com

[24] "Public Backs Affirmative Action, But Not Minority Preferences," Pew Research, June 2, 2009. www.pewresearch.org.

[25] Ruth Davidhizar and Sally Erdel, "Sexual Harassment," *Nursing Management*, vol. 29, no. 2, February 1998, p. 41. EBSCO Host,

Business Source Complete, SUNY Rockland, Suffern, NY. 22 Feb. 2010.

[26] "U.S. Charges Sexual Harassment at a Mitsubishi Plant in Illinois," *New York Times*, April 10, 1996, p. D2. 22 Feb. 2010. http://www.nyt.com; and **Mitsubishi Settles with Women in Sexual Harassment Lawsuit, *New York Times*, August 29, 1997, p. D2. 24 Feb. 2010. http://www.nyt.com**

[27] "U.S. Charges Sexual Harassment at a Mitsubishi Plant in Illinois," *New York Times*, April 10, 1996, p. D2. 22 Feb. 2010. http://www.nyt.com

[28] "A Racy Silicon Valley Lawsuit and More Subtle Questions About Sex Discrimination," *The New York Times*, March 6, 2015. www.nyt.com

[29] "Man Wins $1 Million Sex Harassment Suit," *New York Times*, May 21, 1993, p. A15. 24 Feb. 2010. http://www.nyt.com

[30] Linda Greenhouse, "The Supreme Court: The Workplace: Court Spell Out Rules for Finding Sexual Harassment," *New York Times*, June 27, 1998, p. A1. 24 Feb. 2010. http://www.nyt.com

[31] Ibid.

[32] Amy Gluckman, "Comparable Worth," *Dollars & Sense*, September/October 2002, Issue 243, p. 42. EBSCO Host, Business Source Complete, SUNY Rockland, Suffern, NY. 22 Feb. 2010. http://ezproxy.sunyrockland.edu:2319/login.aspx?direct=true&db=bth&AN=7719251&site=bsi-live.

[33] Joel P. Rudin and Kimble Byrd, "U.S. Pay Equity Legislation: Sheep in Wolves' Clothing," *Employee Responsibilities and Rights Journal*, vol. 14, no. 4, December 2003, p. 184.

[34] *Shultz v. American Can Company-Dixie Products*, No. 19,581, UNITED STATES COURT OF APPEALS FOR THE EIGHTH CIRCUIT, 424 F.2d 356; 1970 U.S. App. LEXIS 10088; 9 Fair Empl. Prac. Cas. (BNA) 524; 62 Lab. Cas. (CCH) P32,309; 2 Empl.

Prac. Dec. (CCH) P10,149, March 30, 1970. LexisNexis, SUNY Rockland, Suffern, NY. 24 Feb. 2010.

[35] *Ellison v. United States*, No. 663-88C, UNITED STATES CLAIMS COURT, 25 Cl. Ct. 481; 121 Lab. Cas. (CCH) P35,609; 1992 U.S. Cl. Ct. LEXIS 90; 30 Wage & Hour Cas. (BNA) 1362; 58 Fair Empl. Prac. Cas. (BNA) 955; 62 Empl. Prac. Dec. (CCH) P42,382, March 13, 1992. . LexisNexis, SUNY Rockland, Suffern, NY. 24 Feb. 2010.

[36] Renae Merle, "Boeing Settles Sex-Bias Lawsuit: Thousands of Women Win in Payout of As Much as $72.5 million," *The Washington Post*, July 17, 2004, p. E01. LexisNexis Academic, SUNY Rockland, Suffern, NY. 24 Feb. 2010.

[37] Ibid.

[38] *Pyramid: Women in S&P 500 Companies* (New York: Catalyst, April 3, 2015).

[39] "Sears Agrees to Settle Disabilities Case," *The New York Times*, September 30, 2009. 24 Feb. 2010. http://www.nyt.com

[40] "Court Says Cruise Lines Must Have Better Access," *The New York Times*, June 7, 2005. 24 Feb. 2010. http://www.nyt.com

[41] Constance L. Hays, "Wal-Mart Is Found Liable in Bias Against Disabled Man," *The New York Times*, May 15, 1994. 24 Feb. 2010. http://www.nyt.com

[42] Ibid.

[43] Linda Saslow, "Island School Districts Bracing to Meet Increases in Expenses," *The New York Times*, May 15, 1994. 24 Feb. 2010. http://www.nyt.com

[44] Steven Greenhouse, "Overweight, But Ready to Fight: Obese People Are Taking Their Bias Claims to Court," *The New York Times*, August 4, 2003, p. B1. 25 Feb. 2010. http://www.nyt.com

[45] Martin J. Lecker, "The Smoking Penalty: Distributive Justice or Smokism?" *Journal of Business Ethics*, vol. 84, Supplement 1, 2009, p. 47.

[46] Barbara Ehrenreich, "Warning: This Is a Rights-Free Workplace," *The New York Times*, March 5, 2000. 25 Feb. 2010. http://www.nyt.com

[47] Jonathan D. Glater, "A Company Computer and Questions About E-Mail Privacy," *The New York Times*, June 27, 2008. 25 Feb. 2010. http://www.nyt.com

[48] Steve Barr, "Election E-Mails Can End Your Term in the Office," *The New York Times*, April 21, 2008, p. D1. 25 Feb. 2010. http://www.nyt.com

[49] "Review Privacy and Surveillance Policies in Light of New California Supreme Court Ruling," *HR Specialist California Employment Law*, vol. 3, no. 10, October 2009, p. 2. EBSCO Host, Business Source Complete, SUNY Rockland, Suffern, N.Y. 22 Feb. 2010.

[50] Elizabeth Kolbert, "Test of Teachers for Use of Drugs is Ruled Illegal," *The New York Times*, June 10, 1987, p. A1. 25 Feb 2010. http://www.nyt.com

[51] Steve Lohr, "IBM Pledges to Assure Privacy of Employees' Genetic Profile, *The New York Times*, October 10, 2005. 25 Feb. 2010. http://www.nyt.com

[52] Ibid.

[53] Frank Pennachio, "Going Beyond the Limits," *Occupational Hazards*, September, 2008, p. 35. EBSCO Host, Business Source Complete, SUNY Rockland, Suffern, NY. 26 Feb. 2010.

[missing notes for 54, 55]

[56] Steven Greenhouse, "Broad Survey of Day Laborers Finds High Level of Injuries and Pay Violations," *The New York Times*, January 22, 2006. 26 Feb. 2010. http://www.nyt.com

[57] Ibid.

[58] Shaila Dewan, "Report Cites Lack of Precautions in 2008 Sugar Plant Fire," *The New York Times*, September 24, 2009, p. A17. 26 Feb. 2010. http://www.nyt.com

[59] Ibid.

[60] Steven Greenhouse, "BP Faces Record Fine for 2005 Refinery Explosion," *The New York*

Times, October 30, 2009, p. B1. 26 Feb. 2010. http://www.nyt.com

61 Ibid.

62 Marci Bortman, Peter Brimblecombe, and Mary Ann Cunniham (Eds.), "Occupational Safety and Health Administration," *Environmental Encyclopedia*, 3d ed., vol. 2 (Detroit: Gale, 2003), p. 1006. Gale Virtual Reference Library, SUNY Rockland, Suffern, NY. 27 Feb. 2010. http://go.galegroup.com/ps/i.do?&id =GALE%7CCCX340480 1069&v=2.1&u=rocklandcc&it= r&p=GVRL&sw=w

63 Jena McGregor (Ed.), "Benefits: More Coverage for Domestic Partners," *Business Week*, September 28, 2009, p. 68.

64 "Ex-Ford Engineer Charged with Stealing Secrets," *Automotive News*, vol. 84, no. 6382, 2009. EBSCO Host, Business Source Complete, SUNY Rockland, Suffern, NY. 28 Feb. 2010.,

65 "Amaranth Sues Touradji for Contract Breach," *Total Alternatives*, September 21, 2009, p. 26. EBSCO Host, Business Source Complete, SUNY Rockland, Suffern, NY. 28 Feb. 2010.

66 "Gibraltar Metals Files Lawsuit vs. Competitor, Ex-sales Exec," *Metal Bulletin Daily*, no. 174, August 8, 2009, p. 64. EBSCO Host, Business Source Complete, SUNY Rockland, Suffern, NY. 28 Feb. 2010.

67 "Atmel Ousts CEO, Other Execs," *Electronic News*, vol. 52, no. 33, August 14, 2006, p. 3. EBSCO Host, Business Source Complete, SUNY Rockland, Suffern, NY. 28 Feb. 2010.

68 David Wellman, "Wal-Mart Sues Former Vice Chairman," *Retail Merchandiser*, vol. 45, no. 8, August 2005, **p. 10. EBSCO Host, Business Source Complete, SUNY Rockland, Suffern, NY. 28 Feb. 2010.**

69 "Dark Days for Volkswagen, "*The Economist,* vol. 376, no. 8435, July 16, 2005, pp. 57-58. EBSCO Host, Business Source Complete, SUNY Rockland, Suffern, NY. 28 Feb. 2010.

70 Reuters, "Guilty Verdict Reached in Tyco Trial," *The New York Times*, June 17, 2005. 28 Feb. 2010. http://nyt.com

71 Lisa Meulbroek, "An Empirical Analysis of Illegal Insider Trading," *The Journal of Finance*, vol. 47, no. 5, December, 1992, p. 1661. 01 March 2010. http://www.jstor.org/stable/2328992

72 Thomas Landon Jr., "Martha Stewart Settles Civil Insider Trading Case," *The New York Times*, August 7, 2006. 01 March 2010. http://www.nyt.com

73 Constance L. Hays and Maria Newman, "Stewart Sentenced to 5 months in Prison for Lying to Investigators," *The New York Times*, July 16, 2004. 01 March 2010. http://www.nyt.com

74 Barry Schwartz, "Outside Shot: The Dark Side of Incentives," *Business Week*, November 23, 2009, p. 84.

75 Ibid.

76 Edmund L. Andrews and Peter Baker, "At A.I.G., Huge Bonuses After $170 Billion Bailout," *The New York Times,* March 15, 2009, p. A1.

77 Michael J. de la Merced, "After Turmoil at Merrill, Thain Will Lead the Lender CIT," *The New York Times*, February 2, 2010, pp. B1, B2.

78 Ibid.

79 Gretchen Morgenson, "Comparing Paychecks With C.E.O.'s," *The New York Times*, April 12, 2015, pp. B1, B6.

80 William Neuman, "Hidden Ingredient: The Sweetener," *The New York Times*, February 25, 2010, p. B1.

81 Ibid.

82 *Bloomsbury Business Library Business and Management Dictionary*, 2007, p. 1082. EBSCO Host, Business Source Complete, SUNY Rockland, Suffern, NY. 01 March 2010.

83 Mark Mazzetti and James Risen, "Blackwater Said to Pursue Bribes to Iraq After 17 Died,"

The New York Times, November 10, 2009, p. A1. 10 March 2010. http://www.nyt.com

84 Mark Mazzetti, James Risen, and Steven Meyers, "U.S. Examines Whether Blackwater Tried Bribery," *The New York Times*, January 31, 2010, p. A1. 01 March 2010. http://www.nyt.com

85 Phyllis Korkki, "With Jobs Few, Most Workers Aren't Satisfied," *The New York Times*, January 10, 2010, p. B2. 02 March 2010. http://www.nyt.com

86 Julie Moran Alterio, "IBM applies for patent to aid outsourcing jobs," *The Journal News*, October 4, 2007. 03 March 2010. http://www.proquest.com/

87 Bruce Stokes, "Aerospace Jobs Landing in Asia," *National Journal*, February 21, 2007, pp. 58-59. 03 March 2010. http://www.proquest.com/

88 Ibid.

89 Julie Moran Alterio, "IBM applies for patent to aid outsourcing jobs," *The Journal News*, October 4, 2007. 03 March 2010. http://www.proquest.com/

90 Sarith Raj, "India Outsourcing Workers Stressed to the Limit," ZDNet.News, August 26, 2009. 03 March 2010. ZDNet News

91 Nancy Cleeland, "Dark and Bitter," *The American Prospect*, vol. 20, no. 8, October 1, 2009, p. A7. 03 March 2010. http://www.proquest.com/

92 Robert Gavin, "Jobless Plight Growing Longer: Millions Remain out 6 months Pressing Hard US Recovery," *Boston Globe*, September 7, 2009, p. B1. 03 March 2010. http://www.proquest.com

93 Pugan Roka, *Bhagavad Gita on Effective Leadership* (New York: iUniverse Incorporated, 2006), p. 59.

94 Robert Gaven, "Easing the Pain of a Shutdown: Company is Called a Model as It Helps Laid Off Workers Find Jobs," *Boston Globe*, August 28, 2009, p. B7. 03 March 2010. http://www.proquest.com

95 Lydia Harris, "Flowserve plant closing shop in June," *McClatchy - Tribune Business News*, February 27, 2010. ABI/INFORM Dateline, ProQuest. 4 March 2010. http://www.proquest.com

96 Ibid.

97 Michael Orey, "They're Employees. No, They're Not," *Business Week*, November 16, 2009, p. 73.

98 Ibid.

99 Nancy Kaffer, "Contract Hiring Under Scrutiny," *Crain's Detroit Business*, July 7, 2008. LexisNexis Library Express, Suffern Free Library, Suffern, NY. 04 March 2010.

100 Kathryn Larkin and John Nixon, "The Hidden Pitfalls of Worker Misclassification: Employer Costs Pile Up When Independent Contractors Are Misclassified," *Employee Benefit News*, July 1, 2008. LexisNexis Library Express, Suffern Free Library, Suffern, NY. 04 March 2010.

101 Ivan Penn, "Contractors Feeling Used, Abused," *St. Petersburg Times*, December 13, 2009, p. 1D. LexisNexis Library Express, Suffern Free Library, Suffern, NY. 04 March 2010.

102 Lisa Rein, "Labor Proposal Targets Builders; Low-Wage Workers' Treatment a Worry, *The Washington Post*, February 9, 2009, p. B1. LexisNexis Library Express, Suffern Free Library, Suffern, NY. 04 March 2010.

103 David C. Yamada, "Dignity, Rankism, and Hierarchy in the Workplace: Creating a Dignitarian Agenda for American Employments, Law," *Berkeley Journal of Employment & Labor Law*, vol. 28, no. 1, 2007, p. 305.

104 Mike Cottrill, "Taking Care: How To Create More Dignity For Your Employees," *Smart Business Cleveland*, 2008, p. 26. EBSCO Host, Business Source Complete, SUNY Rockland, Suffern, NY. 04 March 10.

105 "PsychoTerror: Action is Needed to End Bullying in the Workplace," *Hazards Fact Sheet 70*, 2000. Hazards Organization Website. 04 March 2010. http://www.hazards.org/bullying.pdf

106 Ibid.

107 Mike Cottrill, "Taking Care: How To Create More Dignity For Your Employees," *Smart Business Cleveland*, 2008, p. 26. EBSCO Host, Business Source Complete, SUNY Rockland, Suffern, NY. 04 March 2010.

108 Michelle Leder, "The CEO BFF: Find More Like This," *Conde Nast Portfolio*, vol. 3, no. 4, May 2009, p. 34. EBSCO Host, Business Source Complete, SUNY Rockland, Suffern, NY. 04 March 2010.

109 "Picketing," *Columbia Electronic Encyclopedia*, 6th ed., October 1, 2009. EBSCO Host, History Reference Center, SUNY Rockland, Suffern, NY. 04 March 2010. http://ezproxy.sunyrockland.edu:2048/login?url=http://search.ebscohost.com/login.aspx?direct=true&db=khh&AN=39004050&site=ehost-live

110 "Congress Passes the National Labor Relations Act," *Great Events: 1931-1939,* vol. 3, p. 367. EBSCO Host, History Reference Center, SUNY Rockland, Suffern, NY. 04 March 2010. ttp://ezproxy.sunyrockland.edu:2048/login?url=http://search.ebscohost.com/login.as

111 "Taft-Harley Labor Act," *Columbia Electronic Encyclopedia*, 6th ed., October 1, 2009. EBSCO Host, History Reference Center, SUNY Rockland, Suffern, NY. 04 March 2010. http://ezproxy.sunyrockland.edu:2048/login?url=http://search.ebscohost.com/login.as

112 "Landrum-Griffin Act," *Columbia Electronic Encyclopedia*, 6th ed., October 1, 2009. EBSCO Host, History Reference Center, SUNY Rockland, Suffern, NY. 04 March 2010. http://ezproxy.sunyrockland.edu:2048/login?url=http://search.ebscohost.com/login.aspx?direct=true&db=khh&AN=39017285&site=ehost-live

113 Steven Greenhouse, "Study Says Antiunion Tactics Are Becoming More Common," *The New York Times*, May 20, 2009, p. B5. 06 March 2010. http://www.nyt.com

114 Steven Greenhouse, "Some Organizers Protest Their Union's Tactics," *The New York Times*, November 19, 2009, p. B1. 06 March 2010.

http://www.nyt.com

115 Ibid.

116 Tom Redburn, "Enron's Many Strands," *The New York Times*, January 27, 2002. 06 March 2010. http://www.nyt.com

117 Joyce Purnick, "Metro Matters; A Whistle Still Ringing in Wall St. Ears," *The New York Times*, December 11, 2003. 06 March 2010. http://www.nyt.com

118 Ronald Parisi, "The Fine Art of Whistleblowing," *CPA Journal*, vol. 79, no. 11, November 2009, EBSCO Host, Business Source Complete, SUNY Rockland, Suffern, NY. 06 March 2010. http://ezproxy.sunyrockland.edu:2319/login.aspx?direct=true&db=bth&AN=45410626&site=bsi-live

119 Robert Chew, "Calling All Whistleblowers! The SEC Wants You," *InsiderTime.com*. February 14, 2009, CNN Website. http://www.time.com/time/business/article/0,8599,1881318,00.html#ixzz0hPogjTCP.

120 Ibid.

121 This case was rewritten using some data from an article by Mary Williams Walsh, "A Trial of Broken Pipes," *The New York Times,* February 12, 2010, pp. B1, B5.

122 This case was written using the following sources: Eidelson, et al. "Unions Trying to Get Between Banks and Their Customers," *Bloomberg Businessweek,* March 23–April 5, 2015, pp. 50-51; and "Definition of Moral Hazard," The Economic Times, n.d. 18 March 2015. www.economictimes.indiatimes.com

123 This case was from an article by this textook's author: "Workplace Romances: A Platonic Perspective," *Research in Ethical Issues in Organizations, Volume 7, Insurance Ethics For a More Ethical World*, Patrick Flanagan, Patrick Primeaux, and William Ferguson, Eds., pp. 253-255; David Streitfeld, "Lawsuit Shakes Foundation Of a Man's World of Tech," *The New York Times*, June 3, 2012, p. BU1; and Dan Levine, "Pao Faces Tough Court if She Appeals Kleiner Bias Suit," *The New York Times*, March 31, 2015. www.nyt.com

CHAPTER 8

MARKETPLACE ETHICS

In 2010, as a result of subpoenas by the House Committee on Oversight and Government Reform, it was revealed that Toyota estimated that it saved $100 million by negotiating with the National Highway Traffic Safety Administration (NHTSA) so it could avoid an equipment recall.[1] However, in February of the same year, Toyota was forced to recall more than 8 million vehicles as a result of faulty braking systems for more than 400,000 hybrid

© Tupungato/Shutterstock, Inc.

automobiles and for front driveshaft defects for 8,000 Tacoma pickups, as a result of public pressure and the subpoenas which found evidence that Toyota had allegedly hid this information from the NHTSA about these defects for several years.[2] This situation demonstrated once again, "caveat emptor," let the buyer beware, is a philosophy that still exists.

This chapter will address some of the issues consumers must face in the marketplace and the role of businesses in being fair to its consumers. The topics include corporations, deceptive financial practices, laws governing the securities industry, deceptive marketing practices, product safety concerns, racial retail profiling, and planned obsolescence.

Corporations

A **corporation** *is a form of ownership where the owners are separate from the business and as such have certain rights such as limited liability (cannot be sued individually), potential to sell stock ownership to the public (if a public corporation), or can increase consumer acceptability as a result of this classification.* The disadvantages include: costly in terms of incorporation and attorney fees; increased recordkeeping; public access to financial data; and dual taxation (corporate profits are taxed and then owners are taxed for their income usually in the form of dividends or capital gains if their stock is sold at a greater price than purchased). **Stock** *is the individual owner's share of a business.*

The corporation consists primarily of three levels; stockholders, a board of directors, and employees. Stockholders are those who own

CORPORATION

a form of ownership where the owners are separate from the business and as such have certain rights such as limited liability.

STOCK

the individual owner's share of a business.

©Songquan Deng/Shutterstock, Inc.

stock. There are two types of stock; preferred and common. Preferred stock is when the owners are generally promised a defined amount of **dividends** (*part of the profits earned by the corporation*) and in the case of dissolution receives the remaining assets before the common stockholders. Common stockholders do not have any given rights except to vote (one vote for each share owned) for issues brought to them by the board of directors, who formulate the policies, and have them executed by the executive officers such as Chief Executive Officer, President, and Vice President, who are employees of the company. It is possible for executive officers to be part of the board of directors as well as being shareholders.

According to the *2010 U.S. Statistical Abstract* published by the Census Bureau, corporations accounted for 67% of all profits generated from businesses, followed by partnerships (23%) and sole proprietorships (10%). A partnership is a business with two or more owners, whereas a sole proprietorship is a business with only one owner. Both partnerships and sole proprietorships may be sued personally, if their business assets do not contain enough funds to pay their liabilities (debts owed by the business); however, neither ownership form of these businesses are taxed as businesses, which corporation are. For this reason, the majority of this chapter will include corporations, but other forms of businesses may be added to our discussion about the consumer marketplace.

Deceptive Financial Practices

In 2001, after hiding more than $1 billion in losses, Enron, an energy-related corporation, filed for bankruptcy protection after it was found that they misstated $586 million in revenue of "off-book partnerships," which should have been stated as a loss.[3] Arthur Andersen Worldwide Societe Cooperative was the auditing firm that breached their accounting ethics for allowing this misrepresentation.[4] As a result of companies such as Enron and Arthur Andersen for their unethical financial reporting, as well as other unethical practices in the securities field, in 2002, the Sarbanes-Oxley Act was passed and will be discussed later on in this chapter. In this section, we will discuss some of these unethical

practices found in the financial field. These practices are churning, the Ponzi scheme, and subprime mortgage rate loans.

Although discussed in Chapter Seven, insider trading should be briefly revisited. This practice is illegal and unethical and begins with stockbrokers or the people who they tell about an unannounced event that will result in changing stock prices. Unfortunately, the majority of public sellers or buyers, who are uninformed about the event, will be victimized when the stock prices increase for these investors if they were to purchase the stock (or decrease in stock prices if they were to sell the stock) after the event is announced.

CHURNING

CHURNING

occurs when a broker engages in excessive trading in order to generate commissions and other revenue without regard for the customer's investment objectives.

Churning is an unethical practice conducted by some investment brokerage firms. According to the Securities Exchange Commission (SEC), **churning** *"occurs when a broker engages in excessive trading in order to generate commissions and other revenue without regard for the customer's investment objectives."* [5] One example of churning occurred when a Maryland Wachovia Securities' broker boasted on radio of how his investors earned a 50% rate of return, when the broadcast was heard by a former investor whose $7.8 million account was churned 540 times in 14 months, and lost $90,000, plus $3,400 in margin interest, in addition to tens of thousands of dollars in commissions earned by this broker; the investor filed a complaint and the broker was eventually barred from the securities industry for life.[6] In addition to the unethical nature of this practice, there is a cost not only to the individual who is responsible for churning the accounts of his unsuspecting investors, but also to the company. In fact, in one situation, the SEC ordered one firm, First Allied, to pay $2 million in fines and interest for failing to supervise a broker who allegedly engaged in churning the accounts of two municipal clients in Florida.[7] As a result of cases such as this, there have been several proposals to introduce legislation to stiffen the penalties for churning accounts, in an effort to protect investors from this practice, including the state of Florida which has tried to pass a bill specifically protecting its senior citizens from having their accounts churned.

PONZI SCHEME

A **Ponzi scheme** *is when a dishonest person convinces unsuspecting customers that they will receive high returns in a short period of time, but actually is taking money from one set of investors to pay off other investors, without the intention of either making a profit for his clients or paying them back.* The name comes from Charles Ponzi who in the early 1920s convinced thousands of Boston investors that he could provide a 50% return in 45 days, when in actuality took money from new investors to pay off early

© Elnur/Shutterstock, Inc.

PONZI SCHEME
when a dishonest person convinces unsuspecting customers that they will receive high returns in a short period of time and uses the funds of one set of investors to pay back the others.

© davidundderriese/Shutterstock, Inc.

investors, and once reported to have taken in $1 million in just three hours.[8] Ponzi's scheme was based upon international reply coupons. In his era, several countries would prepay international postage (like a self-addressed stamped envelope) which could be purchased in Rome, redeemed in Boston, and since the fixed price of the coupons did not reflect the post-World War I devaluation of money, for a $1 worth of lira you could redeem it for $3.30 worth of stamps in Boston.[9] Unfortunately, the postage stamps were what Ponzi used to convince his investors, but as other defrauders emulated his concept, they would just change the "financial prize."

Perhaps, none will be as famous as the Ponzi scheme that led to the loss of over $65 billion conducted by Bernard Madoff who was sentenced to 150 years in prison in 2009 for securities fraud which began as early as the 1980s.[10] What made this case so unusual was that, first, the Securities Exchange Commission had been tipped off earlier allegedly about Madoff's actions but had not investigated it properly; and second, the largest targets of Madoff's fraud were his friends or "friends of friends," even though due to their stockbrokers' actions, many average citizens lost their pensions and life savings. In terms of how he was able to mislead so many, the details of his scheme came to light at a federal court hearing by one of his friends, who helped Madoff with this elaborate scam. In 2009, Frank DiPascali testified how he helped Madoff use historical stock data from the Internet to create fake trade blotters, sent out fraudulent account statements to his clients, and arranged wire transfers between Madoff's London and New York offices to create the impression that the firm was earning commissions from stock trades.[11] Yet, is should be pointed out that the rate of returns were so much higher than other investors were receiving, some sort of red flag should have indicated to his clients, that Madoff was doing something out of the ordinary to yield such positive results.

SUBPRIME MORTGAGE RATE LOANS

In 2008, according to the Mortgage Bankers Association, nearly 4% of prime mortgages and 7.3% of all mortgages were past due or in foreclosure; the highest rate since the group started tracking prime and subprime mortgages in 1979.[12] **Subprime mortgages** *are those where* *the rates are lower initially, usually for clients who could not be approved at prime rates, but could qualify for the subprime rates.* However, within a few years, the rates would then rise as high as 12%, causing many of the borrowers to pay mortgage rates they could not afford. Second, as the value of homes declined, given that banks loaned mortgages on the market value of the homes, mortgage rates were adjusted upwardly to reflect these new market values. As an example, if a homeowner purchases a $200,000 home and puts down $20,000, for the first year the owner has paid less than $1,000 back in principal (since most mortgage payments in the first few years are for interest payments), and the market value of the house was devalued to say, $100,000, the borrower had to make up 20% of the dropped value, which would be $20,000. Subprime mortgage borrowers, who likely lacked these funds to begin with, could not pay the additional $20,000 or the higher mortgage rate, and could only sell their homes for a loss. There had been reports that some homeowners were so frustrated with their inability to pay their mortgages or sell their homes that some just left their houses as is, resulting in the banks having to sell homes that were not properly maintained, in addition to the defaults which harmed their overall profits.

In 2000, Edward Gramlic, a Federal Reserve governor, warned that these subprime mortgages were luring people into risky mortgages,

© ChameleonsEye/Shutterstock, Inc.

while a year later Sheila Bair tried to convince subprime lenders to adopt a code of "best practices," but their voices were ignored for this new market which accounted for $540 billion in mortgages to the bank in 2004 and $625 billion in 2006, before the housing market declined.[13] It is believed by many scholars and financial experts that the banks were guilty of negligence or at the least unsound lending practices since they were luring potential homeowners who did not have the ability to pay their mortgages; but, the banks thought that as a last resort they could foreclose on the property and sell the property at a price high enough to recoup their losses; unfortunately, they did not expect the housing market bubble to burst, which resulted in many banks going out of business. But even more disconcerting was that firms such as AIG purchased these mortgages from the banks at a lower rate, expecting to earn profits, and were left holding mortgages from customers who lacked the resources to pay them back. AIG was on the verge of bankruptcy when the federal government loaned money to them so they could avoid going out of business. This caused many U.S. taxpayers to criticize the government for the billions of dollars used for this "bailout," as well as the many other bailouts that followed.

Laws Governing the Securities Industry

MARTIN ACT OF 1921 ("blue sky" law): law enacted in order to protect investors from securities fraud, giving the state attorney generals greater power when investigating the alleged perpetrators.

Several laws were enacted to protect consumers in the financial securities field which will be discussed briefly. These laws were the Martin Act of 1921 (Blue Sky Law); Securities Act of 1933; Securities Exchange Act of 1934; Trust Indenture Act of 1939; Investment Company Act of 1940; and the Sarbanes-Oxley Act of 2002. The **Martin Act of 1921** *("blue sky" law) was enacted in order to protect investors from securities fraud and gave the state attorney generals the ability to file civil or criminal charges of securities fraud transactions; subpoena along with investigative powers; require those subpoenaed to testify and not hide behind the Fifth Amendment (right against self-incrimination); and that any failure to comply with the investigative subpoena is prima facie proof of fraud.*[14] This gave the attorney generals much needed latitude in investigating and prosecuting securities fraud and was a crucial legislation, not only before the SEC laws, but has been used quite recently by several state attorney generals.

A second set of acts were the Securities Act of 1933 and the Securities Exchange Act of 1934. The Securities Act of 1933 had two objectives: (1) require that investors receive significant financial information concerning publicly offered securities, and (2) prohibit deceit, misrepresentations, and other frauds in the sale of securities.[15] Securities sold in the United States had to be registered and contain a description of the company's properties and business; the actual security offered for sale; information about the management of the company; and financial statements certified by independent auditors.[16] The Securities Exchange Act of 1934, granted by Congress, created the Securities and Exchange Commission (SEC) which had extensive authority over all aspects of the securities industry, including the power to register, regulate, and oversee brokerage firms, clearing agencies, the stock exchanges, and the transfer agents.[17] The act also identified and prohibited certain types of conduct in the markets as well as empowering the SEC to require periodic reporting of information by companies with publicly traded securities; in addition, it prohibited insider trading and required public disclosure of information for any firm trying to purchase more than 5% of a publicly traded company.[18]

A third set of acts included the Trust Indenture Act of 1939 and the Investment Company Act of 1940. The first act applied to debt securities such as bonds, debentures, and notes offered for public sale which must have a formal agreement between the issuer of the bond and the bondholder (known as a trust indenture); while the second act regulated companies offering securities like mutual funds to publicly disclose their financial records as well but were not monitored by the SEC.[19]

The final act to be presented is the Sarbanes-Oxley Act of 2002, which was a result of the Enron scandal. First developed by Senator Paul

Sarbanes and Representative Michael Oxley, it contained eleven titles (or sections) which included: creating a board to oversee its implementation and continued execution; requiring the chief executive and other fiscal officers to sign the reports after reviewing them and attesting to their accuracy and compliance with generally accepted accounting principles; prohibiting the avoidance of these requirements by transferring their activities outside the United States; presenting the financial information in an understandable format; and imposing penalties and fines including up to twenty years imprisonment for altering, destroying, mutilating, concealing, or falsifying records, including up to ten years for any accountant who knowingly violates the auditing requirements which comply with proper auditing practices.[20]

Deceptive Marketing Practices

Unfortunately, there are many deceptive marketing practices conducted in the business world to entice consumers to purchase their products at the highest price possible. However, only a few prevalent ones will be discussed here. The unethical marketing methods used by businesses in this section are price fixing, price gouging, bait and switch advertising, and false advertising.

©3Dstock/Shutterstock, Inc.

CONDUCTING BUSINESS ETHICALLY

PRICE FIXING

Price fixing *is when two or more businesses will charge the same price so consumers cannot shop and compare for the lowest price among the competition.* Under the Sherman Anti-Trust Act, price fixing is illegal and does not distinguish whether the price agreed upon by competition is high, low, or remains the same, since it does not allow the free market to operate using the laws of supply and demand. Within the last few years, price fixing is still an issue. One example includes Bayer, a rubber chemical company, which pleaded guilty to one felony count of suppressing competition and agreed to pay a $66 million fine since several of their employees were found guilty of price fixing actions from 1995 to 2001. Joining their co-conspirators were DuPont Dow Elastomers ($84 million fine); Syndial ($9 million); and Zeon Chemicals ($10.5 million), who were fined by the European Commission.[21]

Another example of price fixing was in 2004 by Samsung and its U.S. subsidiary, Samsung Semiconductor for dynamic random access memory (DRAM) computer memory chips. They agreed to pay a $300 million fine, along with Infineon Technology and Hynix Semiconductor, who jointly paid $350 million in fines in 2004.[22] No industry appears to be immune from this type of price maneuvering: Lufthansa agreed to settle an $85 million class action suit relating to cargo price fixing; in 2007 British Airways was fined $200 million, Korean Air $100 million, and Quantas $61 million.[23] Between the United States Department of Justice and the European Community, businesses must ensure that neither they nor their employees are responsible for any price fixing.

PRICE GOUGING

In 2010, New York City's Taxi and Limousine Commission found that about 3,000 of their taxi drivers overcharged 1.8 million passengers an average of $4.50 per trip resulting in over $8 million for a twenty-six-month period of time, which some had described as the biggest fraud in the taxi industry's history.[24] **Price gouging** *is selling a product or service for an amount that is unfairly higher than it is normally sold for.*

Another example of price gouging occurred in 2009, in the pharmaceutical industry during the flu season when the Centers for Disease Control and Prevention (CDC) had fifteen complaints of price gauging in addition to one physician who was approached by a sales representative to pay $60 a dose for a flu vaccine which prior to the shortage was selling for $8.50.[25] This is reminiscent of 2004, when a British plant cut the flu vaccine supply in half, causing prices as high as $90 a dose, which had been around $8.50 a dose before the cut.[26]

The last example of price gouging is the fuel industry. In 2009, TransMontaigne Product Services (Morgan Stanley Capital Group) agreed to a $2.3 million settlement in what is believed to be the first case in the nation in which a fuel supplier, not a retailer, has agreed to pay for price gouging during a declared state of emergency, which occurred in Florida as an aftermath to Hurricane Ike.[27] During the infamous Hurricane Katrina in Louisiana, several businesses were reportedly conducting price gouging. However, some libertarian philosophers and economists disagree with the law and believe that price gouging is merely capitalism at its highest level.

BAIT AND SWITCH ADVERTISING

BAIT AND SWITCH ADVERTISING

the advertising of a highly discounted product or service with the intention not to sell it in order to convince the consumer to purchase another product or service at a higher price (switch).

Bait and switch advertising *is the advertising of a highly discounted product or service (bait) with the intention not to sell it in order to convince the consumer to purchase another product or service at a higher price (switch).* In 2009, Dell Computers Incorporated paid $4 million in restitution, penalties, and costs for advertising cheap financing and warranties in the form of no interest and no down payment for qualified purchasers who had high credit scores and then had to pay as high as 20% in interest fees.[28] In addition, the warranties and services were not performed as advertised.[29] In another case, an owner of twenty-two Midas automobile repair shops advertised $79 brake specials and often charged an additional $110 for unnecessary brake-rotor resurfacing.[30] In 2010, the owner agreed to pay $1.8 million and Midas took over his shops.[31] Yet, the securities field is not immune either. Two former Credit Suisse Securities brokers misled their investors for almost $2 billion outside the United States by convincing them that they were purchasing liquid money market funds but actually were purchasing higher yielding, but riskier investments, without any government backing which included subprime mortgages and mobile home contracts.[32] The SEC filed a civil suit against the two brokers. The last example involves a time share bait and switch. An unsuspecting victim received a birthday card, explaining that the company had been trying to find him since he won two airplane tickets and a seven-day automobile rental, but learned only after taking advantage of it that the travel agency that contacted him would select the midweek flight and airplane and would require him to sit through a ninety-minute seminar on time shares.[33] But, unknown to the Travel Agency, in California, where the victim lived, there is a law that makes this illegal unless the offer is clear and discloses in writing anything that would not be understood by the prize recipients and include all pertinent information (Section 17537.1 of the California Business and Professional Code).[34]

© Aleutie/Shutterstock, Inc.

FALSE ADVERTISING

Another deceptive marketing practice is false advertising. However, it should be noted that there is a form of advertising that is sometimes misconstrued as false advertising, but it is not. The form is called "sales puffery." **Sales puffery** *is making statements that are known to be exaggerated and that the Federal Trade Commission (FTC) does not consider as false advertising.* For example, if a company states that their bread is the best tasting in the world, it is considered "sales puffery," as it is an opinion. However, if a company states that its bread is lower in calories than every other bread, this may be considered false advertising. In the same vein, if a company states that its bread is less in calories than all other breads and the reason is because it cuts its loaf into forty slices rather than thirty-two slices, like its competitors, this may also be considered false advertising.

In 2010, trade schools such as culinary institutes or automobile trade schools were found to aggressively push their programs, which cost $30,000, to lower income students in an effort to convince them that they would earn middle-class salaries. Unfortunately, most experts concurred that the loans and interest which were borrowed from some of these trade schools by their graduates did not compensate for their anticipated incomes. As an example, one student was promised by the recruiter that he would earn $38,000 a year and found that many of the school's graduates were earning $8 an hour as dishwashers; while another student who attended an automobile trade program who was promised earning at least $50,000 after graduation could not find work and was earning $12 an hour weatherizing foreclosed houses.[35] In another example, veterans returning from the current wars were enticed to take their coursework online or through other schools, which may be less competitive, especially for admission. Not only did these soldiers and veteran soldiers find that their degrees did not result in the same job opportunities from these "non-profit institutions" as the traditional academic institution graduates may have, but these institutions were more interested in gaining the government loans received by these students plus were not as concerned with these veterans' academic and professional goals. For example, many students were earning MBAs (Masters of Business Administration degree) in ten months rather than the usual two years it would take for most MBAs to earn their degrees.[36] In one case, one of the schools accepted a student with a brain injury which impaired his ability to concentrate and probably would have not benefited at all academically or professionally.[37] These promises are misleading and question the legality given the expectations of the students and the use of taxpayers' money.

False advertising to young children is the last deceptive marketing practice we'll discuss. The children's cereal Frosted Mini-Wheats was advertised as improving "asserted attentiveness" in nearly 20% of all children who ate it, but the FTC found the study's results applied to only half the children who ate this product and even then only 11% of the children's attention improved 20%.[38]   In another false advertising case, Disney agreed to the FTC's demand that they change an advertisement for their "Baby Einstein" DVDs after a study by the University of Washington found that infants watching the DVDs understood six to eight fewer words than babies who did not watch them at all, so Disney removed the word "educational" in its advertising.[39] The last example was in 2009, when in Canada it was found that drug companies such as Johnson and Johnson, Novartis, Pfizer, Proctor and Gamble, among others, allegedly knew that their over-the-counter syrups and chewable tablets did not relieve cough and cold symptoms in children under the age of six as advertised and had to change their labels as a result of a planned $8 million class action lawsuit by a group of Quebec consumers.[40]   Historically, several businesses have been criticized for using their advertising to exploit children or their parents. According to one Harvard Medical psychiatrist and co-founder of a non-profit organization "Campaign for a Commercial-Free Childhood," today marketers spend at least $15 billion a year targeting children who are estimated to view 40,0000 advertisements annually.[41]

Product Safety Concerns

In 2010, the Consumer Product Safety Commission investigated at least thirteen deaths associated with the sling-style infant carriers over the last twenty years, including three deaths in 2009, when all but one involved a baby younger than four months of age.[42] In another incident in the same year, Do It Best Corporation voluntarily recalled a series of children's bicycle bells because the product contained too much of the chemical element, lead.[43] Also in 2010, importer Byer California voluntarily recalled girls' and boys' jackets due to strangulation hazards.[44]

© Sisacorn/Shutterstock, Inc.

Consumers are exposed daily to the potential of using products that may be unsafe for them or their families. The Consumer Product Safety Commission, created in 1972 by Congress, has been charged with protecting the public from serious injury or death from unsafe products and is believed to have reduced the rate of deaths and injuries by 30% due to their diligence.[45] Three industries involving product safety will be discussed in this section: the pharmaceutical industry, the automotive industry, and the food industry.

PHARMACEUTICAL INDUSTRY

In 2009, a whistleblower revealed that Pfizer would pay $50 for each physician whom a sales representative could persuade to add Bextra to the standard care for surgery patients, even though the FDA rejected the company's application.[46] Five years earlier, the FDA released a statement warning that Bextra had been shown to increase risks of heart problems after bypass surgery, when it was used as a painkiller. [47] In the same year, although the FDA announced that clinical trials indicated that Celebrex could carry an increased risk of heart attacks and strokes, unlike Merck & Company who pulled its pain reliever Vioxx from the market for similar reasons, Pfizer had still not pulled this drug from the shelves.[48] Also in 2004, the FDA warned users of the drug naproxen, known as

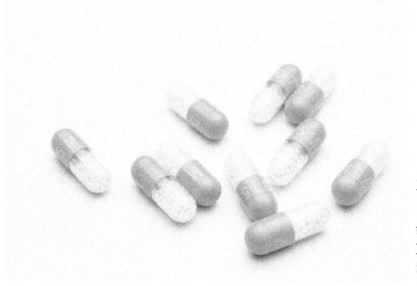

Aleve by the pharmaceutical manufacturers Bayer Healthcare AG, of an increase in risks of heart attacks, which also raised another question, what type of job is the FDA doing if it originally permitted these drugs to be sold in the first place? [49]

Even when it is in its experimental stages, sometimes companies will not risk producing a drug if it has any safety concerns. For example, Sanof-Aventis, Merck, and Pfizer discontinued work on an experimental obesity drug because the trials indicated that these drugs could contribute to depression and suicide.[50] On the other hand, three other drug companies had decided to continue their experiments, even though in one case the results indicated mediocre results in its goal of reducing weight, which amounted to less than a 6% reduction over the period of a year.[51]

The last example involves the power of marketing. The oral contraceptives Yaz and Yasmin which had been heavily advertised were found to be linked with placing women using the drugs at higher risks for blood clots, strokes, and other health-related issues. They agreed to spend $20 million on a corrective advertising campaign.[52] The new advertisements released in 2009 describe the potential risks associated with taking these drugs. What has been occurring in more recent years is that pharmaceutical companies are now advertising to potential patients, as much as their physicians, which brings up an ethical issue regarding whether the patients have the medical knowledge to request these advertised drugs from their physicians. In light of the questions that surrounded the death of pop-star Michael Jackson in 2009, one may question why certain physicians do not play a greater role in refusing pharmaceutical requests from their patients if it could cause them potential harm?

AUTOMOTIVE SAFETY ISSUES

In 1916, in a landmark case, *MacPherson v. Buick Motor Company*, consumers were given the right to sue the manufacturers directly, instead of only the retailers who they purchased their goods from.[53] The case originated when Donald C. MacPherson suffered injuries when one of the wheels collapsed on his Buick automobile and he wanted to

sue Buick Motor Company directly but was prohibited at the time since he did not purchase the wheel from Buick, but a retailer; however, the Court of Appeals in New York (highest court in the state) ruled in his favor confirming that he also had a contract with not only the retailer but the original manufacturer.[54] This strengthened the rights of the consumer, and increased the obligations of the manufacturer,   since before this ruling, the retailers would lack the assets for a wronged customer to be fairly compensated compared to the manufacturer who possessed more assets than the retailers. Basically, it would mean that instead of suing a small "mom and pop" drug store, a consumer now could sue a multi-billion-dollar pharmaceutical company, who could not hide under the old rule that they were immune from a lawsuit since they did not sell the product to the consumer directly, (called privity of contract) and therefore had no direct contract with the consumer and would not have been liable.

Throughout the years, there have been several cases of product safety issues. One of them was the Ford Pinto case discussed in Chapter Six of our text. Although Ford Motor Company knew that it produced a dangerous automobile, the Pinto, because when it was tested, they found that if there was a rear-end collision, since the gas tank was too close to the bumper, there was the potential for the gas tank to explode upon impact. Instead of moving the gas tank further away from the bumper, since it was too costly and it would have set back the production date and result in their competition benefiting, Ford Motor Company decided not to make the change. Years later it was found that their actuaries had computed that it would have been less expensive to be sued for the deaths, physical injuries, and automotive damage attributed to the crashes than the production costs for repairing the problem. In 2010, the same allegations occurred with Toyota Motors when documentation was purportedly found indicating that instead of making the necessary changes in their malfunctioning computerized systems, they saved around $100 million for not rectifying the problem.   In a 2010

Business Week article, an electronic automobile manufacturer, Hughes Telematics, found that currently manufactured automobiles may have between 80 and 100 microprocessors, compared to one central internal computer ten years prior to the article; this may have explained why 1.2 million vehicles were recalled for software glitches in 2007 compared to 420,000 automobile recalls in 2003, all for the same reason.[55] Based upon this information it is apparent that with the increased number of microprocessors, potentially more software glitches may occur which was why there have been increases in the recalls each year.

Yet, Toyota and Ford were not the only ones with recalls. Audi/ Volkswagen models for 2009 and 2010 were recalled after it was found that the temperature sensor might falsely detect gearbox oil temperature which could result in the transmission suddenly shifting into neutral and leading to a crash. In 2009, three major automobile manufacturers, General Motors, Chrysler, and Hyundai Motors, collectively recalled more than 2.5 million automobiles for problems such as oil leaks which could lead to engine fires and frame corrosion or crashes, from various year models produced between 1998 and 2008.[56]

In another recall, Honda Motors, in 2014, was reported to have known of defective airbags manufactured by Takata Corporation, which resulted in five deaths. When one of Honda's employees in 2011 found the problem, it took several years before Honda hired an outside law firm to audit the defects and found that 1,729 written claims, injuries, or deaths from 2003 to 2014, were not reported. Furthermore, federal regulators contacted Honda of possible underreporting of these claims in early 2012, but did not take any action until September 2014.[57]

FOOD SAFETY

As consumers, every time a food and safety warning is announced consumers question how effective the FDA and Department of Agriculture is in terms of protecting the public from unsafe food. After all, in 2004 there was salmonella in California almonds; in 2006 an E. coli outbreak in California-grown spinach, and in 2009 a suspected salmonella contamination in California pistachios.[58] In 2009, Peanut Corporation of America (PCOA) experienced the largest food recall

in history by the Food and Drug Administration; it was reported that PCOA supplied over 3,900 peanut-based products that resulted in more than 690 people in forty-six states including the death of nine.[59] Annually it has been estimated that food-borne contamination has caused an estimated 76 million illnesses, 325,000 hospitalizations, and 5,000 deaths in the United States alone.[60]

According to Frank Yiannas, Vice President of Food Safety for Wal-Mart, a thriving food safety culture is effective when top management sets the tone.[61] Allen Sayler, Vice President of Regulatory Affairs and International Standards at the International Dairy Foods Association believes that this responsible corporate behavior may be done when management encourages its employees to improve their food safety knowledge by offering access to training; participates in state and national professional organizations, such as the International Association of Food Protection or the Institute of Food Technologists; and ensures that the firms selling food products are certified under a Global Food Safety Initiative–recognized third party such as Safe Quality Foods or the British Retail Consortium.[62] In an article in the June 2009 issue of *Consumer Reports*, Consumer Union recommended the following three steps should be taken to avoid further salmonella outbreaks:

Congress should give the FDA the mandate and budget to inspect every food processing facility annually, as well as the authority to order a recall when needed (although pressured by the FDA, currently it is up to the companies to do the recalls); companies must test for specific contaminants, report their findings to the FDA and what they will do with the food, if contaminants are found in the food; and the federal government must form a single food safety agency, not the more than dozen units currently in operation.[63]

Racial Retail Profiling

In 2000, although not admitting any wrongdoing, The Children's Place, a national chain of clothing stores, was found to have allegedly told their employees that in order to prevent theft, they should follow African American customers around and not give them large shopping bags, which, according to "testers," confirmed that this occurred.[64] Also, it was allegedly reported that salespersons were told to refrain from inviting African Americans to apply for store credit cards or tell them about sales.[65]

In 1997, a jury awarded a shopper, Paula Hampton, $1.16 million for race discrimination when she was detained at a Kansas Dillard's store, the same year a jury ordered Eddie Bauer to pay $1 million to three men

© Piotr Marcinski/Shutterstock, Inc.

in Maryland for false imprisonment and other charges.[66] Racial profiling in retailing has been problematic for many minorities and unfortunately, these were not the only cases involving this type of discrimination.

In 2005, Makan Magassa, an immigrant from Mali, West Africa, heard a Macy's saleswoman tell another employee to "keep an eye on the suspicious black man"; after looking around he eventually realized they were talking about him and after filing a complaint with the attorney general's office, Macy's paid $600,000 as a settlement.[67] In the same year, after a 911 call, which could not be traced, the caller said she saw ten youths with a gun coming out of a car she observed in a mall parking lot; but, as the six males and four females entered a tuxedo rental store, they were ordered by police in West Orange, New Jersey, to lie face down, then they were handcuffed and patted down. Police found no guns on any of these youths; they were in the store to purchase a tuxedo for the prom that night.[68]

Of the racial profiling cases involving consumers, the most ironic was when the Newark Airport security personnel questioned Shah Rukh Khan, a "Bollywood" star because his name was on a "computer alert" list; he was in the United States to promote his film, "My Name is Khan," which exposed the racial profiling of Muslims after September 11, 2001.[69] Unfortunately, there have been many cases involving this "shopping racism," but unless retail stores are given more diversity training, have corporate policies prohibiting this type of profiling, and have management from top down support antidiscriminatory behavior, this type of unethical behavior will continue.

Targeting Minorities in Marketing

Another area where minorities are being discriminated is when marketers target them for products or prices when they are not in a position to negotiate on their own behalf. One such example was the subprime mortgage rates discussed earlier. In 2009, a *New York Times* analysis found that 85% of the worst hit neighborhoods for default were African Americans and Latinos, and that if they earned more than $68,000 they were almost five times as likely to hold high interest subprime mortgages compared to their white counterparts in the same income class, who were approved for conventional loans.[70] In another study by New York University, 33% of the subprime mortgages given out in New York City in 2007 went to borrowers with credit scores that should have qualified them for conventional, prevailing rate loans.[71] Yet, this was not the only case where marketers have negatively focused upon minorities. In 1990, R.J. Reynolds Tobacco Company decided to test-market their menthol cigarette "Uptown" in Philadelphia with the intention of enticing mostly African Americans to smoke their new brand.[72] However, the American Cancer Society believed that this was an exploitation of African Americans living "in the ghetto," which is who R.J. Reynolds was targeting.[73]

The last product to demonstrate this targeting toward minorities occurred in New York City when a few small delicatessen stores were selling St. Ides Special Brew Freeze, an ice cold fruit flavored malt liquor which was being sold to underaged minorities.[74] In 1992, this same company agreed without admitting any wrongdoing to stop advertising its malt liquor which suggested that it could increase male sexual prowess and used rap musicians in its media advertisements in order to entice African American males to purchases this product.[75] This type of advertising to lower income consumers also questions the ethicality of some businesses in terms of their marketing practices.

PLANNED OBSOLESCENCE

Another area where manufacturers take advantage is through a process called **planned obsolescence**, *a practice of intentionally developing and marketing products with a limited lifespan.*[76] One example of a compulsory planned obsolescence occurred in 2009 when the transition to digital television was enacted affecting everyone including the poor, elderly, and minorities who could not use the analog television and had to convert their sets so they could be used.[77] A second example is women's sports apparel. Julie Baxter, Vice President of Moving Comfort, a sports apparel manufacturer stated, "Women like to buy sports apparel for fitness classes, and there is some planned obsolescence in terms of fashion and colors, so women buy in this category with good frequency."[78] Although there are many examples of planned obsolescence including automobiles, computers, appliances, and

PLANNED OBSO-
LESCENCE
a practice of intentionally developing and marketing products with a limited lifespan.

© iQoncept/Shutterstock, Inc.

clothes, in some instances consumers have been resisting. For example, in the case of computers, some consumers will wait until the next model is out, since there appears to be a new model annually and they know that the price will drop to make way for the new model. The problem, however, is when technological manufacturers will no longer produce replacement parts, so consumers must purchase the newest model or will sell the replacement parts at such a prohibitive price that the repair bills, due to the replacement costs, are higher than the product itself. In 2009, the Blue-ray digital video recorder began replacing the DVD and VCR. In addition, in 2010, the 3-D screen began replacing flat panel HD (high definition) television sets. Yet, perhaps another question should be posed; is it the manufacturer or the consumer who is driving the planned obsolescence movement?

The twenty-first century will be bringing in many new ethical questions given the rapid advancement of technology. Yet, the basic issues will remain, and that is, what obligation does business have towards its consumers? The pendulum seems to be constantly swinging from caveat emptor (let the buyer beware) to increased legislation on behalf of the consumer so perhaps it will be caveat venditor (let the seller beware). If businesses would remember that they too are consumers there would be less of a tug of war, but only time will tell.

Summary

This chapter discusses some of the ethical issues in the consumer marketplace. Given that of the three major forms of business ownership, corporations generate 67% of all the profits earned in the United States and may use their assets to their advantage, to the disadvantage of the consumer,

CONDUCTING BUSINESS ETHICALLY

corporations were mostly discussed. Since one advantage of the corporate form of ownership is limited liability when the individual owners may have less exposure with their personal assets (usually none unless fraud or malpractice is involved), there are several examples in the corporate world of deceptive financial practices, deceptive marketing practices, product safety breaches, racial retail discriminatory practices, and planned obsolescence.

Deceptive financial practices include churning, the Ponzi scheme, and subprime mortgage rate loans, which resulted in various laws protecting the consumer against these unethical practices. Churning is when a financial adviser engages in excessive trading in order to generate commissions without regard to the customer's financial well-being. Another unethical practice is when an unsuspecting investor is convinced he will earn a higher than usual rate of return, is shown this high rate, and then decides to continue the investment with the anticipation of earning more on the investment. Unbeknownst to this investor, the money shown to earn this rate is not the investment, but the money of others, who just entered this "scheme." Unfortunately, when all the investors want their money, the whole scheme fails, because a bona fide investment never existed in the first place.

The subprime rate mortgage was another deception as a result of unsuspecting borrowers who generally could not have qualified for a conventional mortgage with their credit rating, but were given a very low mortgage rate which balloons (increases) within a few years. This caused the borrower to either pay a rate that would require income, few, if any could earn to pay it back, or have the bank take over the house (foreclosure). Unfortunately, the value of the home market decreased leaving many of the banks who owned the loans (or those who bought the loans from these banks and now own the mortgage) into bankruptcy.

In an effort to reduce investor abuses, several laws were enacted. These include the Martin Act; 1921 Blue Sky Law; Securities Act of 1933; Securities Exchange Act of 1934; Trust Indenture Act of 1939; Investment Company Act of 1940; and the Sarbanes-Oxley Act of 2002. As a result of these laws, the consumers were better protected against fraudulent practices in their financial dealings.

Deceptive marketing practices were also problematic for unsuspecting consumers. These included pricing fixing, price gouging, bait and switch advertising, and false advertising. Price fixing is when two or more businesses will charge the same price so consumers are forced to pay the price determined by the producers, and cannot control the prices by their demand, which is a fundamental principle in capitalism. Price gouging is selling a product or service for an amount higher than it normally is sold, which usually exploits a consumer. For example, during Hurricane Katrina in Louisiana, some retailers charged exorbitant prices which otherwise they would not have been able to obtain.

Bait and switch advertising was another method of consumers being exploited. Products being advertised at a low price would entice consumers into the business, only to find out that the advertised product was either unavailable or told by the sales personnel that the product was inferior; however, a better product was available for a higher price, but at a greater discount. Other methods of false advertising were discussed bringing up the question whether the term, caveat emptor, let the buyer beware, is still a marketing practice among businesses.

Product safety is also a consumer concern. Areas discussed include the pharmaceutical, automotive, and food industries. All three industries have breached the safety laws which many critics believe need to be strengthened.

Racial retail profiling has also been a situation which historically has plagued African Americans. Whether African Americans are being followed by security, accused of shoplifting, or discouraged from opening a store credit card, retailers need to ensure their customers that they will not tolerate this type of behavior. Along the same lines are the marketers who target minorities in their advertising campaigns for subprime mortgage loans, alcoholic beverages, and cigarettes.

The last issue discussed in this chapter was planned obsolescence by the manufacturers. Yet, if consumers are willing to purchase the most updated, newest, contemporary product model, who is really to blame?

KEY TERMS

Bait and switch advertising: the advertising of a highly discounted product or service with the intention not to sell it in order to convince the consumer to purchase another product or service at a higher price (switch).

Churning: occurs when a broker engages in excessive trading in order to generate commissions and other revenue without regard for the customer's investment objectives.

Corporation: a form of ownership where the owners are separate from the business and as such have certain rights such as limited liability.

Dividends: part of the profits earned by the corporation.

Martin Act of 1921 ("blue sky" law): law enacted in order to protect investors from securities fraud, giving the state attorney generals greater power when investigating the alleged perpetrators.

Planned obsolescence: a practice of intentionally developing and marketing products with a limited lifespan.

Ponzi scheme: when a dishonest person convinces unsuspecting customers that they will receive high returns in a short period of time and uses the funds of one set of investors to pay back the others.

Price fixing: when two or more businesses will charge the same price so consumers cannot shop and compare the lowest price among the competition.

Price gouging: selling a product or service for an amount that is unfairly higher than it is normally sold for.

Sales puffery: making statements that are known to be exaggerated, but that the Federal Trade Commission does not consider as false advertising.

Stock: the individual owner's share of a business.

Subprime mortgages: loans to individuals below the prime rate to borrowers who might not qualify for conventional prime rate loans since they could not afford the monthly payments of prime rate loans.

CHAPTER REVIEW QUESTIONS

1. What are two deceptive financial practices found in the chapter? Give specific examples.
2. Discuss two deceptive marketing practices discussed in the chapter.
3. Are consumers being protected adequately from unsafe products? Give two specific examples found in the chapter.
4. What are two examples of racial profiling in retailing?
5. How have minorities been targeted by marketers? Give two examples.

CASES FOR DISCUSSION

CASE 8.1 LOW RATES AND HIGH REPOSSESSION [79]

Within the last few years, people with credit scores of 640 or below have been obtaining credit for new cars, resulting in one in four new auto loans being approved to subprime borrowers. A subprime borrower is a person who takes out a loan at a rate lower than the prime market rate for those with impeccable credit. In June 2014, total automobile loans have skyrocketed to the highest level before the financial crisis caused by subprime mortgage loans. As a result there are examples of Zheng Hui Dong, a Chinese immigrant who paid $42,000 over the life of her loan for a 2010 Honda Civic or Beatriz Rodriquez who filed for bankruptcy but is still fighting to keep up her $900 monthly payments for the Honda that she needed to take care of her grandchildren. These examples are not atypical where many families are paying 110% of their car's value over seven years. No wonder why delinquent automobile loans of sixty days or more have risen 24% from January 2014 to January 2015.

Compounding this problem are the dealers who inflate the borrower's income or falsify employment records, where in some cases, even the unemployed without any source of income may qualify for loans. With an increase in supply of used cars, the ability to repossess and recoup losses are becoming so problematic for lenders that Wells Fargo is now placing a ceiling on subprime automobile loans to 10% of all its loans. Prior to this, there were no ceilings. In fact, Wells Fargo competitor, Capital One, is considering to follow suit and place a limit on these subprime loans.

Although extending subprime loans to borrowers who normally would not qualify is a legal practice, many credit analysts are questioning the wisdom of bankers who encourage such liberal lending practices.

DISCUSSION QUESTIONS

If you were the president of a local bank, knowing that many of your competitors may be tightening their credit policies which may open up a market for lenders who will continue to have more liberal subprime automobile loan qualifications for their borrowers, given the potential for an overall profit for the majority who do pay their loans, would you follow Wells Fargo and tighten your credit requirements for subprime automobile loans, or encourage loans to anyone who may remotely qualify?

(a) Defend your response, using the **full** S.E.A. method (state the philosophy, explain the philosophy in your own words, give a general example, and apply the philosophy to your response).

(Supplemental question b) Apply the seven-step Velasquez decision-making model found in Chapter 6.

CASE 8.2 MARKETING E-CIGARETTES [80]

Although a rudimentary, smokeless non-tobacco device was patented as early as 1963, it was not until a Chinese pharmacist, Hon Lik, commercially marketed the modern e-cigarettes in 2004, when they first entered the small shops in areas such as Viet Nam, that their popularity picked up. E-cigarettes, short for electronic cigarettes "are battery operated devices designed to deliver a liquid containing highly addictive nicotine, flavoring, and other chemicals by heating it into an aerosol that is inhaled."

In 2015, there were no restriction on how e-cigarettes could be advertised and the U.S. Food and Drug Administration is not expected to place any safeguards which may crucial to preventing children using the e-cigarettes for candy flavored nicotine-infused solutions.

DISCUSSION QUESTIONS

At this point, many cigarette companies, including your competitors, are entering the market. Assume you are the Chief Executive Officer of a major cigarette company who is considering whether to manufacture the e-cigarette or not and if you do so, what marketing restrictions, if any, would you impose?

(a) Defend your response, using the full S.E.A. method (state the philosophy, explain the philosophy in your own words, give a general example, and apply the philosophy to your response).

(Supplemental question b) Apply the seven-step Velasquez decision-making model found in Chapter 6.

ENDNOTES

[1] Micheline Maynard, "Toyota Cited $100 Million Savings After Limiting Recall," *The New York Times*, February 21, 2010, p. B1. 10 March 2010. http://www.nyt.com

[2] Hiroko Tabuchi and Nick Bunkley, "Toyota Announces Steps to Restore Confidence on Safety," *The New York Times*, February 17, 2010. 10 March 2010. http://www.nyt.com

[3] "Ex-Andersen Firms Will Pay $40 Million Enron Settlement," *The New York Times*, July 15, 2003, p. C11. LexisNexis Academic, SUNY Rockland, Suffern, NY. 10 March 2010.

[4] Ibid.

[5] Andrew Ackerman, "The SEC Charges Broker With 'Churning' Florida Accounts," *Bond Buyer*, vol. 370, no. 33241, December 30, 2009, p. 4. EBSCO Host, Business Source Complete, SUNY Rockland, Suffern, NY. 11 March 2010.

[6] "NASD Bars Maryland Broker from Industry," *Money Management Executive*, vol. 15, no. 31, August 6, 2007, p. 5. EBSCO Host, Business Source Complete, SUNY Rockland, Suffern, NY. 11 March 2010.

[7] "At the Bell," *Investment News*, March 8, 2010, p. 1. LexisNexis Academic, SUNY Rockland, Suffern, NY. 12 March 2010.

[8] "1921: Charles Ponzi," *The Strait Times* (Singapore), February 8, 2009. LexisNexis Academic, SUNY Rockland, Suffern, NY. 12 March 2010.

[9] David Montgomery, "One Name Stands Alone in the Grand Scheme of It All: Madoff? Meh, History Puts Its Money on Ponzi," *The Washington Post*, December 20, 2008, p. C1. LexisNexis Academic, SUNY Rockland, Suffern, NY. 12 March 2010.

[10] William K. Rashbaum and Diana B. Henriques, "Accountant for Madoff is Arrested and Charged with Securities Fraud," *The New York Times*, March 18, 2009, p. B1. 13 March 2010. http://www.nyt.com

[11] Jack Healy and Diana B. Henriques, "Madoff Aide Reveals Details of Ponzi Scheme," *The New York Times*, August 11, 2009, p. A1; *The New York Times*, March 18, 2009, p. B1. 13 March 2010. http://www.nyt.com

[12] Vikas Bajaj and Louise Story, "Mortgage Crisis Spreads Past Subprime Loans," *The New York Times*, February 12, 2008, p. A1. 13 March 2010. http://www.nyt.com

[13] Edmund L. Andrews, "Fed Shrugged as Subprime Crisis Spread," *The New York Times*, December 18, 2007. 13 March 2010. http://www.nyt.com

[14] "The Martin Act: Using New York's 'Blue Sky' Law to Require Enhanced Disclosure by CO_2 Emitters," Paul, Weiss, Rifind, Wharton, and Garrison, LLP, January 9, 2009. 13 March 2010. http://www.paulweiss.com

[15] "Securities Act of 1933," U.S. Securities and Exchange Commission Website. 13 March 2010. http://www.sec.gov/about/laws.shtml

[16] Ibid.

[17] Ibid.

[18] Ibid.

[19] Ibid.

[20] "A Guide to the Sarbanes-Oxley Act." 13 March 2010. http://www.soxlaw.com

[21] Nancy Seewald, "Two Former Bayer Execs Indicated for Price Fixing," *Chemical Week*, August 17, 2005, p. 6. LexisNexis Academic, SUNY Rockland, Suffern, NY. 13 March 2010.

[22] Jayne O'Donnell, "Samsung Guilty of Price Fixing," *USA Today*, October 14, 2005, p. 1B. LexisNexis Academic, SUNY Rockland, Suffern, NY. 13 March 2010.

23 Kerry Izard, "Briefing: Introduction," *Airline Business*, March 17, 2008. LexisNexis Academic,   SUNY Rockland, Suffern, NY. 13 March 2010.

24 Michael Barbaro, "Cabbies Gouged Over $8 million from Passengers," *The New York Times*, March 13, 2010, pp. A1, A16.

25 Donald G. McNeill, Jr., "Shifting Vaccine for Flu to Elderly," *The New York Times*, November 23, 2009, p. D1. 14 March 2010. http://www.nyt.com

26 Ibid.

27 Leslie More Mira, "Exxon Seeks Clear Price Gouging Law," *Platt Oilgram News*, p. 10. LexisNexis Academic, SUNY Rockland, Suffern, NY. 13 March 2010.

28 Noreen O'Leary, "Dell Pays $4 million in deceptive ads," *Adweek.com*. September 17, 2009. LexisNexis Academic, SUNY Rockland, Suffern, NY. 13 March 2010.

29 Ibid.

30 Nathan Olivarez-Giles, "Owner of 22 Midas Auto Shops Settles Fraud Claims" *Los Angeles Times,* January 26, 2010, p. B7. LexisNexis Academic, SUNY Rockland, Suffern, NY. 13 March 2010.

31 Ibid.

32 Adam Shell, "Two brokers accused of defrauding investors, SEC says scan cost $1B," *USA   Today*, September 4, 2008, p. 3B. LexisNexis Academic, SUNY Rockland, Suffern, NY. 13 March 2010.

33 David Lazarus, "Thrown a Curve in Time Share Pitch," *The Los Angeles Times*, December 9,   2009, p. B. LexisNexis Academic, SUNY Rockland, Suffern, NY. 13 March 2010.

34 Ibid.

35 Peter Goodman, "In Hard Times, Lured into Trade School and Debt," *The New York Times*, March 14, 2010, pp. A1, A22.

36 Daniel Golden, "G.I. Bill of Goods," *Business Week*, January 11, 2010, p. 39.

37 Ibid., 36.

38 "Kellogg To Settle Charges of False Advertising," *The Globe and Mail*, April 21, 2009. LexisNexis Academic, SUNY Rockland, Suffern, NY. 17 March 2010.

39 Jacquie Bowser, "Disney Refunds Parents for Baby Einstein DVDs Following Legal Threats," *Brand Republic News Releases*, October 28, 2009, p. 1. LexisNexis Academic, SUNY Rockland, Suffern, NY. 17 March 2010.

40 Aaron Derfel, "Class Action Sought on Cold Remedies," *The Gazette* (Montreal), March 26, 2009, p. A4. LexisNexis Academic, SUNY Rockland, Suffern, NY. 17 March 2010.

41 Ninotchka Beavers, "Bull's Eye: Advertisers Are Targeting Our Kid," Kaboose Website. 19 March 2010. http://parenting.kaboose.com/behavior/bulls-eye.html

42 "Infant Deaths Prompt Government Warning on Slings," *The New York Times*, March 12, 2010. 19 March 2010. http://www.nyt.com

43 "Bicycle Bells Recalled for High Lead Level," *The New York Times*, March 18, 2010. 19 March 2010. http://www.nyt.com

44 "Children's Jackets Recalled Because of Drawstrings," *The New York Times*, March 10, 2010. 19 March 2010. http://www.nyt.com

45 "CPSC Overview," U.S. Consumer Product Safety Commission Website. 19 March 2010. http://www.cpsc.gov

46 Scott Hensley, "Pfizer Whistleblower Tells His Bextra Story," September 3, 2009, NPR.org website. 19 March 2010. http://www.npr.org

47 "FDA: Consider 'Alternative' to Celebrex." CNN.com, December 17, 2004. 19 March 2010. http://www.cnn.com/2004/HEALTH/conditions/12/17/celebrex.heart/index.html.

48 "FDA Urges Limits on Celebrex, Bextra," CNN.com, December 23, 2004. 19 March 2010. http://www.cnn.com/2004/HEALTH/12/23/pain.warning/index.html

49 "FDA Warns Naproxen Users," CNN.com, December 21, 2004. 19 March 2010. http://www.cnn.com/2004/HEALTH/conditions/12/17/celebrex.heart/index.html

50 Andrew Pollack, "Obesity Drug Clears Trial, Arena Says," *The New York Times*, March 31, 2009, p. B3. 19 March 2010. http://www.nyt.com

51 Ibid.

52 Natasha Singer, "Health Concerns Over Popular Contraceptives," *The New York Times*, September 26, 2009, p. B1. 19 March 2010. http://www.nyt.com

53 University of St. Thomas, School of Law Website. 19 March 2010. http://courseweb.stthomas.edu/law/macpherson.htm

54 Ibid.

55 "Recipe for Recall," *Business Week*, February 22, 2010, pp. 42-43. EBSCO Host, Business Source Complete, SUNY Rockland, Suffern, NY. 20 March 2010.

56 "Recalls," *Consumer Reports*, vol. 74, no. 11, November 2009, p. 14. EBSCO Host, Business Source Complete, SUNY Rockland, Suffern, NY. 20 March 2010; and "2.5 Million Vehicles Face Recall," *Consumer Reports*, vol. 74, no. 7, July 2009, p. 14. EBSCO Host, Business Source Complete, SUNY Rockland, Suffern, NY. 20 March 2010.

57 Hiroko Tabuchi, "Honda Failed to Report Defects' Full Human Toll," *The New York Times*, November 25, 2014, pp. B1-B2.

58 Cary Blake, "Food Safety Requires a Village of Many," *Western Farm Press*, vol. 32, no. 4, February 6, 2010, p. 12. EBSCO Host, Business Source Complete, SUNY Rockland, Suffern, NY. 20 March 2010.

59 Joseph Bermudez, "Tainted Food Recalls Create Widespread Risks to Manage," *National/Underwriter/Property & Casual Risk & Benefits Management*, vol. 113, no. 32, August 31, 2009, p. 23. EBSCO Host, Business Source Complete, SUNY Rockland, Suffern, NY. 20 March 2010.

60 Ibid.

61 Allen Sayler, "2009 Product Recalls: Lesson to be Learned," *Dairy Foods*, vol. 111, no. 1, January, 2010, p. 106. EBSCO Host, Business Source Complete, SUNY Rockland, Suffern, NY. 20 March 2010.

62 Ibid.

63 "Recipe for Safer Food," *Consumer Reports*, vol. 74, no. 6, p. 5. EBSCO Host, Business Source Complete, SUNY Rockland, Suffern, NY. 20 March 2010.

64 Carey Goldberg, "Retail Racial Profiling," *The New York Times*, December 24, 2000. 20 March 2010. http://www.nyt.com

65 "Accused of Discrimination, Clothing Chain Settles Case," *The New York Times*, December 22, 2000. 20 March 2010. http://www.nyt.com

66 Andrea Elliot, "In Stores, Private Handcuffs for Sticky Fingers," *The New York Times*, June 17, 2003, p. B4. 20 March 2010. http://www.nyt.com

67 Nicholas Confessor, "Both Sides Voice Satisfaction In Settling Macy's Profiling Case," *The New York Times*, January 15, 2005. 20 March 2010. http://www.nyt.com

68 "Police Procedure Investigated After Search of 10 Teenagers," *The New York Times*, May 25, 2001. 20 March 2010. http://www.nyt.com

69 Rachel Lee Harris, "Bollywood Star Detained at Newark Airport," *The New York Times*, August 16, 2009, p. C2. 20 March 2010. http://www.nyt.com

70 Michael Powell and Janet Roberts, *The New York Times*, May 15, 2009, p. A1. 20 March 2010. http://www.nyt.com

71 Ibid.

72 Anthony Ramirez, "A Cigarette Campaign Under Fire," *The New York Times*, January 12, 1990. 20 March 2010. http://www.nyt.com

73 Ibid.

74 David M. Halbfinger, "Icy, Fruity Malt Liquor Lures Minors, Critics Say," *The New York Times*, July 24, 1997. 20 March 2010. http://www.nyt.com

75 Ibid.

76 "Your Toaster Will Self-Destruct," *The Korea Herald*, July 11, 2008. LexisNexis Academic, SUNY Rockland, Suffern, NY. 20 March 2010.

77 "Switching to Digital TV: Is This a Mess or What?" *The New York Times*, January 16, 2009, p. 28. LexisNexis Academic, SUNY Rockland, Suffern, NY. 20 March 2010.

78 Nancy Pritchard Bouchard, *SGB*, vol. 42, no. 3, p. 3. EBSCO Host, Business Source Complete, SUNY Rockland, Suffern, NY. 20 March 2010.

79 This case was rewritten based upon the following article: Michael Corkery and Jessica Silver-Greenberg, "Wells Fargo Puts a Ceiling on Subprime Auto Loans," *The New York Times*, March 2, 2015, p. B1.

80 This case was written using the following sources: Megan McCardle, "Thank You For E-Smoking," *Bloomberg Businessweek*, no. 4366, February 10, 2014, pp. 54-58. Business Source Alumni Edition, EBSCOhost. 18 March 2015; "E-Cigarettes: Not Safe, Not Harmless," Tobacco Free California, n.d., n.p., 2015. 18 March 2015; and "Protecting Teens From the Allure of E-Cigs," *Bloomberg Businessweek*, no. 4377, May 5, 2014, p. 16. Business Source Alumni Edition, EBSCOhost. 18 March 2015.

CHAPTER 9

ENVIRONMENTAL ETHICS

Studies have shown that the high levels of greenhouse gas emissions have been continually increasing for the last century and a half as a result of industrial activity. In 1997, thirty-seven industrialized countries and the European Community signed an agreement in Japan, called the **Kyoto Protocol**, *which set targets to reduce greenhouse gas emissions by approximately 5% against the 1990 levels over a five-year period spanning 2008-2012.*[1] Yet, the United States and China were the only two industrialized countries that refused to sign the agreement. Ironically, the United States was the world's largest emitter of greenhouse gas emissions (17% increase since 1990) since the Kyoto Protocol was signed.[2] In fact, in another study, researchers found that the United States, which accounted for 5% of the population was responsible for 30% of the cumulative carbon emissions, while India with 17% of the world's population accounted for less than 2% of the emissions.[3] At the heat of this issue is the question, To what extent are businesses responsible for the environmental sustainability of our planet? This chapter will analyze the effect business has had on our environment, in the name of profits, and what, if any, responsibilities do businesses have beyond those of

KYOTO PROTOCOL
set targets to reduce greenhouse gas emissions by approximately 5% against the 1990 levels over a five-year period spanning 2008-2012.

their stockholders. The areas to be covered are pollution control issues, environmental classism, animal rights, conservation of resources, and energy renewal and possible pollution reduction solutions.

Pollution Control Issues

Water pollution and air pollution have been problematic since the inception of the industrialization of the United States. Although businesses have been responsible for polluting our planet, consumers are not blameless, since their demand of products is primary, with little regard given to either the manufacturing process or its effect on our environment. This section will be divided into three parts: air pollution, water pollution, and land pollution and the issues that surround these pollutants.

AIR POLLUTION

There are several causes of air pollution. One of them is the **greenhouse effect**, *which is when large quantities of carbon dioxide are released into* *the atmosphere for a time and warm the earth's surface.*[4] The carbon dioxide is a result of fossil fuels emitted from fuel manufacturers of products such as petroleum or coal during the production process. *A term used to measure the total carbon dioxide emitted as a result of these greenhouse gas emissions which are produced by a business, process, or individual is called a **carbon footprint**.*[5] China and the United States are the world's top energy producers, consumers, and emitters and account for 40% of the greenhouse gases emitted annually, and would be high on the carbon footprint list.[6]

In December 2009, the Environmental Protection Agency issued a ruling which acknowledged that greenhouse gases pose a danger to human health and the environment, in an effort to pave the way for the further regulation of carbon dioxide emissions which originated from sources such as vehicles, power plants, factories, and refineries. [7] This Environmental Protection Agency (EPA) ruling was a result of a 2007 Supreme Court decision which required the agency to determine whether carbon dioxide and five other climate altering gases (methane, nitrous oxide, hydrofluorocarbons, perfluorocarbons, and sulfur hexafluoride) threatened human health and welfare, and to take steps to regulate the emissions of these gases, should the findings confirm that they were a danger.[8] In the 2007 ruling, the Supreme

© Thomas.LENNE/Shutterstock, Inc.

Court found that the EPA had the authority to regulate "heat trapping gases" in automobile emissions if it could prove that these gases were air pollutants.[9] Prior to this 2007 ruling and 2009 findings, several state courts contended that under the Clean Air Act, the EPA lacked authority to regulate actions involving greenhouse gases, since it had not been established that these gases were harmful to the humans or the environment, which was required under the act.

Although carbon dioxide may be number one in emitting gases resulting in the greenhouse effect, additional research has shown that methane, which originates from landfills, livestock, and oil and gas facilities, is a close second in leaving a carbon footprint.[10] In addition to the health hazards, at stake are retreating shorelines, an increased number and intensity of tropical cyclones, and ice sheet eroding, all which are uncertain to the time and extent when all of this will occur.[11] However, it should be pointed out that carbon dioxide is the most dangerous of the greenhouse gases because it can remain in the atmosphere for a century or more.[12]

In one southern region of the United States, a meteorologist for News Channel 8, who covered Virginia and Maryland, had monitored the greenhouse phenomena and linked how warmer conditions had affected life in the Chesapeake Bay area, and on the air asked his viewers, "Will your children and grandchildren still be able to go crabbing?" [13] This led to many other inquiries and created quite a stir in this area. Perhaps not tangentially, but still in an effort to address this concern, in September 2009, the Obama administration proposed that it would impose a nationwide limit on greenhouse gas emissions from vehicles and require a nearly 40% increase in fuel efficiency for cars and light trucks sold in the United States by 2016.[14] It is believed that this will result in a predicted increased retail cost for new automobiles and trucks by an average of $1,100 and will save automobile consumers $3,000 over the life of their vehicles in fuel bills and reduce carbon dioxide emissions by nearly a billion tons, in addition to cutting consumption of oil by 1.8 billion barrels from the year 2012 to 2016.[15]

Another form of atmospheric pollution is the **depletion of the ozone layer**. *This is the gradual breaking up of ozone gas in the stratosphere,* *which protects all life on earth from harmful ultraviolet radiation and is produced by the use of aerosol cans, refrigerators, air conditioners, industrial solvents, and industrial foam blowers.*[16] The hole in the earth's ozone shield reduces the filtering out of cancer-causing ultraviolet rays, damages crops, and can cause cataracts.[17] As a result of this ozone depletion, studies have predicted that besides the addition of several hundred thousand new cases of skin cancer, it may cause destruction for as much as 75% of the world's crops and that the plankton which floats on the ocean's surface layer given that the entire food chain of the world's oceans is dependent upon this plant life, and it will have severe negative consequences if it suffers the mass destruction which is predicted.[18] In another study, it was predicted that in the state of Georgia, the farm industry loses $250 million annually as a result of ozone-related crop damage.[19] This depletion of the ozone layer is a grave atmospheric issue.

A third form of air pollution is **acid rain**, *the emission of nitrogen oxide and sulfuric oxide as a result of fossil fuels* (coal, oil, natural gas, etc.) and has been defined by the Environmental Defense as follows:

> Atmospheric deposition is the process whereby airborne particles and gases are deposited on the earth's surface. These pollutants come either from natural sources, such as forest fires, volcanoes, and oceanic salt, or from power plants, newly plowed fields, motor vehicles, and other human activities. Wet deposition is the fraction of atmospheric deposition contained in precipitation— predominantly rain and snow. Dry deposition (the remainder) is the fraction deposited in dry weather through such processes as settling, impaction, and adsorption. Atmospheric deposition that is acidic is called acid deposition. Acidic wet deposition is called acid precipitation or, more commonly, acid rain.[20]

Acid rain then falls down affecting trees, lakes, drinking water, soil, vegetation, our food supply, and is a danger to the health of all members of our planet as a result of its existence. Acid rain is responsible for the corrosion of buildings such as the Taj Mahal in India, the Acropolis in Athens, and in one case was attributed to the death of dozens of people

the gradual breaking up of ozone gas in the stratosphere, which protects all life on earth from harmful ultraviolet radiation and is produced by products such as aerosol cans or refrigerators.

the emission of nitrogen oxide and sulfuric oxide as a result of fossil fuels (coal, oil, natural gas, etc.) which damages the crops, soil, trees, drinking water, etc.

in West Virginia when a steel bridge collapsed as a result of this acid rain corrosion.[21] In the 2000 report by the Environmental Defense Agency, it was predicted that 43% of the Adirondack lakes may become acidified by the year 2040.[22]

In their report, the agency recommended the following to eliminate some of this air pollution: (1) instead of just cutting down the amount of sulfuric acid emitted during the summer, which is mandated, it should be year round; (2) increase emission standards for large diesel trucks and buses, and (3) emissions standards should be set for other harmful contaminants such as non-road vehicles and engines which would include marine vessels, locomotives, and construction equipment.[23]

WATER POLLUTION

In a 1972 Gallup Poll, 72% of American said they worried a great deal about pollution of rivers and reservoirs compared to 2010 when only 46% were concerned.[24] Yet, this may be a false perception. For example, it was reported by environmentalists that the Tennessee Valley Authority's Kingston coal-fired power plant released forty-five times the amount of toxic pollutants in the nearby Emory River in 2008 than it did in 2007 which included: 140,000 pounds of arsenic, 320 tons of vanadium, and similarly huge amounts of chromium, lead, manganese, nickel as well as increased discharges of mercury, barium, copper, and zinc.[25] In 2009, Exxon-Mobil was found liable for $105 million for contaminating New York City well water, used for drinking, from its underground storage tanks at gas stations which contained the banned gasoline additive methyl tertiary butylether (MTBE), which followed another lawsuit of the same, for Shell, BP, Chevron, Citgo, Hess, and Sunoco all who had settled previously for claims totaling $15 million.[26] Ironically, at the time the decision was announced, Exxon-Mobil wanted to review its findings with it attorneys, when twenty years earlier it was responsible for one of the greatest oil spills in the history of water pollution, the 1989 *Exxon Valdez* debacle.

In March 1989, Exxon's supertanker, the *Exxon Valdez* ran aground on Bligh Reef, when it ruptured and spilled 11 million gallons of crude oil into Alaska's Prince William Sound, contaminating about 900 miles of shoreline and killing an unknown amount of wildlife. Exxon agreed to pay over $900 million in lawsuits to a trust fund administered by local and federal agencies, as well as $5 billion in punitive damages, as a result of a host of several human errors including an inebriated captain, who was charged.[27] However, on June 25, 2008, the Supreme Court reduced the punitive damages from $5 billion to about $500 million since Exxon-Mobil (Exxon merged with Mobil after this disaster) had paid about $507 million to compensate more than 32,000 Native Alaskans, landowners, and commercial fishermen for the damages caused by the spill and in a 5-3 split, felt that the plaintiffs (Exxon-Mobil) should not have to pay more than that amount in punitive damages.[28] Unfortunately, there lies the problem. Many businesses just look at their lack of social responsibility, when fined, as a cost of doing business, and to add insult to injury, the victims are not always supported by the courts.

In a 2007 case, a pipe manufacturer in Alabama, a division of McWane Incorporated, was convicted and fined millions of dollars for dumping oil, lead, zinc, and other chemicals into a large creek, but the case was overturned by an appellate court on the grounds that the Supreme Court had exempted the waterway from the Clean Water Act.[29] However, recent Supreme Court decisions have weakened the authority of the EPA and the Clean Water Act, in general. In one of its several rulings against the

EPA's regulatory authority under the Clean Water Act (*Coeur Alaska Inc. v. Southeast Alaska Conservation Council*, 2009), the Supreme Court found that the Army Corps of Engineers, not the EPA, had the authority to issue permits over mine-waste discharges.[30] In 2005, the Army Corps issued permits to the mine developer, Coeur Alaska, to dump mine tailings—waste rock left after the extraction of metals— into the Lower Slate Lake and the Southern Alaska Conservation Club, the Sierra Club, and Lynn Canal Conservation Incorporated filed a lawsuit arguing that it breached several sections of the Clean Water Act and would affect the waterways across the country from an environmental viewpoint.[31]

A second case was in 2001, *Solid Waste Agency of Northern Cook County v. United States*, when the Supreme Court found that the EPA only had federal control over navigable water, while the state had jurisdiction even though it was an isolated quarry filled with water used by migratory birds, which would have otherwise been protected under the EPA's authority.[32] A third case decided in 2006 by the Supreme Court in the 5-4 case, *Rapanos v. United States*, ruled on an appeal by the defendant John Rapanos who cleared and filled regulated wetlands without obtaining a permit under the Clean Water Act, that he was justified according to the Court, because "a wetland needs to have a 'significant nexus' to a body of water that is actually navigable." [33] With these two latter cases, the Supreme Court has enabled the EPA to lose its authority in many of its jurisdictions.

LAND POLLUTION

The third form of pollution is land pollution, which will include any pollution besides air and water, although land pollution can affect the atmosphere as well as the water. One example of land pollution involved the farm industry, where the farm animals' byproducts were found to be problematic. In Brown County of Wisconsin, 41,000 dairy cows produce more than 260 million gallons of manure yearly, which is spread on nearby fields, but if the amounts are excessive, bacterial and chemicals can pollute the land and even seep into the ground and contaminate the resident's tap water.[34] Unfortunately, the Clean Water Act of 1972 regulates only chemicals or contaminants that move through pipes or ditches, which means it does not typically apply to waste that is sprayed on a field and enters downwards into the groundwater, contaminating it.[34]

In 2015, a judge of the Federal District Court in New Orleans issued a forty-four-page finding that BP could be penalized for nearly $14 billion for the 2010 Deepwater Horizon oil spill into the Gulf of Mexico which amounted to a spillage of almost 3.2 million barrels (134 million gallons) of oil. Eleven men were killed as a result and at that time caused the largest marine spill in the nation's history.[35]

© joreks/Shutterstock, Inc.

In another situation, Tessera Solar, a solar dish company, planned to erect 34,000 dishes, 40 feet high and 38 feet wide, on 8,320 acres of the Mojave Desert in Southern California.[36] But, still, many environmentalists are concerned about its impact on such protected wildlife as the desert tortoise, the Nelson's bighorn sheep, and the Mojave fringe-toed lizard.[37] One major issue in the question of what is best for the environment must involve weighing between how much energy can be saved by such projects such as solar dishes, offshore drilling, or nuclear reactors and how it effects the wildlife, land, water, or even the atmosphere. These effects are not so easy to measure.

Even the military has been involved in land pollution. In 2003, the United States Navy ceased military training operations in Vieques, Puerto Rico, and has been removing hazardous unexploded bombs by detonating them, resulting in the burning of almost 100 acres of dense tropical vegetation from hazardous substances such as TNT, napalm, depleted uranium, mercury, lead, and PCBs which has caused a disproportionate amount of illnesses such as cancer, hypertension, and liver disease to the inhabitants of this island.[38]

Land pollution exists also in the construction industry. Although lead paint has been banned since 1978, it still exists in many homes and has been linked to neurological damage in young children and in addition was found to lower their I.Q. and even may be responsible for increasing behavioral problems with them.[39] Still, contractors resist any proposed plans such as mandating construction workers to be trained and certified in lead-safe work practices, claiming it would cost approximately $1,000 more for each job.[40] Once again, profits over people.

But even farmlands abroad are affected by land pollution. Officials in China found that over 10% of its farmlands have experienced an annual loss of 20 billion yuan ($2.8 billion) in pollution from chemical plants, steel factories, and crude oil storage facilities resulting in the contamination of 12 million tons of grain annually.[41] Even in India, 100 acres of agriculture land were damaged by an industrial chemical discharges including sponge-iron and ferro-alloy elements by a company whose outcries by surrounding farmers were unheeded. Unfortunately, even the Indian authorities did not take the matter seriously.[42] Evidently, lack of support for protecting the land environment against pollution when compared to the costs which could be incurred by the business to prevent its occurrence is a global problem.

K-Cups are also a problem regarding land pollution. It has been estimated that the number of K-Cups sold in 2014 could form a circle 10.5 times around the world, if placed end to end. Not being recyclable, Keurig Green Mountain has promised by 2020 to develop a fully recyclable version of the K-Cup. Even the inventor, John Sylvan, has expressed regret for developing the K-Cup, knowing now the environmental damage it has caused, but can take some solace in the 2014 K-Cup Sustainability Report where President and CEO Brian Kelley has made a commitment to reduce, and hopefully reverse, the amount of negative land environmental impact it has created.[43]

Environmental Classism

In 2010, a government report found that India's poor suffered some form of land degradation in 45% of the country's geographic area.[44] For example, in the city of Edayanchavadi, a group of men armed with shovels and saws, and an excavator, cleared 8 acres of road as they cut down hoards of trees, by paying a family five times the amount they had been offered two years earlier by a wealthy realtor.[45] Even in Vietnam, in the Province of Vinh Phuc, thousands of people were driven from their land for a golf course which provided jobs for only thirty local residents, while farmers were compensated for their land at an average rate of $2.50 a square meter, which was the cost equivalent of a sack of rice.[46] But it does not only happen in other countries.

In a study by the Associated Press, it was found that African Americans were 79% more likely than whites to live in neighborhoods with the highest pollution scores and where those living in these neighborhoods had an unemployment rate almost 20% higher than the national average, and were less likely to have a college degree.[47] In this same research it was shown that short-term exposure to air pollution worsens existing lung and heart disease and is linked to asthma, bronchitis, and cancer; and long-term exposure magnifies the risks.[48] Furthermore, it was found that one in every six people in the high-risk area lived in poverty.[49]

But, the environmental inequity of the poor is not a new concept. Back in the late 1960s, in Syracuse, New York, when I-81 was constructed, city planners designed a highway and road system that created a

© De Visu/Shutterstock, Inc.

schism between the suburbs and urban areas, or more plainly between the worlds of the rich overclass and poor underclass, leaving the poor communities with excessive noise, automobile exhaust, and much pollution, compared to their more affluent citizens whose areas were kept more pristine.[50] In addition, sewage and water treatment plants within the city's poor communities resulted in asthma rates being thirteen times higher than in the rest of the county of Onondaga, where Syracuse was situated.[51] Even more compelling was the fact that for almost a century, companies located on the lake's shore disposed 165,000 pounds of mercy, phosphorus, and chlorine compounds from a company called Allied Chemical which was scheduled to be cleaned up; but three decades later it still was and the reason attributed to its lack of completion was cost.[52] Yet, a newer costly sewage plant was being built in the area for $122 million for the more affluent citizens, which leads many to speculate that had the impacted community been white and affluent this matter would have been long resolved.[53]

Another issue demonstrating a problem of environmental classism is when a more affluent country will take advantage of a less affluent one by dumping waste into these other less wealthy countries. For example, in 2009, with the conversion of analog to digital television, a Seattle-based group estimated that at least one in four households were expected to dump their old television sets, which would result in 28 million cathode ray tubes, containing approximately 5 pounds of lead, and may eventually end up on foreign soil.[54] In its study, BAN (Basel Action Network) traced electronic waste from the United States to a processing facility in Guiyu, China, which included old desktop computers, laptops, and television sets where residents there suffer some of the highest dioxin and lead poisoning in the world. It is believed that 80% of this electronic waste will be shipped to China and Africa.[55] Unfortunately, there appears to be a "loophole" that does not legally prevent the U.S. domestic companies from dumping electronic waste to less developed countries, which is very problematic from a global environmental perspective.

In terms of pollution, the state of Alabama seems to have had its share. In 2009 alone, 8,500 tons of coal ash, which contains arsenic and lead, were being hauled in daily from a disaster 350 miles away to be placed in Arrowhead Landfill, in Perry County, Alabama, a poor African American community, while its wealthier white community leaders were scheduled to receive a "per ton host fee" which will add more than $3 million to a county budget that previously consisted of $4.5 million.[56] Residents of this area were concerned about the toxic wastes found there, based upon the experiences of other water supply sites nationwide. This problem was all due to equipment failure, flooding, tornadoes, or a lack of oversight at the landfill, especially since the Alabama Department of Environment had such a poor record in terms of regulating their landfills.[57]

But this was not the only environmental situation Alabama residents experienced, especially the residents who were African American and mostly poor. Two major catastrophic events occurred in West Anniston, Alabama, consisting of poor neighborhoods, when a chemical plant located there produced thousands of pounds of potentially deadly PCBs (polychlorinated biphenyls) annually and even worse, were uninformed about it until later on when some residents were found to have high concentrations of PCBs in their blood.[58] In a second debacle, in 2003, the military began burning chemical weapons which emitted dioxins, PCBs, furan, heavy metals, and trace amounts of nerve and mustard gas agents, in an area also equally as poor.[59]

One commonality among all these examples of environmental irresponsibility is a new class of discrimination, which may be termed **environmental classism**, *defined as discrimination from any action that results in a negative environmental impact on a group of individuals who lack economic and political power to oppose it.* Some writers classify these types of action as environmental racism; however, class is a more overriding factor since an affluent member of a minority group will generally not be living in a poor community.

To support this notion, was a *New York Times* article written by Robert F. Kennedy Jr. and Dennis Rivera in which they state: "It is a popular perception that environmental protection is the exclusive concern of the privileged. In fact, it is the poor and disfranchised who are at greatest risk from environmental abuse."[60] Once again, all you need to do is look

ENVIRONMENTAL CLASSISM
discrimination from any action that results in a negative environmental impact on a group of individuals who lack economic and political power to oppose it.

at the facts. In eastern Mississippi, two waste management companies have sought to build huge toxic waste disposal plants where 70% of the residents were low income and without a job.[61]

In the New York metropolitan area, the EPA even merged census data and lists of hazardous waste sites to determine whether wealthier communities were getting preferential treatment under the federal Superfund program, designed to clean up abandoned chemical waste dumps in a move to create "environmental equity."[62] This followed a federal study by the EPA when it found that that "racial minority and low-income populations experienced higher than average exposures to selected air pollutants, hazardous waste facilities, contaminated fish and agricultural pesticides," and that epidemiologists had found decades ago that blacks from poorer communities faced greater health risks from lead poisoning largely from old paint, than whites which was largely attributed to housing discrimination and inadequate public housing.[63]

Finally, in a study comparing the proximity of 9 million people from 1987-2007, it was found that 20% of those studied lived within 1 kilometer of the nation's 413 commercial hazardous waste facilities; 18.3% within 1–3 kilometers; and 16.9% within 1 kilometer, for a total of 20.9% and were 1.5 times as likely to be in poverty validating the premise that classism in environmental hazard exposure to toxic wastes exists in the United States and is still a contemporary problem.[64] Environmental classism is endemic in all parts of the world and environmental distributive justice should be a factor when making decisions about the placement of toxic wastes and not economic distributive justice. In other words, factors when making environmental decisions should include the effect on every member of the population, not just those who are more affluent.

Animal Rights

CRUELTY TO ANIMALS

Three weeks after a logging company cleared the land in one Congo forest, the density of animals dropped more than 25%; a year after a logging road went into a Malaysian forest area in Sarawak, not a single animal remained.[65] But construction is not the only threat facing wildlife; hunting is a major issue where in some cases in the jungle, animals are being slaughtered without any purpose, while others are being killed because of their meat or body parts. Hunting is a multi-million-dollar business according to some experts, who found that in one single Laotian province, $3.6 million worth of wildlife was exported annually which included pangolins, cats, bears, and primates; in addition, in another report it was found that fifty-one tigers were killed in Sumtra in an area where only an estimated 350 tigers were still on the island, and even more disturbing, was the fact that there were 1,000 more tigers during the 1980s.[66] Even the number of hippopotamuses have declined as much as 20% because they were being hunted illegally for meat and ivory from 1997-2007.[67]

© Ajayptp/Shutterstock, Inc.

In the Congo, which is home to an estimated 60% of the world's surviving mountain gorillas, it was reported that seven in one month had been killed not for their meat or pelts, but for their internal organs, which some consider a delicacy.[68] In a second unrelated case in the Congo, a twelve-member family of mountain gorillas were massacred in one of the worst slaughters of these type of gorillas in the last twenty-five years, and were just left there.[69] The ones responsible for their deaths left them without taking any meat or body parts and had killed them for no apparent reason.

In his book, *Defense of Animals*, philosopher Peter Singer discusses **speciesism**, which he defines as *a prejudice against animals by humans who believe they are superior to them*.[70] Furthermore, he argues that "nonhumans are of equal value to humans and worthy of equal consideration, and that an animal's ability to feel pain should also give

SPECIESISM

a term philosopher Peter Singer defines as a prejudice against animals by humans who believe they are superior to them.

him protection under the moral umbrella that humans typically reserve for themselves." [71]   Anyone who has ever owned a pet would probably agree that animals, as sentient beings, do deserve a certain amount of protection and to be treated in a humane manner, so to speak. Animal cruelty is morally abominable; but there seems to be a mixed reaction as to whether or not animals have any rights and whether individuals will abide by their own moral compasses when it involves profits.

In an effort to protect its wildlife, the Spanish Parliament passed a resolution granting legal rights to apes, which included not using apes in circuses and banning research that harms apes, which Peter Singer lauded as being of "world historical significance."[72] Although legal rights such as this are somewhat rare, animal advocates find other ways to protest the inhumane way of treating animals. For example in East Millstone, New Jersey, a company called Huntingdon Life Sciences had been accused of mistreating dogs in its testing of an antibacterial agent for which its client Colgate-Palmolive wanted to add to its toothpaste.[73] Unfortunately, an undercover employee for the animal rights group PETA (People for Ethical Treatment of Animals) revealed to the public this situation and informed the president of this New Jersey testing firm that his company's services would no longer be required for this project since there is a movement by animal activists to stage a major consumer boycott against Colgate-Palmolive's products as a result of this animal testing.[74] In another "sting" by the PETA group, a second investigator found that monkeys had been tortured during the testing for a new Proctor & Gamble (P&G) drug being developed to alleviate migraine headaches, but this time Huntingdon lost their account with P&G permanently.[75] P&G was the parent company for Colgate-Palmolive.

This was not the only situation where animal rights advocates intervened. Members from PETA pressured Coca-Cola and PepsiCo. to stop financing research that used animals to test or develop their products unless required by law.[76] This was the result of PETA discovering that these companies used rats and chimpanzees to test taste perceptions, but even more alarmingly it was reported that a Coco-Cola scientist, financed by Nutrasweet, cut open the faces of chimpanzees to study nerve impulses used in the perception of these sweet tastes.[77]

ANIMALS AS PART OF OUR FOOD CHAIN

PETA also protects animals when they are slaughtered for food. In a move to sue Kentucky Fried Chicken (KFC) for falsely advertising on its website about the welfare of its chickens, and after organizing a six-month boycott to seek an improvement in the way its 700 million chickens were raised and slaughtered every year, KFC agreed to expand its living space for their chickens by 30% and would put cameras in the slaughterhouses to monitor whether the animals were killed as painlessly as possible.[78] But, PETA is not the only agency that attempts to protect animals awaiting their slaughter. For example, in some four-star New York City restaurants, they offer a delicacy called foie gras, which is made from the engorged livers of ducks and geese, who are force fed, usually with long plastic tubes for four weeks before their slaughter, which causes the livers of these ducks and geese to grow at least six times in size. The Humane Society is against such a practice and even went to court in an attempt to stop these restaurants from selling these delicacies.[79]

Sometimes, with public pressure, corporations change to a more ethical path. Take Burger King for instance, when several animal rights advocates had criticized them for cruelty to the animals it would

© rCarner/Shutterstock, Inc.

slaughter. Some of the accusations against Burger King included: cows were feeling their throats being slit, some livestock showed up at the slaughterhouse frozen to the wall of the truck, and pigs were found so cramped that they would go "mad."[80] Now Burger King has pledged to serve meat only from animals housed, treated, and slaughtered with care, which will include giving the chickens extra leg room in their cages, not branding cows more times than necessary, and not dragging livestock to the slaughterhouse by their limbs when they fall lame.[81]

Undercover operations have been extremely helpful in discovering abuses of animals, especially those slated for the slaughterhouse. In a hidden video by someone from the Humane Society, it was found that emaciated cows were being shocked and "manhandled" improperly in the Westland/Hallmark plant located in Chino, California, and was eventually pressured by the United States Department of Agriculture to shut down.[82]

Hogs are also abused during the slaughtering process. For example, in some cases not enough electricity is used to kill them because doing so would damage their loins and reduce their value in the marketplace.[83] Prior to their slaughtering, the pigs are raised in crates and are unable to turn around and are in this confined position for about 75% of their lives.[84] Another example of animal cruelty included some of the pigs were found to be conscious and then thrown into the boiling vats while for all intent purposes they were still alive.[85]

Another issue is cows used to produce milk. In one dairy farm, operated by milk producer Horizon, according to *New York Times* writer, Michael Pollen, "thousands of cows that never encounter a blade of grass spend their days confined to a fenced dry lot, eating (certified organic) grain and tethered to milking machines three times a day."[86] Just because they are not being slaughtered does not mean the cows should not be treated humanely.

Animal compas-
SIONATE
indicates that the animals were raised in a humane manner.

On the other hand, you have companies that want to do the right thing. For example, Whole Foods Market is planning to display labels claiming "**animal compassionate**," *indicating that the animals were raised in a* *humane manner.* [87] It appears more and more food suppliers are leaning toward this direction of being compassionate to animals. Cage-free eggs and wild salmon are just two examples of companies being cognizant of the animals, although many may be more concerned with how they are perceived by their consumers and the media.

POACHING

With ivory now taking in $1,500 each, along with the cruelty to these animals which goes along with this poaching of African elephants, in March 2010, the 175-nation Convention on International Trade in Endangered Species of Wild and Fauna and Flora, turned down a proposal from Tanzania and Zambia to permit a one-time sale of 90 tons of its ivory stock, and maintained its twenty-one-year ban on the sale of ivory.[88] Yet, the week before, an American-sponsored plan to ban international trade in bluefin tuna and to protect polar bears was denied.[89]

Another animal on the extinct list is the South American tapir, known to frequent salt licks in an effort to consumer minerals like calcium and iron and which makes them predictable and therefore vulnerable for poaching.[90] Since they take thirteen months to reproduce, it is predicted that even if twenty are killed, it could jeopardize their existence in certain areas.[91]

One hour south of Playa Junquillal, Costa Rico, young people are paid $2 a night to scoop up newly laid eggs of the leatherback turtles which are threatened for extinction due to elements such as global warming and the rising seas as a result.[92] Given this poaching, it is no wonder that in 2007, scientists were only able to find thirty-two leatherback turtles in this area, when dozens use to appear for tourists as an attraction.[93]

© defotoberg/Shutterstock, Inc.

Unfortunately, the prevention of poaching is problematic. First, there have been several incidents throughout history where law enforcement agents protecting wildlife from poaching have actually been killed. Second, due to financial reasons, many countries will not protect a certain group of species from being on an endangered species list. Third, in some countries penalties are not severe. In Russia, for example, where scientists estimate that humans cause from 65% to 80% of tiger deaths, mostly by poaching, those poachers who are caught suffer only minor penalties.[94] Poachers will kill tigers for parts such as bones, internal organs, and whiskers which result in huge profits especially in the Asian market.[95] In one study by the Wildlife Conservation Society of New York, along with other Russian organizations, it was found over the years 1987-2009 there was a 41% drop in the Amur tiger population in Russia. It is no doubt that more severe poaching penalties would be a greater deterrent, given that the penalty in Russia for poaching tigers is 1,000 rubles, the equivalent of U.S. $35.[96]

Yet, perhaps as consumers we must take responsibility for encouraging businesses to sell us products that have been garnered by poachers or even those who do not treat animals humanely. For example, purchasing cage-free eggs, organically raised meat or chicken, and wild fish (rather than farm raised); and refusing to purchase furs, given the cruel trapping methods used to capture the animals; and many other purchasing choices can deter unethical businesses from profiting by their apathy to the health and care of animals.

Unfortunately, some consumers appreciate being able to partake in a delicacy that is illegal. One such case occurred in Santa Monica where a Japanese restaurant was accused of violating the federal Marine Mammal Protection Act by serving the endangered Sei whale as sushi.[97] The chef, charged with illegal selling of a marine mammal product for an unauthorized purpose, was sentenced to a year in federal prison and a fine of $100,000 for an individual, and $200,000 for the organization (the maximum sentence).[98] Yet, one question still remains: How culpable were the diners in this situation?

Still, there are laws that do protect wildlife, especially in the United States. One of them is the Endangered Species Act of 1973, which "provides for the conservation of species that are endangered or threatened throughout all or a significant portion of their range, and the conservation of the ecosystems on which they depend."[99] There are approximately 1,900 total species covered under this act, of which 1,320 are found in part or entirely in the United States and include species such as the grizzly bear, California tiger salamander, Chinook salmon, green sea turtle, gray wolf, Stellar Sea-lion leopard, and saltwater crocodile.[100] Another law is the United State Marine Mammal Protection Act, which sets standards for domestic fishing and for countries fishing in the domestic waters of the United States. One standard found under this law is that when fishing for yellowfin tuna, precautions must be taken so that dolphins are not taken in error. Breaching this law could result in an embargo, such as one where Mexico's yellowfin tuna to the United States were banned.[101] More laws such as these are necessary to ensure that our animal life is protected but it is the ethical responsibility of everyone to join in their role as advocates for animal rights.

Conservation of Resources

Based upon research by the Environmental Data Services, the world population in 1900 was about 1.6 billion and is expected to exceed 8 billion by the year 2025; oil is being spilled into the oceans at ten times

© doomu/Shutterstock, Inc.

the rate of the already substantial natural seepage from oil fields; and due to human pressure, the world is losing hundreds of species of all kinds daily (e.g., trees from tropical forests).[102] Given this and other research, it is incumbent on our society to identify how we are going to preserve the resources for our future generations. "*Development that meets the needs of the present world without compromising the ability to future generations to meet their own needs,*" is termed **sustainable development**.[103] John Elkington believes that *businesses have three obligations* which he termed the **triple bottom line**: *economic prosperity (profits), environmental quality (planet), and social justice (people).*[104] The focus in Chapters Seven, Eight, and Ten is on social justice for people; this chapter, however, focuses on the environment (i.e., planet Earth).

In an attempt to ensure that organizations are committed to sustainable development a network-based organization, **Global Reporting Initiative (GRI),** has pioneered *a sustainable reporting framework to be used as a benchmark for organizational performance with respect to its continuous improvement to economic, environmental, and social performance.*[105] Conceived in 1998 by a Boston-based non-profit organization called CERES, along with others the GRI drafted Sustainability Reporting Guidelines; a year later, twenty organizations released sustainability reports based upon these guidelines.[106] In 2001, CERES separated from the GRI so it could form its own independent institution, and as of 2009, over 1,000 organizations from sixty countries filed sustainability reports based upon GRI guidelines.[107] To the extent that so many organizations are now conducting sustainability reporting, their chief financial officers will have to accept this as part of their own annual reporting, and be resigned to the fact that it is here to stay and that it would behoove them to be part of this movement.

Whether or not companies have joined the GRI sustainability reporting movement, they are addressing the triple bottom line in their own policies. Clorox's "GreenWorks" natural cleaning products are recyclable; GE has cut its nitrogen oxide emissions, created Energy Star appliances which reduce energy output and water usage; Timberland manufactures biodegradable boots and shoes, has added more renewable and reusable waste materials, less waste, and less chemicals; and Toyota has reduced its greenhouse gas reductions, reduced its water consumption, and lowered the carbon dioxide emissions.[108] These companies have also joined another movement called **green marketing**, *the production of goods or services that will enable the continuation of a sustainable development of our resources for future generations.*

Besides Clorox, GE, Timberland, and Toyota, other companies are doing their share as well. Wal-Mart made a commitment to invest $500 million in technologies to reduce its greenhouse emissions from stores and distribution centers by 20% over seven years and the fuel efficiency of its truck fleet by 25% over three years, and will double the figures within ten years by designing stores that are at least 25% more energy efficient than they had been four years prior to their announcement.[109]

In another type of move, Vinod Khosla of Khosla Ventures has pledged $1.1 billion in green technology and information technology startups.[110] As of 2009, he invested $400 million of his own funds for companies that reduce dependence on coal, oil, and those that manufacture materials like concrete or plastic in an environmentally efficient manner which include projects such as these: one project by a company demonstrating that membrane chemistry could manufacture desalination plants more energy efficiently; another company is designing a compressor-free air conditioner; a third company takes carbon dioxide produced by burning coal and by putting it through water converts it to carbonate and then cement.[111]

Surfing, which is a sport that enthusiasts find protesting against those polluting our waters, have actually been guilty of not being as environmentally friendly as thought of because simply put, their surfboards are made with a chemical called toluene diisocyanate (TDI).[112] However, in San Clemente, a startup company called Green Foam Blanks is changing that by manufacturing a surfboard with a recycled polyurethane blank—the foam core of a surfboard—which will reduce the production of TDI at the same time.[113]

Several small businesses have joined this push by green marketing their products or production processes to save our planet. One such business is Chicago's Consolidated Printing, whose mission is "to eliminate all of the toxic chemicals from her operation," as according to owner Marilyn Jones, "printing is one of the top 10 most toxic businesses."[114] In place of petroleum, normally used to clean various printing tools, her business uses reprocessed restaurant grease in its place; in addition, she uses metal-free inks and modifies her digital prepress system to work without toxic chemicals.[115] Other businesses include Recycle Technologies, which manufactures and sells recycled antifreeze, is one fifth less expensive and has a four fifths smaller carbon footprint; New York Beverage Wholesalers, which installed seventy-two solar panels to power its 7,000 square foot facility, upgraded the refrigeration gear to lower electricity consumption and uses a diesel truck and more energy efficient forklift; Pet Camp purchased a giant 20-foot fan from a dairy industrial facility to use to cool canines and cats, cutting energy consumption; Ripe, a graphic design firm, moved to electronic communication and consolidates marketing material to consume less paper; and Taylor Companies, a furniture maker, consolidated its facility with new energy-efficient equipment.[116] It is no wonder that "green companies" both large or small are expected to raise $9.6 billion as an initial public offering (IPO), according to Bloomberg New Energy Finance.[117] An **initial public offering** *is when a new company offers its stock to the public for the first time.*

INITIAL PUBLIC
OFFERING
when a new company offers its stock to the public for the first time.

However, as pointed out earlier in this section, large companies also are developing approaches to conserve our planet's resources. One example is Nike. In an effort to eliminate leather hides from deforested locales in the Amazon basin, Nike requires since 2010 that leather suppliers in Brazil document the original sources of its hides and prove that the farmlands are properly licensed or will do not business with them.[118] As a large superpower in the athletic shoe industry, the suppliers are sure to adhere to their criteria for exercising environmental responsibility.

Fiat is also involved in reducing the carbon footprints in our environment. It has developed a new technology called Multiair, which is expected to reduce fuel consumption by up to 25% while boosting power and reducing harmful emissions by at least 10%.[119] In addition, it plans on offering an automatic transmission that reduces carbon dioxide emissions by 10% and "flex" engines that switch between gasoline, methane, and other biofuels.[120] But businesses are not the only ones directly involved in reducing toxicity in our environment.

Even countries are becoming competitive in their green marketing strategies. In 2009, President Barack Obama stated that he wanted to make the United States "the world's leading exporter of renewable energy," but China has seemed to rise to the challenge.[121] In an effort to become number one in green energy, especially solar power, Shi Zhengrong, the Chief Executive of China's largest solar power producer, Suntech Power Holdings, stated that in order to build its market share, it will be selling solar panels in the United States for less than the cost of the materials, assembly, and shipping.[122] This will create an interesting dilemma, because if the United States attempts to be protectionist, and gives a tariff to a country that is promoting saving energy, how will that look in terms of a "green policy," but by not doing so, the United States may be losing out to being a dominant exporter of renewable energy.

Energy Renewal and Possible Pollution Reduction Solutions

Several attempts have been made to renew our energy resources and to reverse the pollution currently found in our environment. A few of these will be discussed in this section, which will be followed by the question of whose cost responsibility it is for these solutions to be implemented. One such potential solution is a full-scale floating wind turbine found in Norway. Statoil, an oil and gas company in Norway has found that by hooking up this wind turbine, electricity can be supplied; and it is currently being studied by the University of Maine for use in the United States.[123] Another possibility is through legislation and a pledge by California's governor, Arnold Schwarzenegger, after he signed a 2009 executive order requiring his state to obtain 33% of its electricity from renewable sources like solar and wind power by 2020, which followed Hawaii's pledge for a 40% renewable requirement by the year 2030.[124] However, such a mandate is not new. In 1999, Texas under then governor, George W. Bush, a strong

renewable requirement was mandated which it quickly exceeded; in fact, in 2008, 5% of the state's electricity came from wind power.[125] Adding to this, once again California concerned that the new flat screen panel televisions are energy guzzlers compared to their standard television counterparts require retailers to sell only television sets (i.e., flat panel screens) that consume about a third less than they did in 2009.[126] According to Adam Gottlieb, Energy Commission spokesperson, if nothing is done by California, by 2020 energy usage in the state will double.[127]

Besides reducing energy consumption, the other issue on the minds of governments worldwide is pollution reduction. Since energy plants burn thousands of tons of household garbage and industrial waste, twenty-four hours a day, in Denmark they have been using a new type of technology where local trash is converted into heat and electricity, and dozens of filters catch toxic pollutants that would have emerged from smokestacks years ago.[128] Not only has it reduced the country's energy costs and reliance on oil and gas, but it diminished the use of landfills and cut carbon dioxide emissions into the atmosphere.[129] The United State is reluctant to follow suit due to some **NIMBY** issues, *which means "not in my backyard."* In other words, no one wants such a plant near them so at this point, the United States is studying it but not actively implementing it. This brings up another issue, What should be done to improve the quality of air, water, and land?

NIMBY
an acronym for "not in my backyard"; in other words, no one wants a landfill or nuclear reactor near them, even if it would benefit the environment overall.

CONDUCTING BUSINESS ETHICALLY

Economist Paul Krugman, a Nobel Prize winner, believes there are several solutions to alleviate what is termed "negative externalities" in our environment. **Negative externalities** *are costs that economic actors impose on others without paying a price for their actions.*[130] In the case of the environment, it can be the factories emitting sulfur dioxide into the atmosphere or polluting our waters, or even those driving automobiles emitting carbon dioxide and thus increasing the greenhouse effect. These solutions are (1) setting standards to limit the pollution produced by the products that create pollution, such as the amount of automobile emissions which pollute our atmosphere; or which would require fossil fuel businesses (like the coal industry) to retrofit their older factories or require their newer factories to have scrubbers to remove sulfur dioxide from their emissions as they did in the late 1970s; (2) taxing those who generate these negative externalities, similar to the Dutch who taxed businesses discharging water containing organic material; (3) charging businesses that create pollution in the form of licenses which they can also sell (known as "cap and trade," where the government auctions off licenses, collects the revenue like a tax but instead of the revenue going to the government it goes to the industry, which will issue the revenue back to businesses who create methods to reduce pollution); (4) having a "cap-and-trade" setup for greenhouse gases by selling licenses and taxing businesses for the carbon they emit, which Krugman calls a "hybrid solution"; (5) banning emission producers such as coal-fired power plants; (6) having an emissions tariff such as a carbon tax on production that creates pollution; and (7) charging a fee to consumers or users of the product, such as having a tailpipe device used to measure the emissions generated and then charging the vehicle owner accordingly.[131]

Although several businesses are trying to use more recycled materials in their products, it is extremely challenging pragmatically and financially. For example, Coca-Cola promised to use at least 25% recycled plastic in its containers by 2015, but decreased this commitment because the quantity of recycled plastic from products and packaging will make it difficult to do so. Yet, the problems experienced by these firms include the following: Americans are notorious for not recycling their recyclable items; the machinery used to recycle these items is often antiquated and cannot handle the volume; initial capital investments for these landfills

NEGATIVE EXTER-
NALITIES
costs that economic actors impose on others without paying a price for their actions.

and its processing are prohibitive to many of the towns and cities; and sorting is problematic. With bigger bins, residents dump soiled diapers, dead animals, and in one case a 6-foot shark. Still, there may be a glimmer of hope: Wal-Mart, Coca-Cola, and other large firms have created a $100 million closed loop fund, offering zero and low-interest loans to cites to pay for better bins and more efficient sorting plants.[132]

All of these solutions then lead to the following questions: Who should pay for these negative externalities? Businesses? Consumers? Taxpayers? How do we know that what we are trying to sustain may even be used in the future? In other words, maybe gasoline will not be as important a commodity to future generations as it is currently. How can we enforce other countries to be environmentally responsible? How can we involve more individuals in our own country of the severity of our environmental problems and get them to be more supportive of measures to ensure the sustainability of resources and reduction in pollution for our future generations? These concerns are legitimate and must be resolved before it is too late for our children and their children.

Finally, for the decision makers faced with an ethical dilemma focused upon an environmental issue, perhaps a modification of the seven-step method could be used in its place, as follows:
- What are the facts?
- What is the environmentally related ethical issue?
- What are the alternatives?
- Who are the stakeholders (those influenced by your decision)?
- Which alternative(s) would satisfy the people and the planet from an ethical viewpoint?
- What would the tradeoffs be for selecting the most environmentally ethical alternative?
- What alternative would you select?

Although similar to the model that has been used throughout the text, from an environmental viewpoint, this modified model would emphasize the importance of considering an action and the impact it would have on the environment. Using John Rawls's veil of ignorance principle, if we were to live in the future, what courses of action would we have wanted our past generations to follow to ensure our resource sustainability and a pollution-free environment?

Summary

Air pollution air, water pollution, and land pollution have been problematic since the inception of the industrialization of the United States. Yet, who is really to blame, business or the consumers who dictate what businesses are suppose to do to meet their needs, regardless of the effect on our environment? There are several causes of pollution but since air, water, and land are most prevalent, these three were mainly discussed in the chapter. Some examples of air pollution are the greenhouse effect, which is when large quantities of carbon dioxide is released in the atmosphere for a time and warms the earth's surface. A second type of air pollution involves the depletion of the ozone layer, which is the gradual breaking up of ozone gas in the stratosphere, which protects all life on earth from harmful ultraviolet radiation and increases the chances for skin cancer, damage to the crops, and has even been known to cause cataracts. A third form of air pollution is acid rain, the emission of nitrogen oxide and sulfuric oxide as a result of fossil fuels (coal, oil, natural gas, etc.). Acid rain then falls down affecting trees, lakes, drinking water, soil, vegetation, and food supply, and is a danger to the health of all members of our planet as a result of its existence.

Water pollution is another problem where oil companies such as Exxon (now EXXON-Mobil) were negligent in maintaining the proper precautionary measures should a disaster occur such as an oil tanker leaking out gasoline in the water. Unfortunately, the courts have not been helpful regarding the protection of the population from water pollution, including the Supreme Court, which defined the jurisdiction of the Environmental Protection Agency for only navigable waters, often neglecting the effects toxic chemicals had on drinking water from bodies not classified as navigable, such as a creek or pond.

Land pollution, another problem, includes not only toxic wastes from irresponsible businesses but even the military. For example, after the United States Navy ceased military training operations in Vieques,

Puerto Rico, it removed hazardous unexploded bombs by detonating them, resulting in the burning of almost 100 acres of dense tropical vegetation from hazardous substances such as TNT, mercury, lead, and PCBs which has caused a disproportionate amount of illnesses such as cancer, hypertension, and liver disease to the inhabitants of this island.

In a study by the Associated Press, it was found that African Americans were 79% more likely than whites to live in neighborhoods with the highest pollution scores and where those living in these neighborhoods had an unemployment rate almost 20% higher than the national average, and were less likely to have a college degree. In 2010, a government report found that India's poor suffered some form of land degradation in 45% of the country's geographic area. One commonality among these examples of environmental irresponsibility is a new class of discrimination, termed environmental classism, and defined as discrimination from any action that results in a negative environmental impact on a group of individuals who lack economic and political power to oppose it.

Animal rights is another environmental issue, but unfortunately animals do not have an active voice for these rights. Although a source of our food chain, how animals are treated is an issue that needs to be examined. Cases of animals being crowded, force fed, and brutally slaughtered are all against the mores of our fundamental beliefs in being humane to animals. Yet, there are companies, such as Whole Foods, who will only purchase food from suppliers who treat animals compassionately before they become part of our food chain. Poaching is another problem, where individuals will needlessly hunt and kill animals for sport or for profit. Endangered species are hunted and in some cases used in restaurants as a delicacy, which questions what role the consumer has in encouraging these businesses to continue their operations.

Based upon research, it is incumbent on our society to identify how we are going to preserve the resources for our future generations, or very little will be available. John Elkington believes that businesses have three obligations, which he termed the triple bottom line: economic prosperity (profits), environmental quality (planet), and social justice (people). In an attempt to ensure that organizations are committed to sustainable development, a network-based organization, Global Reporting Initiative (GRI), has pioneered a sustainable reporting framework to be used as a benchmark for organizational performance with respect to its continuous improvement to economic, environmental, and social performance. Although GRI has created a method for reporting the triple bottom line for companies that have joined this initiative, many companies are using green marketing, by advertising that their products and services are complying with the continuation of our resources for future generations. Such companies include Clorox, Timberland, Wal-Mart, and many small businesses that are doing their share of saving our planet.

Government regulations such as in California and Texas mandate emissions standards reduce the carbon dioxide produced from automobiles. Proposals by Nobel Prize–winning economist Paul Krugman include placing a tariff on imported goods that create pollution, issuing licenses for polluters, and collecting revenue for projects that will reduce such pollution. In all, efforts are being made to follow ethical actions to make our planet a better place for future generations. Crucial to this is who should pay for pollution and maintaining a sustainable environment, and how decisions will take into consideration the environmental impact on our planet. A modification of our seven-step method has been proposed to respond to the question of decision making; the issue of who will pay the costs needs to be resolved.

KEY TERMS

Acid rain: the emission of nitrogen oxide and sulfuric oxide as a result of fossil fuels (coal, oil, natural gas, etc.) which damages the crops, soil, trees, drinking water, etc.

Animal compassionate: indicates that the animals were raised in a humane manner.

Carbon footprint: term used to measure the total carbon dioxide emitted as a result of these greenhouse gas emissions which are produced by a business, process, or individual.

Depletion of ozone layer: the gradual breaking up of ozone gas in the stratosphere, which protects all life on earth from harmful ultraviolet radiation and is produced by products such as aerosol cans or refrigerators.

Environmental classism: discrimination from any action that results in a negative environmental impact on a group of individuals who lack economic and political power to oppose it.

Global Reporting Initiative (GRI): organization that pioneered a sustainable reporting framework to be used as a benchmark for organizational performance with respect to its continuous improvement to economic, environmental, and social performance.

Greenhouse effect: when large quantities of carbon dioxide are released in the atmosphere for a time and warm the earth's surface.

Green marketing: the production of goods or services which will enable the continuation of a sustainable development of our resources for future generations.

Initial public offering: when a new company offers its stock to the public for the first time.

Kyoto Protocol: set targets to reduce greenhouse gas emissions by approximately 5% against the 1990 levels over a five-year period spanning 2008-2012.

Negative externalities: costs that economic actors impose on others without paying a price for their actions.

NIMBY: an acronym for "not in my backyard"; in other words, no one wants a landfill or nuclear reactor near them, even if it would benefit the environment overall.

Speciesism: a term philosopher Peter Singer defines as a prejudice against animals by humans who believe they are superior to them.

Sustainable development: development that meets the needs of the present world without compromising the ability of future generations to meet their own needs.

Triple bottom line: businesses have three obligations: economic prosperity (profits), environmental quality (planet), and social justice (people).

CHAPTER REVIEW QUESTIONS

1. What are some examples of how businesses are polluting our planet as presented in this chapter?
2. What is environmental classism and what are some examples of its existence?
3. How have the rights of animals been compromised? What has or can be done to ensure their rights?
4. What has been done to help conserve our resources?
5. What are some potential solutions to our environmental challenges? Which ones do you believe will be most successful?

CASES FOR DISCUSSION

CASE 9.1 ADMITTING THERE IS AN ELEPHANT IN THE ROOM[133]

In Africa, every fifteen minutes an elephant is killed for its ivory tusks and other body parts. Furthermore, a 76% decrease in their population in central Africa from 2002 to 2015 has been reported. In February 2014, the United States Interior Department's Fish and Wildlife announced a complete ban on the commercial sale of ivory in the United States with very few exceptions. Some of these exceptions include if the antiques are over 100 years old and can be certified as such or if the seller can demonstrate that the ivory was lawfully imported before 1990 (permissible under the ban), then they may be sold.

One issue confronting this ban is that there may not be enough officials who can enforce it and there are ways of using certain chemical procedures that give the impression the ivory is older than it actually is. Given that unless the individual is an experienced ivory tusk expert, it can deceive even those who legitimately are trying to certify the tusks' age and therefore may prevent those who are trying to comply with the law unable to legitimately do so. In addition, the rules do not prohibit private ownership but mainly interstate sales of ivory items.

Complicating this is the fallout on innocent owners of ivory products, when they were obtained legally. For example, Grammy Award winner Vince Gill is concerned that if he brings over his forty classic Martin guitars, which consist of ivory pegs and bridges, he will be unable to take them overseas. In another case, a Commack, New York, attorney will now be prevented from selling the hundreds of chess sets with antique ivory pieces he has spent years on collecting. A final case is that of Mike Clark, who owns Collectors Firearms in Houston, Texas, and will not be able to sell his handguns and rifles with ivory even though he purchased them before the ban.

DISCUSSION QUESTIONS

If you were to draft this law in a state that has not yet developed an intrastate (within the state) ban on the sale of ivory tusks, what would your law include?

(a) Defend your response, using the **full** S.E.A. method (state the philosophy, explain the philosophy in your own words, give a general example, and apply the philosophy to your response). (Supplemental question b) Apply the seven-step Velasquez decision-making model found in Chapter 6.

CASE 9.2 ONE BIN FOR ALL[134]

An environmental proposal for the city of Houston will allow residents to throw their recycling and trash items in a single bin instead of separating them first. Supporters of the plan cite the fact that the national average of facilities that dispose their recyclable items in an environmental responsible manner is 34.5% compared to Houston's 6% and it would help reduce greenhouse gas emissions and costs. One reason attributed to this pollution reduction is that it would cut traffic since there would be only one pickup compared to two.

However, Dr. Robert Bullard, Dean of the School of Public Affairs at Texas Southern University, found that there is mostly a lower income, minority population surrounding the landfill. Placing a new waste-sorting plant near an existing landfill will once again demonstrate how his research on environmental racism continues to be practiced, in this case by the Houston officials. Environmental racism represents the proximity of minority neighborhoods being exposed to environmental risks at a higher rate than their "non-minority" counterparts because they lack the political and financial clout to challenge the environmental threats.

Houston's director of sustainability, Laura Spanjian, disagrees and believes the proposed sorting center is an advanced manufacturing facility and not a landfill. But, she admits that while this facility would receive a fair amount of truck traffic, it would improve the environmental quality of the neighborhood by diverting the waste from the existing landfills. Bullard disagrees and believes that the landfills he was able to get closed in these minority neighborhoods in the late 1960s and 1970s are now being replaced by new facilities.

DISCUSSION QUESTIONS

As a city councilor of Houston, would you be in favor of the new advanced manufacturing facility in the proposed minority neighborhood?

(a) Defend your response, using the **full** S.E.A. method (state the philosophy, explain the philosophy in your own words, give a general example, and apply the philosophy to your response). (Supplemental question b) Apply the seven-step Velasquez decision-making model found in Chapter 6.

Endnotes

1 "Kyoto Protocol," United Nations Framework Convention on Climate Change Website. 24 March 2010. http://unfccc.int/kyoto_protocol/items/2830.php

2 Bill Chameides, "Did the Kyoto Protocol Miss the Target?" *The Huffington Post*, March 24, 2010. 24 March 2010. http://www.huffingtonpost.com/bill-chameides/did-the-kyoto-protocol-mi_b_317855.html

3 Peter Singer, *One World: The Ethics of Globalization*, 2d ed. (New Haven, CT: Yale University Press, 2002), p. 32.

4 "Greenhouse Gas Definitions," *Aviation Week & Space Technology*, August 20, 2007, vol. 167, no. 8, August 20, 2007. EBSCO Business Source Complete, SUNY Rockland, Suffern, NY. 9 April 2010.

5 Andrew Kaplan, "Learning the Lingo," *Beverage World*, vol. 128, no. 4, April 15, 2009. EBSCO Business Source Complete, SUNY Rockland, Suffern, NY. 9 April 2010.

6 Joshua Kucera, "Side by Side in Need for Green Growth," *U.S. News and World Report*, vol. 147, no. 4, April 2010. EBSCO Business Source Complete, SUNY Rockland, Suffern, NY. 9 April 2010.

7 John Broder, "Greenhouse Gases Imperil Health, E.P.A. Announces," *The New York Times*,

December 7, 2009, p. A18. 9 April 2010. http://www.nyt.com

8 Ibid.

9 Linda Greenhouse, "Justice Says E.P.A. Has Power to Act on Harmful Gases," *The New York Times*, April 3, 2007. 9 April 2010. http://www.nyt.com

10 Andrew C. Revkin, "Global Warming," *The New York Times*, Science section, December 8, 2009. 9 April 2010. http://www.nyt.com

11 Ibid.

12 Andrew C. Revkin and John Broder, "In Face of Skeptics, Experts Affirm Climate Peril," *The New York Times*, December 6, 2009, p. A1. 9 April 2010. http://www.nyt.com

13 James Kanter, "New Voices on Climate Change," *The New York Times*, November 22, 2009. 9 April 2010. http://www.nyt.com

14 John M. Broder, "New Standard Links Mileage and Gas Emissions," *The New York Times*, September 15, 2009, p. B4. 9 April 2010. http://www.nyt.com

15 Ibid.

16 Manuel G. Velasquez, *Business Ethics: Concepts and Cases*, 5th ed. (Upper Saddle River, NJ: Prentice Hall, 2002), p. 271.

17 "Ozone Decay in '95 Is Unparalleled," *The New York Times*, November 29, 1995. 9 April 2010. http://www.nyt.com

18 Manuel G. Velasquez, *Business Ethics: Concepts and Cases*, 5th ed. (Upper Saddle River, NJ: Prentice Hall, 2002), p. 271.

19 *Building on Thirty Years of Clean Air Success: The Case for Reducing NOx Air Pollution* (Boulder,CO: Environmental Defense, 2000), p. 15.

20 Ibid., 29.

21 Manuel G. Velasquez, *Business Ethics: Concepts and Cases*, 5th ed. (Upper Saddle River, NJ: Prentice Hall, 2002), p. 272.

22 *Building on Thirty Years of Clean Air Success: The Case for Reducing NOx Air Pollution* (Boulder,CO: Environmental Defense, 2000), p. 29.

23 Ibid., 42.

24 Jeffrey Jones, "In U.S., Many Environmental Issues at 20-Year-Low Concern, " *Gallup Poll Briefing*, March 16, 2010, p. 1. EBSCO Business Source Complete, SUNY Rockland, Suffern, NY. 10 April 2010.

25 Jonathan Rickman, "TVA Coal Ash Spill Caused Huge Toxic Metal Release," *Energy Daily*, December 9, 2009. EBSCO Business Source Complete, SUNY Rockland, Suffern, NY. 10 April 2010.

26 Daniel Hays, "Exxon Mobil Hit With $105M Damage Award For New York Pollution," *National Underwriter / Property & Casualty Risk & Benefits Management*, vol. 114, no. 44, November 23, 2009, pp. 17-18. EBSCO Business Source Complete, SUNY Rockland, Suffern, NY. 10 April 2010.

27 Felicity Barringer, "$92 Million Sought for Exxon Valdez Cleanup," *The New York Times*, June 2, 2006. 11 April 2010. http://www.nyt.com

28 Adam Liptak, "Damages Cut Against Exxon in Valdez Case," *The New York Times*, June 26, 2008. 11 April 2010. http://www.nyt.com

29 Charles Duhigg and Janet Robert, "Rulings Restrict Clean Water Act, Hampering E.P.A.," *The New York Times*, March 1, 2010, p. A 17.

11 April 2010. http://www.nyt.com

30 Jennifer Koons, "Supreme Court Backs Army Corps, Mining Company in Alaska Water Case," *The New York Times*, June 22, 2009. 11 April 2010. http://www.nyt.com

31 Felicity Barringer, "Reach in Clean Water Is An Issue in Two Supreme Court Cases," *The New York Times*, June 22, 2009. 11 April 2010. http://www.nyt.com

32 Ibid.

33 Linda Greenhouse, "Court Splits Over Wetlands Protection," *The New York Times*, June 19, 2006. 11 April 2010. http://www.nyt.com

34 Charles Duhigg, "Health Ills Abound As Farm Runoff Fouls Wells," *The New York Times*, September 17, 2009. 11 April 2010. http://www.nyt.com

35 John Schwartz. "Judge's Ruling on Gulf Oil Spill Lowers Ceiling on the Fine BP Is Facing," *The New York Times,* January 16, 2015, p. B3.

36 Todd Woody, "Battle Brewing Over Giant Desert Solar Farm," *The New York Times*, August 5, 2009. 11 April 2010. http://www.nyt.com

37 Ibid.

38 Mireya Navarro, "New Battle on Vieques, Over Navy's Cleanup of Munitions," *The New York Times,* August 7, 2009, p. A10. 12 April 2010. http://www.nyt.com

39 Mireya Navarro, "Rule on Lead Safety Set to Take Effect," *The New York Times*, April 9, 2010, p. A18.

40 Ibid.

41 "Government Targets Land Pollution," Financial Times Ltd. China.com.cn. June 20, 2008. LexisNexis Academics, SUNY Rockland, Suffern, NY. 13 April 2010.

42 "Factory Effluents Damages Agricultural Land," *The Statesman* (India), November 17, 2005. LexisNexis Academics, SUNY Rockland, Suffern, NY. 13 April 2010.

43 James Hamblin, "A Brewing Problem: What's the Healthiest Way to Keep Everyone Caffeinated?" *The Atlantic*, March 2, 2015. www.theatlantic.com

44 Akash Kapur, "Pollution As Another Form of Poverty," *The New York Times*, October 8, 2009. 11 April 2010. http://www.nyt.com

45 Ibid.

46 Seth Mydans, "A Harvest of Golf Courses From Vietnam's Farmland," *The New York Times*, October 20, 2009, p. A10. 13 April 2010. http://www.nyt.com

47 The Associated Press, "More Blacks Live with Pollution," in Paul S. Rothenberg, Ed., *Race, Class, and Gender in The United States,* 8th ed. (New York: Worth Publishers, 2010), pp. 294-295.

48 Ibid.

49 Ibid.

50 Linda Carty, "The Dirty Saga of Onondaga County," *Experiencing Race, Class, and Gender in the United States*, 5th ed. (New York: McGraw-Hill Company, 2009), p. 266.

51 Ibid.

52 Ibid.

53 Ibid.

54 Nathanial Gronewold, "Some See E-Waste Crisis Trailing Switch to Digital TV," *The New York Times*, June 15, 2009. 14 April 2010. http://www.nyt.com

55 Ibid.

56 Shalia DeWan, "Clash in Alabama Over Tennessee Coal Ash," *The New York Times*, August 30, 2009, p. A12. 14 April 2010. http://www.nyt.com

57 Ibid.

58 Bob Herbert, "Poor, Black, and Dumped On," *The New York Times*, October 5, 2006. 14 April 2010. http://www.nyt.com

59 Ibid.

60 Robert F. Kennedy Jr. and Dennis Rivera, "Pollution's Chief Victims: The Poor," *The New York Times*, August 15, 2010. 14 April 2010. http://www.nyt.com

61 Keith Schneider, "Black Fighting Blacks On Plan for Dump Site," *The New York Times*, December 13, 1993. 14 April 2010. http://www.nyt.com

62 John Cushman Jr., "Environmental Hazards to Poor Gain New Focus at E.P.A.," *The New York Times*, January 21, 1992. 15 April 2010. http://www.nyt.com

63 John Cushman Jr., "Clinton to Order Pollution Policy Cleared of Bias," *The New York Times*, February 10, 1994. 15 April 2010. http://www.nyt.com

64 Robert Bullard, Paul Mohai, Robin Saha, and Beverly Wright, *Toxic Wastes and Race at Twenty: 1987-2007* (Cleveland: United Church of Christ, 2007), pp. 37, 46. 16 April 2010. www.ejnet.org/ej

65 Sharon Begley, "Cry of the Wild," *Newsweek*, vol. 150, no. 6, August 6, 2007, p. 23.

66 Ibid.

67 Ibid.

68 Scott Johnson, "Gorilla Warfare," *Newsweek*, vol. 150, no. 6, August 6, 2007, p. 28.

69 Ibid., 25.

70 Charlotte Laws, "Guess Who's Coming to Dinner? The Controversial Peter Singer!," *Philosophy Now*, no. 67, May/June 2008, p. 11.

71 Ibid.

72 Adam Cohen, "What's Next in the Law? The Unalienable Rights for Chimps," *The New York Times*, July 14, 2008. 16 April 2010. http://www.nyt.com

73 Gina Kolata, "Tough Tactics in One Battle Over Animals in the Lab," *The New York Times*, March 24, 1998. 16 April 2010. http://www.nyt.com

74 Ibid.

75 Ibid.

76 Brenda Goodman, "Coco-Cola and PepsiCo Agree to Curb Animal Tests," *The New York Times*, May 31, 2007. 16 April 2010. http://www.nyt.com

77 Ibid.

78 Elizabeth Becker, "Animal Rights Group to Sue Fast Food Chain," *The New York Times*, July 3, 2003. 16 April 2010. http://www.nyt.com

79 Anthony Ramirez, "Animal Rights Group Asks New York to Ban Foie Gras, *The New York Times*, June 22, 2006. 16 April 2010. http://www.nyt.com

80 Greg Winter, "Burger King Pledges Human Use of Animals," *The New York Times*, June 29, 2001. 16 April 2010. http://www.nyt.com

81 Ibid.

82 Joe Nocera, "A Case of Abuse, Heightened," *The New York Times*, March 8, 2008. 16 April 2010. http://www.nyt.com

83 Ava Park, "The Dark Side of White Meat," *Business and Society Review*, no. 89, Spring 1994, p. 61. EBSCO Business Source Complete, SUNY Rockland, Suffern, NY. 16 April 2010.

84 Ibid.

85 Ibid.

86 Marian Burros, "You Are What You Eat: 2006 and the Politics of Food," *The New York Times*, December 27, 2006. 16 April 2010. http://www.nyt.com

87 Andrew Martin, "Meat Labels Hoping to Lure Sensitive Carnivores," *The New York Times*, October 24, 2006. 16 April 2010. http://www.nyt.com

88 Alan Cowell, "Bid to Relax International Ban on the Sale of Ivory is Rejected," *The New York Times*, March 22, 2010. 16 April 2010. http://www.nyt.com

89 Ibid.

90 Anthony King, "New Research on Malaysia's Odd, Elusive Tapir," *The New York Times*, June 2, 2009, p. D4. 16 April 2010. http://www.nyt.com

92 Elisabeth Rosenthal, "Turtles Are Casualties of Global Warning in Costa Rico," *The New York Times*, November 14, 2009, June 2, 2009, p. A8. 16 April 2010. http://www.nyt.com

93 Ibid.

94 Michael Schwirtz, "Data Show a Decline for Tigers in Russia," *The New York Times*, November 24, 2009, p. D4. 17 April 2010. http://www.nyt.com

95 Ibid.

96 Ibid.

97 Jennifer Steinhauser, "Sushi Spot Is Charged With Serving Whale Meat, *The New York Times*, March 10, 2010, p. A20. 17 April 2010. http://www.nyt.com

98 Ibid.

99 "Endangered Species Act of 1973," Office of Protected Resources Website. 17 April 2010. www.*nmfs.noaa.gov*/pr/species/turtles

100 Ibid.

101 Peter Singer, *One World: The Ethics of Globalization*, 2d ed. (New Haven: Yale University Press, 2004), p. 59.

102 John Elkington, *Cannibals with Forks: The Triple Bottom Line of 21st Century Business* (Gabriola Island, Canada: New Society Publishers, 1998), p. 54.

103 Ibid., 55.

104 Ibid., 2.

105 "What Is GRI?" Global Reporting Initiative Website. 17 April 2010. www.globalreporting.org

106 "History," Global Reporting Initiative Website. 17 April 2010. www.globalreporting.org

107 Gary Cokins, "Measuring the New 'Triple' Bottom Line: People, Profits, and the Planet," *Financial Executive*, November, 2009, p. 37. 10 April 2010. www.financialexectuvies.org

108 Satinder Dhiman, "Products, People, and Planet: The Triple Bottom-Line Sustainability Imperative," *The Journal of Global Business*, vol. 2, no. 2, July 2007.

109 Michael Barbaro and Felicity Barringer, "Wal-Mart Says It Will Cut Fuel and Energy Use," *The New York Times*, October 26, 2005. 17 April 2010. http://www.nyt.com

[110] Claire Cain Miller, "Venture Firms 'Green' Funds Top $1 Billion," *The New York Times*, August 31, 2009, p. B1. 17 April 2010. http://www.nyt.com

[111] Ibid.

[112] Todd Woody, "Business of Green: Surf's Up, Waste's Down," *The New York Times*, November 19, 2009, p. F4. 17 April 2010. http://www.nyt.com

[113] Ibid.

[114] Amy Barrett, "Lean and Green," *Small Biz*, August/September 2009, p. 38.

[115] Ibid.

[116] Ibid.,39, 40, 42, 44.

[117] Mark Scott and Alex Morales, "A Gold Rush In Green Technology," *Bloomberg BusinessWeek*, April 25, 2010, p. 24.

[118] Adam Aston (Ed.), "Can Nike Help Save the Amazon?" *BusinessWeek*, August 10, 2009, p. 54.

[119] Carol Matlack, "The Hidden Edge At Fiat," *BusinessWeek*, August 24 & 31, 2009, p. 28.

[120] Ibid.

[121] Keith Bradsher, "China Racing Ahead U.S. in Drive to Go Solar," *The New York Times*, August 25, 2009, p. A1. 17 April 2010. http://www.nyt.com

[122] Ibid.

[123] Henry Fountain, "Seeking Wind Energy, Some Consider the Sea," *The New York Times*, November 19, 2009, p. F6. 17 April 2010. http://www.nyt.com

[124] Kate Galbraith, "Schwarzenegger Orders Renewables Goals," Green Inc. *The New York Times*, September 15, 2009. 17 April 2010. http://www.nyt.com

[125] Kate Galbraith, "California and Texas: Renewable Energies Odd Couple," *The New York Times*, October 18, 2009, p. WK3. 17 April 2010. http://www.nyt.com

[126] Cliff Edwards, "Hasta La Vista, Power-Hungary TVs," *BusinessWeek*, November 9, 2009, p. 33.

[127] Ibid.

[128] Elisabeth Rosenthal, "Europe Finds Clean Fuel; U.S. Sits Back," *The New York Times*, April 13, 2010, p. A1.

[129] Ibid.

[130] Paul Krugman, "Green Economics: How We Can Afford to Tackle Climate Change," *The New York Times*, Magazine Section, April 11, 2010, p. 36.

[130] Ibid., 36-38, 41.

[131] Ibid.

[132] "Recycling in America: In the Bin," *The Economist*, April 22, 2015. www.economist.com

[133] This case was rewritten based upon the following articles: Melissa Mahony, "The Elephant in the Room," *Unearthed*, February 13, 2014. www.onearth.org; New York Times Editorial Board, "Banning Ivory Sales in America," *The New York Times*, February 18, 2014, p. A22; and Tom Machberg, "Limits on Ivory Sales, Meant to Protect Elephants, Set Off Wide Concerns," *The New York Times*, A15, March 21, 2014.

[134] This case was rewritten based upon the following article: Neena Satija, "A Waste Solution May Lean on a Low Income Area," *The Texas Tribune*, August 23, 2014, p. A23A.

CHAPTER 10

GLOBAL MARKETPLACE ETHICS

Tang Yinghong had problems. His employer, Ningbo Beifa Group, had successfully supplied pens, mechanical pencils, and highlighters to Wal-Mart stores; however, he learned that where he was an administrator in the Chinese coastal city of Ningbo, Wal-Mart was planning to inspect the labor conditions at his factory.[1] On three occasions Wal-Mart had found that Beifa was paying its 3,000 workers less than China's minimum wages

© underworld/Shutterstock, Inc.

and was violating its overtime rules, and should there be a fourth offense, their relationship with Wal-Mart would be terminated.[2] In March 2010, two months after threatening to leave China because of their censorship and hacking, Google closed its Internet search service and directed its users to its Hong Kong site.[3] And, in Paris, United States employees of Sodexo, a food service business, earn less than France's minimum wage of $12.28 an hour.[4] The role of ethical relativism is a challenge when dealing with the global marketplace; and comparing it to the mores of the United States can be quite problematic. But are we Americans any better? Remember the low wages earned by outsourced foreign employees, for American businesses under the names of celebrities such as Kathy Lee Gifford where fifteen-year-old girls earned $0.31 an hour and worked seventy-five hours weeks for her sportswear, or Shaquille O'Neal and Michael Jordan for endorsing athletic shoes that were made by $0.25-an-hour Indonesian and Filipino workers?[5] These celebrities may have lacked the knowledge of these unconscionable conditions, but the fact is that these outsourced workers were working in conditions that would be illegal in the United States. This chapter will present the following topics: child labor and sweatshops, international bribery, the Foreign Corrupt Practices Act of 1977, protectionism, and unethical foreign marketing practices.

Child Labor and Sweatshops

In a 2009 *Political Science Quarterly* study, it was reported that 62% of the Americans surveyed were willing to pay $5 extra for a $20 sweater which was produced under more ethical conditions and 75% would spend 50 cents more on a pound of fair-trade coffee.[6] Although this is a step in the right direction, abuses of workers still exist. According to the United Nations Children's Fund (UNICEF), an estimated 158 million children aged five to fourteen are engaged in child labor, of which 69 million are from in Sub-Saharan Africa and 44 million from South Asia, where they work in hazardous conditions such as being in mines, having contact with chemicals or pesticides in agricultural jobs, working with dangerous machinery, being employed at private homes as domestic servants, or being hidden behind the walls of factory workshops.[7]

UNICEF defines child labor with a criteria including at least twenty-eight hours of domestic work for those aged fourteen or less, and at least forty-three hours for those aged fifteen to seventeen; and for economic work (working for businesses) at least one hour for those eleven years of less, at least fourteen hours for those aged twelve to fourteen, and at least forty-three hours for those age fifteen to seventeen.[8] For this reason, child labor will be discussed separately from the abusive working condition found in "sweatshops."

CHILD LABOR

The number of cases involving children working in unsafe working conditions with low pay is astronomical. A sampling of some of these abuses will be discussed. For example, in the Guandong Province, near Hong Kong, more than 100 children were found working for factories in the city of Dongguan, one of China's largest manufacturing centers for electronics and consumer goods worldwide, where most who were between thirteen and fifteen were found to be either tricked or kidnapped from their rural homes into almost slave-like conditions for low pay, before they were rescued by the government.[8] Many of these children were paid about $0.42 an hour, far below the local minimum wage of about $0.64 an hour, and some were even reported to have

© paul prescott/Shutterstock, Inc.

been lined up based upon their body type, which was indicative of their ability to do a given job prior to being taken.[9]

In another documented case, a Shanghai man claimed his children were brought to a brick factory around midnight of the day they vanished and were told, "you will start working in the morning, so get some sleep, and don't lose your bowls, or you will have to pay for them," and that they were charged 50 renminbi ($6.50) for a blanket to keep them warm.[10] Forced to work under severe conditions which included being scantily clothed, unpaid, and often fed water and steamed buns, they would have remained there as "slaves," but fortunately they were rescued by government officials.[11]

Even though these abuses occurred in China, some of their child labor is an indirect result of American businesses using foreign workers abroad. In 2007, several American companies including Wal-Mart, Disney, and Dell were accused of using child labor from Chinese factories where some worked sixteen-hour days on a fast-moving assembly line and were paid less than the minimum wage of $0.55 an hour.[12] Although the executives went on record claiming they had no knowledge of these conditions, historically there have been issues which these firms have been accused of, but denied, such allegations. In 1992, an NBC *Dateline* documentary program showed children as young as eleven years old sewing Wal-Mart labels into garments manufactured from a Bangladesh factory.[13] This was the same factory where two years prior to this television program, twenty-five workers including several children had died; but, just as appalling, at the time Bangladesh had no laws against child labor.[14]

Another example of American businesses using child labor is the GapKids clothing chain. It was reported that in 2007, in Delhi, India, child workers were found to be hand-embroidering their clothes even though India has a law against employing children that young, The Child Labor Prohibition and Regulation Act in India prohibited the employment of children younger than fourteen years old in hazardous jobs which included work in the embroidery industry.[15] After finding out that children were being used like that, GapKids announced a grant of $200,000 to improve working conditions and pledged to organize an international conference to develop solutions to alleviate or improve the working conditions found in child labor.[16] Yet, it should be noted that in 2000, it was due to the pressure of college students which led some factories for mega-conglomerates Nike and Gap to cut back on its child labor.[17]

In fact, in one 2000 case, the U.S. Customs Service banned clothing imported from a Chinese-owned factory in Mongolia when it found out that the company, Dong Fan International, employed underage workers and forced them to stay at their posts for marathon shifts.[18] Historically, this ban was rarely imposed by the U.S. Customs Service. Yet, it should not go unnoticed that these companies, whether aware of it or not, seem not to be concerned about how their products were being manufactured, as much as they were of how they could keep their labor costs down. Which brings up another issue: How culpable are American businesses for looking the other way?

According to Jeremy Snyder, Assistant Professor of Canada's Simon Fraser University in the British Columbia, companies such as Wal-Mart have been accused of using their dominant purchasing position to exert influence over their suppliers to set prices well below their level of comfort of these suppliers, in terms of profit, and force them to reduce the wage levels of their own employees, which includes loss of benefits and improving working conditions, forcing them to be placed into a position so they exploit their own employees.[19] Child labor is just another method to ensure low prices; and since many foreign governments may have minimal child labor laws and do not enforce them, many American businesses are complicit with this exploitative process.

But in a 2009 research study, J. Lawrence French found that perhaps ethical relativism should be explored as a rationale for encouraging child labor in these less developed countries. His study involved 461 children working in Franca, Brazil's shoe factories, and found that instead of calling for an end to such employment, there should be more of a focus on improving the working conditions of these child laborers.[20] For example, he found that in the shoe manufacturing process, they used glue regularly which resulted in more health problems and a lower life satisfaction than non-users, but if water-based glue was used it would be safer for them. The issue with their employers, however, was that the water-based glue took longer to dry and slowed down the production process.[21] Still, he found that the economic conditions for the families of these child laborers have improved as a result of their working and was actually seen as an opportunity rather than as exploitation by some.

However, there are individuals who are striving to make some progress. For example, Kailash Satyarthi created the South Asian Coalition on Child Servitude, which has raided factories in India, where more than 40,000 bonded laborers, many of them children, have been freed. He won the Nobel Peace Prize in 2014 for his continued work to campaign for the strengthening of laws that ban child labor practices and for reaching out to more than 2,000 civil society organizations worldwide.[22]

In 1993, when Congress proposed that the U.S. Child Labor Deterrence Act had passed, which would have banned imports manufactured by children, the garment factories in Bangladesh, where the child labor laws were weak, if they even existed or were enforced at all, would have resulted in 50,000 children being fired from their garment factory jobs and some would have ended up in worse jobs, such as prostitution, according to one report.[23] Perhaps, we can consider how John Rawls discussed his difference principle, which involved looking at the least advantaged group and determining whether an action is *just* by measuring whether this group was in a better position than before the action. It goes without saying that from an American standard, child labor is unjust; however, if the living standards for the children who are working are better and instead of outlawing child labor in third-world countries, their working conditions could be improved, the Rawlsian difference principle may apply in these cases.

SWEATSHOPS

In an effort to hide their unethical activities, and auditing efforts by American companies, some foreign factories had been found to produce inaccurate payroll records which did not reflect the over forty-hour weeks their employees had been working, so they could avoid overtime payments.[24] In addition, workers and managers rehearsed how to answer the auditors' questions about hours, pay, and safety conditions so they could pass their scrutiny.[25] This, however, does not change the fact that sweatshops still exist in the same factories where American businesses are outsourcing their labor in an effort to reduce their costs and be more competitive.

Besides traditional factory work, there is a new type of sweatshop used in the buying and selling of virtual currencies found in online gaming. Placed in cramped corners, *young people play online games to earn credits which they sell for a profit to overseas customers in Taiwan, South Korea, and even the United States.*[26] These online factories are called **gold farming**.[27] Primarily in China, there is a concern that this will affect China's real economy and as a result the government placed a warning against these practices; but these impressionable young workers find illegal "gold farms," to play for low wages, long hours, and poor working conditions, anyway.

Yet, the United States and China are not the only countries who take advantage of low wages. For example, it was found that British companies such as Diesel, House of Fraser, Moss Brothers, and River Island were using sweatshops in Cambodia where they were paid 5 pence an hour and Bangladesh where they earned 16 pounds a month (about U.S.$25).[28]

GOLD FARMING
factories where young workers are placed in cramped corners, to play on-line games to earn credits which they sell for a profit to overseas markets.

© chippix/Shutterstock, Inc.

But, it should be pointed out that sweatshops exist beyond Asia. For example, a shirt manufacturer by hip-hop artist Sean Combs, who claimed he had no knowledge, was informed that in Choloma, Honduras, female workers were ordered to take pregnancy tests and if found to be pregnant, were fired to help the company save on medical expenses and maternity leaves, while fourteen other workers were fired when they tried to organize a union.[29] In addition, the factory managers would shout and use profanities, as well as force this primarily female workforce to work overtime and not be paid for that time.[30]

In California, the United States Department of Labor (USDOL) found eight employees from India were paid under the required minimum wages while helping their California company move from Foster City to Fremont. The USDOL found that some of the Indian workers worked as much as 122 hours in a week and received, in many cases, $1.21 an hour. The company, Electronics for Imaging, claimed to inadvertently overlook that they were actually being paid based upon what they earned when employed in Bangalore, India, and were even paid in rupees, while in the United States.[31]

Given this problem is so prevalent, perhaps we should ask, what can be done to discourage these pervasive sweatshops from existing?

PREVENTING CHILD LABOR AND SWEATSHOPS

Child labor and sweatshops are pervasive issues and solutions are needed. One potential solution is education and access to better medical care. *New York Times* writer Nicholas Kristoff found two programs that he believed would be helpful in resolving these issues involving child labor: (1) deworming the children—the annual cost is about $0.50 and reduces absenteeism from anemia, sickness, and malnutrition based upon a study in Kenya; and (2) paying a monthly stipend to impoverished mothers to send their children to school, as was done in Mexico.[32] The program was called Oportunidades and after its implementation, it resulted in an increase in high school enrollment in some rural areas by 85%.[33]

Another potential solution is for the big chains to market only fair-trade products. All the espresso sold at Dunkin' Donuts stores in the

United States and all McDonald's stores in New England sell only fair-trade coffee, and in 2006, Starbucks bought 50% more fair-trade coffee than in 2005.[34] A **fair trade**–certified *product is one where as a member they agree "to four principles: pay at least a price to producers that covers the costs of sustainable production (the Fairtrade Minimum Price), pay a premium that producers can invest in development (the Fairtrade Premium), partially pay in advance when producers ask for it, and sign contracts that allow for long-term planning and sustainable production practices; it also establishes specific product standards that govern the trade of each commodity to which licensees must subscribe."*[35] Robert Pollin, a University of Massachusetts economist, found that if the wages of a worker, say in Mexico, is increased by 30%, it would add only 1.2% to the price of the shirt, which is $0.24 for a $20 shirt.[36] Pollin's research reverts the issues of unfair working conditions and wages back to the consumer and whether they will take their social responsibility seriously enough to pay for the production process of a product so it was manufactured in an ethical manner.

© Gustavo Frazao/Shutterstock, Inc.

FAIR TRADE guarantees that the product purchased is by a member who complies with fair wages, working conditions, product standards, and other ethical practices established by the Fair Trade Federation.

A third solution is by having businesses work in partnership with developing countries, in order to bring up their economies and living standards. Peet's Coffee, in conjunction with Technoserve, a nonprofit organization funded by the Gates Foundation, has been working with poor sub-Saharan Africa coffee farmers in Kenya, Rwanda, Tanzia, and Uganda by linking their products with coffee drinkers in the developing countries.[37] An arduous process, Peet's Coffee has taught the farmers how to cultivate, process, and market their gourmet coffee to countries where coffee is not consumed. Its goal is to sell the product online and at its cafés. Technoserve is also working with Starbucks and Green Mountain Coffee Roasters.[38] Altruistic partnerships such as these improve not only the economies of these less developed countries but will eliminate the desperation many of its citizens will experience which often forces them to work for businesses that exploit them.

The final solution would be to organize either an international labor union or have labor unions work in conjunction with each other. For example, besides Sodexo, which was discussed in the beginning paragraph of this chapter, other companies such as Detsche Telekom in German, Tesco in Britain, or H&M in Sweden, which have been accused of not treating their workers fairly, have been under the scrutiny of several foreign unions.[39] If international unions form strategic partnership alliances or form an international union, global employees would be treated more fairly. However, in less developed countries this would be problematic on many counts, including aggressive government intervention, lack of support from some locals, fear of locals to go against the government, and cultural antiunion sentiments.

International Bribery

In one of China's highest profile case in 2010, four executives arranged a plea bargain for accepting bribes from Chinese steel makers, which allowed Rio Tinto, an Australian major seller of iron ore to raise prices, which would increase the profit that this firm would receive for its raw materials.[40] This actually brings up two major concerns: the first one is an ethical relative issue and the other is Aristotelian; if bribery is accepted in foreign countries, is it acceptable to bribe an official? On the other hand, just because everyone else does it, does that make it an acceptable practice? Let us look at the first premise, that bribery should be acceptable. The Greek philosopher Protagoras, an ethical relativist, once stated, "Man is the measure of all things." According to his statement, he believed that if bribery is acceptable in Country A, regardless of whether it is acceptable in Country B, in terms of conducting business in Country A, bribery should be permitted. This brings one to think of the eighteenth century when there was the French and Indian War, fought between France, England, and the Native Americans. Lore has it that during battle, the British would line up in rows against their enemies, who would do the same thing. The front row would then fire upon each other, then line up in the back row (if they survived the shootings), load up their muskets (guns), and continue until one of the sides retreated or were all killed. The Native Americans, however, had a different plan. They would hide behind the rocks and shoot their opponents. When they fought the British, they hid behind the rocks, while the British would line up, and you can probably guess the rest….you could say that the British were "sitting ducks." This is no different from Protagoras's viewpoint. If everyone else is taking bribes, are not the Americans like the British and will find themselves losing to the competition because the Americans are not offering the bribes to their potential clients?

On the other hand, according to Aristotle we must always aim for the highest good or virtue since, as he said, "virtue of character comes from habit." By not bribing their potential clients, these American business executives are practicing virtue by conducting business in an ethical manner. After all, if everyone steals, does it make it right for you to steal? But what happens if a foreign firm is found guilty in the United States of bribery?

In a federal case brought forth by the Justice Department, German automobile manufacturer Daimler agreed to pay $185 million for

© Kritchanut/Shutterstock, Inc.

violating American bribery laws when they paid $56 million for more than 200 transactions in twenty countries which earned them $1.9 billion for bribery payments which included luxury European vacations, armored Mercedes vehicles for a high ranking Turkmenistan official, and other gifts and monies.[41] This turned the tables on bribery and follows Protagoras's viewpoint since it is not legal to bribe in the United States under the Foreign Practices Corrupt Act of 1977, which will be briefly discussed later.

In a study conducted by the Moscow-based Information Science for Democracy Foundation, more than $300 billion is paid in bribes annually, which represented more than 25% of Russia's 2009 gross domestic product (GDP) and as a result had persuaded more than fifty international companies to pledge a zero-tolerance of bribery in Russia. Still, Hewlett-Packard, world-renown personal computer manufacturer, was accused of paying $11 million in bribes to win business in Russia while German electronics manufacturer Seimens had agreed in 2008 to pay $1.3 billion in fines to end corruption accusations in the United States and Germany.[42]

The next example occurred in 2014, when Hewlett-Packard's Russian subsidiary pleaded guilty to bribery charges in a San Francisco federal court in order to win a large technology contract with the Office of the Prosecutor General of the Russian Federation. These illegal payments continued for ten years, through a "slush fund" created for bribery payments by its executives. Two sets of books to "launder" or hide money paid for the bribes and using anonymous email accounts to arrange secret meetings to hand over bags of cash were tactics used, costing Hewlett-Packard $108 million in penalties. In addition, falsified books and other internal control irregularities were uncovered from 2006 to 2010 for bribes given to Poland's national police agency, which amounted to more than $600,000.[43]

Bribery is extremely pervasive in the business world.

FOREIGN CORRUPT PRACTICES ACT OF 1977

The **Foreign Corrupt Practices Act of 1977 (FCPA)** *"was enacted for the purpose of making it unlawful for certain classes of persons and entities to make payments to foreign government officials to assist in obtaining or retaining business."* [44] When it was first enacted the FCPA applied to all U.S. persons and certain foreign issuers of securities, but in 1998 was modified to include an anti-bribery provision that would apply to foreign firms and persons or their agents who breach any of the sections found in the FCPA within the territory of the United States.[45] However, the FCPA is vague when it comes to "grease payments." A **grease payment** *is when individuals or firms are permitted to pay "facilitating payments," a small amount of cash which sometimes may be needed to expedite what it calls "routine governmental action."* [46] Grease payments are like unofficial exceptions such as when a government official is given a few dollars to process a visa or work order; they provide police protection, ensure smooth mail phone or power service, protect perishable products for bananas, let us say, or to schedule timely inspections.[47] The difference between a grease payment and a breach of the FCPA is that the former is minimal and without payment would negate any type of business activity, while the latter is an outright bribe and is antithetical to its purpose. The logic behind the FCPA is that in reality the purchaser is making a decision not based upon the product or what is best for the company, but is acting egotistically. In addition, when businesses employ bribery as part of their business activities, the additional cost is actually being borne by the consumer, since bribery would be considered a cost of doing business when computing the marked up retail price. Therefore, the consumer is penalized on the retail sticker price and by the original decision to purchase a product or supply which under other anti-bribery actions may not have been selected in the first place, which ultimately is compromising the quality of the product, as well.

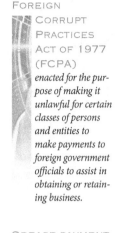

© Muellek Josef/Shutterstock, Inc.

In 2005, The Titan Corporation, a top military and intelligence contractor, agreed to settle criminal and civil charges when it bribed Mathieu Kérékou, president of the West African country of Benin, and was ordered to pay $28.5 million, the largest penalty in the history of the FCPA at the time.[48] The Securities Exchange Commission found that from 1999 to 2001, $3.5 million went to the president's business advisor and about $2 million to the president's election campaign.[49] Three years later, as mentioned, Siemens paid the largest legal settlement ($1.3 billion) under the FCPA. Up until then, the enforcement of the FCPA had been modest.[50]

The last bribery case involves the selling of guns and, in 2010, represented the largest single investigation and prosecution against individuals in the history of the Department of Justice's enforcement of the FCPA.[51] For two and a half years, the Federal Bureau of Investigation (FBI) had been setting up twenty-two suspects, where they posed as defense officials of an African country seeking pistols, tear-gas launchers, bulletproof vests, and other supplies for a 20% commission.[52] Finally, in one large swoop, 150 FBI agents executed fourteen search warrants throughout the country.[53] A federal grand jury found that one of those arrested was the vice-president of sales for Smith&Wesson Inc., the largest manufacturer of hand guns, who was looking for the kickback to clinch the sale of 1,825 pistols for violating the FCPA. [54]

In a 2008 study on enforcing the FCPA, there had only been sixty-one criminal prosecution cases and forty-seven civil cases from 1977 to 2007. In a study by the Commerce Department it was estimated that from 1994 to 2001, U.S. businesses lost contracts valued at $200 billion to over 400 foreign companies that allegedly used bribery in their business transactions.[55]

Yet, you would think that due to the FCPA, the perception of the United States with other countries would be one of ethicality. In a 2002 study, the Bribe Payers Index ranked the United States as thirteenth among the twenty-one leading exporting nations to possess the most propensity of the "multinational corporations to bribe," by Transparency International. [56] In another survey, they asked respondents to name three countries most likely to use an "unfair" advantage in international and trade investment, other than bribery, and found that the United States was selected most frequently in 58% of the cases.[57]

However, there is a silver lining for complying with the FCPA and for its existence. Since its inception, many companies have been able to use the FCPA as an excuse not to pay bribes. In one case, the former president of Texaco, James Kinnear, stated that the FCPA allows companies to refuse to pay bribes by claiming it is against the law and they did not want their company to be exposed to a lawsuit, plus it saved the company from having to pay bribes.[58] In another situation, Colgate-Palmolive cited the FCPA when it refused to pay a bribe from the Chinese officials regarding the construction of a factory, which ultimately opened up anyway, without the payment of bribes.[59] It should be noted, however, that it is not a judgment of China, because in their country, bribery may be more acceptable than in the United States. In light of all that has been written perhaps considering what you would do if faced with a situation of potential bribery, you should consider what Peter Drucker said, as quoted in Chapter Six: "What kind of person do I want to see when I shave myself in the morning or put on my lipstick?" Or, what if your actions were to appear on the front page of tomorrow's pages; what would it say and how would you feel?

PROTECTIONISM
the intervention through any government action into the marketplace on behalf of its own domestic markets to insulate them from their foreign competition.

Protectionism

Perhaps best known for his thoughts on free trade, Adam Smith believed in what he termed the "invisible hand," which was the belief that the free market system and not the government should be involved in determining for producers what and how many goods should be manufactured and for consumers at what price these products should be sold for. *The intervention through any government action into the marketplace on behalf of its own domestic markets is called* **protectionism.** Protectionism can consist of tariffs, subsidies, embargos, trade quotas, restrictive standards, or any other governmental actions that insulate a domestic

© Photosani/Shutterstock, Inc.

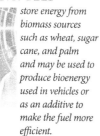
company or industry from foreign companies or industries and prevent the free market system of supply and demand to run its natural course. Each of these protectionism techniques will be discussed and will be followed by the question: Is a country ever justified in following a protectionist policy?

TARIFFS

A **tariff** *is a tax on imported goods or services to reduce the amount of imports entering the domestic country, although sometimes it is imposed for retaliatory reasons.* In 2009, the United States imposed a tariff on tires being imported by China which amounted to 35% after millions of U.S. manufacturing jobs were being lost to outsourced Chinese labor.[60] At this time for every $4.46 worth of Chinese goods purchased by U.S. consumers, only $1 of American goods were being sold to China which amounted to a trade deficit with China of $268 billion in 2008.[61] A **trade deficit** *is when imports (foreign purchased goods or services) exceed exports (goods or services purchased by foreign consumers). A* **trade surplus** *is when exports exceed imports.*

As a result of the tariff, when it was first announced, China immediately responded by threatening to retaliate against America automobile producers and chicken suppliers.[62] In the same year, the United States

was on the receiving end of provisional tariffs by the European Union (EU) for its biodiesel industry, which has been weak in Europe as a result of U.S. subsidization for this industry.[63] Their tariffs would vary from $328 to $511 on a ton of American biodiesel and based upon how much the company was being subsidized by the United States.[64] **Biofuels** *store energy from biomass sources such as wheat, sugar cane, and palm and may be used to produce bioenergy, which in some cases may be used in vehicles or can be used as an additive to make the fuel more efficient.*[65]

In another tariff confrontation, Brazil threatened to raise duty taxes (tariffs) on a wide range of American-made imported goods, including automobiles and cosmetics, and was supported by the World Trade Organization to do so, since the United States was found to be in violation of its agreements because it was subsidizing its cotton growers.[66] By the United States supporting these cotton growers, their costs and selling prices were reduced, leaving Brazil in a situation whereby they were unable to compete equally with the American imported cotton industry and believed by threatening to impose tariffs of $591 million as a retaliatory measure, the United States would cease subsidizing this industry.[67] However, one day before Brazil was to begin imposing its tariff sanctions, the United States agreed to modify its export loan program and establish temporary assistance for the Brazilian cotton industry.[68]

SUBSIDY

when the government funds an industry so the exporting producers are able to sell their products or services at a price equal to cost or lower than cost of the domestic country.

SUBSIDIES

Another protectionism technique is a ***subsidy***, *which is when the government funds an industry so the exporting producers are able to sell their products or services at a price equal to cost or lower than cost of the domestic country where they are exporting the goods (or services).* For example, in the 1970s, Japanese automobile manufacturers were being partially funded by their government, so when they exported their cars to the United States, who were not being subsidized by the American government, the prices of the exported Japanese automobiles were far lower than the domestic, American automobiles' prices. As an example, consumers would purchase a Japanese automobile for $3,000 rather an American automobile for $6,000.

SUBSIDIES

© arka38/Shutterstock, Inc.

In 2004, the United States agreed to cut 20% in subsidies it paid to American farmers after being pressured from developing West African countries, including Benin, Burkina Faso, Chad, and Mali, who claimed that tens of thousands of their farmers were left destitute as a result of this protectionist technique.[69] Furthermore, the World Bank, the United

Nations, the International Monetary Fund, and Oxfam International all believed that these subsidies by affluent countries like the United States made it impossible for largely rural, poor countries to compete in the global market which could enable these less wealthy countries "to trade their way of poverty."[70]

In an alleged illegal complaint by the United States on behalf of Boeing, it was found out that in a 2009 preliminary report, the European Union (EU) governments funneled billions of dollars in illegal subsidies to Airbus from 1970 to 2004, in an effort to win a $35 billion contact to build new aerial refuel tankers for the U.S. Air Force.[71] Although still not settled, this case raised not the question, "are subsidies ethical?" but instead, "are subsidies legal?"

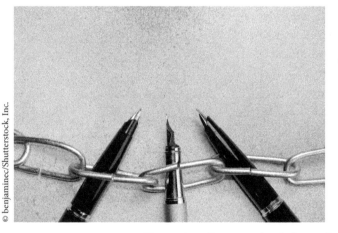

EMBARGO

a form of protectionism; the banning of a product or service from being sold in a given country.

EMBARGOES

An **embargo** is a third form of protectionism and is *the banning of a product or service from being sold in a given country.* For example, due to political reasons, Cuban cigars have been banned from being sold in the United States since 1962. It should be noted that at the time of this writing, relations between the United States and Cuba appear to be changing. In 1972, there was an embargo against OPEC (Organization for Petroleum Exporting Countries) oil for political and economic reasons given the great dependency the United States had on foreign oil. In 1997, the United States imposed a strict trade embargo against Sudan until it would terminate its support for terrorist groups and the genocide of its own people; as of 2010, it was still in effect.[72]

In 2008, Russia lifted an embargo against Poland for its meat, claiming it did not satisfy the EU's strict standards, but after several Eastern European countries placed pressure on Russia to lift the ban in an effort to

CONDUCTING BUSINESS ETHICALLY

support Poland, it did so eighteen months later, and watched its exports surge.[73] In late 2009, the United States threatened to cut off investments to Iran's oil and gas industry and other restrictions on Iranian banks over their nuclear program.[74] The use of embargoes is used generally for economic and political reasons.

Another reason an embargo may be used is if an exported product is feared to be dangerous. Generally, the Food and Drug Administration (FDA), which has the power to sanction an embargo, will block imports of individual food products rather than an entire category of one country's foods.[75] For example, instead of placing an embargo on all seafood, it may place an embargo on farm-raised seafood. In 2008, the FDA did exactly that when it banned the selling of farm-raised seafood as well as vegetable protein because of repeated instances of contamination.[76] Based upon the limited number of embargo cases, it should be noted that this protectionist technique is usually imposed as a last resort.

TRADE QUOTAS

Trade quotas *are the limiting of imported goods permitted to enter a given country.* In 1993, the European Union set quotas favoring banana imports from the Ivory Coast, the Windward Islands, and other former colonies at the expense of imports from Latin America, as well as American banana companies.[77] Sixteen years later, after the EU was sued by these countries under the General Agreement on Tariffs and Trade (GATT) and then the World Trade Organization (WTO) accusing them of rigging an unfair trade deal, the EU rescinded its sanctions against the Latin American and American banana companies.[78]

It should be pointed out that there are organizations working to reduce protectionism. One of them is GATT, which was organized in 1947 to encourage free trade between member states by regulating and reducing protectionist techniques (such as tariff, embargoes, trade quotas, etc.) and act as a mechanism for resolving

© Lisa S./Shutterstock, Inc.

trade disputes among its more than 110 member countries.[79] Another such organization is the WTO. With over 150 members, the World Trade Organization was created in 1995, as the only international organization dealing with the rules of trade between nations to ensure trade exchanges are conducted as free as possible.[80]

One of the functions of the WTO is to reduce disputes regarding protectionist techniques that member countries may impose on each other. In 2009, the United States and the European Union accused China of unfair practices stating that the Chinese government was restricting exports of raw materials to give manufacturers in its country a competitive advantage in the production of steel, chemicals, and aluminum.[81] Both countries filed a complaint with the WTO, but unless the parties agree to some settlement, it will take at least a year to resolve.[82] However, it should be pointed out that since China and the United States are major trade partners for each other, China was willing to make some modifications to alleviate these protectionist measures. As a general rule, many times countries will attempt to impose certain trade restrictions, but if there is a strong possibility of retaliation, there usually are rollbacks or sometimes the restrictions may even be rescinded.

RESTRICTIVE STANDARDS

RESTRICTIVE STANDARDS *reduce the opportunity of exported goods or services to compete with the domestic country's products or services.*

Another form of protectionism is setting up **restrictive standards** *which reduces the opportunity of exported goods or services to compete with the domestic country's products or services.* China has created a policy called "indigenous innovation," whereby its government will offer tax breaks and subsidies to Chinese companies and give them preference in state contracts.[83] As an example, Shanghai had released a list of over 500 approved products which was not in violation of WTO rules, since China has not yet signed an agreement that covered government procurement (purchases).[84]

Patent laws are another example of protectionism. In October 2009, there was a rule that forced companies to file patents or trademarks in China before doing so overseas if they wanted to qualify for government procurement.[85] In April of the same year, French electronic manufacturer Schneider

Electric settled a three-year patent dispute with Chint Group, a maker of products such as transformers and circuit breakers, for $23 million, even though Western attorneys believed it was the Chint Group infringing upon the French company; but when the trial came to court, the evidence was ignored.[86] One reason China was victorious in all these situations was due to the potential market volume generated by its large consumer population.

The last example involves China's currency. China had been devaluing its renminbi (the Chinese "dollar") in 2010 so its exported products would be less expensive and would attract more consumers.[87] Along with its lower labor costs, from a legal viewpoint, China may not be breaking any laws but may be breaching some ethical ones. Workers must be paid fair wages and devaluing their currency to an extreme low could jeopardize their own economy in time. However, as a retaliatory measure, in 2010, the United States threatened to impose tariffs to make their products more expensive and American products more competitive.

DUMPING

Dumping *is the selling a product or service below cost or substantially lower than is being sold in the domestic country.* There are two types of

DUMPING

selling a product at lower than cost or the price sold in the domestic country or selling a domestically banned product abroad.

dumping. According to the WTO when "there is a genuine ('material') injury to the competing domestic industry" and that "the government has to be able to show that dumping is taking place, can calculate the extent of the dumping (how much the lower the export price is compared to the exporter's home market price), and show that the dumping is causing injury or threatening to do so," it then satisfied the definition of dumping and could be liable for any penalties imposed by the WTO. For example, if Ford Motor Company sold it automobiles in the United States for $25,000 and in Canada for $15,000, it would probably be considered dumping.[88] The second definition of dumping will be discussed later in the chapter.

In 2009, the European Union sanctioned the Chinese and Vietnamese shoe exporters for a tariff of 16.5% and 10% for a minimum of fifteen months for it antidumping actions.[89] But, even the United States is guilty of such actions, as in 2009 when the WTO ruled in favor of Japan against the Americans for dumping ball bearings in Japan by selling them for less than they cost in the United States.[90]

The second form of dumping is when a company sells a product abroad when it is banned in the domestic country, such as a foreign country selling lead paint to American consumers. One of these dumping cases involved the 1977 selling of 2.4 million pairs of TRIS-treated children's pajamas banned in the United States because the fabric caused kidney cancer, and was banned the next year.[91] In a second dumping case, between 1971 and 1976, nearly 14 million pounds of pesticides which contained a banned dangerous nerve toxin was sold in fifty countries, resulting in the deaths of 1,000 water buffaloes and injury or death of many farmers in Egypt.[92] Just because in certain instances, dumping is legal, it does not mean it is ethical.

In another dumping situation, Cutter Biological, a division of German drug manufacturer Bayer, and some pharmaceutical manufacturers in China were involved with selling blood-clotting drugs abroad, knowing that they were dangerous to the patients who would be using them. In another case which occurred in the mid-1980s, Bayer sold $4 million of unheated Factor VIII, a blood-clotting drug for hemophiliacs, to Argentina, Taiwan, Singapore, Malaysia, and Indonesia, although it carried a high risk of transmitting AIDS; yet Bayer sold a safer product to more developed countries like the United States, according to papers found by *The New York Times* in 2003.[93] In the last case, in 2008, Chinese manufacturers shipped overseas, substituted dried pig intestines to produce the drug heparin which was administered to dialysis and surgery patients to prevent blood clotting, which was useless in clotting the patients' blood and also baby formula, which contained an illegal toxic chemical called melamine which resulted in several deaths.[94] Although these are examples of unethical marketing practices, since they are examples, it was discussed in this section.

TRADING BLOCS

A **trading bloc** *is an organization in which its members agree to reduce protectionist measures against each other, such as having no or reduced tariffs; however these actions are not given to those outside of their membership.* Although many of these trading blocs exist, for brevity purposes only a few of them most familiar with American businesses will be discussed. The first is the twenty-seven member (2010) European Community, established as a common market in 1973 under a 1957 treaty which made it possible to abolish custom barriers within the Community, establish common tariffs to non-EU members, use a common currency adopted in 2004 (but not by England who still uses the British pound), abolish border controls on EU goods, recognize national

TRADE BLOC
an organization in which its members agree to reduce protectionist measures against each other, such as no or reduced tariffs, but not to those outside of their membership.

rules for the majority of products, enact a partial alignment of national VAT (value added tax) rates to reduce tax barriers, develop an agreement of tax investment income with some of the member states, have the opportunity to bid on member public contracts (many times these are not given to those outside the country seeking the bid for the product or service), and have an integrated market for financial services to save the costs of borrowing for businesses and consumers (i.e., reduced bank charges for cross-border payments).[95]

The second trading bloc is the North American Free Trade Agreement (NAFTA) established in 1994 to eliminate tariffs and other protectionist techniques among Canada, United States, and Mexico. Given the differences of all three countries, it was quite challenging to establish this particular trading bloc, but from an economic viewpoint it has successfully reduced several trade barriers, such as tariffs and quotas, formerly imposed prior to the signing of NAFTA.

The ten-member Association of Southeast Asian Nations, founded in 1967 (Indonesia, Malaysia, the Philippines, Singapore, and Thailand) was established to accelerate the economic growth, social progress, and cultural development in their regions through joint endeavors and collaboration; abide by the principles of the United Nations Charter; assist each other in training and research; collaborate for greater utilization of their agriculture and other industries; expand their trade; improvement their infrastructures; and raise peoples' living standards.[96]

Another trading bloc of which the United States is a member is the twenty-one-member Asia Pacific Economic Cooperation (APEC) established in 1989 in an effort to support sustainable economic growth and prosperity in the Asia-Pacific region with a goal of eliminating trade and tariff barriers among its members.[97]

Mercosur is the final trading bloc, which began under the 1991 Treaty of Asuncion to allow free trade among its four full members (Argentina, Brazil, Paraguay, and Uruguay), one pending full member (Venezuela), and two other members awaiting their ratification (Brazil and Paraguay) and whose purpose has been to eliminate trade barriers.[98] However, there has been some division over its purpose, such as Brazil where they want to keep Mercosur focused on regional trade issues, while other countries, such as Venezuela, want the group to expand its focus on political issues.[99] In 2008, Unasur—which consists of Argentina, Bolivia, Brazil, Chile, Columbia, Ecuador, Guyana, Paraguay, Peru, Surinam, Uruguay, and Venezuela—pledged to "establish a mechanism of mutual trust regarding defense and security," based upon their August 2009 Summit meeting, and hope eventually to emulate the European Union; but at that Summit, Columbia and Venezuela seemed diametrically opposed politically, so it is not quite yet evident how successful this latter goal will be.[100] One question which may be posed is: By having a trade bloc, is this free trade or protectionism? Questions such as this one will now be addressed.

PROTECTIONISM OR FREE TRADE?

In 1929, the Smoot-Hawley Tariff Act increased the price of 20,000 items produced abroad and for the next four years imports from Europe into the United States declined by 67%; U.S. exports were more than halved; overall world trade declined by 66%; and unemployment rose from 9% in 1930 to 25% in 1933.[101] So, the question still remains: protectionism or free trade? According to Adam Smith, we should allow the market to determine our course of actions in identifying how much and what to produce, and at what cost. Yet, by doing so, one takes the risk of failing, and given that economics is about power, the one way not to lose your power is to protect your resource holdings, through another approach, protectionism by government intervention. Let us briefly look at both approaches and a rationale for each.

First, the free trade approach. If we followed utilitarian Peter Singer's philosophy, we can hypothesize that the most affluent countries will impose the greatest protectionist measures so they will not lose their resources which would then fall into the hands of the less developed nations. So, from a Singerian perspective, one may argue that free trade is best for everyone, because otherwise, the more affluent nations will stay that way forever, given their power to protect against the less developed

© Zerbor/Shutterstock, Inc.

countries. Even if we look from the perspective of consumers, free trade works better. For example, if the United States imposed a 10% tax on electronic equipment entering the country from China, American consumers will now have to pay $1,100 on their Chinese-manufactured flat panel screen televisions which would have cost them $1,000 before the tariff. Now, what if the Chinese retaliate and charge a 10% tariff on American automobiles? The Chinese now have to pay 10% more ($2,500 on their $25,000 American-produced automobile) than before the tariff, also. The net results are that both Chinese and American consumers are paying 10% more on their goods, and by having these tariffs, they will also reduce the amount of goods they can export, resulting in less jobs, much like what happened with the Smoot-Hawley Tariff Act in 1929. From these examples, it is apparent that in a perfect world protectionism techniques are not ideal from a utilitarian perspective. But, we are not in a perfect world.

If Thrasymachus's philosophy "justice is in the advantage of the stronger," was applied, and even if a country like the United States wanted to "play by the rules of the free market," would this not be the same as the British during the French and Indian Wars where the Indians were "not playing by the rules"? During the 1970s, the Japanese were subsidizing their automobile industry and the American automobile manufacturers were unable to compete with the lower Japanese vehicle retail prices, because the U.S. government would not practice protectionism. So maybe, in this case, would not the United States be justified in protecting its markets by tariffs or quotas to equalize the Japanese government's subsidization intervention, or should they just allow the free market system to prevail? Most entrepreneurs would probably agree that the former approach would be most advisable in this situation. However, a utilitarian may state that the less developed country will now have a chance if free trade exists.

One last thought: Are trading blocs free trade or protectionist? To simplify this question, the response will be based upon a qualitative approach. If the country is part of the trading bloc, evidently it will encourage free trade, but only between the trading partners and those who are excluded will be, by far, more disadvantaged. Given this premise, if a less developed country is not a member of a trading bloc, there will be an even greater gap between economic prosperity and poverty. Yet, in some instances it actually improved the living standards of less affluent countries. Take NAFTA, for instance; as part of the NAFTA trading bloc, due to its lower labor costs, many American jobs and factories have been moved to Mexico, which improved the living standards of many Mexican citizens who prospered from this trade pact. Even from a utilitarian perspective, if you compared the living standards of those Americans who lost their jobs to the Mexicans who at the time lacked employment and then compared the living standards of both citizens after NAFTA, most likely, from a utilitarian viewpoint, the collective living standards of both the country's people improved. However, if you looked from a Rawlsian approach, if we could agree that the least advantaged group was the displaced American workers (Rawls might not agree and claim the Mexican citizens were), would they pass Rawls's difference test? Most likely according to Rawls, the displaced workers are in a worse position than before, which reverts back to the question, Is free trade or protectionism better? With an even more expanding global economy, the answers are not as clear; however, it should be pointed out that whenever a less affluent group of individuals have the ability to improve their living standard at a higher rate than their affluent counterparts, perhaps whichever approach would benefit the least advantaged group may be the best approach, and that using a Rawlsian lens may be the clearest path to this rhetorical question.

Unethical International Practices

Besides the cases discussed, before demonstrating the dumping of tainted products which were shipped to foreign countries because they were either dangerous or outlawed in their domestic countries, there were other unethical practices which existed and will be mentioned in this section. The first is marketing tobacco products in foreign countries because they are not legally allowed to do so in their domestic country. In a 2004 study, conducted by the World Health Organization and the Centers for Disease Control and Prevention, it was found that about 11% of the children in Latin America and the Caribbean, 17% in Russia, and 25% in Jordan were given free cigarettes by teenaged tobacco marketers representing companies like Philip Morris.[102] Using peers to push a harmful, addictive product is appalling.

Another type of unethical practice is overcharging customers. In a defense contract audit in 2004 a "suspected irregularity" involving a Halliburton contract to provide gasoline to Iraqi citizens found that its Kuwaiti fuel supplier, the Altanmia Marketing Company, may have overcharged the Army $61 million over a four-month period.[103] However, instead of the investigation focusing upon the company, the auditors' efforts were on the individual workers.[104] In this situation, what would happen if the fuel supplier was guilty and refused to pay? Should it be necessary to go to trial, taking this case to a court in a foreign country would be very difficult, given that the legal system of Kuwait is much different from the American judicial system. So, if the supplier knows this, from a legal breach it becomes an ethical one.

In the United States, the Internal Revenue Service is always being challenged on finding those who avoid taxes. Foreign tax collectors have the same issue. Fortunately, for the Swedish tax collectors, a whistleblower, who ultimately lost his job, informed outside sources (after contacting the company's ethics officer) that the pharmaceutical company, Wyeth, had a worldwide practice of tax invasion against foreign governments, as well as abuse of marketing funds, using sales of excessive inventory to distributors to give the impression of higher sales, and using nepotism when issuing business contracts.[105] Without the

CONDUCTING BUSINESS ETHICALLY

potential of whistleblowers informing others of the unethical actions of their companies, more unethical actions would occur in the business world.

In another type of conflict, three American countries wanted to sell genetically modified crops to the European Union, but they were culturally opposed to its sale; so they filed a complaint with the WTO, which supported the claims by the United States, Argentina, and Canada.[106] Yet this brings up another ethical issue: Why should a group of countries be forced to have a product enter its

market that it is culturally opposed to? Protagoras would surely agree.

But other unethical practices occur globally, and one of them is by an American beverage company. Coco-Cola was accused of "channel stuffing," which is shipping more concentrate than their bottlers actually needed in an effort to inflate their actual sales and net income numbers, and did so by offering the bottlers in Japan cash incentives of up to $25 million; and in addition, they programmed their computer systems to appear as if the concentrates were sold even if they were not.[107] Manipulating numbers in this case was not only unethical, but it was also illegal.

The last practice concerns a medical patient from another country, who is part of an experimental trial. The drug used in the trial by the patient is not lifesaving, so when the trial is over, is there a responsibility to the patient or the stockholder? Several drug companies such as CV Therapeutics in Palo Alto, California, tested their products overseas because it was easier to find patients who were eager to participate and be tested than in the United States; of the 1,104 patients tested, 600 were from Russia.[108] Yet, as stated, legally, after the trials were terminated, companies were no longer responsible to continue to dispense the drugs

© Piyaphat Detbun/Shutterstock, Inc.

to these "patients," although if it had been a lifesaving drug morally they would be. This leaves another ethical issue unanswered: What should these companies do?

There are many international marketing and business activities that bring others to question the ethicality of companies. In the first situation, the marketing of addictive products to the youth would not be viewed as ethical, nor would the Kuwaiti fuel supplier overcharging of a client or Wyeth's alleged tax evasion. The Coco-Cola example would also be unethical and like the Kuwaiti fuel supplier and Wyeth, would not be legal either. Enforcement of these illegal activities is sometimes problematic because they cannot be enforced sometimes; and, if the agent conducting the act is aware of it, the action although illegal in the agent's domestic company may then become an ethical issue (since the enforcement will not occur). However, in one of the other examples, should the European Union be obliged to take genetic foods into its market? Using Rawls's "veil of ignorance," what if a company forced the United States to offer in their food markets, snake or water rats (they do in some European countries as a delicacy), what would their reaction be? And, should not the culture of the consumer market take precedence over that of the manufacturer's business plan? Respecting the cultural differences of other countries is an ethical issue and one not easily answered. Finally, do the pharmaceutical firms have an obligation to their trial patients or to their stockholders, or to both?

Final Thoughts

In an experiment at Northeastern University, subjects were given a coin and told to flip it to see whether they would have to undertake the completion of a long, laborious task or a short, fun one. The participants were instructed to privately flip the coin and tell the professor the results. What they did not know was that they were being taped. Only 10% of them honestly informed their professor of the results. The other 90% either never flipped the coin or flipped the coin until it resulted in their favor (i.e., selecting the easier, fund task).[109] Given these research subjects are the next business leaders, we need to determine why it is when individuals believe they will get away with an unethical action, they will do so. Would a video camera deter this type of behavior? Do the rewards of immoral actions supersede one's moral compass?

Perhaps Aristotle stated it best in Book 2 of his *Nicomachean Ethics:* "Virtue, then, is a state of character concerned with choice, Lying in a mean…by which the man of practical wisdom (phronesis, prudence) would determine it….a mean between two vices, the one involving excess, the other deficiency, and that it is such because its character is to aim at what is intermediate in passions and in actions…For in everything it is no easy task to find the middle." What constitutes doing the right thing is a very delicate seesaw; where ultimately, your balance must be precise, and where the entrepreneur who can figure it out by possessing a strong moral compass, will then be told that he or she has been *conducting business ethically*.

SUMMARY

In the global world, there are issues that sometimes make it more difficult to determine what the ethical path may be to take, since each country's values are different. One of these issues is child labor, which by most standards are not moral. Yet, there is a viewpoint that if children were not able to work, then they would be forced into more oppressive situations, so instead of focusing on eliminating child labor, the focus should be on bettering the working conditions. As for sweatshops, regardless of the living standards, the same applies and efforts should be made to ensure that all workers are employed in safe and healthy environments and to be fairly compensated. Unfortunately, when this does not occur, many times it is found that the businesses indirectly responsible for these unconscionable conditions are not the outsourced foreign factories but the American corporations who may look the other way in the name of profits. Better education, fair-trade products, strategic partnerships, and unions are potential solutions.

International bribery is extremely problematic since American businesses must compete with foreign businesses that consider bribery as a normal course of action when conducting business. In the United States it is illegal, and most believe unethical, and those breaching the Foreign Corrupt Practices Act of 1977 (FCPA) will probably pay a penalty—either monetarily or by imprisonment. The pressure of playing on a level playing field creates the conflict with those working in an ethical environment. Yet, in some instances, business executives found that by adhering to the FCPA, the pressure to negotiate bribes was alleviated and could still result in a favorable contract acceptance.

Protectionism is the intervention of the government in foreign trade and consists of such techniques as tariffs, subsidies, embargoes, trade quotas, restrictive standards, dumping, and even trade blocs in some cases. A tariff is a tax on imported goods or services to reduce the amount of imports entering the domestic country. A subsidy is when the government funds an industry so the exporting producers are able to sell their products or services at a price equal to cost or lower than cost of the domestic country where they are exporting the goods (or services). An embargo is a third form of protectionism and is the banning of a product or service from being sold in a given country. Trade quotas are the limiting of imported goods permitted to enter a given country. Restrictive standards reduce the opportunity of exported goods or services to compete with the domestic country's products or services. Dumping is the selling of a product at lower than cost or the price sold in the domestic country (or selling a domestically banned product abroad). The former part of the definition is a form of protectionism, while the latter refers to an unethical marketing technique. To some, a trade bloc is also a form of protectionism as it is exclusionary to those not in the trading bloc. A trading bloc is an organization in which its members agree to reduce protectionist measures against each other, such as having no tariffs or reduced tariffs. Yet, it does not help those outside of their membership.

The question of whether protectionism or free trade is a more ethical policy may be more of a rhetorical one. If you are a utilitarian like Peter Singer, free trade is the most equitable for the majority, since its focus is on not having any government intervention protecting the overclass from the underclass. If you are Thrasymachus, protectionism would be supported, since if you were in power and believed you needed to protect your economic resources from those who currently do not posses such resources, in his words, "might makes right."

Besides the dumping of tainted products which are shipped to foreign countries because they may be dangerous or outlawed in the domestic countries, there are other unethical practices that exist. The first is marketing tobacco products in foreign countries because they are not legally allowed to do so in their domestic country. Another type of an unethical practice is overcharging a customer, which was exemplified by a Kuwaiti fuel supplier charging the Air Force $61 million more than they should have. Tax evaders were also problematic, especially for the domestic countries of the evaders when they are earning revenue in another country. Another ethical issue was why should a group of countries be forced to have a product enter its market that it is culturally opposed to? This question was posed when the United States, Canada, and Argentina forced the World Trade Organization to allow them to sell genetically modified crops into the European Union market, which opposed it for cultural reasons. In another situation, Coco-Cola was accused of "channel stuffing," which is shipping more concentrate than their bottlers actually needed in an effort to inflate their actual sales and net income numbers. The last ethical dilemma is to determine when a patient from another country is part of a trial and the drug is not lifesaving, when the trial is over, is there a responsibility to the patient or the stockholder? This chapter examined the ethical issues that often arise during the course of doing business in a global market.

KEY TERMS

Biofuels: store energy from biomass sources such as wheat, sugar cane, and palm and may be used to produce bioenergy used in vehicles or as an additive to make the fuel more efficient.

Dumping: selling a product at lower than cost or the price sold in the domestic country or selling a domestically banned product abroad.

Embargo: a form of protectionism; the banning of a product or service from being sold in a given country.

Fair trade: guarantees that the product purchased is by a member who complies with fair wages, working conditions, product standards, and other ethical practices established by the Fair Trade Federation.

Foreign Corrupt Practices Act of 1977 (FCPA): enacted for the purpose of making it unlawful for certain classes of persons and entities to make payments to foreign government officials to assist in obtaining or retaining business.

Gold farming: factories where young workers are placed in cramped corners, to play online games to earn credits which they sell for a profit to overseas markets.

Grease payment: when an individual or firm is permitted to pay "facilitating payments," a small amount of cash that might sometimes be needed to expedite what it calls "routine governmental action," such as processing a visa.

Protectionism: the intervention through any government action into the marketplace on behalf of its own domestic markets to insulate them from their foreign competition.

Restrictive standards: reduce the opportunity of exported goods or services to compete with the domestic country's products or services.

Subsidy: when the government funds an industry so the exporting producers are able to sell their products or services at a price equal to cost or lower than cost of the domestic country.

Tariff: a tax on imported goods or services to reduce the amount of imports entering the domestic country.

Trade deficit: when imports (foreign purchased goods or services) exceed exports (goods or services purchased by foreign consumers).

Trade quotas: the limiting of imported goods permitted to enter a given country.

Trade surplus: when exports exceed imports.

Trading bloc: an organization in which its members agree to reduce protectionist measures against each other, such as no or reduced tariffs, but not to those outside of their membership.

CHAPTER REVIEW QUESTIONS

1. What are some examples of unfair child labor practices discussed in the chapter?
2. What are some potential solutions to eliminate sweatshops?
3. What are some examples of international bribery?
4. How effective is the Foreign Corrupt Practices Act of 1977?
5. Is protectionism good or bad? Use examples from the chapter to support your response.
6. What are some examples of unethical business practices?

CASES FOR DISCUSSION

CASE 10.1 IS BRIBERY REALLY BRIBERY?[110]

According to the Foreign Practices Corrupt Act (FPCA), "anything of value to government officials in obtaining or retaining business" is illegal. However, when foreign subsidiaries of the United States, whose domestic firms are issuing these bribes, do so, they should be on a level playing field with their foreign competitors. For example, Wal-Mart was accused of paying bribes to secure building permits that helped its Mexican subsidiary to open a number of new stores.

However, even more challenging is if a company finds that its own employees have breached the FPCA, the costs to monitor their activities is more costly than the actual fines. For example, Avon had to pay more than $300 million in professional fees to examine the charges, while Wal-Mart spent more than $400 million in its internal investigation and their newly formed compliance programs after its Mexican situation.

Pressuring these companies are the whistleblower laws, which require companies to pay their whistleblowers, as in the case of Bank America which had to pay out $170 million to four whistleblowers. Between the costs for paying whistleblowers, paying fines, and developing compliance programs or losing profits and business opportunities in foreign countries where the Foreign Corrupt Practices Act is not a law, the challenges for U.S. businesses in foreign countries are even more challenging.

DISCUSSION QUESTIONS

If you were the Vice President of International Business Development for a U.S. corporation, and were offered bribes to expedite paperwork required to open a branch ahead of foreign competitors, what would you do?

(a) Defend your response, using the **full** S.E.A. method (state the philosophy, explain the philosophy in your own words, give a general example, and apply the philosophy to your response). (Supplemental question b) Apply the seven-step Velasquez decision-making model found in Chapter 6.

(Supplement question c) If you were hired as a consultant to identify what steps a company in this situation should undertake to prevent breaking the Foreign Corrupt Practices Act, what would you recommend, using the **full** S.E.A. method (state the philosophy, explain the philosophy in your own words, give a general example, and apply the philosophy to your response)?

(Supplemental question d) Apply the seven-step Velasquez decision-making model found in Chapter 6.

CASE 10. 2 CHILD LABOR: OPPORTUNITY OR EXPLOITATION? [111]

In an ITV undercover UK documentary, Bangladesh factories producing clothes for British retailers were forcing young girls to work up to eleven hours where they were physically and verbally abused. Some of these thirteen-year-olds were slapped, kicked, and attacked with a used fabric roll. Bangladesh employment laws prohibit anyone under age eighteen working more than five hours, as well as allowing employees mistreating workers, especially those younger employees.

Uzbekistan also uses child labor for its cotton harvest, which many U.S. suppliers look the other way or claim they are inspecting the facilities or will not use them. However, this is not always the case. The Uzbekistan government denies the charges.

In addition, the China Labor Watch (CLW) allegedly discovered ten children working for Samsung Electronics and the Lenovo Group, which is denying it, even though, according to the CLW, this is the second time they found underage workers employed at these companies. Child workers were also found working at Foxconn, the trade name of the Taiwanese company, Hon Har Precision Industry, who supplies technology firms such as Apple. In addition, CLW found other multinational firms engaging in this same practice of using underage children for their manufacturing plants.

Yet, one fourteen-year-old told a reporter that she had to work to eat. Some even argue that allowing these children the opportunity to work in manufacturing plants may be better than low-poverty families forcing their children into more illicit acts such as drug selling, prostitution, or other crimes.

DISCUSSION QUESTIONS

As a U.S. retailer, would you do business with a supplier whose products are dramatically lower in price, if you knew they were using child labor?
(a) Defend your response, using the **full** S.E.A. method (state the philosophy, explain the philosophy in your own words, give a general example, and apply the philosophy to your response). (Supplemental question b) Apply the seven-step Velasquez decision-making model found in Chapter 6.

As a U.S. retailer with a business in a less developed country such as Uzbekistan, since the law is rarely enforced, would you use child labor?
(c) Defend your response, using the **full** S.E.A. method (state the philosophy, explain the philosophy in your own words, give a general example, and apply the philosophy to your response). (Supplemental question d) Apply the seven-step Velasquez decision-making model found in Chapter 6.

Endnotes

1 "Dexter Roberts and Pete Engardio, "Secrets, Lies, and Sweatshop," *Business Week*, no. 4011, November 27, 2006, p. 50.

2 Ibid.

3 Miguel Helft and David Barboza, "Google Closes Search Service Based in China," *The New York Times*, March 23, 2010, p. A1.

4 Carol Matlack, "A European Tour for U.S. Labor," *Bloomberg Business Week*, February 15, 2010, p. 59.

5 Steve Greenhouse, "A Crusader Makes Celebrities Tremble," *The New York Times*, June 18, 1996. 20 April 2010. www.nyt.com

6 Anand Giridharadas, "Expressing Convictions at the Mall," *The New York Times*, October 9, 2009. 20 April 2010. www.nyt.com

7 "Child Protection From Violence, Exploitation, and Abuse," UNICEF Website. 21 April 2010. www.unicef.org

8 David Barboza, "China Says Abusive Child Labor Ring Is Exposed," *The New York Times*, May 1, 2008. 20 April 2010. www.nyt.com

9 Ibid.

10 Howard W. French, "Reports of Forced Labor, Unsettle China," *The New York Times*, June 16, 2007. 20 April 2010. www.nyt.com

11 Ibid.

12 David Barboza, "In Chinese Factory, Lost Fingers and Lost Pay," *The New York Times*, January 5, 2008. 20 April 2010. www.nyt.com

13 Thomas C. Hayes, "Wal-Mart Disputes Report on Labor," *The New York Times*, December 24, 1992. 20 April 2010. www.nyt.com

14 Ibid.

15 Amelia Gentleman, "Gap Campaigns Against Child Labor," *The New York Times*, November 16, 2007. 20 April 2010. www.nyt.com

16 Ibid.

17 Steven Greenhouse, "Anti-Sweatshop Movement Is Achieving Gains Overseas," *The New York Times*, January 26, 2000. 20 April 2010. www.nyt.com

18 Joseph Kahn, "Citing Child Labor, U.S. Bans Apparel from Mongolia Plant," *The New York Times*, November 29, 2000. 20 April 2010. www.nyt.com

19 Jeremy Snyder, "Exploitation and Sweatshop Labor: Perspectives and Issues," *Business Ethics Quarterly*, vol. 20, no. 2, April, 2010, p. 204.

20 J. Lawrence French, "Children's Labor Market Involvement, Household Work, and Welfare: A Brazilian Case Study," *Journal of Business*, vol. 92, no. 1, March 2010, p. 63.

21 Ibid., 74-75.

22 Charles Kenny, "Child Labor Is Still Prevalent Around the World: Here's How to Eliminate It," *Bloomberg Businessweek,* October 20, 2014. www.Bloomberg.com.

23 Nicholas D. Krisof, "Put Your Money Where Their Mouths Are," *The New York Times*, April 23, 2004. 20 April 2010. www.nyt.com

24 "Dexter Roberts and Pete Engardio, "Secrets, Lies, and Sweatshop," *BusinessWeek*, no. 4011, November 27, 2006, p. 52.

25 Ibid.

26 David Barboza, "In China, New Limits on Virtual Currency," *The New York Times*, June 30, 2009. 20 April 20104. www.nyt.com

27 Ibid.

28 Emily Nash, "Stores Sweat Shop Shame, Report Slams Workers' Pay," *Daily Record*, September 14, 2007. LexisNexis Academic. SUNY Rockland, Suffern, NY. 20 April 2010.

29 Steven Greenhouse, "Activists Rap Hip Hop Star, Clothing Label Said to Use Foreign Sweatshop," *The International Herald Tribune*, October 29, 2003. LexisNexis Academic. SUNY Rockland, Suffern, NY. 20 April 2010.

30 Ibid.

31 The Associated Press. "U.S. Tech Firm Fined for Underpaying Indian Workers," *The New York Times*, October 23, 2014. www.nyt.com

32 Nicholas D. Kristof, "How Can We Help the World's Poor?" *The New York Times*, November 20, 2009. 20 April 2010. www.nyt.com

33 Ibid.

34 Andrew Downe, "Fair Trade in Bloom," *The New York Times*, October 2, 2007. 20 April 2010. www.nyt.com

35 "Certification and Membership," Fair Trade Federation Website. 20 April 2010. www.fairtradeorganization.org

36 Laura Shapiro, "Nothing for Nothing," *The New York Times*, July 16, 2009. 20 April 2010. www.nyt.com

37 Steve Hamm, "Into Africa: Capitalism From the Ground Up," *Businessweek*, May 4, 2009, pp. 60-61.

38 Ibid., 61.

39 Carol Matlack, "A European Tour for U.S. Labor," *Bloomberg BusinessWeek,* February 15, 2010, p. 59.

40 David Barboza, "Mining Case Out of China Takes a Turn: Executives Confess to Bribery, Not Spying," *The New York Times*, March 23, 2010, p. A1.

41 "Daimler's Bribery Settlement Is Approved," Reuters, *The New York Times*, April 1, 2010. 21 April 2010. www.nyt.com

42 Lidia Kelly, "Multinationals Pledge No Corruption In Russia," *The New York Times*, April 20, 2010. 21 April 2010. www.nyt.com

43 Doug Carroll, "HP's Russia Unit Pleads Guilty in Bribery Case," *USA Today*, September 12, 2014. www.usatoday.com

44 "Foreign Corrupt Practices Act: An Overview," The Department of Justice Website. 21 April 2010. www.justice.gov/criminal/fraud/fcpa

45 Ibid.

46 Jeffrey Seglin, "The Right Thing: When Bribery Is Lost In Translation," *The New York Times*, October 15, 2000. 21 April 2010. www.nyt.com

47 Ibid.

48 Tim Weiner, "Titan Corp. To Pay $28.5 Million in Fines for Foreign Bribery," *The New York Times*, March 2, 2005. 21 April 2010. www.nyt.com

49 Ibid.

50 Masako N. Darrough, "The FCPA and the OED Convention: Some Lessons from the U.S. Experience," *The Journal of Business Ethics*, vol. 93, no. 2, p. 255. Business Source Complete. SUNY Rockland, Suffern, NY. 21 April 2010.

51 Robert Tirgaux, "Is Foreign Bribery Sting More Than Show?" *St. Petersburg Times* (Florida), January 21, 2010, p. 4B. LexisNexis Academic. SUNY Rockland, Suffern, NY. 21 April 2010.

52 Ibid.

53 Ibid.

54 Paul M. Barrett, "Big Shots Go Down at Gun Show," *Bloomberg Businessweek*, February 1 & 8, 2010, p. 17.

55 Ibid., 259.

56 Ibid., 256.

57 Ibid.

58 Tor Krever, "Curbing Corruption? The Efficacy of the Foreign Corrupt Practices Act," *North Caroline Journal of International Law & Commercial Regulations*, vol. 33, no. 1, 2007, p. 91. Business Source Complete. SUNY Rockland, Suffern, NY. 21 April 2010.

59 Ibid.

60 Keith Bradsher, "China Moves to Retaliate Against U.S. Tire Tariff," *The New York Times*, September 14, 2009, p. A1. 24 April 2010. www.nyt.com

61 Ibid.

62 Steven Greenhouse, "Tire Tariffs Cheered By Labor," *The New York Times*, September 15, 2009, p. B1. 24 April 2010. www.nyt.com

63 James Kanter, "Europe Backs Tariff on U.S. Biofuel Imports," *The New York Times*, March 3, 2009, p. B1. 24 April 2010. www.nyt.com

64 Ibid.

65 "Products," Biofuel Africa Website. 24 April 2010. www.biofuel.no

66 Sewell Chan, "Obama Faced Criticism Over Slow Pace Of Action on Trade Issues," *The New York Times*, March 11, 2010. 24 April 2010. www.nyt.com

67 Ibid.

68 Sewell Chan, "U.S. and Brazil Reach Agreement on Cotton Dispute," *The New York Times*, April 6, 2010. 24 April 2010. www.nyt.com

69 Elizabeth Becker, "International Business: U.S. Will Cut Farm Subsidies In Trade Deal," *The New York Times*, July 31, 2004, p. C3. 24 April 2010. www.nyt.com

70 Ibid.

71 Nicola Clark and Christopher Drew, "W.T.O. Says Aid to Airbus Was Illegal," *The New York Times*, September 5, 2009, p. B1. 24 April 2010. www.nyt.com

72 Ginger Thompson, "State Department Official Turned Lobbyist Is Accused for Illegally Working for Sudan," *The New York Times*, October 28, 2009, p. A14. 24 April 2010. www.nyt.com

73 July Dempsey, "In a Car, A Lesson In Russian-European Trade," *The New York Times*, January 1, 2008. 24 April 2010. www.nyt.com

74 Mark Landler, "U.S. Is Seeking A Range of Sanctions Against Iran," *The New York Times*, September 28, 2009, p. A1. 24 April 2010. www.nyt.com

75 Gardiner Harris and Andrew Harris, "F.D.A. Detains Chinese Imports for Testing," *The New York Times*, November 14, 2008, p. A18. 24 April 2010. www.nyt.com

76 Ibid.

77 Eduardo Porter, "Banana Wars," *The New York Times*, November 14, 2008, p. A18. 24 April 2010. www.nyt.com

78 Ibid.

79 "General Agreement on Tariffs and Trade," CIESIN Thematic Guide on Political Institutions and Global Environmental Change Website. 24 April 2010. www.ciesin.org/TG/PI/TRADE/gatt.html

80 "The WTO in Brief," World Trade Organization Website, July 23, 2008. 24 April 2010. www.wto.org

81 Jack Healy, "China Accused of Trade Restrictions," *The New York Times*, June 23, 2009. 24 April 2010. www.nyt.com

82 Ibid.

83 Dexter Roberts, "Closing for Business," *Bloomberg Businessweek*, April 5, 2010, p. 36.

84 Ibid.

85 Ibid.

86 Ibid., 37.

87 Jeff Sommer, "In Currency Games, the Prize May Be a Trade War," *The New York Times*, April 11, 2010, p. B5.

88 "Anti-dumping, Subsidies, Safeguards: Contingencies, Etc.," World Trade Organization Website. July 23, 2008. 24 April 2010. www.wto.org

89 Stephen Castle, "E.U. Seeks Compromise On Chinese Shoe Exports," *The New York Times*, October 13, 2009. 24 April 2010. www.nyt.com

90 Reuters, "W.T.O. Rules Against U.S. in Dumping Case," *The New York Times*, October 13, 2009. 24 April 2010. www.nyt.com

91 Ann Crittenden, "U.S. Won't Ban Export of Unsafe Products: TRIS Sleepwear Case Would Use   Controls 'Sparing,'" *The New York Times*, September 30, 1980, p. D8. 24 April 2010. www.nyt.com

92 Ibid.

93 Walt Bogdanich and Eric Koli, "2 Paths of Bayer Drugs in 1980's: Riskier One Steered Overseas," *The New York Times*, May 22, 2003, p. C5. 25 April 2010. www.nyt.com

94 Gardiner Harris, "The Safety Gap," *The New York Times*, November 2, 2008, p. MM46. 24 April 2010. www.nyt.com

95 "Europa: Europe on 12 Lessons" Website. 25 April 2010. http:europa.eu

96 "Aim and Purposes," and "The Founding of ASEAN" Overview, The Association of Southeast Asian Nations Website. 25 April 2010. www.aseansec.org

97 "History" and "Mission Statement," Asia Pacific Economic Cooperation Council Website, July 21, 2009. 25 April 2010. www.apec.org

98 Joanna Klonsky and Stephanie Hanson, "Mercosur: South America's Fractious Trade Bloc," Council on Foreign Relations Website, August 20, 2009. 25 April 2010. www.cfr.org/publication/12762

99 Ibid.

100 Alejandra del Palacio, "Unasur Summit Ends With Call for Peace In South America," Chinaview.com, August 29, 2009. 25 April 2010. news.xinhuanet.com/english/2009-08/29/content_11961343.htm

101 David Rockefeller, "Present at the Trade Wars," *The New York Times*, September 20, 2009. 24 April 2010. www.nyt.com

102 Greg Winter, "Enticing Third World Youth; Big Tobacco Is Accused of Crossing an Age Line, " *The New York Times,* August 24, 2001. 24 April 2010. www.nyt.com

103 "Question Raised on Halliburton's Kuwait Contract," *The New York Times*, January 16, 2004. 24 April 2010. www.nyt.com

104 Ibid.

105 David Cay Johnston and Melody Petersen, "Whistleblower Accuses Wyeth of Tax Dodges," *The New York Times*, January 17, 2003. 24 April 2010. www.nyt.com

106 Elisabeth Rosenthal, "Biotech Food Tears Rift in Europe," *The New York Times*, June 6, 2006. 25 April 2010. www.nyt.com

107 Sherri Day, "Coke Employers Are Questioned in Fraud Inquiry," *The New York Times*, January 31, 2004. 25 April 2010. www.nyt.com

108 Richard P. Nielsen, "2008 Society for Business Presidential Address: High-Leverage Finance Capitalism, the Economic Crisis, Structurally Related Ethics, Issue, and Potential Reforms," *Business Ethics Quarterly*, vol. 20, no. 2, April, 2010, p. 312.

109 Alina Tugend, "In Life and Business, Learning to Be Ethical," *The New York Times*, January 10, 2014. www.nyt.com.

110 This case was rewritten based upon the following article: Peter J. Henning, "Foreign Bribery Cases That Can Drag On and On," *The New York Times*, December 22, 2014. www.nyt.com.

111 This case was rewritten based upon the following articles: Miles Brignall and Sarah Butler, "Bangladesh Garment Factories Still Exploiting Child Labour for UK Products," *The Guardian* (U.S. Edition), February 5, 2014. www.theguardian.com; "Uzbekistan: 2013 Findings on the Worst Forms of Child Labor," United States Department of Labor. www.dol.gov/ilab/reports/child-labor/uzbekistan; and "Supplier for Samsung and Lenovo Accused of Using Child Labor," *The New York Times*, August 29, 2014, p. B2. www.nyt.com.

GLOSSARY

A priori: knowledge based upon reasoning rather than experience (a posteriori is knowledge based upon sensory experience).

Acid rain: the emission of nitrogen oxide and sulfuric oxide as a result of fossil fuels (coal, oil, natural gas, etc.) which damages the crops, soil, trees, drinking water, etc.

Aesthetics: basically, the philosophy of art or the value of beauty.

Affirmative Action: policies that require protected groups (African American, Latinos, etc.) be given a special opportunity to be hired or promoted in an effort to reverse past discriminatory practices which now will result in minorities being hired or promoted fairly.

Ageism: discrimination against an individual based upon age.

Alienation: the separation of a worker as an individual from his job and self, as well as from his family, which according to Marx and Engels was a result of capitalism's demands on the proletariat working class.

Animal compassionate: indicates that the animals were raised in a humane manner.

Anuttara-samyaksambodhi: refers to a person who wants to practice Buddhism.

Ascetic: one who denies oneself basic, ordinary pleasures.

Axiology: the branch of philosophy that deals with the study of values.

Bait and switch advertising: the advertising of a highly discounted product or service with the intention not to sell it in order to convince the consumer to purchase another product or service at a higher price (switch).

Bhagavad Gita: the equivalent of a Hindu bible, written around 3000 BCE.

Biofuels: store energy from biomass sources such as wheat, sugar cane, and palm and may be used to produce bioenergy used in vehicles or as an additive to make the fuel more efficient.

Bodhisattva (or Mahasattvas): one who wants to be enlightened and helps others to be so as well.

Bribery: the act of persuading somebody to exercise his or her business judgment in one's favor by offering cash or a gift and thereby gaining an unfair advantage.

Buddha's Dharma: a doctrine depicting the way of life.

Carbon footprint: term used to measure the total carbon dioxide emitted as a result of these greenhouse gas emissions which are produced by a business, process, or individual.

Categorical imperative: the belief that a rule cannot be accepted unless there are no conditions or exceptions to that rule.

Churning: occurs when a broker engages in excessive trading in order to generate commissions and other revenue without regard for the customer's investment objectives.

Common goods approach: an approach where all members of society are ensured agreed upon common goods such as affordable health care, effective public safety, peace among nations, a just legal system, and unpolluted environment.

Communism (Marxist): those who believe that economic resources should be shared by all members of society, by any means necessary, and not just the owners who possessed the abundance of society's wealth at the expense of those workers who actually created it.

Communitarian: commonly believed to be when individual rights are superseded by community rights, but Sandel believes this term refers to all groups who should be considered before deciding on what is the best action to take when faced with an ethical public policy decision.

Comparable worth: also known as pay equity, a broad term for a range of policies developed to reduce the pay gap between occupations traditionally filled by women.

Consequentialism (or the teleological approach): the ends justify the means—in other words, the focus of moral decision making is on the results not the process.

Conventional level: according to Kohlberg's model, it is based upon when you are making a decision. The deciding factor is what others think of your decision. (What will other people think?) In Gilligan's model, it is based upon doing what is best for others and detrimentally neglecting yourself.

Corporation: a form of ownership where the owners are separate from the business and as such have certain rights such as limited liability.

Cultural relativism: the belief that the values of individuals differ from culture to culture, as opposed to being absolute, when values are accepted regardless of cultural background.

Cyrenaic hedonism: a belief that there two states, pleasure and pain, and that one should pursue the former and avoid the latter.

Depletion of ozone layer: the gradual breaking up of ozone gas in the stratosphere, which protects all life on earth from harmful ultraviolet radiation and is produced by products such as aerosol cans or refrigerators.

Diamond Sutra: a written record of a teaching given by the Buddha over 2,500 years ago, which had been passed down from generation to generation.

Difference principle: when expectations are to the advantage of the representative person who is worse off, it is just.

Dividends: part of the profits earned by the corporation.

Doctrine of the superior individual: a social Darwinism theory by Callicles, which justifies why the strong who dominate the weak are constrained by conventional morality.

Domestic partnership benefits: are when primarily gay or lesbians have long-term partnerships, are living together, and can have health insurance for their partners through their partner's company.

Dumping: selling a product at lower than cost or the price sold in the domestic country or selling a domestically banned product abroad.

Embargo: a form of protectionism; the banning of a product or service from being sold in a given country.

Employment at will: when employers have the right to terminate any employee at their discretion.

Entitlement theory: where individuals are entitled to their holdings as long as they have been obtained fairly and may not be taken by anyone else including the government.

Environmental classism: discrimination from any action that results in a negative environmental impact on a group of individuals who lack economic and political power to oppose it.

Epicureans: a group who believed in maximizing pleasure and minimizing pain, but also believed in the importance of mental pleasures. In addition, qualitative pleasures were better than quantitative pleasures.

Epistemology: includes questions about knowledge, such as: What is knowledge? and How do we know what we know?

Ethical dilemma: a situation or decision affecting others when there may not be an obvious solution in terms of what is the right thing to do.

Ethical dilemma: when an individual is faced with making a decision that involves an ethical situation, such as: Should I receive a full travel reimbursement if an unwritten discount was issued?

Ethical hedonism: refers to the view that although it is possible not to seek pleasure and avoid pain, it is morally wrong to do so.

Ethical wisdom: according to Socrates, "the recognition of the fundamental importance of the ethical in the life of man (humankind) and of doing good as the basic principle of human activity."

Ethics: a branch of philosophy that identifies why and if a particular moral standard should be a moral standard.

Exploitation: according to Marx and Engels, a result of capitalism when workers were being taken advantage of in terms of their wages compared to their employers who owned the businesses which the workers actually were creating.

Fair trade: guarantees that the product purchased is by a member who complies with fair wages, working conditions, product standards, and other ethical practices established by the Fair Trade Federation.

Fairness/justice approach: seeks equality for all individuals and asks questions such as: How fair is an action? Does it treat everyone in the same way, or does it show favoritism and discrimination?

Foreign Corrupt Practices Act of 1977 (FCPA): enacted for the purpose of making it unlawful for certain classes of persons and entities to make payments to foreign government officials to assist in obtaining or retaining business.

Glass ceiling: a term defining the inability of women to be promoted into the executive suite compared their male co-workers.

Global Reporting Initiative (GRI): organization that pioneered a sustainable reporting framework to be used as a benchmark for organizational performance with respect to its continuous improvement to economic, environmental, and social performance.

Gold farming: factories where young workers are placed in cramped corners, to play online games to earn credits which they sell for a profit to overseas markets.

Grease payment: when an individual or firm is permitted to pay "facilitating payments," a small amount of cash that might sometimes be needed to expedite what it calls "routine governmental action," such as processing a visa.

Green marketing: the production of goods or services which will enable the continuation of a sustainable development of our resources for future generations.

Greenhouse effect: when large quantities of carbon dioxide are released in the atmosphere for a time and warm the earth's surface.

Gunas: it is believed there are three possessed by all individuals; even though one dominates over the others.

Harvard Case Method: a seven-step approach that identifies the optimum alternative for a specific problem or opportunity faced by an organization, without taking into consideration any ethical consequences to all the stakeholders affected by the selected alternative.

Hedonism: originates from the Greek word *hedone* (pleasure) and may be best described as the philosophy that individuals should maximize pleasure and minimize pain.

Hostile takeovers: those who purchase a business with the intention of selling its assets for a profit at the expense of jobs, local economies, etc., who are sometimes called corporate raiders.

Independent contractors: individuals who work for themselves and are exempt from overtime, fringe benefits, ability to join a union, and are responsible for paying any required taxes which normally are paid by employers, such as Social Security taxes.

Informatics: optically scanned paper transferred to computer screens where a distance away the relevant information is keyed in and then digitized material speedily returned to the home office.

Initial public offering: when a new company offers its stock to the public for the first time.

Insider trading: illegal trading in securities by individuals or firms who possess non-public information.

Institutional or corporate bullying: when bullying is entrenched in an organization and becomes accepted as part of the workplace culture.

Karma capitalism: when good leaders who are selfless take initiative and focus on their duty rather than obsessing over outcomes or financial gain.

Kyoto Protocol: set targets to reduce greenhouse gas emissions by approximately 5% against the 1990
levels over a five-year period spanning 2008-2012.

Least advantaged: the stakeholders who benefit the least from the alternative

Least advantaged: those who are least favored by categories such as family and class origins, natural endowments, or situational events (such as entrepreneur Donald Trump).

Libertarian: one who believes that individuals are free to do what they please, without any government intervention, as long as they do not interfere with the rights of others.

Lifestyle discrimination: discrimination against employees because of their activities outside the work environment, which may include smoking or skydiving.

Logic: a specialized branch of philosophical science first discovered by Aristotle in the fourth century BCE which examines the science of valid defenses.

Lookism: discriminating against an individual because of physical appearance.

Martin Act of 1921 ("blue sky" law): law enacted in order to protect investors from securities fraud, giving the state attorney generals greater power when investigating the alleged perpetrators.

Metaphysics (or ontology): deals with questions of reality: What is appearance? and What is real?

Negative externalities: costs that economic actors impose on others without paying a price for their actions.

Nepotism: the process of favoritism to relatives, especially in appointments to desirable positions.

NIMBY: an acronym for "not in my backyard"; in other words, no one wants a landfill or nuclear reactor near them, even if it would benefit the environment overall.

Non-consequentialist (or deontological thinker): believes that the means is more important than the ends. It is not the results that should be taken into account when faced with a moral dilemma, but the process.

Objectivist philosophy: endorses individualism by stressing "rational self-interest" over charity and the welfare state, as espoused by Ayn Rand.

Original position: developed by John Rawls as part of a thought experiment where you imagine being in a new society free to create whatever rules you wish.

OSHA: under the Occupational Safety and Health Act of 1970, OSHA's purpose is to develop standards, issue regulations, conduct inspections, and issue citations to ensure the safety and health of all workers.

Philosopher: one who looks for a rational explanation of his or her experience of reality, who tries to grasp the real as a matter of understanding, as opposed to a magical, mythical, fictional explanation of things; means a lover of wisdom.

Philosophy: a discipline in which philosophers continue to question the assumptions behind every claim and the most basic beliefs about reality, and then to critically examine those beliefs.

Planned obsolescence: a practice of intentionally developing and marketing products with a limited lifespan.

Political philosophy: the examination of social values and the justification of various political institutions and political relations.

Ponzi scheme: when a dishonest person convinces unsuspecting customers that they will receive high returns in a short period of time and uses the funds of one set of investors to pay back the others.

Postconventional level: according to the Kohlberg model, the determining factor when making a decision is based upon a higher level of development when you act in a manner for the good of humankind, and your motivation is not for any personal reward or motivated by what others may think. In the Gilligan model, it is putting yourself ahead of others, not to be selfish but to be selfless.

Prajnaparamita: loosely interpreted refers to the ability to understand the way (*Tao* or *dharma*).

Preconventional level: based upon when you are making decisions in which the determining factor is how you are benefited by that decision (i.e., motivated by selfishness).

Predatory capitalism: where your intention is to drive competitors out of business.

Price fixing: when two or more businesses will charge the same price so consumers cannot shop and compare the lowest price among the competition.

Price gouging: selling a product or service for an amount that is unfairly higher than it is normally sold for.

Prima facie duty: according to W.D. Ross, when one more important duty (such as saving a life) becomes more important than a lesser duty (being on time for a date).

Protectionism: the intervention through any government action into the marketplace on behalf of its own domestic markets to insulate them from their foreign competition.

Psychological egoism: individuals have been created by nature to maximize pleasure and minimize pain and could not do anything for another person unless it benefited them.

Psychological hedonism: the belief that all humans have been developed to desire pleasure, avoid pain, and that it is impossible for humans to pursue anything else.

Rajasic: describes individuals who perform actions for their own benefit or fulfillment.

Restrictive standards: reduce the opportunity of exported goods or services to compete with the domestic country's products or services.

Rights approach: the right for an individual to choose for oneself (right of privacy, freedom of speech, freedom of religion, etc.).

Sales puffery: making statements that are known to be exaggerated, but that the Federal Trade Commission does not consider as false advertising.

Samsara: endless cycle of rebirth.

Sattwic: one who acts without personal gain in accordance with the teachings of the scripture and its firm belief in righteousness.

SEA method: a teaching method developed by the author to integrate a philosophy with an action to be taken by an individual in a given case study involving an ethical dilemma (state philosophy, explain and exemplify in general terms the philosophy, apply the philosophy to the case).

Skeptics: those who doubted that there was any possibility of true knowledge since the truth seemed to produce conflicting claims.

Social contractarian: an individual who believes that individual citizens have a bilateral contract with the government in terms of how much control and restraint it has over its societal members.

Sophists: those who believed in preparing their students in the art of rhetoric or power of persuasive speech for an usually large fee, unlike their predecessors, the Sophos who did not charge fees.

Sophos: the original philosophers who practiced their craft by raising questions as to the origin of the world and the meaning of a good life.

Speciesism: a term philosopher Peter Singer defines as a prejudice against animals by humans who believe they are superior to them.

Speciesism: discrimination against any species that has sentience or the ability to feel   (pleasure or pain), as created by Peter Singer.

Stakeholders: those parties who influence the organization or are influenced by the organization (e.g., stockholders, employees, clients, society, government agencies).

Stephanus numbers: describe the corresponding page and section of the relevant volume of the Greek text as edited by the French scholar, Henri Estienne (which in Latin is *Stephanus*).

Stock: the individual owner's share of a business.

Subprime mortgages: loans to individuals below the prime rate to borrowers who might not qualify for conventional prime rate loans since they could not afford the monthly payments of prime rate loans.

Subsidy: when the government funds an industry so the exporting producers are able to sell   their products or services at a price equal to cost or lower than cost of the domestic country.

Sustainable development: development that meets the needs of the present world without compromising the ability of future generations to meet their own needs.

Systemic: more than one organization (or its global ramifications). In the case of a systematic ethical issue, it refers to the ethical issue that affects many organizations, such as affirmative action, insider trading, etc.

Tamas: one who is not compassionate, will put people in pain to achieve selfish goals, bring discomfort to their organizations, and are demonic or corrupt.

Tariff: a tax on imported goods or services to reduce the amount of imports entering the domestic country.

Tathagata: a sage or Buddha.
that could be selected by the decision maker in an ethical dilemma.

Three C's theory: consists of three components: *compliance* to laws and principles of morality; *contributions* to society; and *consequences* of actions. In order for a business or one's actions to be ethical all three must be satisfied, according to Robert Solomon.

Trade deficit: when imports (foreign purchased goods or services) exceed exports (goods or services purchased by foreign consumers).

Trade quotas: the limiting of imported goods permitted to enter a given country.

Trade surplus: when exports exceed imports.

Trading bloc: an organization in which its members agree to reduce protectionist measures against each other, such as no or reduced tariffs, but not to those outside of their membership.

Triple bottom line: businesses have three obligations: economic prosperity (profits), environmental quality (planet), and social justice (people).

Ultraminimum state: where all use of force is suspended except for self-defense and only by those who purchase its protection, as believed by Robert Nozick.

Utilitarian approach / utilitarianism: selecting actions that produced the greatest good over evil for the majority of those affected by these actions.

Utilitarianism: advocates pursuing the greatest amount of pleasure for the greatest amount of people, also a consequentialist philosophy.

Values: ideals you believe in and are then compared to one or more moral standards, which would enable you to make the most ethical choice (e.g., friendship, religion, money).

Veil of ignorance: developed by Rawls where after creating societal rules under his original position you modify them since you will not know anything (be ignorant) about what your own circumstances or background will be (e.g., poor, wealthy, old, young).

Veil of ignorance: presupposes that the parties who will be developing a policy or course of action will have no knowledge in terms of their place in that decision (e.g., whether they would be the executives making the decision or the customers affected by the decision).

Velasquez Model of Decision Making: a seven-step method to decision making that considers the ethical consequences for all the stakeholders affected by the decision.

Virtue approach: assumes there are certain virtues or ideals that we should all strive for in order to develop us as better human beings (e.g., honesty, self-control, integrity).

Whistleblower: involves the act of reporting wrongdoing to internal or external parties.

Workplace rankism: when a superior abuses his/her power at the expense of subordinates.

INDEX

Arignote, 23
Aristippus, 62–63
Aristotle, 14–15, 54–59, 335
Arthur Andersen and Company, 180, 185
Arthur Andersen Worldwide Societe Cooperative,
      253
Art of War (Sun-tzu), 94–95
Asia Pacific Economic Cooperation (APEC), 348
Atlas Shrugged (Rand), 145
automotive industry
      decision making, 180–181
      global marketplace ethics, 341
      marketplace ethics, 267–269
      workplace ethics, 222
axiology, 14

B

Bailey, Andrew, 13
Bair, Sheila, 258
bait and switch advertising, 262–263
Bakke, Alan, 211
Bank of America, 226
Baxter, J. Clifford, 237
Baxter, Julie, 273
Bayer, 267, 347
Ben and Jerry's, 81, 149
Bentham, Jeremy, 115–116, 181–182
Best Buy, 234
Bhagavad Gita, 92–94
biofuels, 340
Blackwater Worldwide, 228
Blumenthal, Nathaniel, 145
Bodhisattva, 90
Boeing Company, 215, 244
Bok, Sissela, 153–156, 238
Bollinger, Lee, 211
bourgeoisie, 134
BP, 221, 293
bribery, employment issues of, 227–228

bribery, international, 334–339
Bronfenbrenner, Kat, 236
Buddha's Dharma, 88–89
Buick Motor Company, 267–268
Bullard, Robert, 318
Burger King, 301–302
Bush, George W., 309–310
Byer California, 265

C

California almonds, 269
Callicles, 38–40
cap and trade, 311
Capitalism and Freedom (Friedman), 147–149
Capitalism (Rand), 145–146
carbon footprint, 287
categorical imperative, 121–122
Cathy, S. Truett, 199–200
channel stuffing, 353
charitable organizations, donating profits to, 148–149
Charmides, 25
Chevrolet, 109–110
Chick-fil-A, 199–200
child labor, 326–334, 360
Child Labor Prohibition and Regulation Act
      (India), 328
Children's Place, The, 271
Christianity, St. Augustine and, 60
churning, 254–255
City of New Haven, 209
Cive, De (Hobbes), 112
Civil Rights Act, 206, 209, 211, 214
Clark, Mike, 318
classical philosophers, 33–78
      cases for discussion, 73–75
      hedonists
            Aristippus, 62–63
            Epicurus, 63–66
            hedonism, defined, 62

D

E

R.J. Reynolds Tobacco Company, 273
Rodriquez, Beatriz, 278
Romer v. Evans, 164–165
Ross, William David, 123–125

S

safety issues
    product safety concerns, 265–271
    in workplace, 219–222
sales puffery, 263–264
same-sex marriage (case example), 199–200
samsara, 88
Samsung, 261, 360
Sandel, Michael, 167–169
Sarbanes, Paul, 259–260
Sarbanes-Oxley Act, 253, 259–260
sattwic, 93
Sayler, Allen, 270
S.E.A. method, of ethical decision making, 66–70,
    191
Sears Roebuck, 216–217
Second Principle (Rawls), 152, 153
Second Treatise of Government, The (Locke),
    127–128
Secrets (Bok), 154, 155
Securities Act of 1933, 258, 259
Securities and Exchange Commission (SEC),
    creation of, 259
Securities Exchange Act of 1934, 258, 259
securities industry, laws governing, 258–260
seven-step model to decision making. *see*
    Velasquez Model of Decision Making
sexual harassment, 212–214
"Shallow Pond, The," 1–2, 67–70
Shanks, Thomas, 181
Sherman Anti-trust Act, 261
Shi Zhengrong, 309
Siddhartha Gautama, 87–92
Siemens, 336

Singer, Peter, 161–163, 299–300
"Singer Solution to World Poverty, The" (Singer),
    163
skeptics, 34
Smith, Adam, 129–131, 339, 349
Smith & Wesson, 338
Smoot-Hawley Tariff Act, 349
social and political philosophers, 109–141
    cases for discussion about, 138–139
    Hobbes, 111–114
    non-consequentialist deontologists
        Kant, 119–123
        Ross, 123–125
    overview, 109–111
    political philosophers
        Locke, 126–129
        Marx, 131–134
        Smith, 129–131
    utilitarianism
        Bentham, 115–116
        defined, 114
        Mill, 117–119
social contract, 112
social contractarians, 126
Society for Human Resource Management, 174
Socrates, 4, 15, 16, 25, 35–38, 40–48, 86, 183
Solid Waste Agency of Northern Cook County v.
    United States, 292
Solomon, Robert, 159–161
Sophists
    Aristotle, 14–15, 54–59, 339
    Callicles, 38–40
    defined, 33–34
    Plato, 21, 25, 47–54
    Protagoras, 34–38, 334
    Socrates, 4, 15, 16, 25, 35–38, 40–48, 86, 183
    St. Augustine, 59–62
    Thrasymachus, 40–43
Spanjian, Laura, 318
speciesism, 162, 299–300

CPSIA information can be obtained
at www.ICGtesting.com
Printed in the USA
LVHW06s0143050918
589175LV00005B/17/P

9 781465 273260